VISUALITY AND MATERIALITY IN THE STORY OF TRISTAN AND ISOLDE

VISUALITY AND MATERIALITY

IN THE STORY OF

TRISTAN AND ISOLDE

EDITED BY

Jutta Eming, Ann Marie Rasmussen,

AND *Kathryn Starkey*

University of Notre Dame Press

Notre Dame, Indiana

Library of Congress Cataloging-in-Publication Data

Visuality and materiality in the story of Tristan and Isolde /
edited by Jutta Eming, Ann Marie Rasmussen, and Kathryn Starkey.
    p.   cm.
  Includes bibliographical references and index.
  ISBN 978-0-268-04139-7 (pbk. : alk. paper) —
  ISBN 0-268-04139-3 (pbk. : alk. paper)
  1. Tristan (Legendary character)—Romances—Adaptations—
History and criticism.   2. Iseult (Legendary character)—Romances—
Adaptations—History and criticism.   3. Tristan (Legendary character)
in literature.   4. Iseult (Legendary character) in literature.   5. Tristan
(Legendary character)—Art.   6. Iseult (Legendary character)—Art.
7. Love in literature.   8. Love in art.   I. Eming, Jutta.   II. Rasmussen,
Ann Marie.   III. Starkey, Kathryn.   IV. Title: Tristan and Isolde.
  PN686.T7V57   2012
  809'.933543—dc23

                                                          2012008951

CONTENTS

ACKNOWLEDGMENTS

The idea for this book emerged from the coeditors' research project, "Tristan and Isolde and the Emotional Cultures of the Middle Ages," which was generously supported by a grant from the TransCoop Program of the Alexander von Humboldt Foundation (Germany). The idea was explored in depth at the conference "Visuality and Materiality in the Story of Tristan and Isolde," held March 30 to April 1, 2007, at Duke University and the University of North Carolina at Chapel Hill. The chapters herein began as presentations there. We received generous support for the conference from the TransCoop Program of the Alexander von Humboldt Foundation and the Max Kade Foundation. Additional sponsors from Duke University were the Josiah Charles Trent Memorial Foundation; the Office of the Dean of Arts and Sciences; the Department of Germanic Languages and Literature; the Rare Book, Special Collection, and Manuscript Library Division of Perkins Library; and the Nasher Museum of Art at Duke University. Additional sponsors from the University of North Carolina at Chapel Hill were the Office of the Dean of Arts and Sciences, the Department of Germanic and Slavic Languages and Literatures, and the Wilson Library. We are enormously grateful to the individuals who helped with planning, organizing, and running the conference, including Tracy Carhart, Christophe Fricker, Nick Ostrau, and Elizabeth Schreiber-Byers, whose poise and problem-solving skills were crucial to its success. Nina Nowakowski's research skills were essential to our progress with the book. We are also grateful to Stephen Little, editorial consultant at the University of Notre Dame Press, whose exemplary professionalism and diplomatic skills kept the book intact and moved it forward. And finally, we wish to thank the anonymous readers for the University of Notre Dame Press, whose trenchant criticisms and commentaries improved this volume.

We dedicate this book to our children: Julian and Lukas, Arnbjorn, and Antonia and Isabella.

Jutta Eming

Ann Marie Rasmussen

Kathryn Starkey

Visuality and Materiality in the Story of Tristan and Isolde

JUTTA EMING, ANN MARIE RASMUSSEN,
and KATHRYN STARKEY

The compelling incentive for this volume, which began at a conference held in 2007,[1] is the fact that the tale of Tristan and Isolde was the most widely depicted secular story of the Middle Ages. Material evidence for this medieval fascination includes texts in all Western European vernacular languages. There are versions, reworkings, or adaptations of the Tristan story in poetry, prose, and drama, and visual depictions are found in manuscripts and printed books that contain the story but also appear independent of the text. In addition, pictures and pictorial narratives (sometimes with and sometimes without inscriptions or captions) that conjure the Tristan story occur on an array of objects: stained glass, wall paintings, tiles, tapestries, ivory boxes, combs, mirrors, shoes, misericords.[2] In contrast to many medieval tales that lost their appeal after the Reformation, the story has continued to resonate strongly up to the present.[3]

The pan-European and cross-medial nature of the surviving medieval evidence is not reflected in the scholarship on Tristan, however, which largely falls along disciplinary and linguistic lines. In literary studies, scholars of Old French publish on Thomas and Béroul, with some work on later French adaptations, while scholars of medieval

German focus on their versions of the story by Eilhart von Oberg and Gottfried von Strassburg.[4] There has been little dialogue between these groups of literary scholars and the art historians who are still documenting the vast number of visual representations of the story of Tristan and Isolde. This volume seeks to open up a dialogue across disciplinary boundaries and to propose a new set of intellectual coordinates—the concepts of materiality and visuality—that will give scholars in several disciplines the tools to explore the productive connections between the verbal and the visual in medieval culture.

The concepts *materiality* and *visuality* enable one to think about the ways in which this vast and fascinating textual and visual evidence fits together without losing sight of the historical specificity or the aesthetic character of the individual pieces. *Materiality* refers to the objects, manuscripts, and spaces on and in which the story appears and also, in the broadest sense, to the construction of space, objects, bodies, and material signs that appear in various redactions. It encompasses the material (German *Stoff*) that stands behind the various versions of the story. Materiality is at once a philological concept (textual variability), a medial concept (ivory, parchment, paint, shoe leather), and a critical concept (how a narrator arranges space in the story, or uses a poetics of visibility, or signifies with the human body through gesture and clothing in uniquely adapting the story). *Visuality,* as we define it, refers to depictions that convey specific meanings, as well as to images, objects, performance, and the processes of visually perceiving. Visuality is at once an art historical concept (referring to the archive of depictions in varied media), a psychological concept (referring to the modes of perception expected of medieval audiences, including allegorical, typological, or experiential frames of mind), and a performative concept (e.g., how narrator, actor, artist, or fictional character might show or signify an emotion through ritualized gestures, speech, or actions).

Of course, visuality and materiality can never be entirely separated from each other. To be perceived, the visible needs material form, although that form could be achieved with a rhetorical device such as personification. Thus the concepts *visuality* and *materiality* function like moving indicators along a single scale of analysis. Their inseparability moves these concepts beyond the straightforwardly descriptive and gives them theoretical power. The visual/visibility becomes *visuality* when it refers to the whole complex of the production, perception, and cultural locations of the story. The material/medial becomes *materiality* when it refers to the means of production and materials used and their typical proliferations. Thanks to this theoretical innovation, something new is gained about the dynamics of the entire Tristan tradition, not just the textual part and not just the image part, and by extension about other medieval imbrications of texts and pictures.

Visuality and materiality are salient terms for the Tristan story *tout court*. They are especially useful for understanding Gottfried's thirteenth-century masterpiece, which is the focus of four chapters in this volume (Baisch; Müller; Schultz; Wandhoff). Central scenes rely on staging (in which Mark sees the lovers loving but fails to perceive their guilt), allegory (the visible and material form of abstract concepts), and symbolic objects such as the chessboard that the lovers use to shield the light, signifying that love is a game of strategy, or that love and loss will be combined like the black and white squares. These terms also encompass the tradition's unique ability to be collapsed into one, emblematic scene — the tryst in the orchard — whose visuality (perception as understanding) relies on the sacred iconography of Adam and Eve next to the forbidden tree.[5] Thus the visuality of this single scene enfolds the materiality (*Stoff* and verbal media) of the entire romance tradition and challenges the viewer to perceive its theological subtext.

In part I of this volume, Müller, Wandhoff, and Schultz calibrate the concepts of visuality and materiality to reframe some of the classic debates on Gottfried's *Tristan*: how is the prequel related to the main story (Müller), what is the scope of Gottfried's famous preface or his famous allegory of the cave (Wandhoff), and what does the love potion do (Schultz)? Schultz's chapter, for example, discusses the love potion as the material form of a refusal of the theology of concupiscence. It puts Gottfried's *Tristan* in its rightful place as the signal moment when "a secular elite turns away from the teaching of priests . . . and begins to explore love on its own terms."

Today Gottfried's *Tristan* seems more skilled and complex than ever. Scholars constantly revisit and reevaluate not only the text itself, but its literary and cultural context and the tradition from which it arose and that it helped to shape. Parts II and III explore this larger tradition, as represented by the story's precourtly precursors and its continuations, by its visual representations in a wide variety of media, and by late medieval dramatizations of and responses to the Tristan material. In other versions of the material we find that, for example, certain conflicts and tensions are not developed, or they are resolved or downplayed, or the redactors have focused on different aspects of the story entirely.[6] In the face of this evidence for the popularity and longevity of the Tristan story in a wide variety of media, the chapters in this volume pose questions that are both significant and largely un-answered due to the isolation of art historical and literary discourses: What makes the material uniquely hospitable to visual depictions? Do visual and verbal narratives relate to each other, and if so, how? Do modes of perception or ways of seeing in turn have an impact on the material?

In answer to the question about the remarkable staying power of the Tristan story, Curschmann discusses four "dramatic shifts of venue and medium that create entirely new and different perceptions (i.e., the visuality aspect) of older literary material." His example from the late nineteenth century is a sensible enhancement of the medieval emphasis of this volume. Koch's conceptual discussion of a sixteenth-century Tristan drama shows how love is recast as a dangerous drive coming from within a material human body—and thus capable of being represented, contained, and disciplined by the gestures of stage performers. It works well with Schultz's chapter to delineate the onset of the drive theory as another new step in the history of sexuality. Luyster analyzes the most extensive depiction of a romance in French medieval wall painting. She argues that the frescoes and their texts are cleverly disjunctive to create an illusion of time passing as the viewer strolls through the architectural spaces of the painted chamber. Thus the medieval viewer takes a journey with Tristan in a now time of di-rect experience, analogous to what a medieval Christian might feel walking through a cycle of sacred images but different from what we moderns would likely ever experience looking at an image.

Krüger's theoretically important contribution, the only one that does not focus on Tristan, demonstrates how the visual can collapse into the material, thereby blocking perceptions, when wall paintings of narrative subjects are voided of their standard literary and didactic meanings (courtly deportment, the virtue of love) in highly decorative contexts. Indeed, Krüger points out that an earlier generation of scholars "saw" the Tristan story where it probably did not exist, since many medieval depictions of lovers or aristocratic life are so conventional as to defy any positive identification. His chapter resonates with Van D'Elden's conclusions about generic scenes whose materiality is so opaque that they cannot signify the presence of the Tristan story at all, while others such as the orchard scene visualize the entire myth in one emblem. Brüggen and Ziegeler offer yet another take on the "problem" of formalism in medieval media by showing that the position of illuminations in one important Tristan manuscript is determined not by the textual references but by the location of initials in an earlier, now-lost manuscript. Text and image refuse any neat coherence.

Although the primacy of the visual and the material in the Middle Ages has long been recognized and in recent years discussions of visual culture have become ever more frequent, this visual turn has largely bypassed Tristan scholarship, which has traditionally been focused on other concerns. This is particularly the case for Gottfried von Strassburg's *Tristan*. The variety and number of approaches bear testimony to the complicated and nuanced threads of this text that every generation has sought to unravel anew.[7] While nineteenth-century work seems primarily concerned with the theme of adultery and attempts to distance itself morally from the story, twentieth-century scholars focus on the concept of love and regard its intricate relationship to religious discourses of the time as the romance's most distinguishing feature. The unification of the lovers was idealized and understood as a quasi-religious experience that drew on contemporary mystical concepts, in particular the notion of the mystic union with God.[8] This positive assessment of the romance that arose from scholars' idealization of the lovers' union meant, however, that little attention was paid to the potential for conflict and discord at court and between the lovers themselves.

The focus of scholarly debate has since changed. For the past two decades the discussion has centered on the negative and destructive aspects of the romance.[9] From one perspective, for example, the lovers' sorrow is a result of their social context, which impedes the relationship's consummation but does not change the ideal notion of love.[10] Recent approaches have examined instead the paradox inherent to the concept of love portrayed in the romance; the opposition of *eros* and death; the development of identity and the issue of subjectivity, particularly of the male protagonist; the transgressive and socially destructive behavior of the lovers; and the abrupt and seemingly unmotivated violent scenes that cannot be easily reconciled with the story of the lovers.[11] The aesthetic structure of the romance both complicates the text's interpretation and sheds new light on the romance.[12] Whether the fragmentary nature of Gottfried's version indicates that the poet intended to leave the outcome of his story open is debatable; it is usually assumed, based on references in the text itself, that this version too would have ended with the lovers' deaths.[13] Some recent work has investigated the mythical aspects of the romance and the competing notions of time that arise from the overlap of the different narrative layers. In this context scholars have focused on individual scenes and the text's segmentation into discrete episodes that are not completely autonomous but have their own dynamic and therefore often seem to cast the entire text in a new light.[14]

Today scholars typically do not even attempt to reconcile all the opposing elements of the romance: the idealism and destructiveness of Gottfried's concept of love; the fatality and contingency of the plot; the reflective and anarchic nature of the characters; the allusiveness and concreteness of the narrative; or the utopian and regressive aspects of the romance. These and other issues continue to present a highly complex and puzzling challenge for the story's recipients.[15]

This book is organized as follows. Part I, "Courtly Bodies, Seeing, and Emotions," examines the importance of seeing and visualizing for the representation of love in the text itself. The importance of visually coded communication, like ritual and performance, for courtly society has long been established. In "The Light of Courtly Society: Blanscheflur and Riwalin," Jan-Dirk Müller focuses on Gottfried's *Tristan* and argues that crucial differences between the love of Tristan's parents, Riwalin and Blanscheflur, and that of Tristan and Isolde arise out of the different ways in which these passionate erotic love affairs could accommodate themselves to the all-embracing visuality of courtly culture and its semantics of seeing. The love of Tristan's parents is described in the text as *leal amur,* legitimate love, and this designation arises, according to Müller, because, although it originates as illicit, their love ultimately conforms to an acknowledged and conventional visual paradigm.

James A. Schultz also compares the love of Tristan and Isolde with that of his parents but comes to a different conclusion. In "Why Do Tristan and Isolde Make Love? The Love Potion as a Milestone in the History of Sexuality," Schultz makes the case that for the poets Gottfried and Eilhart, the love of both Tristan and Isolde and Riwalin and Blanscheflur was "legitimate." Schultz argues that both authors refuse to engage Christian theological discourses that explain sexual habits with innate forces like lust as a consequence of original sin. The poets' refusal to explore the question of what impelled their characters to seek sexual relations signals a determination on the part of an emerging secular courtly culture to set off a domain in which writers could explore love and the desire to make love free from the taint of sinfulness that Christian theology had established as the first cause of desire. These authors used the symbol of the love potion to block theological inquiry into sexuality, thereby relieving love of denigration and opening a narrative domain for secular love and sexuality.

Two chapters examine the creation of allegory and visual space in Gottfried's *Tristan* and its reception. In "How to Find Love in Literature: Reading Gottfried von Strassburg's *Tristan* and His Cave of Lovers," Haiko Wandhoff revisits the cave of lovers in Gottfried's *Tristan,* arguing that it is not only the romance's conceptual nucleus but also a *mise-en-abyme,* an internal representation of Gottfried's *Tristan,* that reflects and is reflected in the romance. Reading Gottfried's text as a cave of lovers and the cave as a text sheds new light on his conception of love and literature. Wandhoff argues that love is ultimately transformed into an aesthetic principle in Gottfried's work, that Gottfried constructs his poem as a material manifestation of love and imagines a reader who is able to decode this visualization.

Ludger Lieb's chapter, "Seeing Love in the World of Lovers: Late Medieval Love Literature as a Fulfillment of Gottfried's *Tristan,*" explores the literary afterlife of Tristan love in the late medieval rhymed couplet texts known as *Minnereden*, which use personification, allegory, and the description of love symptoms to fully realize strategies for visualizing love suggested in Gottfried's *Tristan*. Only true lovers, Lieb argues, are able to see love in this "other world."

Part II, "Media, Representation, and Performance," addresses the ways in which the story is reshaped as it is reconceived for different media. These reinterpretations of the material bring into high relief the emotional valence of the story for its different audiences.

In his comparative contribution, "From Myth to Emblem to Panorama," Michael Curschmann considers the historical dynamics of the long Tristan tradition, asking the question, "What are some of the forces or agents that create and maintain consciousness of, and interest in, the subject beyond its initial appeal?" He offers quick sketches of four stages: the initial formulations of the myth in early verse romance, the ascendance of an emblematic representation of the emerging story in a single image; the treatment of the narrative in Thomas Malory's panoramic vision of the Arthurian world; and finally, one late and grand Victorian response to this vision, *Tristram of Lyonesse* by Algernon Charles Swinburne, poet, critic, and medievalist.

Elke Koch's chapter, "Framing Tristan — Taming Tristan? The Materiality of Text and Body in Hans Sachs's *Tragedia*," brings into focus Sachs's moralized sixteenth-century dramatic version of the story. Koch discusses the materiality of the body and the materiality of the text as keys for analyzing the aesthetic strategies that Sachs uses to represent love by employing the genre of drama and the media of performance as well as print. Sachs's emotional pedagogy prepares the ground for a repressive discipline of emotion by reinforcing an understanding of love as dangerous energy and therefore, eventually, as a drive. By constituting love as a drive, Sachs draws on earlier concepts of the affect, but by equating love and desire, by derationalizing the emotion and separating it from the body as a means of communication while at the same time planting it firmly within the body, he takes part in shaping a concept of emotion that still echoes in Norbert Elias's understanding of civilization and its history.

Amanda Luyster, in "Time, Space, and Mind: *Tristan* in Three Dimensions in Fourteenth-Century France," examines the fourteenth-century wall paintings in the great hall of the château of Saint-Floret.

Luyster argues that the overall design draws the viewer into its three-dimensional presence of reality, shaping his or her journey through the distinct segments of the room's architecture so as to mimic the literary protagonists' journey through the narrative. The unusual complexity and focus on re-creating movement through time and space at Saint-Floret are analogous to religious wall paintings of the fourteenth century, and the author proposes formal and historical parallels with Avignon. Saint-Floret is unusual, however, in that the re-creation of space and experience is transferred to the secular realm. Luyster concludes that the murals re-create time and space and a full-body experience, an experience like that of reality, and she suggests that the viewing experience might be understood as a secular pilgrimage, a journey that mirrors that of Tristan and other heroes through the chateaux and forests of legend.

Klaus Krüger's chapter, "Tristan Love: Elite Self-Fashioning in Italian Frescoes of the Thirteenth and Fourteenth Centuries," examines fresco fragments from private houses in Florence. Placing these frescoes against the backdrop of sociopolitical transformation, Krüger argues that they allowed bourgeois householders and patrons in search of a new identity to appropriate the models of social self-fashioning favored by the very nobility they sought to displace. While the representational art in these frescoes originally belonged to the nobility, in its new context it no longer has the same points of reference. The heraldic crests and other insignia of noble elitism, for instance, no longer refer to actual genealogies but symbolize power among the new urban middle-class elite. One curious aspect of the situation in Florence is that the urban elite has moved this representational art out of public spaces and into their private rooms.

In the third and final part of this volume, "The Visual Culture of *Tristan,*" five scholars bring new, yet foundational material evidence to our attention, setting the stage for more nuanced analyses of the striking visual iconicity of this story, that is to say, its significant narrative moments that, translated into depictions, effectively reduce the story to a single scene.

Martin Baisch's study, "Discourses of Curiosity: The Materiality of Meaning in Edition Studies and Cultural Studies," focuses on the question of materiality, which is defined in two ways. First, materiality means the factual transmission of the text, whose relevance and status have been discussed by scholars under the rubric of material philology. Second, materiality functions on a semiotic level to refer to the ways in which texts represent and suggest material presence or absence. A discussion of the poetic commentaries in Gottfried's *Tristan* shows that both definitions of materiality can be used productively. As material texts, the poetic commentaries differ from one manuscript to the next. Further, these different versions produce differing auras of materiality, or effects of authorial presence. The chapter concludes with a discussion of editorial and philological problems within scholarship on Gottfried's *Tristan* regarding materiality.

Although the Tristan material appears frequently in the visual arts, only three manuscripts contain illustrations of Gottfried's *Tristan*. In "Textual Worlds — Pictorial Worlds: Interpreting the Tristan Story in Illuminated Manuscripts," Elke Brüggen and Hans-Joachim Ziegeler compare these three image cycles that appear in the thirteenth-century Munich manuscript (Bayerische Statsbibliothek, Cgm 51), the fourteenth-century Cologne manuscript (Historisches Archiv, W*kl.f°88), and the fifteenth-century Brussels manuscript (Bibliothèque Royale, MS 14697). Focusing on the story of Riwalin and Blanscheflur and Tristan's birth, the authors explore the often surprisingly disjunctive relationship between story and image, arguing that decisions about image making go hand in hand with considerations regarding the medium of the book and its format.

When dealing with written texts, we can identify an illumination by its placement in the manuscript or by an accompanying rubric or inscription. When dealing with ivories, embroideries, wall paintings, and other artifacts, however, there is often no written identification on the object. Then it is necessary to have a specific image, a scene that can be identified from its context no matter what the medium. In "Specific and Generic Scenes in Verse *Tristan* Illustrations," Stephanie Cain Van D'Elden provides a survey of Tristan images in all media and argues for a distinction between specific and generic scenes. The alternation between these specific and generic scenes in the structure of the romance of Tristan and Isolde helps us understand the composer/designer/artist's approach to the story — his intentions in rendering the story either in writing or visually—from a simple courtly tale of bride-winning to a complex account of adultery and intrigue.

Margaret Alison Stones's chapter, "The Artistic Context of Some Northern French Illustrated *Tristan* Manuscripts," similarly addresses source material that has never been published and presents a panorama of stylistic changes in visual representations of the Tristan story in illuminated French manuscripts. Stones outlines the chronology and geography of the reception of Tristan in France through a comparative examination of the illustrations in the manuscripts and their cultural context. Although most of the manuscripts are neither signed nor dated, nor are many of their patrons known, it is often possible to attribute the illustrations by stylistic analogy to workshops or sometimes to artists whose other works are better localized and dated. In this way a pattern of the reception of *Tristan* manuscripts can be reconstructed.

THIS VOLUME ALLOWS READERS TO SURVEY THE RICHNESS OF THE surviving evidence from a variety of disciplinary approaches while also offering new perspectives on the nature of representation in medieval culture. It is our hope that it will stimulate a dialogue in which questions of interest to art historians and literary scholars intersect in productive and exciting ways. Our goal is to facilitate interdisciplinary dialogue and to open up and explore new avenues of inquiry into the well-documented and well-researched story of Tristan and Isolde.

Notes

1. This conference, "Visuality and Materiality in the Story of Tristan and Isolde," was held March 30 to April 1, 2007, at Duke University and the University of North Carolina at Chapel Hill as a part of the collaborative project "Tristan and Isolde and the Emotional Cultures of the Middle Ages."

2. The literature on individual pictorial representations of the Tristan story is too vast to provide a comprehensive survey of it here. The following works provide surveys of objects containing images: Michael Curschmann, "Images of Tristan," in *Gottfried von Strassburg and the Medieval Tristan Legend: Papers from an Anglo–North American Symposium,* ed. A. Stevens

and R. Wisbey (Cambridge: D. S. Brewer, 1990), 1–17; Doris Fouquet, *Wort und Bild in der mittelalterlichen Tristantradition: Der älteste Tristanteppich von Kloster Wienhausen und die textile Tristanüberlieferung des Mittelalters* (Berlin: Erich Schmidt, 1971); Hella Frühmorgen-Voss, "Tristan und Isolde in mittelalterlichen Bildzeugnissen," in *Text und Illustration im Mittelalter: Aufsätze zu den Wechselbeziehungen zwischen Literatur und bildender Kunst,* ed. Norbert H. Ott (Munich: C. H. Beck, 1975), 119–39, figs. 37–53; Norbert H. Ott, "Katalog der Tristan-Bildzeugnisse," in Ott, *Text und Illustration,* 140–71; Norbert H. Ott, "Epische Stoffe in mittelalterlichen Bildzeugnissen," in *Epische Stoffe des Mittelalters,* ed. Volker Mertens and Ulrich Müller (Stuttgart: A. Kröner, 1984), 449–74; Norbert Werner, "Tristan-Darstellungen in der Kunst des Mittelalters," in *Tristan und Isolt im Spätmittelalter: Vorträge eines interdisziplinären Symposiums vom 3. bis 8. Juni 1996 an der Justus-Liebig-Universität Gießen,* ed. Xenja von Ertzdorff (Amsterdam: Rodopi, 1999), 13–59.

3. For example, Richard Wagner's *Tristan* and Thomas Mann's *Tristan.* More recent works that engage with the story of Tristan include Raoul Schrott, *Tristan da Cunha, oder Die Hälfte der Erde* (Munich: Hanser, 2003); and John Updike, *Brazil* (New York: A. A. Knopf, 1994); and the many film versions include Jean Delannoy, *L'Éternel retour* (Art House Classic, 1943); Veith von Fürstenberg, *Feuer und Schwert—Die Legende von Tristan und Isolde* (DNS, 1982); Fabrizio Costa, *Il cuore e la spada* (Sat 1 T. V. Production, 1998); and Kevin Reynolds, *Tristan & Isolde* (ApolloProMedia 1. Filmproduktion KG (I), 2006).

4. There are several exceptions to this rule, such as the comparative studies by Walter Haug, "Erzählen als Suche nach personaler Identität, oder: Gottfrieds von Straßburg Liebeskonzept im Spiegel des neuen *Tristan*-Fragments von Carlisle," in *Erzählungen in Erzählungen: Phänomene der Narration in Mittelalter und Früher Neuzeit,* ed. Harald Haferland and Michael Mecklenburg (München: W. Fink, 1996), 177–87; and "Reinterpreting the Tristan Romances of Thomas and Gotfrid: Implications of a Recent Discovery," *Arthuriana* 7.3 (1997): 44–59, that take into consideration the Carlisle fragment.

5. See Doris Fouquet, "Die Baumgartenszene des Tristan in der mittelalterlichen Kunst und Literatur," *Zeitschrift für deutsche Philologie* 92 (1973): 360–70; Curschmann, "Images of Tristan"; Kathryn Starkey, "Tristan Slippers: An Image of Adultery on a Symbol of Marriage?," in *Medieval Fabrications: Dress, Textiles, Clothwork, and Other Cultural Imaginings,* ed. E. Jane Burns (New York: Palgrave, 2004), 35–53.

6. See, for example, Jan-Dirk Müller, "Die Destruktion des Heros oder wie erzählt Eilhart von passionierter Liebe?," in *Il romanzo di Tristano nella letteratura del Medioevo/Der "Tristan" in der Literatur des Mittelalters: Beiträge der Triester Tagung 1989,* ed. Paola Schulze-Belli and Michael Dallapiazza (Frankfurt am Main: Th. Hector, 1990), 19–37; Peter Strohschneider, "Gotfrit-Fortsetzungen: Tristans Ende im 13. Jahrhundert und die Möglichkeiten nachklassischer Epik," *Deutsche Vierteljahrsschrift* 65 (1991): 70–98; and Monika Schausten, *Erzählwelten der Tristangeschichte im hohen Mittelalter: Untersuchungen zu den deutschsprachigen Tristanfassungen des 12. und 13. Jahrhunderts* (München: W. Fink, 1999).

7. For a survey of secondary literature, see René Wetzel, "Der Tristanstoff in der Literatur des deutschen Mittelalters: Forschungsbericht, 1969–1994," in *Forschungsberichte zur Germanistischen Mediävistik,* ed. Hans-Jochen Schiewer, vol. 5.1 (Bern: Peter Lang, 1996), 190–254; Christoph Huber, *Gottfried von Straßburg: Tristan,* Klassiker-Lektüren 3 (Berlin: Erich Schmidt, 2000; rev. ed., 2001); and Huber's online bibliography, "Bibliographie zum *Tristan* von Gottfried von Straßburg (1984–2002)," *Das altgermanistische Internetportal: Mediaevum.de,* http://bibliographien.mediaevum.de/ bibliographien/bibliographietristan.htm (Feb. 18, 2008), which goes up to 2002. An unpublished extension of this bibliography that incorporates scholarship on other versions of Tristan and continues to 2007 was compiled by the authors as part of the TransCoop Program project "Tristan and Isolde and the Emotional Cultures of the Middle Ages." A comprehensive (or even representational) overview of the extensive secondary literature on the story of Tristan is beyond the scope of this introduction. We refer here to only a few of the seminal works.

8. For a contrasting opinion, see Alois M. Haas, "Mystik oder Erotik? Dialektik von Tod und Leben in Gottfrieds *Tristan,*" in *Todesbilder im Mittelalter: Fakten und Hinweise in der deutschen Literatur,* ed. Alois M. Haas (Darmstadt: Wissenschaftliche Buchgesellschaft, 1989), 148–68. See also Niklaus Largier, "Liebe als Medium der Transgression: Überlegungen zu Affektgemeinschaft und Habitusformung in Gottfrieds *Tristan* (mit einer Anm. zur *Hohelied*-Mystik)," in *Norm und Krise von Kommunikation: Inszenierungen literarischer und sozialer Interaktion im Mittelalter; Für Peter von Moos,* ed. Alois Hahn, Gert Melville, and Werner Röcke (Berlin: Lit, 2006), 209–24.

9. This argument draws on Horst Wenzel, "Negation und Doppelung: Poetische Experimentalformen von Individualgeschichte im *Tristan* Gottfrieds von Straßburg," in *Wege in die Neuzeit,* ed. Thomas Cramer (München: W. Fink, 1988), 229–51. On the conflict with courtly culture, see Urban

Küsters, "Liebe zum Hof. Vorstellungen und Erscheinungsformen einer 'höfischen' Lebensordnung in Gottfrieds *Tristan,*" in *Höfische Literatur, Hofgesellschaft, höfische Lebensformen um 1200: Kolloquium am Zentrum für Interdisziplinäre Forschung der Universität Bielefeld (3. bis 5. November 1983),* ed. Gert Kaiser and Jan-Dirk Müller (Düsseldorf: Droste, 1986), 141–76; Horst Wenzel, "Öffentlichkeit und Heimlichkeit in Gottfrieds 'Tristan,'" *Zeitschrift für Deutsche Philologie* 107 (1988): 335–61; C. Stephen Jaeger, "Mark and Tristan: The Love of Medieval Kings and Their Courts," in *In hôhem prîse: Festschrift für Ernst S. Dick,* ed. Winder McConnell (Göppingen: Kümmerle, 1989), 183–97; Werner Röcke, "Im Schatten höfischen Lichtes. Zur Trennung von Öffentlichkeit und Privatheit im mittelalterlichen Tristan-Roman," in *Licht: Religiöse und literarische Gebrauchsformen,* ed. Walther Gebhardt (Frankfurt am Main: Peter Lang, 1990), 37–75.

10. See Tomas Tomasek, *Die Utopie im "Tristan" Gotfrieds von Straßburg,* Hermaea, N. F. 49 (Tübingen: Niemeyer, 1985); and Rüdiger Schnell, *Suche nach Wahrheit: Gottfrieds "Tristan und Isold" als erkenntniskritischer Roman,* Hermaea, N. F. 67 (Tübingen: Niemeyer, 1992).

11. On the opposition of *eros* and death, see Haug's "Der *Tristan* — eine interarthurische Lektüre," in Walter Haug, *Brechungen auf dem Weg zur Individualität: Kleine Schriften zur Literatur des Mittelalters* (Tübingen: Niemeyer, 1995), 184–96; "Erzählen als Suche"; and "Gottfrieds von Straßburg 'Tristan'—Sexueller Sündenfall oder erotische Utopie," in *Kontroversen, alte und neue: Akten des VII. Internationalen Germanisten-Kongresses Göttingen 1985,* vol. 1, ed. A. Schöne (Tübingen: Niemeyer, 1986), 41–52. On the development of identity and the issue of subjectivity, see, for example, Wenzel, "Negation und Doppelung"; Judith Klinger, "Möglichkeiten und Strategien der Subjekt-Reflexion im höfischen Roman: Tristan und Lancelot," in *Mittelalter: Neue Wege durch einen alten Kontinent,* ed. Jan-Dirk Müller and Horst Wenzel (Stuttgart: Hirzel, 1999), 127–48; Molly C. Robinson, "*Tristan*: A Story of Precarious Belonging," *Tristania* 18 (1998): 1–16; Monika Schausten, "*Ich bin, alse ich hân vernomen, ze wunderlîchen maeren komen*: Zur Funktion biographischer und autobiographischer Figurenrede für die narrative Konstitution von Identität in Gottfrieds von Straßburg 'Tristan,'" *Beiträge zur Geschichte der deutschen Sprache und Literatur* 123 (2001): 24–48; Elke Koch, *Trauer und Identität: Inszenierungen von Emotionen in der deutschen Literatur des Mittelalters* (Berlin: de Gruyter, 2006). On the destructive behavior of the lovers, see Rainer Warning, "Die narrative Lust an der List: Norm und Transgression im Tristan," in *Transgressionen: Literatur als Ethnographie,* ed. Gerhard Neumann and Rainer Warning, Litterae 98 (Freiburg: Rom-

bach, 2003), 175–212; Jan-Dirk Müller, "Gottfried von Straßburg: *Tristan*; Transgression und Ökonomie," in Neumann and Warning, *Transgressionen,* 213–42. And on the seemingly unmotivated violent scenes, see Jutta Eming, "Ritualisierte Konfliktbewältigung bei Eilhart und Gottfried: Der Mordanschlag auf Brangäne und das Gottesurteil," *LiLi* 144 (2006): 9–29.

12. Christian Kiening, "Ästhetik des Liebestods: Am Beispiel von *Tristan* und *Herzmaere,*" in *Das fremde Schöne: Dimensionen des Ästhetischen in der Literatur des Mittelalters,* ed. Manuel Braun and Christopher Young, Trends in Medieval Philology 12 (Berlin: de Gruyter, 2007), 171–93, looks at Tristan from the perspective of a medieval aesthetic.

13. See, for example, Christoph Huber, "Spiegelungen des Liebestodes im 'Tristan' Gottfrieds von Straßburg," in *Tristan und Isolde: Unvergängliches Thema der Weltliteratur,* ed. Danielle Buschinger and Wolfgang Spiewok (Greifswald: Reinecke-Verlag, 1996), 127–40. Warning, "Die narrative Lust," is one exception, however. Ingrid Kasten, "Martyrium und Opfer: Der Liebestod im *Tristan,*" in *Martyrdom in Literature: Visions of Death and Meaningful Suffering in Europe and the Middle East from Antiquity to Modernity,* ed. Friederike Pannewick (Wiesbaden: Reichert, 2004), 245–57, sees a parallel in the poem's structure to martyr legends.

14. Thus Susanne Köbele, "*Iemer niuwe*: Wiederholung in Gottfrieds 'Tristan,'" in *Der "Tristan" Gottfrieds von Straßburg: Symposion Santiago de Compostela, 5. bis 8. April 2000,* ed. Christoph Huber and Victor Millet (Tübingen: Niemeyer, 2002), 97–115; Müller, "Zeit im 'Tristan,'" in Huber and Millet, *Der "Tristan" Gottfrieds von Straßburg,* 379–97; and Uta Störmer-Caysa, "Wer ist der Herr der Zeit? Über die Ungewissheit von Übereinkunft in Gottfrieds *Tristan,*" *Poetica* 33 (2001): 51–68.

15. See, for example, Max Wehrli, "Das Abenteuer von Gottfrieds *Tristan,*" in *Formen mittelalterlicher Erzählung: Aufsätze* (Zürich: Atlantis, 1969), 243–70.

PART I

Courtly Bodies, Seeing, and Emotions

CHAPTER ONE

The Light of Courtly Society

Blanscheflur and Riwalin

JAN-DIRK MÜLLER

Visuality is the core of courtly life.[1] Everything that claims to be legitimate and valuable has to prove itself before the eyes of courtly society. The love of Riwalin and Blanscheflur — in contrast to that of Tristan and Isolde — is called *leal amur,* legitimate love, and as such it must be practiced in accordance with common rules.[2] Yet when the narrator first characterizes Blanscheflur and Riwalin's love as *leal amur,* it is still illicit. Courtly society does not approve of it, and it must be kept secret and hidden. Their love endangers Blanscheflur's honor, for its secrecy gives offense to King Mark and Tristan's conception is premarital. Nevertheless, there must be some quality that justifies the attribute *leal amur* and distinguishes their love from Tristan's passion (which is never referred to as *leal*). How does Gottfried deal with this problem? My thesis is that their love is called *leal* because it is ultimately in agreement with courtly values; it should be respected because it confirms what everybody can see.[3]

The transformation of an illegitimate love into a legitimate one is mirrored in a narrative process that starts with and returns to courtly visuality, remaining only a short period in the darkness of secrecy. The story leads from light to dark and back to light. I show this by describing the origin of Blanscheflur and Riwalin's love and its termination after their flight from Mark's court. To be sure, in the end the picture is not complete, the full restoration of social approval is impeded, and some doubts about legitimacy remain. But later on, these flaws are corrected. Deviant in the beginning, Riwalin and Blanscheflur's love conforms step by step to courtly norms. Hence it finally could have been integrated into courtly order, if an unforeseen accident had not happened. In contrast, the potion love of Tristan and Isolde remains irreconcilable with that order, even though it also depends on it. It seems that in medieval epics this dependence cannot be overcome.

The courtly concept of love always combines individual and social elements.[4] This is obvious in *Minnesang.* Here, the sentence "I love you" is addressed to the lady via the courtly audience. It is also apparent in the rituals of friendship and alliance. The public kissing of an ally or friend can end in a love scene (e.g., in *Reinfrid von Braunschweig*)[5] or the courtly welcome of a noble foreigner and the exchange of representative gifts in an inescapable passion *(Eneit).*[6] The two components can be integrated (as in the first case) or dissociated (as in the second) but never as radically separated as with Tristan and Isolde. In this regard the love of Tristan's parents remains a conventional one.

My starting point is a simple question: I ask how Blanscheflur sees Riwalin and how she sees herself in relation to Riwalin. The answer will tell us something about the importance of visuality and the character of emotion in courtly novels. The Blanscheflur-Riwalin configurations need to be compared with similar configurations in the story of Tristan and Isolde. My aim is to demonstrate some crucial differences in spite of some identical presuppositions. Here I disagree with the Tristan scholarship that describes the relationship as a typological one.[7] In my opinion the term *typology* — suggesting a relation of promise and fulfillment — is not appropriate. I maintain that Tristan's passion is unique, and by telling the story of his parents Gottfried tries to emphasize the differences from usual courtly love. There is no connection from one to the other. But even Tristan's passion is judged by comparison to courtly norms; it can never be freed from them and therefore finally fails. Tristan and Isolde's passion cannot surpass *leal amur* but only countermand it. I shall explain this by analyzing the semantics of light, which are similar in only one respect in the two stories.

The Courtly Feast, or Riwalin in the Focus of Public Desire

The love of Tristan's parents depends in a puzzling way on what anybody can see and what anybody should think.[8] It begins during a courtly festival that displays the splendor of courtly society.[9] Mark's "hohgezit" (524) is a feast for the eyes. Nothing that has ever been seen by human eyes ("keines ougen schouwe" [544]) surpasses what can be seen here: "swaz dem ougen sanfte tuot / und edeliu herze ervröuwen sol" (all that soothes the eye and gladdens noble hearts, 553). The radiance of the flowers and blossoms is reflected in the eyes of the participants ("daz si den lieben gesten / in ir ougen widerglesten" [they reflected from the dear guests' eyes, 567–68]). Vernal nature and courtly society mirror each other:

> diu süeze boumbluot sach den man
> so rehte suoze lachend an,
> daz sich daz herze und al der muot
> wider an die lachende bluot
> mit spilenden ougen machete
> und ir allez widerlachete.
>
> (569–74)

———

> [The delightful blossom on the trees smiled out at one so pleasantly that one's heart and all one's soul answered the smiling blossom with teasing eyes, and gave back all its smiles.]

One may see everything that one desires: "und swes der gerne sehende man ze sehene guoten muot gewan, daz lie diu state da wol geschehen" (And all that a man who loved spectacles wanted to see was there to indulge him, 613–15). Gottfried specifies the panorama of courtly entertainments that people can behold:

> dise vuoren *sehen* vrouwen.
> jene ander tanzen *schouwen*;
> dise *sahen* buhurdieren,
> jene ander justieren.
>
> (617–20)

———

[Some went to look at the ladies, others to see dancing;
some watched the bohort, others jousting.]

People admire the knights' beautiful equipment and the beautiful colors that the summer is displaying.

Gottfried describes less the festivities themselves than how courtly society perceives them ("man *sach*" [one saw, 663]; "lie der sumer wol schouwen" [summer showed clearly, 676]; "*sach* man" [one saw, 679]).[10] This perception is a collective one. There is no special subject of perception, no special agent seeing: courtly society gazing at itself enjoys its own beauty and perfection.[11]

In the center of this display of beauty is Mark's sister Blanscheflur, a "sælige ougenweide" (heavenly vision, 641), a young lady more beautiful than any other:

> ein maget, daz da noch anderswa
> schoener wip nie wart gesehen.
> wir hoeren von ir schoene jehen,
> sine gesæhe nie kein lebende man
> mit inneclichen ougen an,
> ern minnete da nach iemer me
> wip und tugende baz dan e.
> (634–40)

———

[a girl so lovely that you never saw a lovelier [lady], there
 or anywhere. We hear tell of her beauty that no man
 of flesh and blood had ever gazed at her with sincere
 eyes and not loved women and noble qualities better
 ever after.]

The desire that Blanscheflur inspires is a collective one, too. It is not Riwalin who falls in love with her; the focus is on every "lebende man" (living man), and it is not only she who is the object of male desire, but by seeing her everybody will love women and their excellence in general more than before. Gazing in courtly society is a collective act, and what is seen are collective values, not an individual person and his or her uniqueness.

In the same way Riwalin is the object of collective appraisal.[12] Blanscheflur is one of the ladies watching the tournament (Gottfried says they "sazen an ir *schouwe*" [sat watching the display, 690]), a tournament so splendid that all want to see it ("daz ez manic ouge gerne *sach*" [that many loved to watch it, 693]). When Blanscheflur catches sight of Riwalin for the first time during the festivities she sees what everyone sees and reacts as everyone does. In the beginning her love is equivalent to all the ladies' delight in the handsome young knight ("'*seht,*' sprachen si, 'der jungelinc / der ist ein sæliger man'" ["See," they said, "that young man; he is a blissful man," 702–3]). They praise him for his appearance, the beauty of his body, his manners, the way he handles his arms, and so on: "wie süeze ist aller sin gebar" (How charming his whole bearing!, 716; cf. 704–17). Their inference includes every lady, not only Blanscheflur: "o wol si sæligez wip, / der vröude an ime beliben sol" (Fortunate is the woman who can enjoy his virtues, 718–19).

Blanscheflur pays attention to the others' words ("nu marcte ir aller mære wol" [she was taking in what they were all saying, 720]). It is their esteem for him ("ze hohem werde" [their prize of his virtues, 724]) that affects her "muot" (thoughts, 725) and her heart (727–29). Only now does she begin to distance herself from the rest of the court; she herself wants to become the "sælige wip" the ladies talked about. The origin of love is public esteem, esteem of her beauty and his virtues. Yet the separation from the others seems to be precarious. Blanscheflur has to conceal her emotions not only from courtly society but from Riwalin as well. Hence, she talks in riddles to him when he eventually sees her at close range ("als er under ir ougen *sach*" [looking her in the eyes, 741]). It is no longer the courtly gaze but an intimate, private one. In the presence of the others communication is difficult. Blanscheflur has to be evasive, and Riwalin is not sure of the meaning of her words. But in the end he will understand what she intimates and both will realize that they are in love with each other.

For Blanscheflur the others who make up the courtly society continue to be present, even if she feels excluded from them. She explains her affection as bewitchment ("zouberlist") and regards it as a miracle ("diz vremede wunder . . . und disiu wunderlîche nôt" [this strange marvel and miraculous torment, 1004–5]), but she is aware of the fact that the other ladies' opinion stimulated her to fall in love and that she had only to verify with her own eyes what everybody said. Her eyes confirm what she heard before; they are dazzled by Riwalin's virtues:

> do ich so vil manic edele wip
> den sinen keiserlichen lip
> und sinen ritterlichen pris
> mit *lobe gehorte* in ballen wis
> als umbetriben unde tragen
> und sines *lobes* so vil *gesagen*
> und ich mit *ougen* selbe *sach*
> die tugende, der man von im *jach,*
> und allez in min herze las,
> swaz *lobeliches* an im was,
> da von ergouchete min sin:
> hie von geviel min herze an in.
> entriuwen daz *erblante* mich,
> daz was daz zouber, da von ich
> min selber sus vergezzen han.
>   (1027–41)

———

[when I heard so many noble ladies bandying his magnificent body about like a ball, and his fame as a knight, too, with their praises, and saying so much to his credit, and saw with my own eyes the fine virtues they gave him proclaimed, and contemplated in my heart what was to praise in him, I became infatuated, and that is why I lost my heart to him. Yes, it dazzled me, this was the witchery that has made me so forget myself.]

The process from exterior perception to interior emotion is analyzed in a meticulous way: Blanscheflur listens to the other ladies praising Riwalin, scrutinizes it with her own eyes, and considers in her heart what she heard and saw. The result—bedazzlement ("daz erblante mich" [1039]) and loss of herself ("min selber sus vergezzen han" [1041])—is enforced by collective judgment.

In its origin this love is *leal amur,* indirectly approved by the court: the most beautiful lady meets the best knight. But there are still some obstacles to be overcome. Their intimacy cannot reveal itself in full view. So at first nothing happens. To go on, Blanscheflur has to leave the arena of courtly visuality behind her for a while and withdraw into a dark space.

Illegitimate Love and the Seclusion from Courtly Society

Blanscheflur and Riwalin's love leads to an illegitimate affair, and this is indicated by the transition from light to darkness, from the open space of the feast to the seclusion of the sickroom, from visuality to invisibility and secrecy.[13] The following scenes are a series of acts that extinguish sight, question the validity of courtly norms, and endanger the identity of its members.

Riwalin is mortally wounded in a war, and at first public feeling and individual mourning coincide once more. This is expressed by the poem's grammar: first we hear a passive voice: "des wart ein jæmerlîchez clagen in dem hove und in dem lande" (this gave rise to doleful laments, at court and in the country, 1146–47); "in weinde manic edele wîp, manc vrouwe clagete sînen lîp. und swer in ie dâ vor gesach, den erbarmete sîn ungemach" (Many a noble woman wept for Riwalin, many a lady lamented him; and all who had ever seen him were moved to pity by his plight, 1159–62). But then the focus shifts to his beloved: "so was ez iemer eine sin Blanscheflor diu reine" (it was alone his Blanscheflur the beautiful, 1165–66), whose pain exceeds all. She torments her body and, regardless of the others, wants to see him for one last time (1189, 1197; cf. 1232). To do so she has to find a secret way to get to him. The spheres that until now were linked begin to compete.[14]

Even the preparations for her visit to the sickroom must remain unnoticed: "da nieman was niwan si zwo" (there was no one there except those two, 1205), that is, Blanscheflur and a servant. The meeting is prepared secretly ("tougenliche" [1260]). The servant disguises Blanscheflur as a beggar so that she is able to visit Riwalin. She has to hide the overwhelming beauty of her face ("ir antlützes schonheit" [1266]), that is, the quality identifying her as the lady of the best knight. Only thus—and not as the king's sister—may Blanscheflur enter the chamber where the dying Riwalin lies. Riwalin has also to send everyone away, including all the attendants caring for him. Blanscheflur's confidante feigns that she is bringing a doctor, lets her enter, and then leaves the room and locks the door. Society is thus systematically excluded. Gottfried creates a space where courtly visibility, class, and the beauty of the noble body are literally extinguished.

It gets dark. Earlier everything was mirrored in somebody's gaze; now nothing can be seen. Even Blanscheflur's goal to see Riwalin for one last time is frustrated. She loses sight: "saz et blintlichen dar" (sat there blindly, 1292); "ir claren ougen wart der tac trüebe unde vinster als diu naht" (In her clear eyes the day turned dark and somber as night, 1302–3). Her noble appearance vanishes: "ir rosevarwer munt wart bleich, ir lich diu kam vil garwe von der vil liehten varwe" (Her rosy lips grew wan, the hue of her flesh quite lost the glow that dwelt in it before, 1298–1300). No more beauty, no more brilliance. She faints and seems to be dead.

Before, the servant had promised that all would pass according to the laws of decorum and honor ("nach vuogen und nach eren" [1261]), but from the beginning of the scene Gottfried demonstrates the collapse of courtly order in the vanishing of light. When Blanscheflur recovers ("Nu daz si do von dirre not ein lützel wider ze crefte kam" [Now when she had rallied a little from this extremity, 1308–9]), Riwalin embraces her, he comes back to life, and she conceives a child. This appears to be inevitable ("ir beider wille ergienc" [they both fulfilled their desire, 1323]). It is not controlled by reason, by the perception of mutual virtues (as courtly love has to be), but is a result of sensual attraction—an almost anonymous process that does not take into account any social or moral considerations. Later, Riwalin is nearly dead, and Blanscheflur is threatened by death, too.[15] Death marks the utmost distance from courtly life. But the connection between *minne* and *tot* here is different from their connection in the story of Tristan and Isolde: *minne* and *tot* are not identical; *tot* can only be a dangerous consequence of *minne*. The wounded Riwalin risks his life, and Blanscheflur is *entladen* (relieved) from her suffering for her love and *beladen* (burdened) by the child she has conceived, which threatens her with shame and will cost her life (1333). It is in this context that their love is called perfect and characterized as *leal amur* (1362; cf. 1357–72).

Against every hope, Riwalin's wound is healed, and they can continue to enjoy their love. For the time being, this love has to beware of courtly supervision ("swenne sî mit vuogen ir state in ein getruogen" [when they could decently arrange a rendezvous, 1367–68]), but finally their secret is threatened by Riwalin's departure to his country. The danger can be overcome only if the story returns into the light of courtly visibility that it had left only fortuitously and under extreme conditions. This return has several stages.

Blanscheflur's Love and Public Blame

First the impending loss of Riwalin aggravates Blanscheflur's situation. When Blanscheflur finds out that Riwalin has to leave Mark's court she is so frightened that she loses sight and hearing and seems to die:

> von herzeleide ir aber geschach,
> daz sin *gehorte* noch *gesach.*
> ir lich wart an ir libe
> als eime *toten* wibe.
>
> (1389–92)

———

[the sorrow in her heart robbed her of sight and hearing.
The hue of her flesh became like that of a dead woman.]

Once again she faints and seems to be dead (1426–29). In this sense the secret love is still associated with darkness. Therefore they flee from Mark's court at nightfall (1578).

But the response to their imminent separation is rather odd. Blanscheflur complains more about having trespassed courtly norms than she regrets the future of her love. She did not consider the social consequences of an illegitimate affair when she gave herself to Riwalin; but when he wants to leave, she is mainly worried about those consequences. I think it is not possible to interpret her words as mere pretext to force Riwalin to care for her. At least the narrator says nothing about such a stratagem. On the contrary, by explaining what will happen to her she places her love again in the frame of courtly order that she temporarily left:

> herre unde vriunt, ich han von iu
> manc leit und vor den allen driu,
> diu toedic unde unwendic sint.
> (1463–65)

———

> [my lord and friend, you harmed me in three ways,
> each deadly and unalterable.]

First, she is afraid that her pregnancy will cost her her life; second, she is aware of the shame she has brought on Mark and herself and fears his revenge ("der heizet mich verderben und lesterliche ersterben" [he will bid me be destroyed and put to a shameful death, 1473–74]); and third, she suspects that even if Mark does not kill her he will disinherit her and she will fail to maintain her own and her child's status:

> daz er mich aber enterbet
> und nimet mir guot und ere,
> so muoz ich iemer mere
> unwert und swaches namen sin.
> dar zuo muoz ich min kindelin,
> daz einen lebenden vater hat,
> ziehen ane vater rat.
> (1480–86)

———

> [he would nevertheless disinherit me and deprive me of my
> honour and property; so that for the rest of my life I would
> lose my standing and be of no account. I would then have to

rear my child without the support of a father, though it has
a father living.]

And even if she herself could cope with her bad luck, it is not a
question that only concerns herself. She feels that she is the focus
of courtly society; everybody is looking at her ("daz man mich mit
den ougen siht" [1500]), and the shame ("laster") of her extramarital
pregnancy affects the king, the dynasty (her "vil hoch geslehte"), and
even Mark's kingdoms: Cornwall and England. Her blame is everybody's blame:

> Und enwolte ich daz niemer geclagen,
> solt ich daz laster eine tragen,
> daz min vil hoch geslehte
> und der künic min bruoder mehte
> des itewizes unde min
> mit eren ane und ane sin.
> swenn aber alle, die nu sint,
> diu maere sagent, ich habe ein kint
> erworben kebesliche,
> deist disem und jenem riche,
> Curnwale und Engellande
> ein offenbaeriu schande.
> und ouwe, swenne daz geschiht,
> daz man mich mit den ougen siht,
> daz zwei lant von den schulden min
> genidert und geschwechet sin,
> so waerich eine bezzer tot.
>   (1487–1503)

_____

[Nor would I ever complain of this if I could bear the shame
alone, and my most noble family and royal brother live in honor,
and free of the scandal and of me! But when the whole world
gossips it round that I have got a bastard child, this and the other
kingdom, Cornwall and England, will suffer open disgrace.
Ah me, when the day comes that people look at me reproachfully

for having caused two lands to be humiliated, I, lonely woman,
were better dead!]

What Blancheflur fears is by no means gossip about an *affaire de fesses;*
it is the judgment of the society she depends on and which defines her
identity. She worries about the fate of Mark's court whose honor will
be contaminated by her shame. Her shame and the ignominy of the
country will be seen, just as was her perfection and the perfection of
Mark's court before.

Riwalin understands and asks Blancheflur to decide whether he
shall stay with her and abandon his country or whether she will follow him. Blancheflur knows that under the conditions of courtly society neither he nor she can stay. So Riwalin prepares the flight. By
leaving Mark's court she can hope to restore her *ere* (honor). She will
be proven wrong, but this is caused by misadventure; it is not impossible on principle.

Return to Courtly Order: The Sun of Noble Alliance

After the nocturnal flight the story seems to return to the light of
honor. Riwalin's marshal, Rual, praises his lord for his luck, not because he found a loving and beautiful wife, but because he conquered
such a valuable trophy as the sister of King Mark. His is again a courtly
point of view. The noble alliance increases Riwalin's honor; his rank,
his glory, his joy rise like the sun:

> "ich sihe wol, herre," sprach er do
> "iuwer ere wahset alle wis,
> iuwer werdekeit und iuwer pris,
> iuwer vröude und iuwer wunne
> diu stiget als diu sunne.
> irne möhtet uf der erden
> von wibe niemer werden
> so hohes namen als von ir."
>
> (1612–19)

["I can well see, my lord," he said, "that your honor increases in every way! Your esteem and reputation, your happiness and joy mount like the sun! You could advance your name through no other woman in the world so much as her!"]

Now all is prepared for a happy ending: after the imminent war with Morgan the marriage is to be celebrated "herlich unde riche" (1627) (splendid and magnificent). Riwalin will take Blanscheflur "offenliche/ vor magen und vor mannen ze e" (1628–29) (publicly in the presence of kinsmen and vassals). For the time being he has to content himself with taking her in front of his followers ("ze kirchen . . . da ez pfaffen unde leien sehen" [in church, in the sight of priests and laymen, 1631–32]), that is, before witnesses, even if not yet the most noble ones, as Rual points out later on: "in minem huse daz geschach, / daz ichz und manic man sach" (this happened under my roof with myself and many others to witness, 4193–94). Certainly only when this solemn public act takes place before the persons upon whom Riwalin's rulership depends will secret and public spheres be reconciled. This does not happen, and this flaw will determine the beginning of Tristan's life. Nevertheless, it was at least intended to transform *leal amur* into a feudal marriage, and only an unexpected accident prevented it. The reestablishment of honor is once more interrupted but not forever, as Tristan's career at Mark's court will demonstrate.

There are still other differences that distinguish Riwalin and Blanscheflur's story from the story of Tristan and Isolde. Riwalin's death is not caused by love but by feudal strife. Blanscheflur dies speechless, mourning for him after she has given birth to Tristan. Does she die a *Liebestod* or — as did many women in the Middle Ages — in childbed? The narrator does not tell us. The story of Tristan's parents remains embedded in the ups and downs of feudal life.

Be that as it may, the renewed interruption is obvious. Tristan is removed from public attention; Rual and his wife hide him; nobody shall see him; they "namen daz cleine weiselin / und burgen ez vil tougen / den liuten von den ougen" (1824–26) (took the little orphan and hid him away from all eyes). During the first period of his life

Tristan stays in the dark. Nevertheless, already when he comes to Mark's court ("Tristan derst ze huse komen / unwizzend" [Tristan has unwittingly come home, 3379–80]), he is able to display his courtly skills until Rual appears at the court and impresses all by his noble appearance ("nu seht wie herliche er gat" [Now look at the stately way he walks, 4087]). No doubt is left about Tristan's royal heritage. There is no question about Blanscheflur's fears; the alliance is legalized as Mark welcomes Tristan as his relative and heir. The story returns to the light of courtly order and public attention.

Still Tristan has to conceal his wish to avenge himself on Morgan; he suffers secretly ("tougenlichen smerzen" [5289]). When he plans to attack him, he and his followers hide their armor under their clothes. By killing Morgan, who had reproached Tristan for his illegitimate birth, Tristan is reestablished as feudal lord.

Tristan's Love and Courtly Visuality

Only before they drink the potion do Tristan and Isolde live in the sphere of courtly visuality. Afterwards, their sphere is the *clair-obscure,* the in-between. Already the room where they drink the potion is separated from the open space on the ship, a room of secrecy for the comfort of Isolde and her ladies: "ein kielkemenat / nach heinlicher sache / gegeben zuo ir gemache" (a private cabin in the keel to be given for their comfort, 11538–40).

Only Tristan comes in from time to time to console the queen. When the others go ashore to relax Tristan comes to see "die liehten sine vrouwen" (his radiant lady, 11662). It is on this occasion that they drink the fatal potion, which is hidden in a still more secret place: "verborgen unde behalten" (hidden and deposited, 11680).

This disposition of space anticipates the total isolation they will suffer, the several attempts to enjoy their love and at the same time the pressure to dissimulate it before the court, the retreat into the *fossiure a la gent amant,* and finally their separation from each other. At first, dissimulation is successful; they are able to deceive the court, for nobody suspects anything:

daz nie nieman dervan
dekeinen arcwan gewan.
ir gebaerde, ir rede, ir maere
oder swaz ir dinges waere
daz nam in lützel ieman war.
                (12963–67)

———

[nobody grew suspicious. None paid attention to what they said,
to how they comported themselves or to any concern of theirs.]

They are able to look at each other "dicke in dem tage . . . in der me-
nege und unter den liuten . . . naht unde tac . . . vrilich und offen-
baere" (many times in the day . . . in the crowd and in the presence of
others . . . night and day . . . open and unconstrained, 12976, 12979,
12983, 12989). In this respect their love recalls the love of Riwalin and
Blanscheflur: it is secret, but it unfolds in full view of the court:

si verswigen ouch ir dinc
und halen ir haelinc
vil anclich und vil ange.
                (13083–85)

———

[They said not a word of their affairs, they kept their secret
very cautiously and fearfully.]

But once their love is suspected it has to withdraw into the space
between the public and private spheres. I pass over the nocturnal conversations between Mark and Isolde that oscillate between open con-
fession and astute lie, and comment briefly on the orchard episode,
when the lovers try to speak to each other apart from courtly supervision. The place where they meet, the *boumgarte* (orchard), is a space
in-between, not in the privacy of Isolde's *kemenate* (chamber), which
should be reserved for Mark, but nearby; the area is secluded but accessible to the public. It is night (the time of secrecy), but the moon is
shining. Nobody sees clearly, but one can recognize shadows. Tristan
and Isolde meet seemingly alone but in a space normally accessible to

all courtiers; as the others are hidden in the treetop, they have to talk indirectly. In the semidarkness the lovers can speak to each other without compromising themselves. But they have to conceal what they really think and want. Their love has no space in public. The space where they can communicate is an ambiguous in-between.

Therefore, they have to leave the court—only to realize that the problem remains. It seems impossible to imagine a love that is not legitimated by the light of honor, *ere*. This holds true even in the *Minnegrotte*.[16] The grotto is an in-between, too. They live in a closed space, a cave ("hol" [16684]), but even if not everyone is able to enter the cave, the interior can be seen from the outside. The subterranean cave is visually exposed and brightly illuminated by three little windows in the rock—allegorically interpreted as "güete," "diemüete," and "zuht" (17063–65) (kindness, humility, and breeding). The light is at the same time "schone unde tougenlichen" (beautiful and secret, 17064), they are exposed to visibility and—again—hidden. Literally it is the sunshine; allegorically it is the light of *ere*.[17]

> ze disen drin
> da lachet in der süeze schin,
> diu sælige gleste,
> ere, aller liehte beste
> und erliuhtet die fossiure
> werltlicher aventiure.
>   (17065–74)

[Through these three, the sweet light, that blessed radiance smiled in, Honor, dearest of all luminaries, and lit up that cave of earthly adventure.]

In the allegory of the grotto the one thing is granted that courtly society refused to the lovers: *ere*.[18] Their passion seems accepted. But, on the other hand, with the concept of *ere* courtly values determine passion, too. The grotto negates the life in courtly society and at the same time embodies its perfection (cf. the so-called *Gesellschaftswunder*). This also means that the life of the lovers is extremely vulnerable. Tristan and Isolde fear the danger of being discovered, and when the noises of Mark's hunt are to be heard they behave as if the court could see them. Again they try to deceive any observer. Nevertheless, Mark's and the hunter's gazes can immediately destroy a love that tried to withdraw itself from courtly attention. Tristan and Isolde remain dependent on this gaze. They subject themselves to the rules of the others, thus demonstrating that they never abandoned courtly society. Their return to Mark's court affirms only what has already happened.

When Mark breaks in and his gaze penetrates the cave, life in the cave darkens. Mark looks through one window and sees Tristan and Isolde on the bed but separated by a sword. He blocks the window with leaves and grass and by doing so diminishes the light of *ere* that illuminated the life of the lovers. Waking up, they realize at once the lack of light—of *ere:*

> nu si begunden umbe sehen
> und nach dem sunnenschine spehen,
> don schein diu sunne niht dar in
> niwan durch zwei vensterlin.
> nu namen si des dritten war
> und alse in daz niht liehtes bar,
> des wunderte si sere.
>
> (17629–35)

> _____

> [Now they began to look around them for sunshine, but
> the sun was shining through two windows and no more.
> They looked at the third and were very much amazed to
> find that it gave no light.]

Obviously the attempt to reconcile secrecy and courtly honor failed. For Tristan and Isolde it is impossible to do without public approval. They return to the court "durch got und durch ir ere" (for the sake of God and honor their status in society, 17698), to the place where everyone controls everyone else. The price they pay is enormously high. Only for a short time can they outwit Mark's heartless blindness: "herzelose blintheit" (17739).

The next rendezvous once again takes place in the orchard but now in full sunshine, an unambiguous space of shame: "ez was an einem mitten tage / und schein diu sunne sere: / leider uf ir ere" (It was noon, and the sun was shining strongly, alas, upon their honor, 18126–28). The sun is shining again, and courtly visibility is restored, but what is revealed is adultery. When Mark discovers the lovers, they barely save their lives but not their love. The separation is final.

In the end the same courtly order prevails over passionate love as it did in the story of Riwalin and Blanscheflur. Even the radical potion love cannot do completely and forever without the others and their gaze. Therefore, in my opinion it is wrong to call *minne* in Gottfried's *Tristan* "romantic."[19] For example, let us compare Gottfried's couple with Richard Wagner's heroes in his opera *Tristan und Isolde*.[20]

In the opera, romantic love is beyond social consideration. At the end of the second act, when their love is discovered, no king, no Melot, no court can disturb the unity of the lovers. They do not even hear Mark's never-ending but sympathetic and discreet speech trying to understand what he is seeing. What he says, what the others think, is quite unimportant to them. No reduction of light (the light of honor) forces them to return to courtly society. On the contrary, the brutal break of daylight into the night of love finally drives them out of this world—as Tristan moans, "Der öde Tag / zum letzten mal" (For the last time the desolate [bleak, dreary] daylight!).[21] They want to stay in the realm of darkness:

> Dem Land, das Tristan meint,
> der Sonne Licht nicht scheint:
> es ist das dunkel
> nächtge Land,
> daraus die Mutter
> mich entsandt.
>
> (57)

———

[In that land of which Tristan spoke, the sun's light does not shine; it is the dark land of Night out of which my mother sent me.]

When Tristan returns to light in the third act it means renewed suffering for him:

Krachend hört' ich
hinter mir schon des Todes
Tor sich schließen:
weit nun steht es
wieder offen,
der Sonne Strahlen
sprengt es auf.

(64)

———

[I heard the crash of death's door closing behind me. But now it
stands wide open again, the sun's beams have burst it open.]

Only when he dies does he see another light but a light opposed to
the light of honor, the daylight in which Mark and his court live:

O diese Sonne!
Ha, dieser Tag!
Ha, dieser Wonne
sonnigster Tag . . .
Tristan der Held,
in jubelnder Kraft,
hat sich vom Tode
emporgerafft. . . .
Wie, hör ich das Licht?
Die Leuchte, ha!
Die Leuchte verlischt!
Zu ihr! Zu ihr!

(73 ff.)

———

[Oh, this sun! Ah, this day! Ah, this sunniest day of joy! . . .
Tristan the hero rejoicing in his strength has rallied from
death. . . . What, is this the light I hear? The torch, ah!
The torch is extinguished. To her! To her!]

The visual world has to be extinguished, and the gaze of the lovers is
completely detached from the gaze of the rest. What Isolde professes
to see in her last words cannot be seen by anybody else:

Seht ihr's Freunde?
Seht ihr's nicht?
Immer lichter
wie er leuchtet . . .
                    (79)

———

[Can you see it, friends? Can you not see it?
How he glows ever more light . . .]

Gottfried's Blanscheflur by contrast saw Riwalin through the eyes of other women; Tristan and Isolde fear to be seen as lovers by anybody from Mark's court. They want to persist in the light of *ere*. Where Wagner's metaphysics of love stage a transfiguration, Gottfried needs a little bundle of grass and one person's gaze to force his courtier-heroes to return to a courtly society that will finally reveal their shame.

Notes

1. See Horst Wenzel, *Hören und Sehen, Schrift und Bild: Kultur und Gedächtnis im Mittelalter* (München: C. H. Beck, 1995); Kathryn Starkey and Horst Wenzel, eds., *Visual Culture and the German Middle Ages* (New York: Palgrave Macmillan, 2005).

2. Gottfried von Strassburg, *Tristan und Isold,* Friedrich Ranke, ed. Text, 7. Auflage (Berlin: Weidmann, 1963), line 1362. Further citations in the text are to line numbers of the poem. For *leal amur,* see Jan-Dirk Müller, "Gottfried von Straßburg: *Tristan,* Transgression und Ökonomie," in *Transgressionen: Literatur als Ethnographie,* ed. Gerhard Neumann and Rainer Warning, Litterae 98 (Freiburg: Rombach, 2003), 235. About the implicit contradictions, Rainer Warning, "Die narrative Lust an der List: Norm und Transgression im Tristan," in Neumann and Warning, *Transgressionen,* 188 ff., criticized the hidden Wagnerianism of Gottfried's modern readers.

3. A part of the following observations was worked out first in my book *Höfische Kompromisse: Acht Kapitel zur höfischen Epik* (Tübingen: Niemeyer, 2007).

4. James A. Schultz, *Courtly Love, the Love of Courtliness, and the History of Sexuality* (Chicago: University of Chicago Press, 2006), 79–98.

5. Karl Bartsch, ed., *Reinfrid von Braunschweig,* Bibliothek des Litera-rischen Vereins in Stuttgart 109 (Tübingen: Literarischer Verein in Stuttgart, 1871), ll. 2318–61; Heinrich von Veldeke, *Eneasroman: Mittelhochdeutsch/Neuhochdeutsch,* ed. Dieter Kartschoke, Universal-Bibliothek 8303 (Stuttgart: P. Reclam, 1986), ll. 626–39, 730–38, 764–804.

6. Courtly relationships are totally changed when Venus interferes and Dido is "infected" literally by the kiss of Ascanius.

7. For instance, Roy Wisbey, "Living in the Present with the Past: Ex-emplary Perspectives in Gottfried's 'Tristan,'" in *Gottfried von Strassburg and the Medieval Tristan Legend: Papers from an Anglo-North American Symposium,* ed. Adrian Stevens and Roy Wisbey, Arthurian Studies 23, Publications of the Institute of Germanic Studies 44 (Cambridge: D. S. Brewer, 1990), 257–76; and see Tomas Tomasek, *Gottfried von Straßburg,* Universal-Bibliothek 17665 (Stuttgart: P. Reclam, 2007), 96 ff. with references. Tomasek himself seems undecided; he calls Blanscheflur and Riwalin's story a "Präfiguration" of that of Tristan and Isolde but also states differences.

8. Schultz, *Courtly Love,* 74, emphasized that the origin of courtly love is placed "outside the lover"; see also the section "The Exogenesis of Courtly Love," 71–75.

9. Cf. the description and analysis in Wenzel, *Hören und Sehen,* 403–6.

10. Here and below, italics are mine.

11. "It remains here to point out that this love represents the court's love for itself.... When it sees nobility and courtliness realized to a high de-gree in a single individual, it responds with love for that individual—which is at the same time love for the values to which it is most deeply committed" (Schultz, *Courtly Love,* 92).

12. For this scene, see Schultz, *Courtly Love,* 94, and the comment that "visible nobility provokes love" (80); and for Schultz's discussion of matters similar to what I discuss here, see 79–98. Wenzel, *Hören und Sehen,* 409: "Riwalins Schönheit und sein ritterlicher Vorrang werden primär über das wahrnehmende Auge einsichtig—durch einen Zugriff von Außen also, der Blancheflurs persönlichem Eindruck eine allgemeine Geltung sichert, weil sie ihn mit den anderen Frauen und Zuschauern teilt."

13. Wenzel, *Hören und Sehen,* 411; Warning, "Die narrative Lust an der List," 189.

14. Wenzel, *Hören und Sehen,* 412.

15. Christina Lechtermann, *Berührt werden: Narrative Strategien der Präsenz in der höfischen Literatur um 1200,* Philologische Studien und Quellen 191 (Berlin: Erich Schmidt, 2005), 156, has pointed to the importance of touch

in this scene that assimilates Blanscheflur to Riwalin in a symbolic death (1289, 1307, 1320, 1327, 1338, 1340).

16. For their halfhearted retreat from courtly society, see Jan-Dirk Müller, "Zeit im 'Tristan,'" in *Der "Tristan" Gottfrieds von Straßburg: Symposion Santiago de Compostela, 5. bis 8. April 2000,* ed. Christoph Huber and Victor Millet (Tübingen: Niemeyer, 2002), 384; and Müller, "Gottfried von Straßburg: *Tristan,* Transgression und Ökonomie," 227 ff.

17. It is impossible to separate those aspects as Tomasek proposes: *Gottfried von Straßburg,* 160; cf. Susanne Köbele, "Mythos und Metapher: Die Lust der Anspielung in Gottfrieds 'Tristan,'" in *Präsenz des Mythos: Konfigurationen einer Denkform in Mittelalter und Früher Neuzeit,* ed. Udo Friedrich and Bruno Quast, Trends in Medieval Philology 2 (Berlin: W. de Gruyter, 2004), 219–46; and Jan-Dirk Müller, "Tristan's Affinity to Myth," in *Mythes à la cour—Mythes pour la cour: Actes publiés par Alain Corbellari u.a.* (Genève: Droz, 2010), 21–37.

18. See line 16698: "daz was mit ere bespart."

19. C. Stephen Jaeger, *Ennobling Love: In Search of a Lost Sensibility* (Philadelphia: University of Pennsylvania Press, 1999), 155–213, is looking for "romantic solutions" in medieval concepts of love. But I think that the term *romantic* is a modernist projection.

20. See Warning, "Die narrative Lust an der List," 202 ff.

21. Richard Wagner, *Tristan und Isolde: In drei Aufzügen,* Universal-Bibliothek 5638, ed. Wilhelm Zentner (Stuttgart: P. Reclam, 1969), 54. Further citations in the text are to page numbers.

CHAPTER TWO

How to Find Love in Literature

Reading Gottfried von Strassburg's *Tristan*

and His Cave of Lovers

HAIKO WANDHOFF

After the lovers have been banished from the court, Tristan leads Isolde
to a hidden place in the wilderness, where he once, on his way to hunt,
had discovered a wonderful place: "la fossiure a la gent amant" (16700).
Gottfried names it in French and only then translates it into German:
"daz kiut: der minnenden hol" (16701) (which is to say: "the Cave of
Lovers" [261]).[1] In Gottfried von Strassburg's early-thirteenth-century
version of the Tristan story, this place is depicted as a skillfully sculpted
grotto hewn in the savage mountainside, a wide and yet intimate room,
high and mighty but nevertheless smooth and cozy, surrounded by
an idyllic landscape. It is a perfect *locus amoenus,* adorned with ivory
and gems and a precious bed made of crystal on the grass-green marble
floor. Moreover, in almost every material part or quality of the cavern
lies buried a hidden significance, uncovered by the narrator in a long
allegorical interpretation—the first explicit allegorical exegesis performed in German secular poetry: The grotto's roundness denotes
Love's Simplicity, its breadth signifies Love's Power, its height means
Aspiration, and so on, with the crystal bed in the grotto's center finally revealing Love's Transparency. Illuminated by the sun through

41

three small windows in the upper part of the cave, this beautiful refuge for lovers, which was constructed by pagan giants in ancient times,
according to an inscription on the bed, is dedicated to the Goddess of
Love. Pretending to leave for Ireland to provide evidence for their innocence, Tristan and Isolde actually seek shelter in this marvelous
"House of Love" ("der Minnen hûs" [17029]), which at the same time
is a sophisticated allegory *and* an artistic hiding place of love, a site
where lovers can consummate their intimacy beyond the constraints
of society.

The grotto provides an outstanding example of materiality and
visuality in the Tristan story. As an overly graphic exposition of a material artifice hiding and exposing the finest examples of true love, it
leads us directly to the center of Gottfried's conception of love *and* love
poetry. His artistic upgrading of a well-known poetic commonplace
not only differs considerably from the tales of Béroul and Eilhart von
Oberg, the more heroic and less courtly versions of the story, in which
Tristan in the wilderness with great difficulty constructs a poor and
simple bower night after night. It also seems to extend significantly
the dimensions of the love grotto in Thomas of England's version,
which Gottfried introduces as his proper source, the one and only true
reading of the Tristan story, describing the lovers' life in the woods as
pleasing and satisfying. Unfortunately, we have almost no access to
Thomas's work itself but must reconstruct it from Brother Robert's
Tristramsaga, an early-thirteenth-century Norse prose adaptation.[2]

For these reasons, it is not surprising that Gottfried's love grotto
has attracted a lot of scholarly attention in recent decades, leading to
the well-established notion that in it is buried the key to a proper understanding of the entire romance.[3] In this chapter I move a step further, treating Gottfried's amazing re-creation of the cave not only as a
conceptual nucleus but also as a *mise-en-abyme,* that is, an internal
representation of his *Tristan.* In its function to enclose and disclose at
the same time a precious example of true love, the Cave of Lovers mirrors the Romance of Lovers and vice versa. Reading Gottfried's text
as a grotto and the grotto as a text sheds new light on his very conception of love and literature and reveals in particular a dominant meta-
poetical or even metafictional feature of the romance.

I

The very basis of my argument is the assumption that Gottfried's *Tristan* can essentially be understood as a narrative meditation on the relationship of love and art, lovers and artists, negotiating the crucial question of how to hide and find love in art and literature. The romance shows in several episodes that love can and must be covered by art, in order to survive in a hostile world. Gottfried demonstrates that amazing artists like Tristan and Isolde almost inevitably become outstanding lovers, because in a world that has expelled Lady Love from everyday life, only art offers appropriate hiding places for her. Unavoidably, Tristan and Isolde discover their love *with* and *within* their artistic courtliness and courtly craftsmanship. But then, after they have found it, the romance shows as well how the loving artists have to use the very same skills, their very same art of courtliness, to hide their love from society in order to protect it from King Mark and his envious court. The loving artists, who have once found love in their artistry, now turn into artistic lovers, hiding love away with and within the very same outstanding craftsmanship, where neither Mark nor any other simple-minded reader will ever find it. Art and workmanship thus provide a perfect treasury of love, a secret place where it can be discovered by noble-hearted lovers, who search for the very idea of love, and where she can be hidden from the common people, who do not know any longer what love is and mostly confuse it with the mere adoration of female beauty. "Minne ist getriben unde gejaget in die endelesten ort" (12280–81) (Love is hounded to the ends of the world [203]), we learn from Gottfried, but there it can still be found, in a mysterious cave hewn in the savage mountainside, but also in the many marvelous "caves of poetry" as constructed by loving artists from antiquity on.

This dialectics of finding and hiding, discovering and covering love in art provide a basic pattern in Gottfried's *Tristan* that touches on different levels of the narrative. It is for this reason that I agree with Wolfgang Mohr, who called the tale a *Künstlerroman* that focuses on Tristan's amazing rise in society to become an esteemed artist at King Mark's court.[4] Art, of course, must be understood here in the medieval, rhetorical sense of the Latin *ars,* which besides music and poetry, literature and languages, also includes hunting and dancing, fighting and singing, or what Gottfried calls "aller hande hovespil" (2121) (all manner of courtly pastimes [69]), in short, the arts of courtliness. The medieval concept of *artes,* in combining what we would differentiate today as science, art, and workmanship, even includes the womanly arts of healing, dealing with herbs and potions, as represented in the romance particularly by young Isolde's mother and, above all, her crafty creation of the love potion. In his prologue, Gottfried von Strassburg highlights the Middle High German term *kunst,* where he explicitly suggests a close relationship between "cunst und nâhe sehender sin" (33–34) (art and subtlety).[5] But throughout his romance he mostly uses the term *list,* which in addition to all the above-mentioned aspects of *ars* covers a skillful "fake" or "betrayal" as well (as in the New High German word *List*).[6] In contrast to modern notions of the fine arts, Gottfried's concept of *kunst,* thus, includes any skillfully crafted *artificium,* be it a crafty performance at court, a marvelous edifice like the Cave of Lovers (or, in Thomas of England's version, the famous hall of statues), or a skillfully worked love story. What is totally absent or at least not necessarily implied, however, is the aspect of morality or social responsibility. For this is exactly what Gottfried's romance shows in detail time and again — that outstanding artists, like Tristan and Isolde, can entertain, instruct, and ennoble the courtly society for their own benefit, but if necessary, they also are in a position to delude and deceive the public, using the very same artistic skills to create illusions and fictions.

Visuality and materiality therefore play a major role in the story of Tristan and Isolde, because love gets wrapped up in material layers and visual traces of art and craftsmanship over and over again. Love, to be sure, can be hidden and found in so-called *senemaeren,* in sad love songs and love poems as performed by Tristan and Isolde themselves (first at Mark's court, later in the wonderful valley surrounding the grotto, and finally when Tristan invents a famous love song for Isolde of the White Hands). But the lovers also cover and expose their love in beautiful, visual performances at court, covering it in their ongoing role-playing, pretending to be faithful queen and loyal courtier, the king's noble wife and splendid nephew.

Tristan and Isolde thus become skillful actors on the courtly stage, and their debut masterpiece is the crafty faking of an ordeal, in which they use their skills again to create a public fiction. But throughout the text they manipulate many visual traces of their love, and their consistent exchange of intimate, loving looks is artificially woven into numerous situations of public courtly performance. But Tristan and Isolde also communicate their love by inventing material objects, for instance, the carved wooden initials *T* and *I* that float down a stream, resembling the same initials that Gottfried hides and exposes in the acrostic in his prologue. But the climax of these attempts to represent love permanently in visual and material works of art is without doubt the invention of the Cave of Lovers. For a long time the cave provides a refuge. Nobody discovers Tristan and Isolde's intimate love, neither at court nor in the grotto, because, as we learn in Gottfried's *Tristan,* only good and thorough readers are able to find Love when she hides in fine works of art. And even after King Mark has become suspicious, he will never be capable of proving it; he will never be in a position to detect the intimate love hidden in the story of Tristan and Isolde.

What turns the motif of love that is represented in works of art into a basic poetic pattern of the romance, however, is that not only the protagonists experience the interdependency and interconnectedness of *minne* and *kunst,* love and art, but the narrator does as well. Gottfried explicitly tells us that in times when Lady Love has been banished from our lives (like Tristan and Isolde from the court), we can only find her name and her memory in works of art—in poems and songs, narratives and romances that remind us of Love's great heroes and famous places. Especially sad ancient love stories but also Gottfried's own romance, which is itself considered a *senemaere* (125–30), provide such retreats. Works like his *Tristan* render ideal places where Love can be hidden, until we, the readers, discover her later on if (and only if) we are skillful readers with noble hearts. So not only Tristan and Isolde have to deal with the dialectics of finding and hiding love but also Gottfried and his audience. Discovering love in art in this context is a question of thorough reading, and this explains why Gottfried introduces himself as a good reader, someone who means to "read" (and not "tell") the true story of Tristan and Isolde to his audience: "ez ist in sêre guot gelesen" (172) (it is very well read for them).[7]

Due to the essential rhetorical task of invention, of "finding"
the proper topics and places for your own work of art in preexisting
sources, Gottfried the reader, just like his hero, has to find love in art,
particularly in Thomas of England's version of the Tristan tale.[8] This
artistic narrative provides the secret sites and prominent situations
of love, and in the process of invention, which includes reading and
imagining, meditating on and thinking about these precious findings
time and again, Gottfried's heart is finally affected by the deep, true
love hidden in all these precious *topoi*. This is what Gottfried tells us
about his own encounter with the pair, his reading of their story:

> ich hân von in zwein vil gedâht
> und gedenke hiute und alle tage:
> swenne ich liebe und senede klage
> vür mîniu ougen breite
> und ir gelegenheite
> in mînem herzen ahte,
> sô wahsent mîne trahte
> und muot mîn hergeselle,
> als er in die wolken welle.
> swenn' ich bedenke sunder
> daz wunder und daz wunder,
> daz man an liebe funde,
> der ez gesuochen kunde;
> was fröude an liebe laege,
> der ir mit triuwen phlaege:
> sô wirt mîn herze sâ zestunt
> groezer danne Setmunt
>
> (12204–20)

———

[I have thought much about the pair of them, and do so now and
ever shall. When I spread Longing and Affection as a scroll before
my inward eye and inquire into their natures, my yearning grows,
and my comrade, Desire, grows too, as if he would mount to the
clouds! When I consider in detail the unending marvels that a man
would find in love if he but knew where to seek them, and the joy

there would be in love for those who would practice it sincerely, then, all at once, my heart grows larger than Setmunt.] (202)

Although the meaning of *Setmunt* remains unexplained,[9] we can assume that it is conceived of as a huge site, providing the model for the poet's immensely growing heart due to his readings of Tristan and Isolde. Adrian Stevens has convincingly pointed out that Gottfried in this passage explicitly links his conception of love to the poetic task of invention (Latin *inventio*), which is basically a kind of reinvention, relying on memory and memorial recollection. The key term for the cognitive process of invention, deployed by Cicero, Augustine, and others, is *cogitatio* — or in Gottfried's Middle High German translation, "(ge-)denken" (12204–5). In contrast to modern notions of "cogitation" or the modern German *denken,* though, the inventional *cogitatio,* besides rational thought, necessarily implies emotional and imaginative involvement: "As Gottfried reads — whether his own text or the text of Thomas — he cogitates, reviewing through the eyes of memory (cf. 'vür mîniu ougen breite' [12207]) the joy and sorrow of love ('liebe und senede klage' [12206]) and pondering their natures and their places ('ir gelegenheite' [12208]) in his heart ('in mînem herzen ahte' [12209])." And because this cogitation is an emotional process, as Stevens points out, "the more intensely Gottfried meditates (cf. 'sô wahsent mine trahte' [12210]) as he examines in his heart the 'places' where joy and sorrow are kept, the more his desire ('muot' [12211]) for love grows."[10] By meditating and cogitating about the love he reads time and again, the poet himself becomes a lover: his memory stretches until he is finally able to experience the love he has found in literature in his own heart. Only then will he be capable of reinventing and renewing the love he has found in order to create a new text, "to 'find' the 'matter' *(res)* of love, the 'ideas' he needs for its reinvention in his text."[11] In many thorough readings he has meditated on hundreds of commonplaces such as grottoes and wonderful gardens in his heart, but now he is finally prepared to turn them into something new, never before seen. Now he is ready to create *his* own outstanding place of love, *his* artistic masterpiece — *his* one and only Cave of Lovers.

The "finding" of love and the "creation" of love literature, thus, go hand in hand, for both tasks are deeply rooted in poetical invention. Originally the first and basic exercise in rhetorical composition, the "finding" of the matter upon which a new text has to be built, *inventio* suddenly turns out to be a key concept in Gottfried's *Tristan,* as already suggested by Stevens: "The art of love, as Gottfried presents it in his *Tristan,* is an art of invention."[12] I consider this "art of invention," where *finding* and *inventing, reading* and *writing, discovering* and *covering* are interwoven aspects of the same compositional process, crucial to a proper understanding of the romance. The poetics of invention provides the rationale for the union of the *art of love* and the *art of poetry* as presented in Gottfried's text, where both arts find their skillful perfection in the marvelous Cave of Lovers, the fulfillment not only of Tristan and Isolde's love but also of Gottfried's artistic craftsmanship.[13] This precious finding at the end of the world, therefore, is not only an outstanding allegory of love but also a sophisticated allegory of poetry. It is a place in the wilderness and a *topos* of literature altogether, a site where the lovers hide in a cave made of stone and where Love hides in allegory, in a cave made of words.

II

This poetics of invention tears down the wall between Gottfried and Tristan and presents the author and his protagonist in close cooperation. Both are introduced as superlative artists, poets, and courtiers, performing their art of courtliness at the cutting edge. Both are masters of the word, creating fictions, manipulating and subverting texts and speech acts, but also composing sad love poetry. Furthermore, they possess highly developed courtly skills. When Tristan presents his mastery of courtliness by gutting a deer in an artistic manner that had never before been seen at Mark's court, Gottfried frames this stunt as a brilliant poetic showpiece depicting in detail all Tristan's tricks as well as his amazing beauty in over six hundred verses (2759–3379).[14]

Later on, Gottfried and Tristan even collaborate in creating the romance's wonderful female protagonist. For not only does *meister* Gottfried, as he is called in several manuscripts, "invent" the beautiful and crafty Isolde, but *meister* Tristan does so, too (11599, 11654, 11681). Her teacher and master falls in love with her only after he has educated and instructed Isolde with his own poetic skills and courtly crafts, transforming the young queen into a perfect artist as well as an adorable work of art. There is nothing "natural" at all in the love of Tristan and Isolde, who surprisingly have never been attracted by the sole beauty and splendor of one another, as were, for instance, Tristan's parents, Riwalin and Blanscheflur. Tristan and Isolde's love, in contrast, is a thoroughly "artificial" love, which emerges out of their corresponding artistry, a love, furthermore, that is initiated not through a loving gaze but a superb love potion created by Isolde's mother, another artificial object that covers and exposes Love in a world that has banished it from everyday life. Last but not least, their love is an artistic love, because it requires art and craftsmanship to be performed under the noses yet hidden from the eyes of King Mark and his court in Cornwall. Consequently, after Tristan and Isolde have fallen in love their amazing craftsmanship and artistry must increase in order to cover and protect their love from the public.

The famous episode of their falling in love particularly reflects the romance's focus on how to hide and find love in art and literature. On the ship to England after accidentally drinking "einen trank von minnen" (11435) (a love drink [192]), which Isolde's mother "betihtete . . . in ein glasevezzelîn" (11432, 11434) (composed in a vial) to cause everlasting love between the old king and her young daughter, Isolde dares to reveal her love to Tristan.[15] She does not, however, render a plain and straightforward declaration of love but shyly hides it in a narrative, recollecting their story, the story of Tristan and Isolde. And this narrative, skillfully composed and interpreted by the young queen herself, another performance of her language skills, ends up in a pun, wherein only a thorough reader (like Tristan) can actually find her love: "'lameir' sprach sî, 'daz ist mîn nôt, / lameir daz swaeret mir den muot, / lameir ist, daz mir leide tuot'" (11986–88) (*Lameir* is what distresses me," she said, "it is *lameir* that so oppresses me, *lameir* is what pains me so" [199]).

Tristan, the master of languages, poetry, and music, thinks about the three possible meanings of the French term *lameir*: "the sea," "bitterness," and, finally, "love." But thinking and meditating on the poetic work of art Isolde has created, he eventually discovers the word's true meaning. In other words, he finds love covered in and exposed by Isolde's artistic composition. Moreover, Tristan falls in love through a text; he falls in love by "reading" and interpreting Isolde's poetry, finding love hidden in *her* skillful revision of the story of Tristan and Isolde. Love herself has forced the young queen to compose a text about *lameir,* hiding her love in an artistic showpiece of her language skills in which only a skilled reader can find it. And this thorough and careful reader, Tristan, is infected by the very love he has discovered in Isolde's narrative, so that he is in a position now to produce his own composition of love by finding and disclosing his own love story to Isolde.

In this episode, once again, Tristan mirrors his master Gottfried, who, as we have already learned, has found the very same love, the love of Tristan and Isolde, in *his* repeated thorough readings of their story (as presented by Thomas of England). And only because he, like Tristan, has been deeply affected by his findings, by the idea of love as covered and revealed in artful poetic compositions, is he finally able to retell the story in a new way, to create *his own* love story. The crucial boundary between author and protagonist, an undisputed and well-established frontier in modern fiction, thus seems to collapse. Gottfried, the poet of the romance, becomes affected by the love he has found in his readings during the exercise of topical invention, and he eventually turns into a lover, who in his widened heart invents new, wonderful places where love can be covered and exposed. And Tristan, too, turns into a lover by "reading" a text; he actually finds love by interpreting Isolde's poetic composition, meditating and thinking about it, until he is able to retell *his* own love story. The fictional romance thus turns into a highly sophisticated, metafictional treatise on the close relationship between the art of love and the art of poetry.

The climax of this merger of Tristan and Gottfried, protagonist and author, however, can be seen in their common *invention* of the love grotto. Both artists, who have just found love in a text by using their artistic craftsmanship, namely, their art of reading, eventually seek a secret place where this love can be securely performed and protected from society. And for this purpose they "invent"—now and again, in the double rhetorical sense of "finding" and "creating"—a perfect place of love, the marvelous Cave of Lovers in the wilderness. We have already learned that Tristan discovered this place some time ago during a hunt, and hunting provides the overall frame of the episode: A hound leads the lovers in the wilderness, and although they don't need any food because they subsist entirely on their loving gazes, hunting becomes one of their major activities in the wonderful valley. In the end, King Mark discovers their hidden place when he is leading a hunting party. Hunting, though, is not only a courtly sport but also an old allegory of love—in other words, a rather common way of representing love in art that goes back to Ovid and ancient love poetry. The notion of "Finding the Cave of Lovers," that is, "Finding the perfect place of love," *on a hunt,* thus strongly suggests a second metafictional meaning that, again, connects the protagonist with his author. For Gottfried himself has found this marvelous place, the *topos* of a cave of lovers, surrounded by a wonderful *locus amoenus* including a nice well, beautiful trees, and lovely birdsong, "on a hunt," that means in the various poetic hunting allegories from Ovid through the Middle Ages.[16]

There is one famous hunting place in particular that Gottfried obviously has revisited time and again, a well-known place that is one of the most prominent *topoi* of love in the Middle Ages: the sad love story of Dido and Aeneas as told in Vergil's *Aeneid* but also in Ovid's amatory works and in the vernacular versions of the Aeneas story, the French *Roman d'Eneas* and its Middle High German retelling by Heinrich von Veldeke. Gottfried's grotto is full of signs and signals recalling the famous ancient love between Dido and Aeneas, the queen of Carthage and the Trojan duke, the very first example of courtly love, described at length in the vernacular romances of Aeneas. Like the Tristan story, it is a *senemaere,* a tragic love song ending in the death of one lover, Dido. But, first of all, like the love of Tristan and Isolde, the love of Dido and Aeneas finds its fulfillment in a grotto in the wilderness. It is during a hunt, which Dido had arranged in order to disclose her passionate love to Aeneas (a love that in the *Aeneas* as well as in the *Roman d'Eneas* is also initiated by a love potion!), that the loving queen suddenly gets lost in a thunderstorm.

The hunting party scatters and loses track of her; only Aeneas eventually finds Dido and takes care of her—in a sheltering grotto that suddenly becomes a lovers' cave.

"Finding the Cave of Lovers on a hunt" in this context simply means finding it on the most renowned literary hunt, in the hunting episode of Dido and Aeneas, in one of the greatest love stories ever, as told by Vergil, Ovid, and the *Roman d'Eneas*. Only Heinrich von Veldeke, in his Middle High German *Eneas,* changed the setting and replaced the grotto with a wonderful place above ground. According to his version of the romance, Queen Dido and Duke Eneas consummate their love under a tree that provides shelter from the storm, in short, at another topical place of love that is well known from antiquity on and can be found in several songs of *Minnesang.* In Gottfried's *Tristan,* then, we find a combination of both versions, of sheltering grotto *and* sheltering tree, a fusion of two classical commonplaces of love, now revisited, recollected, and rearranged in Gottfried's version of the Tristan story: a grotto with a crystal bed, marvelously rebuilt and adorned, but furthermore surrounded by a *locus amoenus,* a valley with sheltering trees and a well, beautiful flowers, and birdsong—a new benchmark in the invention of an ideal site for lovers!

In Gottfried's rearrangement of these *topoi,* the spatial order of inner and outer realm, grotto and garden, is significant. The grotto, on the one hand, provides the core of the arrangement and reflects the climax of the lovers' life in the wonderful valley, representing the inner realm where Tristan and Isolde actually consummate their love. Here, with hands and voices, Tristan and Isolde play the music of love on one another's bodily instruments while lying on the precious crystal bed. (In a skillful work of art like the Cave of Lovers even the most intimate sexual encounter of the lovers can only be announced in artistic metaphors.) But this is what happens in the grotto itself, in the inner circle of love, as it were. In order to get there, the lovers first have to pass through the wonderful valley surrounding it, which provides an outer place where the idea of love only has to be found (or "invented") before it can be brought to life again in the grotto. On a bench under a sheltering lime tree in the wonderful valley, Tristan and Isolde remember and retell the famous stories of true ancient lovers:

si beredeten unde besageten,
si betrûreten unde beclageten,
daz daz Villîse von Trâze,
daz der armen Canâze
in der minnen namen geschach;
daz Biblîse ir herze brach
durch ir bruoder minne;
daz ez der küniginne
von Tîre und von Sidône,
der seneden Didône
durch sene sô jaemerlîchen ergie.
mit solhen maeren wâren s'ie
unmüezic eteswenne.

(17187–99)

———

[They debated and discussed, they bewept and bewailed how
Phyllis of Thrace and poor Canacea had suffered such misfortune
in Love's name; how Biblis had died broken-hearted for her
brother's love, how love-torn Dido, queen of Tyre and Sidon,
had met so tragic a fate because of unhappy love. To such tales
did they apply themselves from time to time.] (267)

Quite surprisingly, Tristan and Isolde talk and meditate about love
(under the tree in the valley) before they finally make love (in the
grotto). Not only at court but also in their retreat in the wilderness
the pair demonstrates what seems to be a basic pattern of Gottfried's
romance—that our way to true love necessarily leads through literature, leads through love as represented in art. Even the greatest lovers,
Tristan and Isolde, have to find love in the lasting memory of poetry
before they can re-create and renew their own version of it *upon* these
findings, in their own hearts and souls, with their own hands and
tongues, on the crystal bed of the Goddess of Love. Since love is no
longer part of our everyday life, it has to be rediscovered in literature
and redefined by memorial recollection and meditation, until eventually the poetic memory of it in the hearts of the "readers" is converted into love itself. Only after this forgotten and expelled idea of

love has been *invented,* that is, found and reexperienced in repeated readings of sad love stories, can it grow in our hearts.

By performing this transition from valley to grotto, from finding to creating, from love's memorial recollection to love's presence, Tristan and Isolde illustrate the mystic conversion Gottfried has claimed for his romance in the prologue. It is said there that his story of the pair with its close interlacing of *herzelieb* and *herzeleid,* "their hearts' joy and their hearts' sorrow," wherever we hear it, will provide the bread for us, a kind of bread akin to the Christian mass; where bread and wine are transformed into the body and blood of Christ, provided for the community of noble-hearted lovers of our time:

> Deist aller edelen herzen brôt.
> hie mite sô lebet ir beider tôt.
> wir lesen ir leben, wir lesen ir tôt
> und ist uns daz süeze alse brôt.
> Ir leben, ir tôt sint unser brôt.
> Sus lebet ir leben, sus lebet ir tôt.
> Sus lebent si noch und sint doch tôt
> Und ist ir tôt der lebenden brôt.
>   (233–40)

> _____

> [This is bread to all noble hearts. With this their death lives on. We read their life, we read their death, and to us it is sweet as bread. Their life, their death are our bread. Thus lives their life, thus lives their death. Thus they live still and yet are dead, and their death is the bread of the living.] (44)

The mystic conversion of bread into the body of Christ, meaning the conversion of memory into presence, is obviously applied here to the process of poetic invention.[17] The thorough reading and repeated meditation upon the recollected places and heroes of love in the reader's heart suddenly turns into love itself. This is what the "readers" Tristan and Isolde experience and demonstrate in their wonderful valley, and this is what the readers of Gottfried's romance shall experience with his text—as long as they are good readers with noble hearts, suitable for the crucial task of finding love in literature.

The fact that even in a seemingly perfect place like the grotto love is not supposed to just be there but always needs to be *found* and *composed* before it comes to life again shows once again that the concept of love in the Middle Ages — or at least in Gottfried's romance — is different from what we consider it to be today. Above all, love is not conceived of as a mere "feeling," an "emotion," or a "state of mind" (although all this is included) but rather a complex and demanding process of recognition. Love in this context is not "natural" or immediate; instead, it has to be artful, artistic, and artificial, which essentially means that the beauty causing love and affection has to be reworked and refined by a compositional mental activity. Isolde's overwhelming beauty as such, for instance, is as dangerous as Enite's beauty in Chrétien's and Hartmann's *Erec*. It beguiles but also blinds her audience at the court and later on King Mark, when he finally discovers her in the cave. For this reason, Gottfried acknowledges the famous saying, "schoene daz ist hoene" (17803) (in beauty there lurks danger [275]). But there is one way to tame and domesticate this beauty, and this way is called *art*. If you compose the awesome beauty of the courtly lady into a fine work of art like Gottfried *and* Tristan do, then this, and only this, can eventually lead you to the very idea of love. And that explains why only Tristan is a suitable lover for Isolde, because only outstanding artists can handle the amazing beauty of women by transforming their *schoene* into an ideal work of art.

Again, we can watch the artists Gottfried and Tristan work hand in hand. They have to convert physical, sensual beauty into art and artistry before they eventually find love — in the very work of art they have just invented! And this process of finding and renewing love, conceived of as a compositional activity of the mind, finally becomes a means of recognition that, according to the Neoplatonic climate of the twelfth and thirteenth centuries, provides insight into abstract forms, above all, into the very *idea* of beauty, leading over to the overwhelming divine beauty of the cosmos. This is where love can take us, as long as it is understood as a process of invention and composition — and not as the mere adoration of physical beauty. Love, like literature, always requires a mental activity that combines rational and imaginative thought as well as emotional involvement. And like literature, love needs a certain matter to work with, places and incidents to remember and to think about in order to discover new meanings and re-create a love story.

This explains why great love and great love literature, according to Gottfried, share the same aesthetics. Both have to be absolutely transparent and crystal clear, like the bed in the middle of the grotto. We learn about the lovers that immediately after drinking the love potion, "daz ietweder dem andern was / durchlûter alse ein spiegelglas" (11725–26) (each was to the other as limpid as a mirror [195]). Not only is the love between Tristan and Isolde crystal clear and limpid, however, but the same transparency is required for its skillful rendering, for the poetic representation of love in literature. This becomes clear when Gottfried praises the courtly narratives by Hartmann von Aue, his primary stylistic model, whom he admires for his crystal-clear style: "wie lûter und wie reine / sîniu cristallînen wortelîn / beidiu sind und iemer müezen sîn!" (4628–30) (How clear and transparent his crystal words both are and ever must remain! [104]).

III

That the crystal-clear bed in the grotto's center, dedicated to the Goddess of Love, signifies the clarity and transparency not only of love but also of love literature sheds further light on the close correspondence between Gottfried's Cave of Lovers and his Romance of Lovers. Both are marvelous works of art, presenting secret retreats for love that have never before been seen; both were invented by Gottfried von Strassburg, skillfully re-created and rebuilt upon his thorough readings of preceding love stories. And like the romance itself, the grotto is *found in* and *founded on* literature, a symbol of art being the proper refuge of love, a place where it finds shelter in the artistic language of poetry. Living in the cave and its wonderful valley, in a manner of speaking, is like living in a famous commonplace of literature: it is like Tristan and Isolde being Aeneas and Dido, duke and queen, loving one another in a socially inacceptable way but, in contrast to their ancient role models, *not* leaving the grotto, *not* coming back to court, *not* trying to accommodate their fatal love with the constraints of society. In contrast, they are living on a permanent hunt, the famous poetic allegory of love that provides the episode's frame. And when this wonderful love life finally ends, when King Mark the hunter finds the grotto in the wilderness, it seems as if Dido and Aeneas are finally being discovered by *their* hunting party that lost track of *their* queen in Carthage a long time ago.

That the Cave of Lovers actually provides a miniature model, a *mise en abyme* of the romance proper, itself being a spectacular limpid mirror that reflects the constant union of the art of love and the art of poetry, becomes evident when Mark finally finds the lovers—but not love. The house of love now is explicitly turned into "the cave of literature," "la fossiure werltlicher âventiure" (17069–70), a story of love that can and will be read—eventually by Mark himself. Sad and lonely at his court, the king has arranged for a hunt. By chance one of the hunters chases a wonderful white stag and enters the splendid valley. Tristan and Isolde have already heard the noise of the hunting party, and it is Tristan, the amazing artist, who immediately invents a new trick to hide their love away even in this intimate place. The lovers lie down on the bed but like two men, separated by a blank sword. When the hunter discovers their traces in the grass, he finally finds a hidden window to look into the cave, seeing "daz gesinde der minne: / niwan ein wîp unde einen man" (17438–39) (Love's retinue—one man and one woman in all! [271]). The man in the cave seems rather common to him, but the woman is so beautiful that he doubts her human nature and finds her even lovelier than a fairy. Scared by the sword, he interrupts his adoration of this supernatural lady and returns to his king, telling him what he has found, again calling it a "schoene âventiure" (17462) (a beautiful story).[18] In the following dialogue, the story and the cave, *âventiure* and *fossiure,* are united in one rhyming couplet: "sag an, waz âventiure?"—"eine minnen fossiure" (17464–65) ("Tell me, what sort of story?"—"A cave of Love").[19]

Now it becomes evident that the Cave of Lovers, as "found" by Tristan, and the Romance of Lovers, as "found" by Gottfried, are basically two sides of the same object. At least they share the same content, and that is, according to the hunter, "ein man und ein gotinne" (17470) (a man and a goddess [271]). The Cave of Love is explicitly turned into a story of love, finally reflecting the romance proper, which also can be considered "a cave," an artistic building where love can be hidden and found. The huntsman leads Mark to the grotto, and the king himself peeps through the window and discovers his nephew with his beautiful wife. Again, he is torn between trust and distrust, hope and doubt, until eventually the amazing beauty of Isolde, which in the grotto appears even greater than in "real" life, takes command of his heart:

> er schouwete ie genôte
> sînes herzen wunne Îsôte,
> diun gedûhte in ouch dâ vor und ê
> nie sô rehte schoene mê.
> (17557–60)

> ———

> [He gazed and gazed at his heart's delight Isolde, who never before had seemed to him so very lovely as now.] (272)

Isolde's beauty is overwhelming, even rivaling the glory and splendor of the sun, and this stunning appearance of her body eventually inflames love. But it is a blinding and deceiving kind of love that now slips into Mark's heart, finally persuading him to give the queen amnesty and take her back to Cornwall.

Now, if "finding Tristan and Isolde in the grotto" is explicitly rendered as "finding an *âventiure* of Tristan and Isolde" in the wasteland, a story to be read and interpreted, it is not too far-fetched to understand the intimate occasion when Mark looks through a small window into a mysterious world of love as a sophisticated allegory of reading.[20] The sad king, desperately searching for love, peeps into an artificial, skillfully crafted, and somewhat pictorial microcosm, highlighting the stunning beauty of a courtly lady who cannot look back and to whom he — in contrast to other versions of the story (like the *Tristramsaga* or *Sir Tristrem*) — has no access, because the entrance door is closed. Moreover, the adventure of the grotto as seen through the peephole necessarily requires interpretation — and this, again, is different from the other versions of the Tristan story, in which the sword is clearly taken as a proof of the lovers' innocence.[21] In Gottfried's text, however, King Mark does not immediately understand what he sees. Instead, his wonderful finding, the mystery of Tristan and Isolde in a grotto, needs further examination, and while Mark thinks about this work of art created by Gottfried, the *âventiure* of Mark's nephew and Mark's wife united and separated at the same time, the immense beauty of the goddesslike woman affects his heart and lets love come in. The king is so overwhelmed by this beauty that he has just found by "reading" what he sees that love instantly enters his heart, turning the reader into a lover, but a blind lover who is ready to forget all his reasonable doubts. Soon after he has felt the flames of love and desire in his heart, he tries to hide the cave again, covering the window with leaves and immediately finishing the hunt so that nobody else can find and read this wonderful *âventiure*.

Finally, the fire in his heart that the Goddess of Love has ignited eventually leads King Mark to make a decision. He thinks about the *âventiure* of Tristan and Isolde in the grotto, repeatedly talking to himself in the hidden chamber of his heart, until he has found an interpretation of his finding. Now he is ready to compose his own story of Tristan and Isolde for the court, but this is a story without guilt and adultery, a story without love and therefore without truth: a false story of a faithful queen and an honorable nephew, both loyal to the king and just about to return to Cornwall. The court accepts his version, Mark's adaptation of the story of Tristan and Isolde in the grotto, and the lovers are welcomed back.

King Mark, acting as a reader who seeks Love in a mysterious adventure of Tristan and Isolde, obviously provides a model for the reader of Gottfried's text, demonstrating how he or she, too, can eventually find love in the poetic compositions of Tristan and Isolde. Like the sad king, those who cannot find love in their lives are apt to search for it in precious works of art, skillfully crafted poetic mysteries hidden in the wasteland of everyday life, but there is one crucial difference: Mark is a superficial reader, a reader who does *not* find love in the grotto but only beauty, transformed into an imaginary icon. He cannot find the love that is the couple's true love, because he is distracted by the woman's physical appearance. Mark falls victim to a false love, a selfish and one-sided love based on his desire, a love that blinds him and thus prevents him from finding out the truth of the story. Consequently, his own story of Tristan and Isolde that was invented based on his finding in the grotto is not the proper story. It is a story founded on a false reading, and in the process of topical invention an incorrect reading must inevitably lead to an incorrect composition. King Mark, in other words, is one of those readers mentioned in the prologue who "have not read correctly" (niht haben rehte gelesen [147]) about Tristan and Isolde, because he has been affected by an inferior kind of love based on mere desire; he lacks recognition and knowledge, insight and truth.

And this remarkable beauty of the queen seems to be heightened by literature. It has grown in the cave, for Mark has never seen his wife as splendid and beautiful in his "real" life at court, and he has never really fallen in love with her before. The king only recognizes Isolde's beguiling beauty in the very moment when he is "reading" her in an *âventiure,* but the beauty of a literary lady is the beauty of an imaginary icon, the splendor of a feint image that—according to Gottfried—surely brings loving feelings into the readers' hearts, but it is a one-sided love, causing "herzelôse blintheit" (17739) (heartless blindness) and turning the readers into simple-minded lovers who chase icons. A good and thorough reader, however, a reader unlike King Mark, can and will find love in the cave, a proper and intimate, two-sided love that, in contrast to Mark's findings, *does* in fact imply truth and insight.[22] It is a story of true love unfolding in the very moment that it reveals the truth of the whole story. For what is actually hidden in the mystery of the cave is nothing but Love herself as represented in her finest heroes, Tristan and Isolde. Their love is deep, true, and everlasting and clearly represents the very idea of love, and this idea of love *is* the truth of the *âventiure,* the truth of the "small" grotto, itself a miniature replica of Gottfried's "enormous" romance.

In Gottfried's arrangement of the grotto, *finding love* and *finding truth* have become the same operation. For only if a reader finds love in the grotto (i.e., in the story of Tristan and Isolde) will he find out the truth of their *âventiure.* But this is the point where a less talented reader like Mark must necessarily fail. Although he has been hunting for their *love* for a long time, he could never find it, neither in Tristan and Isolde's artistic performances at court nor in the faked ordeal nor in their masterpiece, the Cave of Lovers. Consequently, he has never been able to discover the *truth* of their story. Now the message of Mark's false, misleading reading is laid bare: only if you are able to find love in the grotto, will you be capable of finding the truth of the story. Or let us put it even more generally: only if you are able to find love will you be capable of finding truth. For only love, based on the poetic *composition* of beauty, not physical beauty as such, leads our inner eyes to the higher levels of knowledge and recognition.

To succeed on this path, however, we have to be careful readers, because there are certain dangers to avoid. Above all, there lurks a false sort of love trying to affect and blind us, a dangerous love based only on our desire, which is ignited by the astonishing beauty of women. This splendid beauty is even overestimated by literature, but it fails to be converted into our "real" life. This is exactly what happens to Mark later on: trying to bring the desire-based love he has found in the *âventiure* back to life, that is, from the fictional Cave of Lovers to the prosaic everyday life at court, must end in disaster. His effort to reinstall his beautiful wife, Isolde, as a beloved and loving queen must inevitably fail, because by now she has definitely turned into an imaginary icon of poetry. This breathtaking lady is now and forever a character of literature, an artistic icon that can never be present in real life again.

But there is, of course, a true and proper sort of love to be found in great love literature, in these precious poetic "Caves of Love" created from antiquity on, containing crystal-clear love stories of men and women who in their paradigmatic love life represent the very *idea* of love. In all the songs and stories, in the *senemaeren* about great lovers and their fate, we can find, revisit, and reexperience love's famous deeds, places, and situations, figuring them out and meditating on them in our hearts. The only thing we must withstand is the temptation of falling in love with the beautiful ladies themselves. We should not be blinded by false idols, by imaginary icons belonging to the realm of art and poetry. Instead of falling in love with them, we should rather take their lives as representations of Love herself, to be adopted and reinvented in our own lives.

What we can find in literature, in other words, is love but definitely not a lover. That is what Mark confuses and with him every simple-minded reader. After our repeated readings, we must go out hunting in our own world, finding an appropriate lover in *our* life. This is what Gottfried suggests: go ahead and find your own Isolde, and reexperience with her the models and examples of love you have found in art and literature. The art of love, thus, depends on a thorough and careful art of reading and demands that one search and find love in an appropriate way:

> und hân ez ouch binamen vür daz:
> der suohte, alse er solde,
> ez lebten noch Îsolde,
> an den man ez gâr vünde,
> daz man gesuochen künde.
> (18110–14)

_____

> [And I firmly believe that, were one to seek as one ought, there would still be living Isoldes in whom one would find in plenty whatever one was able to seek.] (279)

Notes

1. This study of Gottfried's *Tristan* owes a lot to a graduate seminar on medieval German literature held at the University of North Carolina at Chapel Hill in 2006. I am indebted to these students for their commitment, their interest, and their stimulating ideas. Quotations are taken from Gottfried von Strassburg, *Tristan,* ed. and trans. Rüdiger Krohn, 3 vols. (Stuttgart: Reclam, 1993–95), cited by line numbers; and translations follow Gottfried von Strassburg, *Tristan,* trans. Arthur T. Hatto (Harmondsworth: Penguin, 1960; reprint, London: Penguin, 2004), cited by page numbers.

2. For a comparison of the grotto episodes, see Sylvia C. Harris, "The Cave of Lovers in the 'Tristramsaga' and Related Tristan Romances," *Romania* 98 (1977): 306–30, 460–500.

3. See Friedrich Ranke, "Die Allegorie der Minnegrotte in Gottfrieds *Tristan,*" in *Gottfried von Straßburg,* ed. Alois Wolf (Darmstadt: Wissenschaftliche Buchgesellschaft, 1973), 1–24; Julius Schwietering, *Der Tristan Gottfrieds von Straßburg und die Bernhardische Mystik* (Berlin: Verlag der Akademie der Wissenschaften, 1943); Herbert Kolb, "Der Minnen hûs: Zur Allegorie der Minnegrotte in Gottfrieds *Tristan,*" in Wolf, *Gottfried von Straßburg,* 305–33; Ulrich Ernst, "Gottfried von Straßburg in komparatistischer Sicht: Form und Funktion der Allegorese im Tristanepos," *Euphorion* 70 (1976): 1–72; Volker Mertens, "Bildersaal–Minnegrotte–Liebestrank: Zu Symbol, Allegorie und Mythos im Tristanroman," *Beiträge zur Geschichte der deutschen Sprache und Literatur* 117 (1995): 40–64.

4. Wolfgang Mohr, "'Tristan und Isold' als Künstlerroman," in Wolf, *Gottfried von Straßburg,* 248–79.

5. Here I differ from Hatto's translation of "nâhe sehender sin" as "criticism."

6. See Georg Benecke, Wilhelm Müller, and Friedrich Zarncke, *Mittelhochdeutsches Wörterbuch,* vol. 1 (Leipzig, 1854–66; reprint, Stuttgart: S. Hirzel, 1990), col. 1010a, 48. According to Jacob Grimm and Wilhelm Grimm, *Deutsches Wörterbuch,* ed. A. Huber et al., vol. 12, Deutsche Akademie der Wissenschaften zu Berlin (Leipzig, 1854–1971; reprint, München: Deutscher Taschenbuch Verlag, 1971–99), MHG *list* is "mit dem alten *kunst* identisch" (col. 1065) but also and increasingly meaning "die schlauheit, das hinterhaltige rechnen zu gunsten eines eigenen vortheils" (col. 1066).

7. Here again I differ from Hatto's translation, "They will find it very good reading" (43).

8. A groundbreaking essay on Gottfried's poetics of invention that has stimulated interpretation is Adrian Stevens, "Memory, Reading, and the Renewal of Love: On the Poetics of Invention in Gottfried's *Tristan,*" in *German Narrative Literature of the Twelfth and Thirteenth Centuries: Studies Presented to Roy Wisbey on His Sixty-Fifth Birthday,* ed. Volker Honemann et al. (Tübingen: Niemeyer, 1994), 319–55.

9. See Krohn, ed. and trans., *Tristan,* 3:181.

10. Stevens, "Memory, Reading, and the Renewal of Love," 327.

11. Ibid., 328.

12. Ibid., 323.

13. Important considerations about "the constant union of the art of love and the art of poetry" in the Middle Ages are provided by Douglas Kelly, *Medieval Imagination: Rhetoric and the Poetry of Courtly Love* (Madison: University of Wisconsin Press, 1978).

14. See Herbert Kolb, "Ars venandi im 'Tristan,'" in *Medium aevum deutsch: Festschrift Kurt Ruh,* ed. Dieter Huschenbett (Tübingen: Niemeyer, 1979), 175–97.

15. My translation "composed in a vial" differs from Hatto's "brewing . . . so subtly devised and prepared" (192).

16. Marcelle Thiébaux, *The Stag of Love: The Chase in Medieval Literature* (Ithaca, NY: Cornell University Press, 1974).

17. See Stevens, "Memory, Reading, and the Renewal of Love," 329–30.

18. My translation differs from Hatto's "a rare marvel" (271).

19. My translation differs from Hatto's "Tell me, what sort of marvel?"— "A lovers' cave!" (271).

20. See Winthrop Wetherbee, "The Theme of Imagination in Medieval Poetry and the Allegorical Figure 'Genius,'" in *Medieval Poetics,* ed. Paul Maurice Clogan, Mediaevalia et Humanistica, n.s. 7 (Cambridge: Cambridge University Press, 1976), 51–52.

21. For a comparison with *Tristramsaga* and *Sir Tristrem,* see Krohn, ed. and trans., *Tristan,* 3:251.

22. See Wetherbee, "The Theme of Imagination," who interprets the king "as the artist of the scene he beholds," as "the poet of *fin amor,* suspended between desire and reverence" (51–52). And further comments: "His intersection of the sunbeam may be seen as an attempt to prolong this moment of suspension and render perfect the image of bliss which he contemplates. All of his emotions are subsumed by the imaginative experience of the state of loving; he is at once the victim and the author of the scene" (52).

CHAPTER THREE

Why Do Tristan and Isolde Make Love?

The Love Potion as a Milestone in the History of Sexuality

JAMES A. SCHULTZ

Why do Tristan and Isolde want to make love? Because they are in love. And why are they in love? The medieval Tristan romances refuse to answer this question, and this refusal is, I believe, both deliberate and significant.

My first question is a question in the history of sexuality. The history of sexuality is a young discipline and has only begun to explore the topics that it might address. So far, it has devoted a great deal of attention to questions of classification, regulation, and social organization. It has asked, for instance, when the classification "heterosexual" was coined and what it meant when women and men once called "normal" were now called "heterosexual." It has studied the regulatory work of disciplines like medicine — how, for example, doctors not long ago believed masturbation was a cause or perhaps a result of illness and how they tried to discourage the practice in order to keep people healthy. Finally, much work has been devoted to the social organization of sexuality, teaching us about the history of prostitution, queer subcultures, families, schools, and other social formations that have shaped sexual life.

The history of sexuality has paid somewhat less attention to first causes: what have people understood to be the motivating force that impels an individual to seek sexual relations? Medieval theologians, we know, would have attributed the urge to have sex to concupiscence or lust, while medieval doctors would have invoked appetite or the memory of past pleasures. This knowledge, however, is imperfect in two ways. First, it is incomplete. With regard to the high Middle Ages, we know what the priests and doctors would have said, but what of those outside the traditions of Latin learning? What, for instance, within the emerging discourse of secular love, was understood to be the motive force that impelled people to want to make love? My inquiry into the Tristan tradition is part of an effort to answer that question.[1] Second, our histories of sexuality continue to be haunted by a very modern notion of sexual desire. Thus John Baldwin, in *The Language of Sex,* treats "concupiscence" and "appetite" along with a number of other medieval notions in a chapter called, simply, "Sexual Desire."[2] For Baldwin, concupiscence and appetite are historically specific, partial understandings of what he takes to be an embracing, universal category: sexual desire. Thus when we have no specific medieval term at hand, it seems perfectly natural to invoke the universal one: Tristan and Isolde are motivated by sexual desire. Who isn't? But sexual desire is actually a relatively recent notion. It seems important to ask whether the writers of and audiences for medieval secular narrative would have assumed that the characters in these texts were affected by anything like what we call sexual desire. I hope to shed some light on this question, at least with regard to the German Tristan romances.[3]

If my first question relates to the history of sexuality, the refusal of the Tristan romances to answer the second question represents an important moment in that history: the moment when a secular elite turns away from the teachings of the priests and doctors and begins to explore love in its own terms. Among the great narratives of the high Middle Ages, the Tristan romances are famous for their preoccupation with questions of love. One would expect them to explain why it is that their hero and heroine fall in love. And of course they do: Tristan and Isolde fall in love because they drink a love potion. On closer examination, however, it turns out that the potion offers a very imperfect answer. Indeed, I believe it represents better than anything else a deliberate refusal to tell us why they fall in love.

In what follows I ask the first question of the two German Tristan romances, expanding it beyond the title hero and heroine to include other lovers as well: Why do characters in the Tristan romances of Eilhart von Oberg and Gottfried von Strassburg want to make love? In most cases, this will lead to the second question: Why are they in love in the first place? In conclusion I argue that the refusal to answer this second question represents a deliberate strategy on the part of Eilhart and Gottfried to stake out a vernacular space in which they can explore love and the desire to make love free from the taint that had always been attached to it in the learned discourse of the priests and doctors.

I am not interested in the nature of love in general, a topic on which a great deal has already been written, at least with regard to Gottfried. Love is relevant to this inquiry only to the extent that *being* in love is advanced as the reason why a man and a woman might want to *make* love. Even then, my focus is limited to that aspect of being in love that is made responsible for the desire to make love. I prefer the phrase "to make love" to other options such as "to have sex" or "sexual intercourse" because it is closer to the Middle High German terms. Eilhart, for instance, speaks of *minne üeben* and *minne phlegen* (2647, 2730–31) in reference to what we would call "having sex." I acknowledge, however, that I am asking a modern question of these medieval texts, one that arises from within the modern inquiry into the history of sexuality. I want to know what it is that serves the function we attribute to sexual desire, what it is that is understood to cause these characters to want to make love. I believe the Tristan romances give an answer that warrants particular attention.

Eilhart von Oberg

Eilhart von Oberg has two ways of responding to the question, why people want to make love. The first is silence. When Rivalin comes to Mark's court, he fights on Mark's behalf because "er gern wolt han sin swester zů ainem wip. mit pein an sinem lip erwarb er, daß er sie beschlieff" (He really wanted to have Mark's sister.[4] By suffering injuries to his body, he succeeded in sleeping with her) (84–87).[5]

Eilhart tells us Rivalin *wants* to sleep with Blanchefleur and that suffering injuries in battle enables him to achieve his goal. But he gives no reason *why* he wants to sleep with her. He does not say Rivalin loves her.

It's the same with Kehenis. On Tristrant's first visit back to Cornwall, he and Kehenis are hiding in the bushes, waiting for Isalde to pass. When Kehenis sees Gymele, one of Isalde's attendants, he is struck by her beauty. Later, when the two of them are alone, "do begund Keheniß zů Gamellinen die minn suchen. do wolt sú sin nit gerůchen" (Kehenis began to seek love from Gymele. She didn't want to grant his request) (6672–74). Should there be any doubt what sort of love Kehenis has in mind, Gymele's response makes her understanding quite clear.

> wǎ tůt ir hin úwer sin?
> ir sehent wol, daß ich bin
> nicht ain gebúrin,
> daß ir mich bittend umb die minne
> in so gar kurtzer zit. . . .
> hettent ir me wann fúnff jǎr
> zů minen gebotten gestan,
> eß wär dannocht zů frů getan,
> daß ir so geringlich wolten haben mich.
> (6679–94)

———

[Have you lost your mind? Surely you can see that I am not a peasant, whom you might ask for love after so short a time. Even if you had stood at my command more than five years, it would still be too early for you to think you could have me so easily.]

By invoking the terms of courtly love service, Gymele puts Kehenis in the position of a knight asking for his "reward," and the reward for loyal service is always sex. There seems little doubt that that is what he has in mind. Why Kehenis wants to sleep with Gymele, however, is not explained, although the effect of her beauty may have something to do with it. Still, he is never said to be in love with her.

The very reticence of episodes like these makes them dangerous. We read them and think, Here we have two young knights, Rivalin already a king, Kehenis the eldest son of a king, filled with youthful self-confidence; they see an opportunity to have sex with beautiful women: of course they want to! Why? Sexual desire. Raging hormones. It's obvious. It was probably obvious to Eilhart, too, which is why he didn't bother to say so.

The reason that is obvious to us, however, may not have been the reason that was obvious to Eilhart. Think of how Parzival behaves when he encounters Jeschute. He too is a young prince, full of youthful self-confidence, only a few weeks away from knighthood, marriage, and kingship. And yet when he throws himself on top of the sleeping beauty, he has not surrendered to an overpowering sexual desire. In fact, he is not thinking of sex at all but of his mother and her parting instructions: "da er mit der herzoginne ranc. dô dâhter an die muoter sîn: diu riet an wîbes vingerlîn" (as he struggled with the duchess; he was thinking of his mother: she advised him to acquire rings from women) (130, 28–30).[6] Parzival is not motivated by sexual desire but by filial obedience.[7] If Parzival were an undergraduate and Jeschute lodged a complaint with the dean of students, it is not likely the dean would find this explanation for his attack very convincing. The dean would know better. We may think we know better, too, but an episode like this should caution us against assuming that characters in these texts are motivated by drives and desires that may seem obvious to us. We must leave Rivalin and Kehenis where they are, at least for the moment: they want to have sex, but we do not know why.

Fortunately there are other cases where Eilhart is more forthcoming, cases in which he does tell us why his characters want to make love. The reason is always the same: they want to *make* love because they are *in* love. The reason comes in two strengths, weak and strong.

The weak version occurs near the end of the narrative, when Eilhart introduces the love of Kehenis and Gardiloÿe. I call it "weak" for two reasons. First, Kehenis and Gardiloÿe have been in love for a long time and, unlike Tristrant and Isalde, have somehow managed to survive without ever having consummated their love. It is not so intense. Second, for each lover, while there is a connection between being in love and making love, there is also some sort of interference. Although the narrator assures us, and Kehenis assures Gardiloÿe, that she has never been absent from his thoughts (7956–61, 7992–93), he understands this less as a reason why he wants to sleep with her than as a reason why she should sleep with him: "[er] sagt ir, sú käm nie uß sinem můt. 'dar umb dú, frow gůt, solt mich deß geniessen lŏn'" (He told her that he had never ceased to think of her. "Therefore, noble lady, you should let me benefit from this") (7992–95). His constancy entitles him to a reward. For her part, once she assures him of her devotion, she regrets the difficulty they have had getting together: "wann daß eß nit mocht sin, so hett all den willen din gar gern williglichen getŏn" (Had it not been impossible, I would have been quite happy to have done your will completely) (7999–8001). It is difficult to tell if she is impelled by a desire of her own to want to make love or if she is merely willing to do what he wants out of love for him.[8] In neither case is it clear that there is a *direct* link between being in love and making love. He wants to make love but formulates this desire as a reward she owes him for his constancy, which is doubtless to be understood as a consequence of his love. She wants to make love because she will do whatever he wants because she loves him so much. In each case love is the *indirect* cause of the desire to make love.

The strong version of the connection between being in love and making love is, as is only appropriate, the case of Tristrant and Isalde. From the moment they drink the potion, their love is presented as a matter of the utmost urgency:

> also schier sie ouch getranck,
> do ducht sie sunder danck,
> sie verlúren baid ir sinne,
> oder sie müsten ain ander minne. . . .
> ÿeglichß wond den tod
> von dem andern gewinnen,
> so grŏß ward daß minnen
> zwúschen in ŏn iren danck:
> daß macht alleß der tranck.
>
> (2353–56, 2364–68)

————

[As soon as they had drunk, they thought, despite themselves,
that they would lose their minds if they did not love one
another. . . . The attraction between them that had arisen
without their wishing it was so strong that each of them thought
the other would be their death: that was all caused by the potion.]

Isalde picks up this theme near the end of her long monologue: "wird
ich nit sin wib, so bin ich sicherlichen tod" (If I do not become his wife,
I will certainly die) (2574–75). And a bit later Brangene expresses a
similar view, telling Kurnewal: "bring mir sie ze samen! . . . oder ir
leben ist verlorn" (Bring them together for me, or their lives are lost)
(2665–67). The love of Tristrant and Isalde is so strong that unless
they make love, they will die.

These are the only cases in Eilhart where we know why someone
wants to make love, and the reason in both cases is the same: they want
to *make* love because they are *in* love. If this is the case, then perhaps
being in love is just another word for sexual desire. Perhaps love makes
them want to have sex, just as sexual desire does. If we step back, however, and ask why they are in love, we will see that the cases are not
the same. The inventory is easy to make. In the case of Kehenis and
Gardiloÿe, we don't know why they fell in love. It happened sometime
in the past, and we are told nothing about the circumstances. In the
case of Tristrant and Isalde, "daß macht alleß der tranck" (The potion
was the cause of it all) (2368). Whatever one thinks of the potion, it is
clearly not the same thing as sexual desire.

Let me return to the original question: Why is it that people want
to make love? In two cases, men who are not in love want to make
love, but we do not know why. In two cases, men and women want to
make love because they are in love. In one case, we do not know why
they are in love. In the other, we do: because they drank the potion.

This may seem like a meager harvest, but that does not mean it
is insignificant. If you ask why, according to Eilhart, people want to
make love, you discover he is not really interested in the question.
If you ask why people *fall* in love, you discover he isn't really interested in that question either. The only time he gives an answer, it

turns out to be the potion. But if you ask further why the potion makes people fall in love, there *is* no answer. That's just the way it is.[9] The refusal to answer says to us: Do not ask why people fall in love and, by extension, do not ask why people want to make love. The silences are not an oversight; they are deliberate: they are part of a general refusal to follow a line of causation that leads back beyond the mere fact that people are in love. This, I believe, is an important function, to which I will return later after seeing what Gottfried has to say on the subject.

Gottfried von Strassburg

Despite the fact that Gottfried has so much to say on the subject of love, he too can be silent on the question of why people want to make love. We never know, for example, why Mark makes love to Brangaene and Isold on his wedding night. Is he overcome by lust? Is he fulfilling the obligations of a husband? Is he responding to a buildup of heat and superfluous fluids? In other cases, however, Gottfried does offer reasons. Actually, there is only one: men and women want to *make* love because they are *in* love, just as in Eilhart.

For Tristan and Isold, it is, again, a matter of life and death. After they confess their love to each other but before they can consummate that love, Tristan tells Brangaene:

> wir sterben von minnen
> und enkunnen niht gewinnen
> weder zit noch state dar zuo,
> ir irret uns spate unde vruo;
> und sicherliche: sterben wir,
> dast nieman schuldic an wan ir.
> (12111–16)[10]

[We are dying from love but can find neither time nor place for it since you are hindering us, both early and late. Truly, if we die, there's no one to blame but you.]

Brangaene sees the urgency of the situation and at once makes it possible for them to consummate their love.[11]

The reason Blanscheflur wants to make love is similar but more abstract. Once Riwalin has been wounded, she is cast into such despair that she would have welcomed death and would indeed have died,

> wan daz si der trost labete
> und der gedinge uf habete,
> daz sin binamen wolte sehen,
> swie soz möhte geschehen;
> und alse sin gesæhe,
> swaz ir dar nach geschæhe,
> daz si daz allez gerne lite.
>   (1187–93)

———

[except that she was sustained by the comfort and supported by the hope that she would actually see him somehow or other, and that, once she saw him, she would suffer gladly whatever might happen afterwards.]

There are two hopes keeping Blanscheflur alive: the hope of seeing Riwalin and the hope of suffering what comes next. There is little doubt that she is thinking about sex. The formulation is similar to that in the mouths of other women — say, Gardiloÿe — combining passivity and eagerness: Gardiloÿe will do whatever Kehenis wants "gar gern willichen"; Blanscheflur will endure whatever happens "allez gerne." And it is typical of the ironic vagueness that MHG narrators often adopt when talking about intimate relations. The narrator does not specify what "might happen afterwards," but we know what he is talking about nevertheless. While Tristan and Isold must actually make love to save their lives, Blanscheflur can avoid death by cherishing the hope that she will make love.

With Riwalin the relation between being in love, making love, and staying alive is even more complex. After he returns wounded from battle and is lying on what all assume is his deathbed, Blanscheflur visits him and faints. She lies there "geliche als ob si wære tot" (just as if she were dead) (1307). When she comes to, she kisses him over and over "unz ime ir munt enzunde sinne unde craft zer minne, wan minne was dar inne" (until her lips inflamed him with the desire and the strength for love, since they contained love) (1314–16). Their love and their desire to make love bring them both back from death or near-death. As in the cases of Tristan, Isold, and Blanscheflur, so also in that of Riwalin, making love is a matter of life and death. But in a slightly different sense. Riwalin is nearly dead until love brings him to life and inspires in him the desire to make love. The exertion nearly kills him (1326–27), but a timely intervention by God restores him to health. Once again we find the threat of death, the desire to make love because of love, and the union of lovers that preserves life.

If *being* in love compels one — on pain of death — to make love, what is it that causes one to fall in love? There are three causes. Most famously, Tristan and Isold fall in love because they drink the love potion.

> Nu daz diu maget unde der man,
> Isot unde Tristan,
> den tranc getrunken beide, sa
> was ouch der werlde unmuoze da,
> Minne, aller herzen lagærin,
> und sleich zir beider herzen in.
> e sis ie wurden gewar,
> do stiez sir sigevannen dar
> und zoch si beide in ir gewalt.
> (11707–15)

———

[The moment the maiden and the man, Isold and Tristan, had drunk the potion, she who keeps all the world busy and sets traps for every heart, Love, was there at once and slipped into both their hearts. Before they were even aware of it, she had planted her victory standard there and drawn them both into her power.]

There can be no question that the potion is in fact the cause of their love.[12]

Riwalin falls in love when he realizes he is the object of love. After Blanscheflur accuses him of having hurt her friend and sighs when she delivers her parting blessing, Riwalin asks himself what this could all mean. He concludes that she uttered the sigh and the blessing

> durch niht niwan durch minne.
> daz enzunte ouch sine sinne
> daz si sa wider vuoren
> und namen Blanschefluoren
> und vuorten si mit in zehant
> in Riwalines herzen lant
> und cronden si dar inne
> im zeiner küniginne.
>
> (805–12)

———

[on account of love alone. That inflamed his thoughts so that they returned to Blanscheflur and took her and led her at once into the kingdom of Riwalin's heart and crowned her there to be his queen.]

It is the realization that she loves him that causes Riwalin to place her in his heart.

The third reason that one falls in love is illustrated by Blanscheflur. We first hear of her love at Mark's festival, as she watches Riwalin ride the bohort and listens to the other ladies praise his skill at riding; his body; the way he moves his imperial legs, holds his shield and lance, his clothes, head and hair, his entire bearing. They conclude with the exclamation: "o wol si sæligez wip, der vröude an ime beliben sol!" (Ah, she will be happy indeed, the lucky woman who will have lasting joy from him) (718–19). When they are done celebrating Riwalin, Gottfried tells us:

> [Blanscheflur] hæte in in ir muot genomen,
> er was ir in ir herze komen;
> er truoc gewaltecliche

in ir herzen künicriche
den cepter und die crone.
                    (725–29)

————

[Blanscheflur had taken him into her thoughts. He had
entered into her heart. With great power he bore the scepter
and the crown in the kingdom of her heart.]

Clearly Gottfried is invoking the commonplace according to which
the lover sees the beloved, whose image enters through the eyes and
lodges in the heart. First we hear how magnificent Riwalin looks, then
that he has conquered Blanscheflur's heart. Surprisingly, however, it
is not Blanscheflur who looks at Riwalin but the ladies of the court.
We do not know what she saw, only what they saw.

As it turns out, Blanscheflur hardly needs to see for herself, as becomes clear a bit later, when she describes what happened at the festival
in her monologue. She says:

do ich so vil manic edele wip
den sinen keiserlichen lip
und sinen ritterlichen pris
mit lobe gehorte in ballen wis
als umbe triben unde tragen
und sines lobes so vil gesagen
und ich mit ougen selbe sach
die tugende, der man von im jach,
und allez in min herze las,
swaz lobeliches an im was:
da von ergouchete min sin,
hie von geviel min herze an in.
                    (1027–38)

————

[When I heard so many noble women passing their praise for
his splendid body and his knightly renown around among
them like a ball, and heaping such praise upon him, and I saw
with my own eyes the excellent qualities that were attributed
to him and gathered into my heart all that was praiseworthy

about him, this caused my mind to play the fool and my heart to fall for him.]

Two things deserve note. First, Blanscheflur hears the noblewomen passing Riwalin's splendid body and knightly renown around among themselves, with praise, like a ball. This rather startling image suggests a surprisingly intimate collective relation to Riwalin's body, his exalted nobility, and his fame as a knight. The women are passing Riwalin around and admiring him. I don't think it is too much to say that they love him—with the version of what I have called "aristophilia," in which those who love nobility and courtliness respond with an intense, erotically charged admiration for someone who represents nobility and courtliness in an exalted form.[13]

Second, the specific features we heard the women praise at the bohort are forgotten and gathered in Blanscheflur's account into the more general "keiserlichen lip und . . . ritterlichen pris" with which she begins. But as soon as she has mentioned these, they too are forgotten in favor of the praise itself. It is the women's praise itself, rather than the things they praise, that incites Blanscheflur to look, at the same time that it predetermines what she sees: not legs and hair and shield and lance, but "die tugende, der man von im jach . . . [und] . . . swaz lobeliches an im was" (the excellent qualities that were attributed to him and everything about him that deserves praise). These are not physical attributes or courtly behaviors or personal judgments on the part of Blanscheflur. They are social values in their most abstract formulation. The excellent qualities are those that courtly women have identified as excellent. That which deserves praise can only be that which deserves praise at court. The sight of courtly excellence and praiseworthiness is what causes Blanscheflur to fall in love.

The image of Riwalin does not pass through Blanscheflur's eyes into her heart. Instead he passes through a courtly screening process, from which he emerges as love and praise. Blanscheflur falls in love with Riwalin because he corresponds to the praise that has been given by the women who pass him around and determine he is worthy of love. Or, to pick up her own strange image, Blanscheflur takes the ball of praise from the women and, like them, loves it. This is a peculiar twist to the familiar paradigm.

There are a couple of instances where Gottfried stays closer to that paradigm. After love has conquered Riwalin, he considers what has happened, looks at Blanscheflur, "und allez sunder ahtete" (and considered each part separately) (924). He notes her hair, her forehead, her temples, her cheeks, her mouth, her chin, and her eyes: "do kam diu rehte minne, diu ware viurærinne und stiez ir seneviuwer an, daz viur, da von sin herze enbran" (Then real love arrived, the true incendiary, and lit the fire of longing, the fire which consumed his heart) (929–32). Note that this is not when Riwalin first falls in love but later, when his passion begins to burn more intensely. The principle involved here is explained by Gottfried just after Tristan and Isold drink the potion but before they confess their love, when they, like Riwalin, take every opportunity to look at the one they love: "die gelieben duhten beide ein ander schœner vil dan e. deist liebe reht, deist minne e" (The lovers each found the other more beautiful than before. This is the custom of love, this is love's law) (11856–58). As Gottfried sees it, looking at a beautiful body does not cause someone to fall in love. It's the other way around: people who have fallen in love find those they love beautiful, so they look at them. Gottfried calls this "diu wuocherhafte minne" (interest-bearing love) (11867). Love causes the lover to look, and looking causes love to increase.

Let me summarize the answers that Gottfried gives to the questions that I posed at the start. Why do people want to make love? There is only one reason: because they are in love. For Gottfried, however, this is a compelling reason: failure to follow love to consummation will kill you. Why do people fall in love? There are three reasons: because of a love potion; because the love of another provokes one to return that love; and because the praise, and collective love, for a courtly paragon causes one to confirm that praise and thereby fall in love.

In other words, there is no cause for love except love itself. It takes three forms: magical, individual, social. Love is in the potion itself that forces Tristan and Isold to fall in love. Love of a single individual for himself causes Riwalin to return that love. Love that is defined, evaluated, and presented to her in terms of shared social values is what causes Blanscheflur to fall in love. There is no getting behind love to discover the cause of love. Love is the cause.

The Great Refusal

I began by asking why the characters in the MHG Tristan romances want to make love. It soon became clear that Eilhart and Gottfried do not share my interest in this question. Eilhart ignores it entirely, except in the case of Tristrant and Isalde, where he joins Gottfried to explain the desire to make love as an inescapable consequence of the power of love. This led me to ask why people fall in love. Eilhart is not interested in this question at all. In fact, his silence is so telling, I think it represents a deliberate refusal to ask the question. Gottfried asks the question. But the more one looks at his answers, the more they seem to circle back to the starting point: love is caused by love.

In addition to posing the question about why people make love, I raised a question about the status of desire in the history of sexuality. Here the evidence of Eilhart and Gottfried is unequivocal. There is nothing in these texts that corresponds to what we usually today understand by sexual desire — that is, according to a recent book on the subject, "*an innate motivational force* (e.g. an instinct, drive, need, urge, appetite, wish, or want) that impels the individual to seek out sexual objects or to engage in sexual activities."[14] To be sure, after one has fallen in love, Love takes over one's heart, thereby becoming an internal force that impels the individual to engage in sexual activities. But although it is internal, it is not innate: it is always provoked by something outside the lover. If the history of sexuality is really committed to writing the *history* of sexuality, then it must study for any given period, not only how people understood sexual acts, but also what they thought it was that provoked them to perform these acts.

The medieval culture in which Eilhart and Gottfried wrote had its own explanations for why people want to make love, and some of these ideas involved an innate motivational force. One might find such ideas in a number of discourses, but surely the best known come from Christian theology. Theologians taught that concupiscence and lust are intrinsic elements of all human beings — the consequence of original sin — that cause people to do that which they should not, especially with the organs of generation. If the theology of concupiscence was not widely known outside the church, the related Christian distrust of all things sexual certainly was. In this context, Eilhart's and Gottfried's lack of interest in the question that I posed becomes very interesting indeed.

At this historical moment, when vernacular literature was exploring new themes in the context of a courtly culture that was coming into its own and feeling a new confidence, Eilhart's refusal to ask why people make love and Gottfried's refusal to locate the beginning of love anywhere outside love signal a refusal to engage these discourses. Yes, we write about love. But we refuse even to ask the question where this love might have come from, since the answers we are used to hearing would denigrate love from the start. The potion serves as a telling symbol of this refusal because, as I argued above, it acts out this same refusal. It will not tell you why it causes love, thereby blocking further progress down a path of inquiry that asks why people fall in love and why they want to make love. It makes perfect sense that romances that thwart the question, what causes love, should have at their symbolic center a potion that does just that. The potion then gives material form to what might be called a Great Refusal. The Tristan romances of Eilhart and Gottfried, in refusing to ask why people fall in love and want to have sex, refuse to engage discourses that *do* answer these questions. In doing so, they set off a domain in which secular love and sexuality can be explored, in which they are not tainted in their very nature by sickness and sin. This is a signal moment in the history of European sexuality, the moment when a self-conscious and sophisticated secular discourse on love declared its independence of the related theological and medical teachings on the subject. The love potion in the Tristan romances can stand as a telling symbol of that declaration of independence.[15]

Notes

1. I have discussed this issue more generally in James A. Schultz, *Courtly Love, the Love of Courtliness, and the History of Sexuality* (Chicago: University of Chicago Press, 2006), 51–98.

2. John W. Baldwin, *The Language of Sex: Five Voices from Northern France around 1200* (Chicago: University of Chicago Press, 1994), 116–72.

3. I have asked this question of *Mären* in James A. Schultz, "Love without Desire in *Mären* of the Thirteenth and Fourteenth Centuries," in *Mittelalterliche Novellistik im europäischen Kontext,* ed. Mark Chinca, Timo Reuvekamp-Felber, and Christopher Young, Beihefte zur Zeitschrift für deutsche Philologie 13 (Berlin: Schmidt, 2006), 122–47.

4. Buschinger translates this line as "parce qu'il désirait avoir pour épouse" (Eilhart von Oberg, *Tristrant: Edition diplomatique des manuscrits et traduction en français moderne,* ed. Danielle Buschinger, Göppinger Arbeiten zur Germanistik 202 [Göppingen: Kümmerle, 1976], 9). Buschinger and Spiewok translate "weil er gern Markes Schwester zur Frau gewinnen wollte" (Eilhart von Oberg, *Tristrant und Isalde,* ed. and trans. Danielle Buschinger and Wolfgang Spiewok, Wodan 27 [Greifswald: Reineke, 1993], 3). The dictionaries, however, suggest that if Eilhart had meant "wife" he would have left out the indefinite article: *ze wîbe hân.* Indeed, the very next sentence suggests that Rivalin is more interested in sleeping with Blanchefleur than marrying her.

5. I cite MS H from Eilhart, *Tristrant,* ed. Buschinger.

6. I cite from Wolfram von Eschenbach, *Parzival,* ed. Karl Lachmann, rev. Eberhard Nellmann, trans. Dieter Kühn, 2 vols., Bibliothek des Mittelalters 8 (Frankfurt am Main: Deutscher Klassiker Verlag, 1994).

7. I have discussed this scene in greater detail in James A. Schultz, "Parzival, Courtly Love, and the History of Sexuality," *Poetica* 38 (2006): 35–37.

8. For an analysis of their love that places it within a conflict over feudal sovereignty, see Peter Strohschneider, "Herrschaft und Liebe: Strukturprobleme des Tristanromans bei Eilhart von Oberg," *Zeitschrift für deutsches Altertum* 122 (1993): 42–44.

9. This is not quite the same as Haug's "Einbruch des absolut Unkalkulierbaren" (Walter Haug, "Gottfrieds von Straßburg 'Tristan': Sexueller Sündenfall oder erotische Utopie," in *Kontroversen, alte und neue: Akten des VII. internationalen Germanisten-Kongresses, Göttingen 1985,* ed. Albrecht Schöne [Tübingen: Niemeyer, 1985], 48). Haug understands the potion as the breakthrough into the narrative of a brutal truth. I see it as a strategy to protect the narrative from questions it does not want to address.

10. I cite from Gottfried von Strassburg, *Tristan und Isold,* ed. Friedrich Ranke, 15th ed. (Zürich: Weidmann, 1978).

11. This entire passage (12050–156) corresponds to four lines in the Carlisle fragment, in which the lovers and their companion speak of love and she gives her consent. The point that matters here — that the lovers will

die if they do not consummate their love—is Gottfried's addition. See Günter Eifler, "Das Carlisle-Fragment und Gottfried von Straßburg: Unterschiedliche Liebeskonzepte?" in *Vox Sermo Res: Beiträge zur Sprachreflexion, Literatur- und Sprachgeschichte vom Mittelalter bis zur Neuzeit: Festschrift Uwe Ruberg,* ed. Wolfgang Haubrichs, Wolfgang Kleiber, and Rudolf Voß (Stuttgart/Leipzig: Hirzel, 2001), 119–20.

12.   That the potion causes Tristan and Isold to fall in love seems now to be generally accepted, and interest has turned to figuring out what we should make of those earlier scenes that suggest that Tristan and Isold are made for each other. See Günther Schweikle, "Zum Minnetrank in Gottfrieds 'Tristan': Ein weiterer Annäherungsversuch," in *Uf der mâze pfat: Festschrift für Werner Hoffmann zum 60. Geburtstag,* ed. Waltraud Fritsch-Rößler, Göppinger Arbeiten zur Germanistik 555 (Göppingen: Kümmerle, 1991), 135–48; Christopher Young, "Minnetrank als Literarisierungsprozeß bei Gottfried von Straßburg," in *Der "Tristan" Gottfrieds von Straßburg: Symposion Santiago de Compostela. 5. bis 8, April 2000,* ed. Christoph Huber and Victor Millet (Tübingen: Niemeyer, 2002), 257–79; Mark Chinca, *Gottfried von Strassburg: Tristan* (Cambridge: Cambridge University Press, 1997), 21–32.

13.   Schultz, *Courtly Love,* 91–94.

14.   Pamela C. Regan and Ellen Bescheid, *Lust: What We Know about Human Sexual Desire* (Thousand Oaks, CA: Sage, 1999), 22; my emphasis.

15.   Starting from a completely different question, Ralf-Hennig Steinmetz comes to a surprisingly similar conclusion. He argues that in his references to the fall and to original sin, Gottfried does not mean to invoke this doctrine but, by way of contrast, to highlight the alternative he proposes, an ideal of love that affirms sexual love between men and women. As I do for both Eilhart and Gottfried, so Steinmetz identifies a strategy by which Gottfried distances the love of which he writes from the Christian teachings about concupiscence and lust (Ralf-Hennig Steinmetz, "Tristans *Erbeminne*: Versuch über vier Hapax legomena bei Gottfried von Straßburg," *Zeitschrift für deutsches Altertum* 129 [2000]: 388–408).

Seeing Love in the World of Lovers

Late Medieval Love Literature as a Fulfillment of Gottfried's *Tristan*

LUDGER LIEB

Minnereden: Conventions of Seeing Love

It is no accident and no ornamental flourish when the eavesdropping male narrator of the anonymous, late medieval *Minnerede* known by the title *Minne und Gesellschaft* (Love and Society), surprises two young women reading a book about Tristan and Isolde.

> und hatten by den zyden
> ein buech in ir beyder hant
> und lasen dar an von Tristant
> und von Ysoten der reinen,
> wie einz daz ander meynen
> könd in steter minne.
> mit herczen und mit sinne
> konden sie truwe halten
> gar an allez spalten.[1]

> ———

> [And there they held
> in their hands, together, a book

and they were reading in it about Tristan
and about Isolde the pure,
how each of them longed for the other
in constant love.
With their hearts and with their minds
they were able to remain true to one another
and were never divided.]

This scene emblematizes a central trend governing the entire genre of late medieval German rhymed couplet texts known as *Minnereden* (in English, discourses on love): whether they mention the Tristan tradition or not, *Minnereden* situate themselves as belonging to and continuing the Tristan tradition. They are a sustained response to the Tristan tradition, as they take up and grapple with the central themes of erotic love enacted in the Tristan tales: the power of erotic desire; the conflict between erotic love and loyalty; the incompatibility of erotic love and conventional mores; the dilemmas attending all attempts to reconcile honor and erotic love; the persistent questioning about the nature of erotic desire and its place in the world.

Minnereden extend and elaborate core concepts of Tristan love, especially, as we shall see, the notion that erotic love creates a kind of alternative universe that is more noble than the conventional world and suitable only for the high-minded and pure of heart. At the same time, *Minnereden* explore aspects of Tristan love in new ways. They are especially interested in making Tristan love a visible part of their discourse, whether by personifying it, making it an allegory, or making its effects, as symptoms, visible to all.

The visualization of love is one of the most striking features of medieval love poetry, and *Minnereden,* which represent the largest genre of secular literature from late medieval Germany, are replete with ways of visualizing the abstraction *Minne* (love).[2] This chapter begins by exploring this well-known, and to some perhaps trivial, point. It then steps backward in time to investigate the way *Minne* is visualized in Gottfried's *Tristan.* In conclusion, it returns to the *Minnereden* and argues that they realized Gottfried's sketch of the other-world of *Minne.*[3]

Let us begin our investigation of the visualization of *Minne* by taking a brief look at the more than five hundred surviving *Minnereden*. Their general content can be summarized as follows: *Minnereden* as a whole are a large-scale project for exploring the mystery of love. They can be interpreted as an attempt to come to grips with the unintelligible aspects of love. To put it differently, *Minnereden* can be read as a strategy to break through to and grasp the ever receding aspects of love, as an attempt to get hold of *Minne,* to interrogate *Minne,* to call *Minne* to account. One might think of *Minnereden* as a series of ongoing conversations and negotiations with *Minne* itself.

To achieve all this, *Minne* needs to take shape, to become visible. Of course, under normal conditions love is invisible (in the same way that God is not immediately visible). *Minne* can be seen only indirectly, for example, by means of visible signs signifying it. However, *Minnereden,* like much other medieval literature, explore the possibility of seeing *Minne* by entering an alternative world, or otherworld, of *Minne,* where the general rules of normalcy cease to be effective. The most common modes employed in *Minnereden* to make love visible are personification, allegory, and descriptions of love symptoms.

A few examples will clarify this point. Let us take a largely unknown but typical *Minnerede, Frau Minne weiß Rat* (Lady Love knows what to do).[4] A first-person male narrator (a typical narrative device for *Minnereden*) tells us that one morning, in search of adventure, he came upon a deep valley.[5] There he found first a lovely *locus amoenus* (with the standard equipment of a spring, singing birds, and flowers) and then a castle surrounded by high walls, in front of which there was an orchard enclosed by a huge hedge of roses. Entering this *hortus conclusus,* the narrator meets a most beautiful woman, dressed all in red, Lady *Minne* (Lady Love). To her inquiry regarding the goal of his search, he replies that he is searching for joy and adventure *(aventiure)* and that furthermore:

> "nun hoff ich, ir seyt mir zuo stewr
> komen in des mayen zier."
> die frow sprach: "gesell, ich main, dir
> wone by vil kluoger synn."

ich sprach: "syd irs nit frow Mynn?"—
"ja, gesell, das betütt ich mit der farb rot.
ich mach ouch mengem hertz nott
und kan es wider zuo fröd pringen
allen den die zuo der mynn lieb han gedingen."[6]

———

["Now I hope that you have come to guide me in this beautiful
month of May." The lady spoke: "My friend, it seems to me that
you possess great intelligence." I spoke: "You are Lady *Minne,*
aren't you?" "Yes, friend, that is what I mean by wearing red.
I make trouble for many hearts, yet I can return joy as well to
all those who trust in the kindness of love."][7]

The frequent appearance of this personification, Lady *Minne,* in
late medieval literature is the very best evidence for the period's fascination with the idea of seeing love face-to-face. It is not just that Lady
Minne is called upon as an authority, as, for example, in the poem
by Walter von der Vogelweide, *Frowe Minne, ich clage iu mêre* (Lady
Minne, I have more complaints for you).[8] Nor is it simply the case of
Lady *Minne* occupying the hearts of lovers, as happens when Gottfried speaks of *Minne* as the entrapper of all hearts ("aller herzen
lâgærîn"), sneaking into Tristan and Isolde's hearts after they drink
the potion ("sleich zir beider herzen în" [11715–16]).[9] In the *Minnereden,* we find an entirely different sort of personification. The narrator
speaks here of a real encounter with Lady *Minne*: he sees Lady *Minne*
eye to eye, and he meets her face-to-face in an orchard surrounded by
roses.[10] All is made to sound absolutely real and creates what one might
call a very strong reality effect. If one reads and studies many of these
texts over a long time, one eventually begins to find it quite plausible
that someone walking through the woods might chance upon Lady
Minne and start a conversation.

However, to meet Lady *Minne* it is essential to leave behind the
everyday world and go into the woods and the wilderness, into a world
that exists outside of ordinary life. The woods and wilderness of these
texts can be interpreted as an alternate reality, contrasting with the
quotidian world of ordinary realities. This exit marks a transgression
by the first-person narrator, who crosses over and surpasses the bor-

ders of his ordinary world and reaches another state and another disposition, one that allows Lady *Minne* to enter the stage.[11] Such immediate encounters with Lady *Minne* are a common way in which *Minne* is made visible and present in the *Minnereden*.

In the mode of allegory, *Minne* does not appear in person but takes shape in other objects, as can be seen in the epic world of the *Minnereden*. Following the rules of allegoresis, the qualities of the corresponding object are interpreted in connection with specific characteristics of *Minne*. Allegories are therefore the most suitable means of visualizing the variety and complexity of *Minne*. Most prominent in *Minnereden* are hunting allegories, but there are also castle allegories and allegories of flowers and colors.

A broad range of allegorical visualization of *Minne* is found in the famous *Minnerede* called *Die Minneburg*.[12] First of all, the castle itself is the object of allegorical interpretation. The narrator espies the castle in the far distance, on the other side of a mountain range, and readily explains that it signifies a lady who is hard to conquer:

> Die burk umb floßen und umb graben
> Ist ein reines wyp gar gut,
> Die vor schanden ist wol behut.
> Die lewen, risen und hunde
> Beduttent hut zu aller stunde.
> Der lewe ist selblich hüt und ere,
> Die sie treit in ir selber, die here,
> Vor yenen und vor disen.
> Ir frunde beduttent die risen.
> So betuten auch die hunde
> Brufer, claffer, die uz irem münde
> Manig rede lippen lappen
> Und boses fur daz gut ye snappen.
>   (548–60)[13]

———

[The castle surrounded by waters and moats stands for a pure, good woman, who is well protected from all shame. The lions, giants, and dogs stand for constant guardianship. The lion stands for the guard she places on her honor herself, and which she,

the most exalted one, carries within herself before all others.
The giants stand for her friends and the dogs stand for spies
and gossips who with their mouths give lip and talk twaddle
and snap at the bad rather than the good.]

Then follows the description of the castle. Within the castle a stone
pillar gives shape to the following allegorical scene. Through five windows on the pillar, the picture of a man is reflected onto the pillar, and
the shape of this man is reinforced by a glass figure. Above the glass
figure there is a second figure, a woman made from steel and diamonds.
The latter is softened by the vibrance of the glass figure, bows down to
it, and begets a child with the glass figure, who is born without delay:

> [The pillar] betüt ein reines wyp,
> Der tugenthafter zarter lip
> In eren ist verwaset.
> Die venster funf verglaset
> Daz sint ir funf synne. . . .
> Von glas der berillen man,
> Der hinder den funf fenstern stat,
> Ist ir vernunft mit voller tat. . . .
> Daz frawen bilde von stahel clar
> Und dyamant gesmidet rein
> Daz ist ir fryer wille ein.
>   (581–84, 588–90, 596–98)

———

[The pillar stands for a pure woman whose virtuous, fine body
is founded in great honor. The five glass windows signify her
five senses. . . . The glass figure (within the pillar) standing
behind the five windows signifies the lady's reason in action. . . .
The female figure, forged purely in clear steel and diamond,
stands for her free will alone.]

The child, begotten and born from the union of reason and free will,
is the so-called *Minnekind,* the *Minne* child. This child grows up and
becomes Lady *Minne* herself, who in the last part of the text presides

over and passes judgment in a great *Minne* trial. Here allegory turns into personification.

In the case of personification an immediate encounter with love, the direct seeing of love, is made explicit, whereas in allegory seeing love is mediated, made possible through a third set of references. The otherwise invisible is made visible by means of allegory.

Finally, *Minne* is made visible by means of symptoms. The enumeration of symptoms of love (a pan-European trope) is common in *Minnereden*.[14] Let us take another example from the *Minnerede Frau Minne weiß Rat* (Lady *Minne* knows what to do). Lady *Minne* explains to the first-person narrator how to recognize *Minne* in his beloved:

> wann es sich kain lengeru frist
> in zwain hertzen verbergen kan,
> wa ainß dem andern guottes gan,
> es vint sich mit lieplichen worten,
> mit gesicht an mengen orten,
> liep plick die ains dem andern tuot.
> also kumpt ye guot uß guot.
> noch ains merck vor in allen:
> wann ains dem andern tuot gefallen
> und ains das ander erplickt,
> vor fröd in lieb sein hertz erschrickt
> und erzint sin anplick für rott.
> das macht als der mynne not
> und die lieb die ains dem andern gan
> vor lieb ains nicht wol reden kan.
>
> (194–208)

———

[For it has reached the point that it can no longer hide itself in two hearts when one wishes the other only good and it shows itself with tender words and with frequent looks in many places and by loving glances passing between them. In this way goodness always arises from goodness. Always keep in mind before all else that when one lover pleases the other and sees the beloved, loving tenderness makes the heart tremble with joy and seeing the

beloved makes the lover blush. All this is caused by the affliction
of love and the loving tenderness that one gives the other and he
is unable to speak in the presence of his beloved.]

Loving words and glances, the trembling heart, blushing, and being
unable to speak: these are the typical symptoms of love. They can be
interpreted semiotically as indexical signs. Saint Augustine would
have called them natural signs, clearly corresponding in a cause-and-
effect relation to the thing they signify. These natural characteristics,
especially blushing and the loss of speech, are most important in those
situations where one of the partners is not really sure of the other's
being truly in love. The advantage of such natural symptoms is that
they cannot be manipulated. They show that *Minne* is definitely present. However, it is important to note that the symptoms of *Minne* are
"secondhand" signs in the sense that *Minne* itself is not seen in them;
they only indicate the consequences of love and point toward its existence. *Minne* itself remains invisible.

Allow me a brief remark concerning the allegories of colors in
the *Minnereden*. The interpretation of individual colors functions in
accordance with allegory, insofar as red signifies the burning of love,
blue means true love and constancy, green stands for the beginning
of a love affair, and so on. However, at the same time, we find special
practices related to the colors of love, for example, two lovers wearing
special colors to indicate a special aspect of their love for one other. This
color is intended to signify that which would otherwise be invisible.
Similar to the symptoms of love, these *Minne* colors display the love
between two lovers and the special way they construct it. In contrast to
the symptoms of love, however, these *Minne* colors are arbitrary signs
(Augustine), or symbolic signs (Peirce). Due to the high degree of ar-
bitrariness they are easily manipulated. One can lie with *Minne* colors.
No wonder that *Minnereden* sometimes reflect critically on them! In
the *Minnerede Die acht Farben* (The Eight Colors), for example, the
narrator observes:

> Es sind vil die varb tragen
> Vnd wissen doch nit ze sagen

Von lieb oder von der mynn
Die tuond in ainualtigem synn.[15]

———

[There are many who wear special colors, and yet they do
not know now to talk about tenderness and love. They are
simple and naive.]

Before moving on to a discussion of *Tristan,* a summary is in order.
Minnereden make *Minne* visible. In them *Minne* can be seen, and it can
also take shape in signs, becoming visible through symptoms and by
means of allegory. Whereas these produce only the indirect visibility
of *Minne,* the personification of Lady *Minne* allows direct vision;
Minne becomes visible in a face-to-face encounter.

Gottfried von Strassburg's *Tristan*: The World of Love

How do these phenomena take shape in Gottfried's *Tristan?* It is not
difficult to show that *Tristan* deals with symptoms of *Minne* and also
that allegories of *Minne* are constructed and interpreted in it. Also,
Lady *Minne* appears in person, not as an actor in the epic world of action but rather as a real authority or as an agent acting within the re-
spective persons.

In the following, I try to avoid a simple enumeration of the respec-
tive passages in which *Minne* takes shape and is made visible by the
narrator in *Tristan.* Instead I focus on selected examples, so as to work
out how the text goes beyond the conventional visibility of *Minne* and
attempts to transgress conventions.

The starting point of my thesis is the famous idea formulated in
the *Tristan* prologue, the idea that alongside the world of ordinary reality there exists another world, a second or alternate world, that of the
edelen herzen (noble hearts). As the author figure tells us, the novel was
written for this other, alternate world:

Ich hân mir eine unmüezekeit
der werlt ze liebe vür geleit

und edelen herzen zeiner hage:
den herzen den ich herze trage,
der werlde in die mîn herze siht.
ine meine ir aller werlde niht
als die, von der ich hœre sagen,
diu keine swære müge getragen
und niwan in fröuden welle sweben: . . .
ein ander werlt die meine ich,
diu sament in eime herzen treit
ir süeze sûr, ir liebez leit, . . .
der werlt wil ich gewerldet wesen,
mit ir verderben oder genesen.
(45–53, 58–60, 65–66)

———————

[Thus I have undertaken a labor to please the polite world and
solace noble hearts—those hearts which I hold in affection,
that world which lies open to my heart. I do not mean the word
of the many who (as I hear) are unable to endure sorrow and
wish only to revel in bliss. . . . I have another world in mind which
together in one heart bears its bitter-sweet, its dear sorrow. . . .
Of this world let me part, to be damned or saved with it.][16]

Already in these few verses the most significant points I want to make
can clearly be shown. First, the term *ander werlt* does not mean the
otherworld of utopia, or the other world of fiction about which we
often talk in academic terms.[17] It is also not a heterotopia. *Ander werlt* is
not just an otherworld, but a *second world,* a duplication of the first one.
It is a second world firmly rooted in the first,[18] and—most important—
it is just as real as the first world: it is a *mundus alter et idem* (a world
different and the same). Second, the *edelen herzen,* or noble hearts, of
this second world of *Minne* do not represent some private arrangement
of individual lovers but rather something concerning the whole community, which Gottfried calls the community of the *edelen herzen.*[19]
This second world of love is therefore a second world of lovers.

Third, the idea is expressed in this passage of seeing with the
heart ("der werlde in die mîn herze siht"). To be able to see this second

world of lovers the usual way of seeing must undergo a process of transformation, which is expressed in the text by the metaphor of the heart being able to look into this second world. Thus the world of *Minne* is visible only for one who is able to see with his heart.[20] We are not simply speaking of imagination here, or of working on the basis of a dichotomy between outer reality and inner imagination. Such a conception would not be adequate, since the second world has an outer reality in the same way as the first world. The crucial difference, then, is not a different status of reality but rather another way of seeing. Fourth is the idea of devotion to the world of *Minne*. The world of *Minne* requires the whole person. Within it the author figure, Gottfried, wants to perish ("be damned") or to find redemption ("be saved"). According to Gottfried, *Minne* is not just a game, something that people play at. Rather, it demands an essential decision for a lifetime commitment.[21]

If one reads *Tristan* anew with this passage from the prologue in mind, one soon realizes that these four essential aspects are treated throughout the story, but they do not come true; that is to say, they are not fulfilled. Instead, the concept of *Minne* suggested in the prologue is realized in the text in only rudimentary fashion. A few examples will demonstrate this, with the episode of the *Minnegrotte* (Cave of Lovers) being of critical importance.

The *ander werlt der Minne* (other world of Love) takes shape already in the love between Riwalin and Blanscheflur. When the fire of *Minne* begins burning in Riwalin we are told:

> er greif in ein ander leben,
> ein niuwe leben wart ime gegeben.
> er verwandelte dâ mite
> al sîne sinne und sîne site
> und wart mitalle ein ander man.
>
> (935–39)

———

[For now he laid hold of a new life, a new life was given him;
so that he changed his whole cast of mind and became quite
a different man.]

Love is experienced by the protagonists as an absolutely different world. Neither Riwalin nor Blanscheflur is able to experience this other world as one embedded within the first, the "real" world. For both of them the consequences are equally imperative: the second world of *Minne* destroys the first world of court life. The other world, the *ander werlt* of *Minne,* is discovered by the protagonists, but in the end they cannot conquer and inhabit it.[22]

This aspect becomes even more clear in the episode of the *Minnegrotte.* Tristan and Isolde live in this *locus amoenus* in the middle of a forested wilderness, but this way of life is confined to a very brief period. Moreover, the world of *Minne* in the wilderness is not quite the same as the *ander werlt der Minne,* for it is situated apart from the real world and not embedded in it.[23]

Entirely missing from the plot is the community of those who love, who are dedicated to *Minne.* In both cases, Riwalin and Blanscheflur, and Tristan and Isolde, *Minne* is never embedded in a community of lovers, the community of the *edelen herzen.*[24] It seems that Gottfried is aware of this problem. The lack of community apparently needs compensation. In my view, the tale of the royal household of the birds as well as the references to great lovers of world literature are intended to replace the absent community of lovers. In any case, life in the *Minnegrotte* cannot cover up this substantial lack.

The other way of seeing, the mode of seeing with the heart, is made apparent in the actions of the protagonists only in swift outlines. In the end, only the narrator or authorial persona comes to terms with this idea, which takes place in the well-known passage of the second autobiographical excursus. There we read:

> Diz weiz ich wol, wan ich was dâ. . . .
> ich vant an der fossiure
> den haft und sach die vallen.
> ich bin ze der kristallen
> ouch under stunden geweten. . . .
> ich hân die fossiure erkant
> sît mînen eilif jâren ie
> und enkam ze Kurnewâle nie.
> (17104, 17114–17, 17140–42)

[I know this well, for I have been there. . . . I have found the
lever and seen the latch in that cave and have, on occasion, even
pressed on to the bed of crystal. . . . I have known that cave since
I was eleven, yet I have never set foot in Cornwall.]

The most important point in this passage is not that it marks fictional-
ity but rather that it transgresses the regular mode of seeing. While
seeing actual objects normally presupposes the bodily presence of the
one who sees, the *Minnegrotte* can be seen even in the case of bodily
absence. This does not mean it is fictional. Rather, it means that the reality of the *Minnegrotte* can be conceived only by one who is capable of
another way of seeing. It is visible only if one sees differently.

Finally, there is the devotion to the world of *Minne,* which for Tristan and Isolde is only possible in a restricted way. They are bound to
one another by the love potion, but still the world of *Minne* remains for
them the isolated world of two lovers. The world called by Gottfried
the community of the *edelen herzen* — for Tristan and Isolde it does not
yet exist.

Minnereden: The Other Way of Seeing Love

Returning now to the *Minnereden,* I suggest the following thesis: the
four dimensions or aspects of love suggested by Gottfried's *Tristan*
found realization in the late medieval *Minnereden.*[25] To make this thesis
more plausible, I want to focus on one *Minnerede,* known by the title
Das Kloster der Minne (The Cloister of *Minne*).[26] Most likely written in
the mid-fourteenth century, this text became famous among scholars because of its supposed connection with a real monastery, Ettal in
southern Bavaria.[27]

Again we find a first-person speaker, who in mid-May is wander-
ing through a beautiful forest when he spots a lady riding through the
woods on horseback. He hides behind the trees and then surprises the
lady, grabbing the reins of her horse and asking her to tell him who
she is. She announces that she is a messenger for Lady *Minne,* her mis-
sion being to search for *frouwen, ritter,* and *knechte* (ladies, knights,

and squires) ready to enter the cloister of *Minne,* a huge and most beautiful cloister, in which Lady *Minne* herself has taken up residence.

The narrator asks the lady to describe the cloister in detail. She tells him that it is round, with twelve doors (one for every month), so spacious that even the quickest horse could not complete a circuit around it in a year's time (i.e., it is as spacious as the whole world).[28] Attracted by this description, the narrator himself moves on to the cloister. He arrives in front of the door for the month of May and from there can see the May dance of women and men, quite obviously in love. Some of the dancers he recognizes, but he himself is feeling rather lonely:

> ye ain fro und ain man
> sach ich by ain ander gan
> und lieplichen kosen. . . .
> ich sach nach liebi ringen
> manig hertz in sinem sinne,
> als im die werde Minne
> enpfolchen hat mit ernst. . . .
> doch gab ez mir ain swären müt.
> ich sach mangen gesellen güt,
> der waz von minem lande,
> der mich wenig erkande.
>   (479–81, 498–501, 531–34)[29]

———

[I saw always walking together, one woman and one man, speaking loving words to one another. . . . I saw many hearts struggling with themselves for the sake of love, just as honorable Minne had earnestly advised them. . . . But it made me feel downcast. I saw many good old friends from my land, and only a very few recognized me.]

One of the crucial interpretive points in this text is its description of a community of lovers, who live together just like monks in a cloister. These lovers are partly known to the observer from his ordinary life. The different realities, the two worlds, start mingling right here. The reality of the narrator's ordinary world and the reality of the ideal

otherworld meet in a sort of in-between space called *Minne*. This space
in between is constituted by the community of the lovers, "in the paradoxical space of an earthly paradise as a heavenly Jerusalem existing
in time" ("im paradoxen Raum eines 'irdischen Paradieses' als Himm-
lisches Jerusalem in der Zeit").[30] Here we find the *ander werlt* described
in Gottfried's *Tristan*.

However, we are still in front of the May gate. The observer is still
outside, not yet part of the community of lovers, and not yet recognized by the members of this community. An initiation is needed.[31] A
lovely lady, known to our narrator from his ordinary life, offers help.
She introduces him into the *Minne*-society, into the community of the
lovers. She also gives him a tour of the cloister. They happen to witness a tournament, described in detail, and the lovely lady suggests
meeting others living in the cloister of *Minne*.

However, our narrator is eager to meet Lady *Minne* herself in
person. His companion, the lovely lady, promises to arrange this:

> lieber gesell, wol dan mit mir,
> ich wil dich nach dines hertzen gir
> die minn lassen schowen
> by mannen und by frowen.
>
> (1525–28)

[Dear friend, come along with me. Following your heart's desire,
I will let you see Love, both with men and with women.]

Now, the narrator is so busy looking at everything to be seen in
this *ander werlt* space (more than six times, he takes the initiative to
describe, "ich sach" [I saw]) that his companion rebukes him:

> ich sach uz liechten ogen clar
> die minn spilen mit gewalt.
> si tät sich umb manig valt
> in lib und och in hertzen.
> ich sach viel iren smertzen
> togenlich verdrucken.

min gespil begund mich zucken
und furt mich aber fürbaß
und sprach: "war umb tüstü das?
dü salt nit also sechen!"

(1556–65)

────────

[With bright and shining eyes, I saw *Minne* playing and acting
forcefully. In many different ways she made herself visible in
bodies and in hearts. I saw many who hid their sorrow secretly.
My friend then took me aside and led me away and said:
"Why are you doing this? Stop looking around like this!"]

The narrator quite obviously needs to learn the proper and adequate
way of seeing. The fact that he is unable to see in the right way is formulated in the following scene.

ich sprach: "liebi fro, sagt an,
wenn nü kömt die Minne?"
si sprach: "hastü nit sinne,
ald wie ist dir beschechen?
wiltü nit minne sechen
hie uff diesem theras,
so frag nach minn nit fürbaß!"
ich sprach: "ich red, als ez mir kompt.
ich han gehört tüsent stunt
Minn wisser vor mir sagen
und von der Minne clagen,
si hab in lib und hertz enzünt
und och tusent stunt verwünt
mit ir minne strale
und in der senden quale
ir genaden wil warten,"
sprach ich zu der vil zarten.
"als wönd ich Minn hie sechen."
"daz mag nit beschechen,"
sprach min gespil da zu mir.

(1574–93)

[I said, "Tell me, dear Lady, when will Lady *Minne* arrive?"
She said: "Have you gone mad? Has something happened to you?
If you cannot see *Minne* here, on this platform, you need ask no
further." I said, "I say what I think. I have heard a thousand times
from those who know about love and who know about the sorrows
of love that *Minne* enflamed body and soul and wounded them a
thousand times with her arrow of love and that they, in the pains
of love, await her grace." This I said to the lovely lady. "That is
why I thought to see Lady *Minne* here." "That cannot happen,"
said my friend to me.]

Here the narrator justifies his expectation to meet Lady *Minne* in person. Yet according to his companion, this expectation is a form of seeing love that must be overcome, since *Minne* has become manifest in
the community of lovers.

A modest and conventional text such as *Das Kloster der Minne*
expresses a basic understanding of *Minne* in the late Middle Ages
that is shared across the entire corpus of *Minnereden*. The tradition of
Minnereden, then, can be read as a realization of Gottfried's *ander werlt
der Minne.*[32]

LET ME BRIEFLY SUMMARIZE. FIRST, *MINNEREDEN* SEEM TO TALK
about nothing else but the otherworld of *Minne*. *Das Kloster der Minne*
describes this world as a sort of para-reality in which the normal first
world is in constant contact with the second, other world. The two
worlds permeate and penetrate one another permanently. Second, love
presents itself, in *Das Kloster der Minne,* in the fulfillment of *Minne*
within its community, the *edelen herzen*. This seems to me a solution
to the *Tristan* problem. Community is taken right into the center of
Minne, which is no longer an affair between two persons but a matter
of the heart of the "*Minne* community." In regard to the *Minnereden,*
one might conclude that once the community of the *edelen herzen* starts
to become literarily active, it produces *Minnereden,* the self-reflective
texts of a *Minne* community.

Third, the otherworld of the *edelen herzen* is visible only to those
who see with the heart, to lovers. Lady *Minne* appears in person or by

means of allegory always and exclusively to lovers. To love, then, also means to undergo a transformation of normal visuality. Fourth, the first-person speakers of the *Minnereden* tell us about their involvement in or initiation into the otherworld of *Minne*. They always stress the completeness of devotion as a form of lifelong commitment.

Fifth and finally, the first-person narrators are not poets.[33] Their self-understanding starts with *Minne,* with their qualities as those who love and as those who want to participate in the world of *Minne.* The aim of their speaking about *Minne,* the aim of the *Minnereden,* is to inscribe themselves into the world of *Minne.* In general this implies an aesthetic descent but at the same time a practical gain. One can sum this up by saying that *Minnereden* attempt to come to terms with the problem of Tristan love by means of a textual practice. This practice is produced and established by a community of lovers, within which the fascinating possibility of seeing love turns into permanent reality.

Notes

1. "Minne und Gesellschaft," in *Mittelhochdeutsche Minnereden I,* ed. Kurt Matthaei (Dublin and Zurich: Weidmann, 1967), 65–73; here 66, lines 60–68.

2. Alois Wolf, *Das Faszinosum der mittelalterlichen Minne,* Wolfgang Stammler Gastprofessur für Germanische Philologie, Vorträge 5 (Freiburg: Universitätsverlag, 1996), 18–22; Walter Blank, *Die deutsche Minneallegorie: Gestaltung und Funktion einer spätmittelalterlichen Dichtungsform,* Germanistische Abhandlungen 34 (Stuttgart: Metzler, 1970); Christian Kiening, "Personifikation: Begegnungen mit dem Fremd-Vertrauten in mittelalterlicher Literatur," in *Personenbeziehungen in der mittelalterlichen Literatur,* ed. Helmut Brall, Barbara Haupt, and Urban Küsters, Studia humaniora 25 (Düsseldorf: Droste, 1994), 347–87; Rüdiger Schnell, "Wer sieht das Unsichtbare? *Homo exterior* und *homo interior* in monastischen und laikalen Erziehungsschriften," in *Anima und sêle: Darstellungen und Systematisierungen von Seele im Mittelalter,* ed. Katharina Philipowski and Anne Prior, Philologische Studien und Quellen 197 (Berlin: Erich Schmidt, 2006), 83–112. A catalog of most of the *Minnereden* can be found in Tilo Brandis, *Mittelhochdeutsche, mittelniederdeutsche und mittelniederländische Minnereden: Verzeichnis der Handschriften und Drucke,* Münchener Texte und Untersuchungen 25 (München: Beck,

1968) (hereafter cited as *Minnereden*). In the following, the *Minnereden* are identified by name and number given by Brandis. A new and revised edition of Brandis's catalog is forthcoming, *Handbuch Minnereden (mit Auswahledition)*, eds. Jacob Klingner and Ludger Lieb (Berlin: de Gruyter, 2012).

3. On the thesis in relation to the *edelen herzen* and the *Minne* cloister, see Ingeborg Glier, *Artes amandi: Untersuchung zu Geschichte, Überlieferung und Typologie der deutschen Minnereden*, Münchener Texte und Untersuchungen 34 (München: Beck, 1971), 180, who already points out "[d]aß alle wahrhaft Liebenden einer—in gewissem Sinne—esoterischen Gemeinschaft angehören, ist eine alte Vorstellung, welche den *edelen herzen* Gottfrieds von Straßburg ähnlich, dort aber mit wesentlich höherem Anspruch, zugrunde liegt wie dem Orden in der 'Sekte der Minner.'"

4. Klingner and Lieb, eds., *Handbuch Minnereden*, no. B422; Matthaei, ed., *Mittelhochdeutsche Minnereden I*, no. 14; hereafter cited by line numbers.

5. See David F. Tinsley, "When the Hero Tells the Tale: Narrative Studies in the Late-Medieval 'Minnerede'" (Ph.D. diss., Princeton University, 1985).

6. Matthaei, ed., *Mittelhochdeutsche Minnereden I*, no. 14, lines 66–74.

7. Unless otherwise noted, all translations into English are by Ludger Lieb and Ann Marie Rasmussen.

8. Walther von der Vogelweide, *Leich, Lieder, Sangsprüche*, 14., völlig neubearbeitete Auflage der Ausgabe Karl Lachmanns, ed. Christoph Cormeau (Berlin: de Gruyter, 1996), no. 17 II, line 1 (= L. 40,27).

9. All citations of Gottfried von Strassburg, *Tristan*, are from *Tristan*, ed. Karl Marold and Werner Schröder, trans. Peter Knecht, vol. 1 (Berlin: de Gruyter, 2004), by line numbers.

10. Essential for an understanding of medieval personification fiction, see Kiening, "Personifikation," esp. 360–62, 383–87.

11. Ludger Lieb and Peter Strohschneider, "Zur Konventionalität der Minnerede: Eine Skizze am Beispiel von des Elenden Knaben 'Minnegericht,'" in *Literatur und Wandmalerei II: Konventionalität und Konversation*, ed. Eckart Conrad Lutz, Johanna Thali, and René Wetzel (Tübingen: Niemeyer, 2005), 109–38.

12. Klingner and Lieb, eds., *Handbuch Minnereden*, no. B385. For the most recent research on the field, see Dorothea Klein, "Allegorische Burgen: Variationen eines Bildthemas," in *Die Burg im Minnesang und als Allegorie im deutschen Mittelalter*, ed. Ricarda Bauschke, Kultur, Wissenschaft, Literatur, Beiträge zur Mittelalterforschung 10 (Frankfurt am Main: Peter Lang, 2006), 113–37; Klein, "Zur Metaphorik der Gewalt in der Minneburg," in

Würzburg, der große Löwenhof und die deutsche Literatur des Spätmittelalters, ed. Horst Brunner (Wiesbaden: Reichert, 2004), 103–19.

13. Citations are from *Die Minneburg: Nach der Heidelberger Pergamenthandschrift (CPG 455) unter Heranziehung der Kölner Handschrift und der Donaueschinger und Prager Fragmente,* ed. Hans Pyritz (Berlin: Akademie Verlag, 1950), given by line numbers.

14. See Urban Küsters, "Die Liebe und der zweite Blick: Wahrnehmungshaltungen in höfischen Liebesbegegnungen," in Brall, Haupt, and Küsters, *Personenbeziehungen in der mittelalterlichen Literatur,* 271–320; Rüdiger Schnell, *Causa amoris: Liebeskonzeption und Liebesdarstellung in der mittelalterlichen Literatur,* Bibliotheca Germanica 27 (Bern: Francke, 1985). On the symptom of falling silent, see also Katharina Wallmann, *Minnebedingtes Schweigen in Minnesang, Lied und Minnerede des 12. bis 16. Jahrhunderts,* Mikrokosmos 13 (Frankfurt am Main: Peter Lang, 1985).

15. Klingner and Lieb, eds., *Handbuch Minnereden,* no. B377. The following citations are from Carl Halthaus, ed., *Liederbuch der Clara Hätzlerin,* Bibliothek der gesammten deutschen National-Literatur 8, Quedlinburg (1840; reprint, with an afterword by Hanns Fischer, Berlin: de Gruyter, 1966), no. II, 19, lines 79–82.

16. Translations throughout of Gottfried's *Tristan* are from Hatto's translation: *Tristan,* trans. Arthur T. Hatto (Harmondsworth: Penguin, 1960; reprint, London: Penguin, 2004).

17. Tomas Tomasek, *Die Utopie im "Tristan" Gotfrids von Straßburg,* Hermaea, N. F. 49 (Tübingen: Niemeyer, 1985).

18. Klaus Speckenbach, *Studien zum Begriff "edelez herze" im Tristan Gottfrieds von Straßburg,* Medium Aevum 6 (München: Eidos, 1965), 36, 67–68, passim.

19. See Franziska Wessel, *Probleme der Metaphorik und die Minnemetaphorik in Gottfrieds von Straßburg "Tristan und Isolde,"* Münstersche Mittelalter-Schriften 54 (München: Fink, 1984), 584–89; Speckenbach, *Studien zum Begriff,* 52.

20. Rüdiger Schnell, *Suche nach Wahrheit: Gottfrieds "Tristan und Isold" als erkenntniskritischer Roman,* Hermaea, N. F. 67 (Tübingen: Niemeyer, 1992), 164–65, 226–28.

21. Franz Josef Worstbrock, "Der Zufall und das Ziel: Über die Handlungsstruktur in Gottfrieds 'Tristan,'" in *Fortuna,* ed. Walter Haug and Burghart Wachinger, Fortuna vitrea 15 (Tübingen: Niemeyer, 1995), 44.

22. Schnell, *Suche nach Wahrheit,* 48–49, stresses the utopian character of the Tristan-*Minne.* He sees it as not yet entwined with the general values

of society. However, he sees a glimpse of utopia in Tristan, that such an entanglement between the world of lovers and courtly world might eventually take shape. See also Tomasek, *Utopie.*

23. Worstbrock, "Der Zufall und das Ziel," 46–47, 51.

24. Of course, Curvenal and Brangaene form with Tristan and Isolde a sort of community; however, both "helper-figures" are not members of the community of lovers, because they themselves are not lovers. See Speckenbach, *Studien zum Begriff,* 37, 60–61. The narrator explicitly says that Curvenal was "von edeles herzen art" (2261).

25. Jan-Dirk Müller, "Gottfried von Straßburg: *Tristan,* Transgression und Ökonomie," in *Transgressionen: Literatur als Ethnographie,* ed. Gerhard Neumann and Rainer Warning, Litterae 98 (Freiburg: Rombach, 2003), 219, diagnoses the fact "daß das in der Tristan-Sage thematisierte Problem der radikalen, gesellschaftliche Ordnungen beiseite schiebenden Geschlechterliebe innerhalb der hochmittelalterlichen Kultur weder diskursiv noch narrativ bewältigt werden kann." The same can be said for the *Minnereden*; however, they fulfill Gottfried's vision of the "Minnekommunikationsgemeinschaft"; see Ludger Lieb and Peter Strohschneider, "Die Grenzen der Minnekommunikation: Interpretationsskizzen. Über Zugangsregulierungen und Verschwiegenheitsgebote im Diskurs spätmittelalterlicher Minnereden," in *Das Öffentliche und Private in der Vormoderne,* ed. Gert Melville and Peter von Moos (Köln: Böhlau, 1998), 275–305. For an immediate influence of the term *edele herzen* on the narrative literature after Gottfried, see Speckenbach, *Studien zum Begriff,* 121–29; a community of lovers is, however, rarely intended (127).

26. See Blank, *Deutsche Minneallegorie,* 162–72; Glier, *Artes amandi,* 178–84; Maria Schierling, ed., *Das Kloster der Minne: Edition und Untersuchung, Anhang; Vier weitere Minnereden der Donaueschinger Liedersaal-Handschrift,* Göppinger Arbeiten zur Germanistik 208 (Göppingen: Kümmerle, 1980); Wolfgang Achnitz, *"De monte feneris agitur hic*: Liebe als symbolischer Code und als Affekt im Kloster der Minne," in Bauschke, *Die Burg im Minnesang und als Allegorie im deutschen Mittelalter,* 161–86. For discussion I thank Rebekka Rehbach in Munich, whose thesis, "Das Phantasma höfischer Liebe und seine Institutionalisierung im 'Kloster der Minne,'" I directed.

27. Schierling, *Kloster der Minne,* 73–115, discusses the links with Ettal in detail and comes to the conclusion that mutual influences are rather implausible.

28. Achnitz, *"De monte feneris agitur hic,"* 168.

29. The following citations are from Schierling, *Kloster der Minne.*

30. See Schierling, *Kloster der Minne,* 136–38, 146–47.

31. Achnitz, *"De monte feneris agitur hic."*

32. In this case one could argue that Gottfried's narrative strategy, namely, to make the impossible possible, is followed up in the building of communities, which within the epistemic order of this world remains impossible (Mark Chinca, "Mögliche Welten: Alternatives Erzählen und Fiktionalität im Tristanroman Gottfrieds von Straßburg," *Poetica* 35 [2003]: 332).

33. Ludger Lieb, "Eine Poetik der Wiederholung: Regeln und Funktionen der Minnerede," in *Text und Kultur: Mittelalterliche Literatur, 1150–1450,* ed. Ursula Peters, Germanistische Symposien: Berichtsbände 23 (Stuttgart: Metzler, 2001), 524–28.

PART II

Media, Representation, and Performance

CHAPTER FIVE

From Myth to Emblem to Panorama

MICHAEL CURSCHMANN

The *matière de Bretagne* is one of the most potent and fascinating literary subjects that still connect us directly with the medieval period—through a long chain of textual, pictorial, and musical manifestations.[1] As such it invites consideration of what I call its historical dynamics. What are some of the forces or agents that create and maintain consciousness of, and interest in, the subject beyond its initial appeal? Where in the well-documented and broadly researched advancement of the story through the ages can we perhaps identify turning points or divergences of particular significance and thereby learn something about how literature "works"? The methodological framework for such considerations must be both comparative and intermedial, and for that reason alone the topic is potentially inexhaustible. This chapter sketches four stages in this general progression in the hope that the overview it provides may be useful to scholars from two very different cultures, where this particular literary topic has been nourished along very different paths. First, it addresses the presentation, what we might also call the literarization, in early verse romance of what for better or worse I have called the "myth";[2] second, the ascendance of an emblematic representation of the emerging story in one single image; third, the treatment of the narrative in Thomas Malory's panoramic vision of the Arthurian world; and finally, one late and grand Victorian response to this vision: *Tristram of Lyonesse,* by Algernon Charles Swinburne, poet, critic, and medievalist.

I

Those who first undertook to recast the *matière de Bretagne* in written verse were keenly aware of competing versions, a dilemma summarized by Thomas of Britain when he allowed that "those who narrate and tell the tale of Tristan tell it in a variety of ways" *(diversement).*[3] Everyone seems to have felt the need to stake his or her own explicit claim against this background of intrinsic diversity. These claims may crystallize in expressions of authorial self-definition and rivalry, as with Gottfried, but taken together they point to an imagined entity beyond the individual rendering, a mythic constellation of people and events that resists easy adaptation and, to this day, easy categorization.[4]

The essential intractability and instability of this myth is of course reflected further in actual composition. The fatal attraction that so appealed to the emerging lay culture is the very thing that defies integration into the evolving concepts of what we would today call civilized society, as exemplified in the Arthurian paradigm.[5] Or conversely, a relationship caused by poisonous magic simply cannot be socialized without loss of the original impetus. Eilhart's solution, for example, namely, Tristrant's inability to refuse what he is asked to do in the name of Isalde, is but a feeble ("courtly") substitute for the waning power of the potion. And structurally, the story of the roaming hero, whether his movements are self-directed or forced into the systolic pattern generated by this attraction to a sedentary heroine, is essentially episodic and open-ended. Hence the fragmentation into short compositions that depict just one of these perennial returns into the arms of the queen.[6] Those poets who undertook epic versions not infrequently struggled in vain to make smooth connections. Even Gottfried's deliberately rationalized rendering is not susceptible to harmonizing interpretations, quite apart from being unfinished.[7] Elsewhere death provides a conclusion, but it does not provide closure in the societal or structural sense, as Thomas, for one, makes quite clear.[8] And all the while even some of the most salient motifs are subject to negotiation: What is the role of Tristan's sword and Mark's glove in the famous discovery scene?[9] What exactly does the love potion do? How long does its poison last? Where, if at all, does King Arthur enter the picture? There are almost as many answers as there are texts.

Finally, both the French and the German manuscript traditions reflect these conditions, albeit in rather different ways. The early Norman and Anglo-Norman verse compositions disappear from the scene after just a few decades, except for isolated Norse and English offshoots of Thomas of Britain's version.[10] They are replaced in the Romance-speaking world by one huge prose compilation, *Tristan en prose,* and its Italian and Spanish descendants.[11] In Germany, where there is no prose outside the verse tradition and where the verse poems continue to be copied well into the fifteenth century, we have instead that crazy quilt of different continuations characterizing the transmission of Gottfried's unfinished work.

II

As the first wave of verse romances ebbs away, consolidation of the myth is achieved in France in two completely different ways. Textually this occurs in the medium of prose, as was mentioned above, through the *Tristan en prose* in conjunction with other such compilations. This comes at a price, however: Arthurianization or "normalization," as it has also been called—the merger with the Arthurian paradigm as it developed in the Vulgate cycle.[12] Quite another sort of consolidation occurs, not much later, in the visual arts. As artistic workshops begin to reflect on the story, one image emerges that serves to epitomize the conflict between the demands of love and society: the secret tryst at night by the brook in the orchard under the eyes of King Mark in the tree above (figs. 5.1, 5.2).[13] This single scene achieves notoriety well beyond text and parchment—as sculpture in stone and wood, in religious as well as profane spaces, or as delicate carving in all kinds of minor media. Especially striking is the number and variety of objects used in toiletry in fourteenth-century France, from mirror cases to jewelry boxes (see figs. 5.1, 5.2) and from hair parters to combs (figs. 5.3, 5.4).

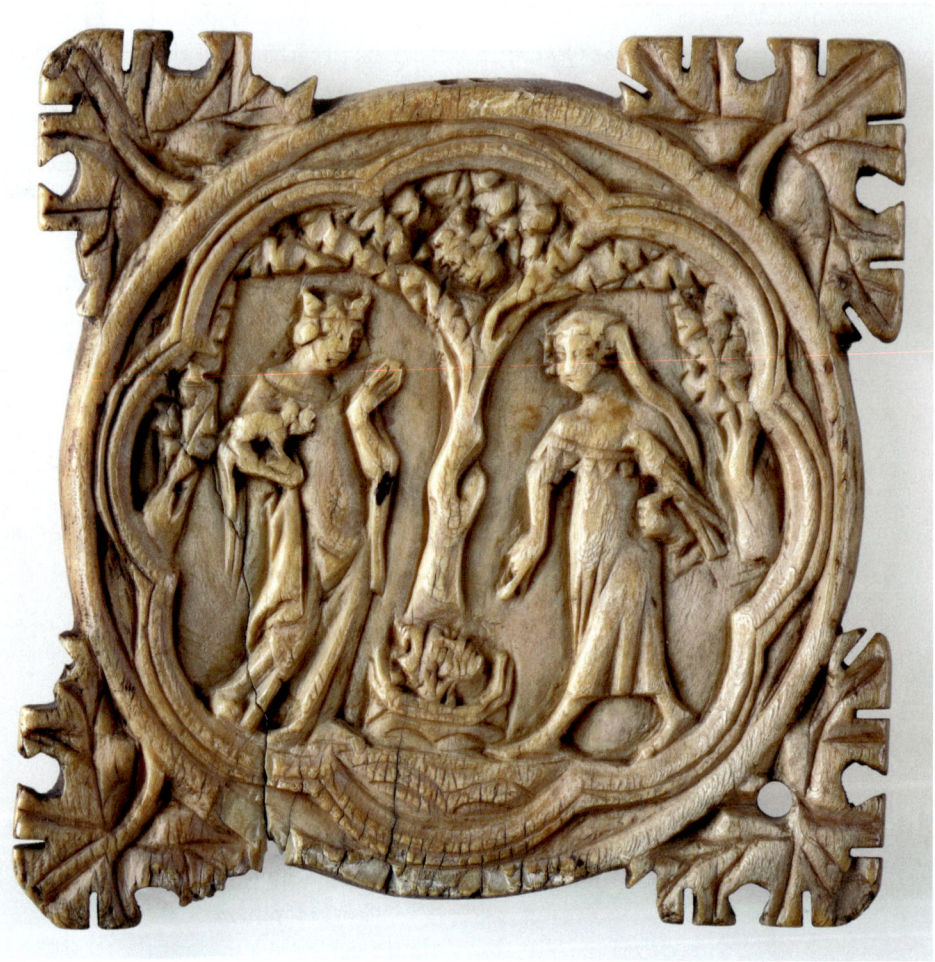

Figure 5.1. Tristan and Iseult's secret tryst. Ivory mirror case, northern France, mid-fourteenth century. Paris, Musée de Cluny. Courtesy of Musée national du Moyen Age–Thermes de Cluny. Photo Réunion des Musées Nationaux/Art Resource, NY.

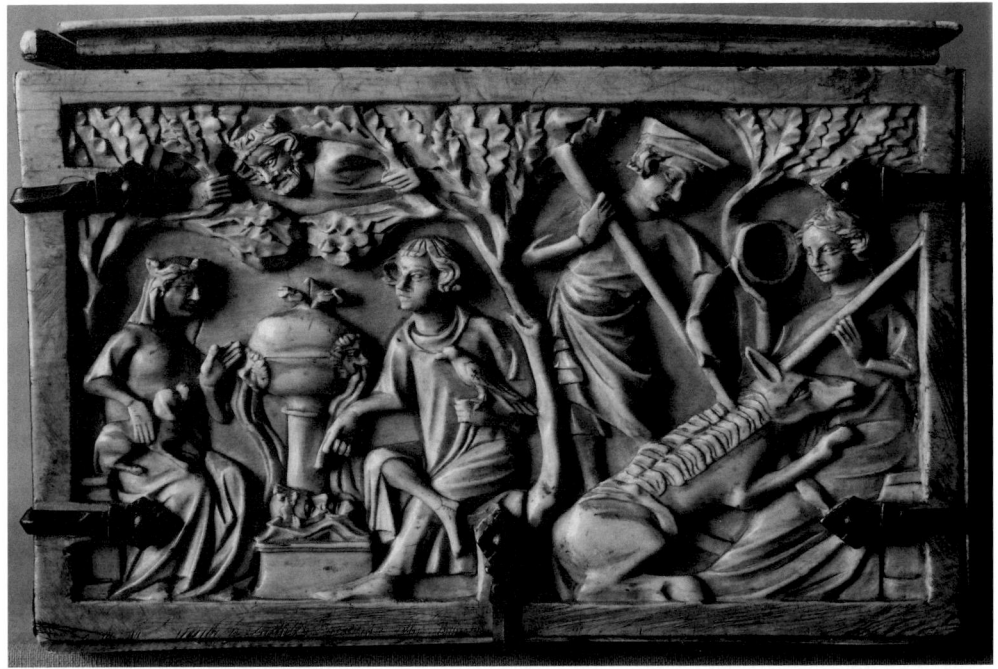

Figure 5.2. Tristan and Iseult's secret tryst. Ivory casket, Paris, 1300–1350. New York, Metropolitan Museum of Art. By permission. Image © Metropolitan Museum of Art.

What causes the selection of this motif as the dominant visual emblem of the whole? As literary construct, this scene, with its dramatic physical triangulation in a clearly defined space, almost cries out for a picture. And as it happened, there existed in religious art a prominent iconographic formula that could easily be adapted for this new secular use: the Fall of Adam and Eve with the serpent in the tree between them (fig. 5.5). The example from Lorenzo Maitani's Genesis cycle in Orvieto speaks for itself; it even includes the element of water beneath the tree, the rivers of Paradise in this instance. The close iconographic analogy holds even when the couple sits, as the example from the Trivulzio Bible shows (fig. 5.6).

The result of this crossover from religious to secular iconography is an image of quite remarkable power and a perfect example of the

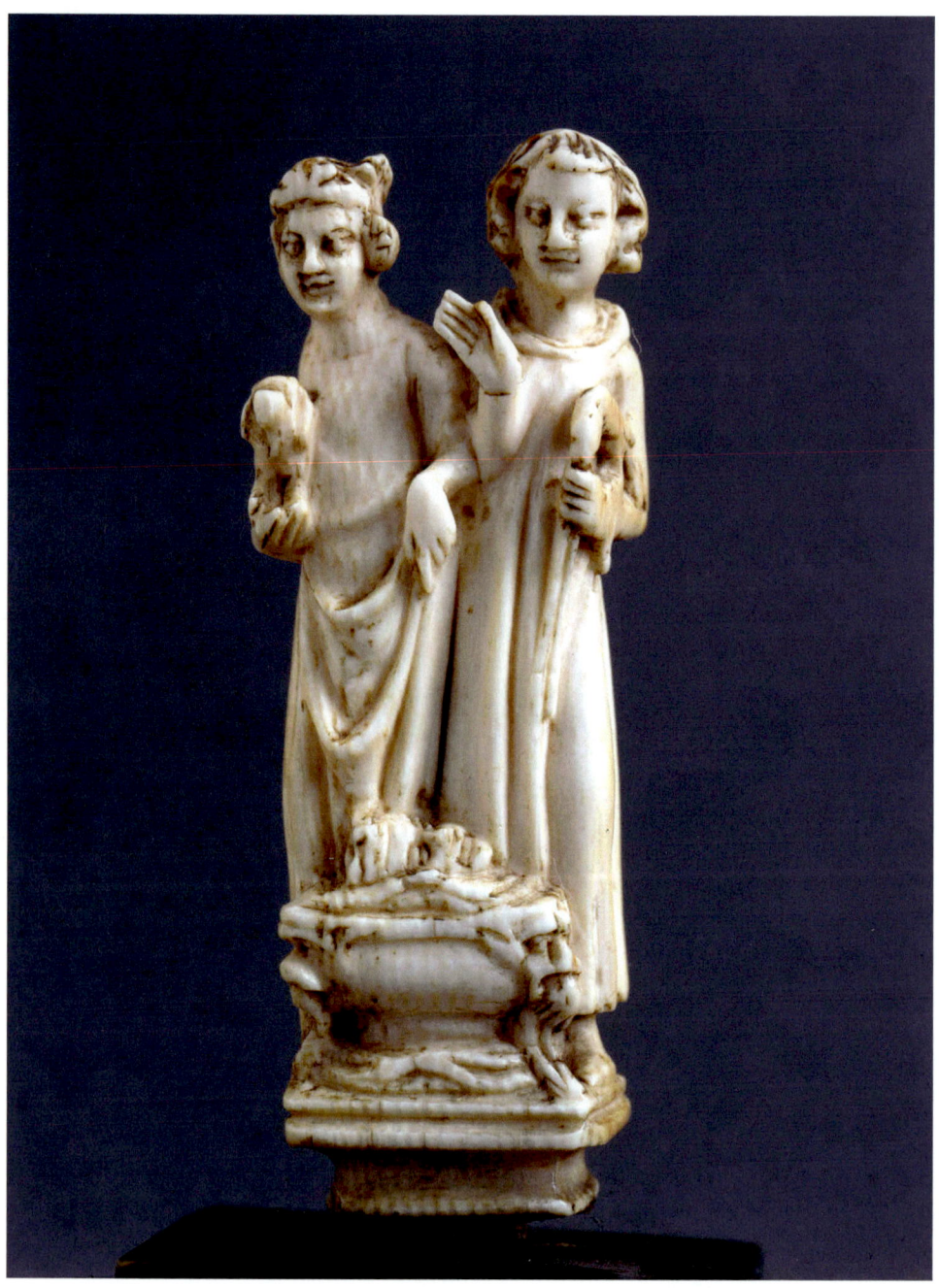

Figure 5.3. Tristan and Iseult's secret tryst. Grip of an ivory hair-parter *(gravoir),* Paris, 1300–1350. Turin, Museo Civico. Courtesy of Museo Civico d'Arte Antica, Turin.

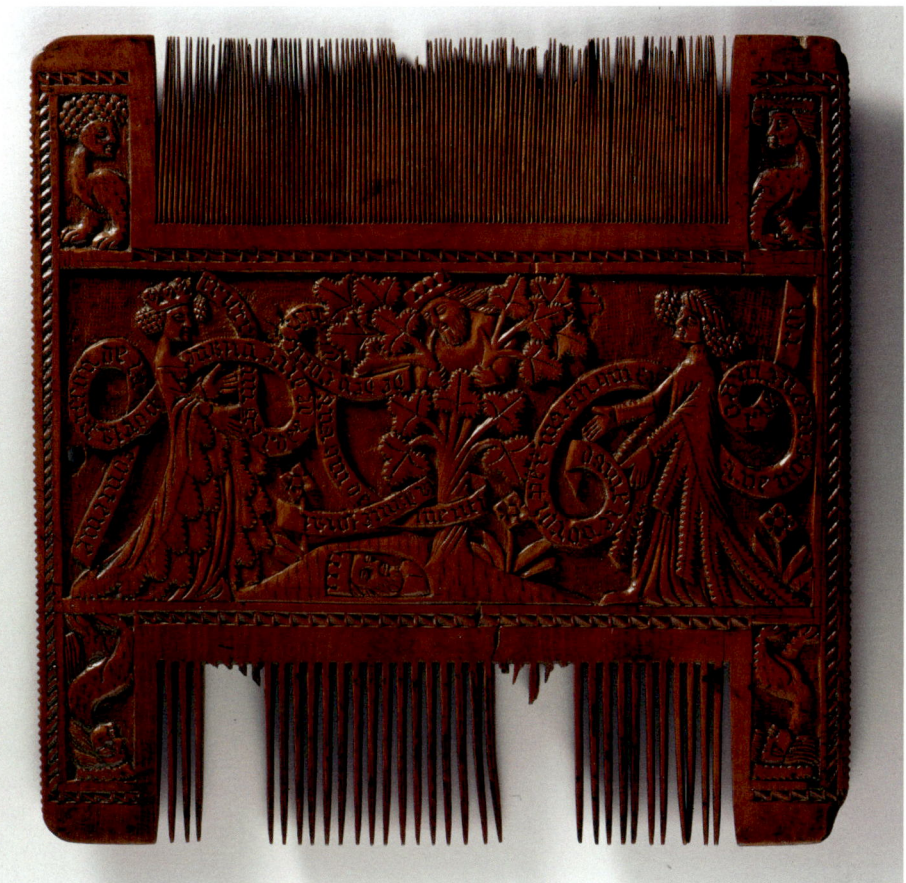

Figure 5.4. Tristan and Iseult's secret tryst. Wooden comb, Rhinelands (?), 1400–1425. Bamberg, Sammlung des Historischen Vereins. Courtesy of Historisches Museum Bamberg.

independence gained ultimately by such pictorial encapsulation of literary themes. It focuses meaning derived from a large literary context and transports and maintains this message even after its initial textual base has largely fallen away. For by now the amplification of the material in the *Tristan en prose* and its descendants had diminished the importance of this very scene in significant ways: details that are constitutive for the image had been omitted, and the whole encounter had

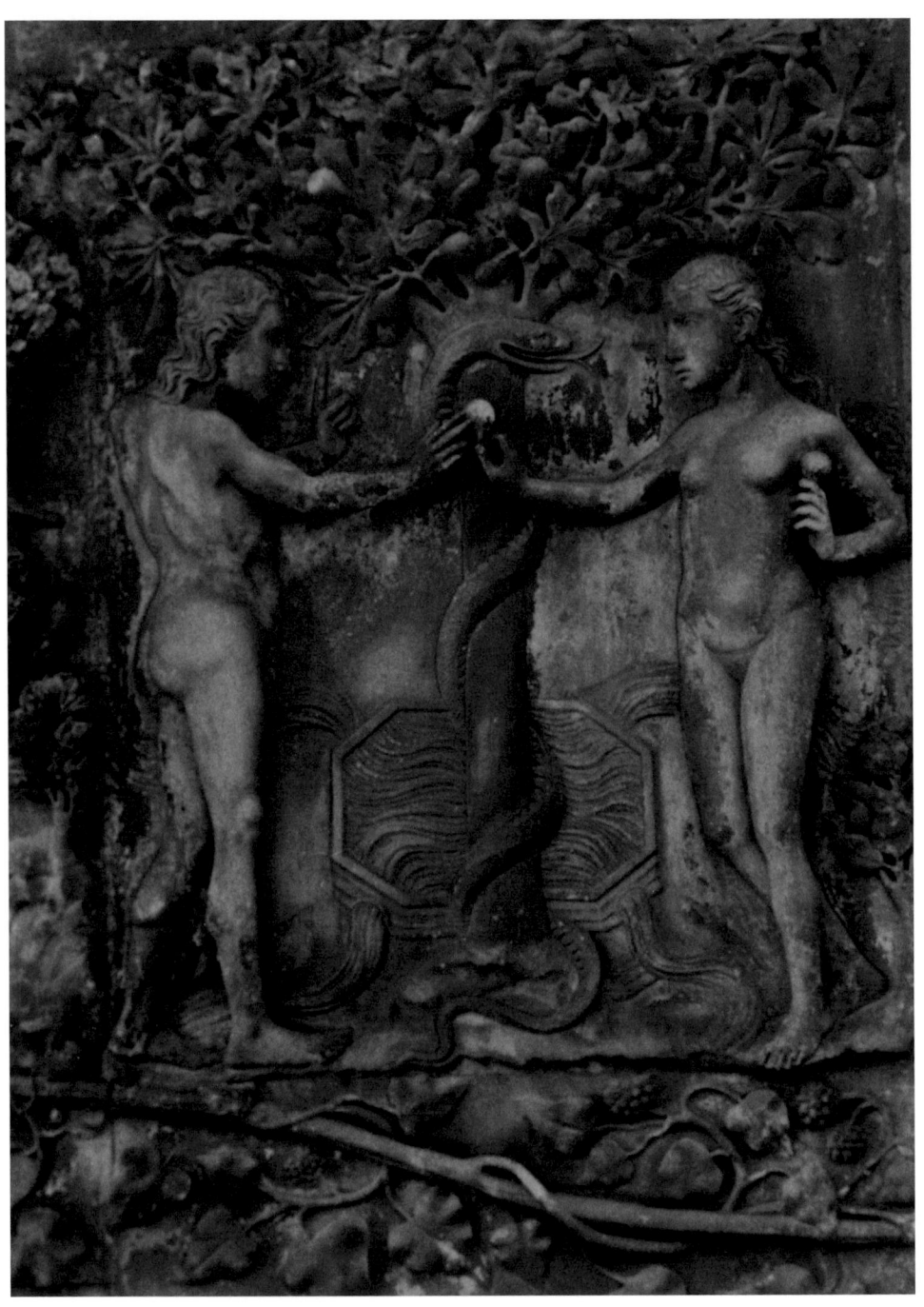

Figure 5.5. Adam and Eve at the Fall. Detail from Lorenzo Maitani, Genesis cycle in marble relief, Orvieto Cathedral, west façade, beginning of the fourteenth century. Photo by the author.

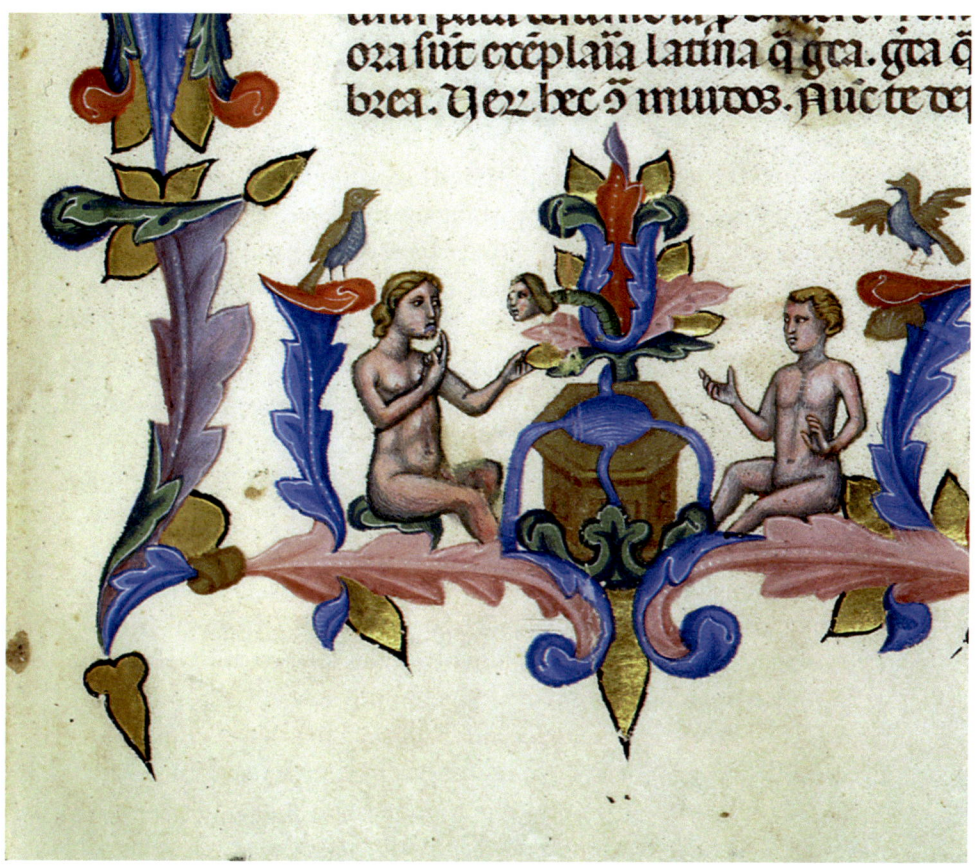

Figure 5.6. Adam and Eve at the Fall. Detail from the Genesis cycle of the "Trivulzio Bible," Milan, Biblioteca Trivulziana, Cod. 2139, fol. 4r. Workshop of Pacino di Buanaguida, beginning of the fourteenth century. Courtesy of Biblioteca Trivulziana. Photo Saporetti Immagini d'Arte.

moved to a marginal position in a totally different context.[14] It is this image alone that carries forward the tradition of the verse romances, while people read different texts.

Such longevity also means that the image has broadened its scope along the way. This tableau of a sitting couple in particular (see fig. 5.2), while still reminiscent of Tristan and Iseult, no longer connotes a furtive meeting quickly summoned and quickly abandoned. These are courtly personages consorting in broad daylight and at relative leisure in a formal environment, thus claiming attention beyond their textual heritage. In the course of the fourteenth century, this pictorial tradition even acquires its own verbal accompaniment, as can be seen in the comb from the Rhinelands (see fig. 5.4). In crude French and equally bad verse, Iseult warns Tristan by pointing to a presumably fictitious fish in the water, he responds by wishing the king were here with them, and Mark curses whoever "has falsely accused the loyal lady."[15] That text seems to have been well established by the middle of the fourteenth century, for it is alluded to in the fresco representation of the tryst in the castle at Saint-Floret in the Auvergne.[16]

The generic relationship to the Fall of Man iconography added a measure of titillating ambiguity to the whole scene. Context does not necessarily resolve this ambiguity, but it tilts perception in one direction or another. Thus surely those toiletry articles display the Tristan emblem and similarly suggestive constellations (in this instance, the hunt of the unicorn, as seen in fig. 5.2) as the archetype of triumphant love that guilefully and gleefully defies convention.[17] In a real world where social and religious regulation of gender relationships left little room for what we have come to call romantic love, these pictures must have opened for their owners a window of imaginary opportunity— a vision of choice.[18] Not surprisingly, then, the Dutchman Dirc Potter described this scene with approval in his otherwise quite critical analysis of the ways of love, *Der minne loep* (1410), as an example of well-placed deception.[19] The subversive character of the image is just as obvious when it reappears as religious counterfact about fifty years earlier in France (fig. 5.7). The picture is the same, but it serves as the basis for a moralistic exemplum: just as these two, a queen and a knight, who significantly remain anonymous, change their tune when they notice the presence of the king, so should we avoid sinful thoughts, for our Lord always knows what is in our minds.

III

This form of emblematic representation did not reach beyond the fifteenth century, while the tradition of the prose *Tristan* continued into

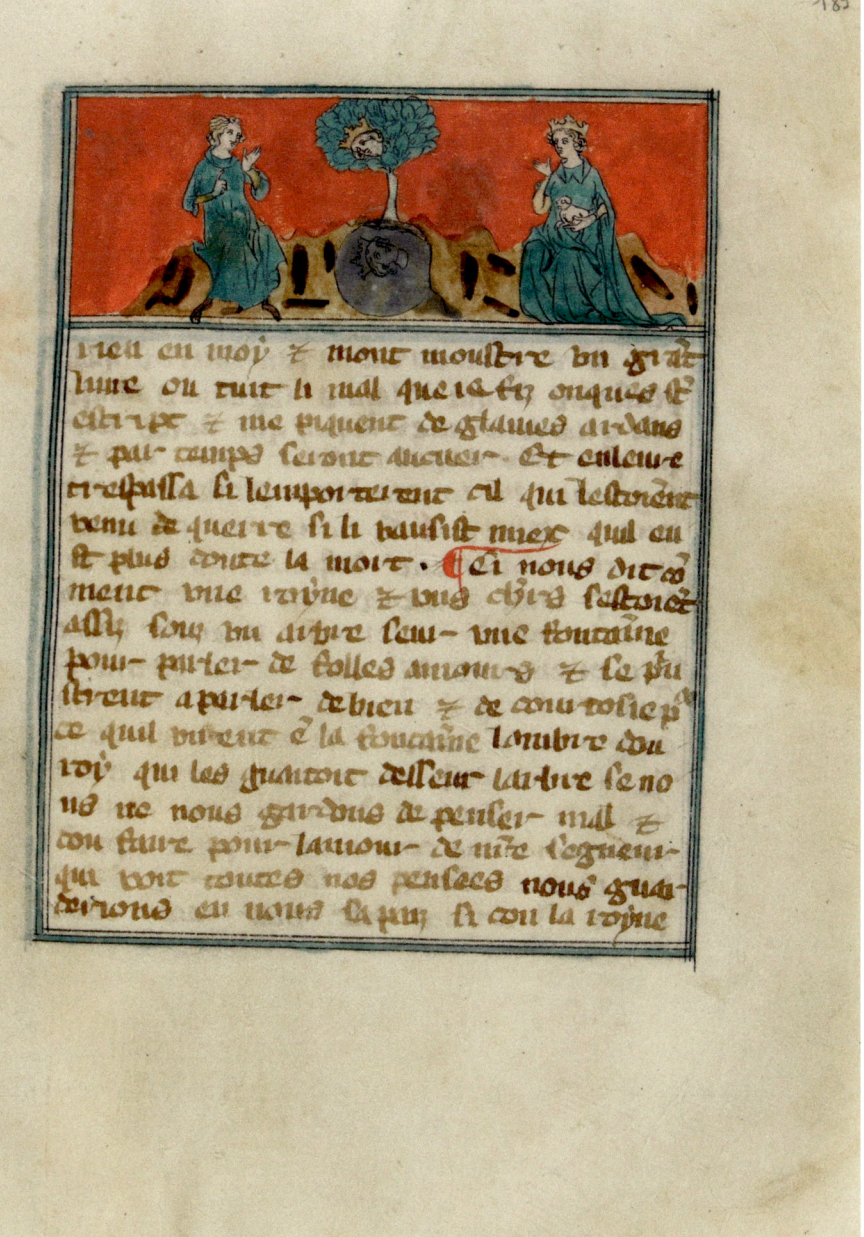

Figure 5.7. A queen and knight overheard by the king. Example in the collection *Ci nous dit* (ca. 1330), Chantilly, Musée Condé, MS 1078 (26), fol. 189r. Courtesy of Musée Condé. Photo Réunion des Musées Nationaux/Art Resource, NY.

print, essentially unchanged.[20] Elsewhere there occurred, however, another one of those dramatic shifts of venue and medium that create entirely new and different perceptions of older literary material. The *matière de Bretagne* found a new vehicle of transmission in England in the vast compilation called *The Whole Book of King Arthur and of the Noble Knights of the Roundtable* by one Thomas Malory, as arranged and published, in 1485, by the printer William Caxton and misnamed *Le morte d'Arthur.*[21]

Malory knew the Tristan story mainly from the French prose version and stretched it further as he wove it as one of several major strands into his panoramic tapestry of the Arthurian world. The first seven books offer only occasional glimpses of Tristram, as he is now called—foreshadowings of his future adventures and his prowess. In books 8 through 10, Malory then reversed the priorities and put Tristram center stage, but developments involving him and—to a much lesser degree—La Beale Isoud are interrupted and redirected constantly by strands of the evolving "Arthuriad" (no fewer than three major tournaments take place!), and Tristram's progress becomes increasingly intertwined with that of Launcelot, his idol and mentor. Accordingly, books 11 and 12 deal primarily with Launcelot's madness. Only at the very end of book 12 do Tristram and Isoud make a final appearance together, living in blissful harmony, as they have done for some time, in Launcelot's castle, Joyous Gard.

Obviously this is no longer the story that had unfolded in the twelfth century.[22] True enough, quite a few of the traditional highpoints remain: Tristram's birth, his fight against Marhaus (Morolt), his two trips to Ireland, the love potion, his marriage to the other Isoud. But constellations have been rearranged, motifs displaced or neutralized, and motivations realigned. All in all, integration into the Arthurian narrative spells disintegration of the Tristan myth: As Tristram, the old trickster Tristan turns into a knight errant, while on the other hand he and Isoud actually establish their own household, with guests and visits and other comings and goings.[23] Tristram's goal is to become an Arthurian knight, and when he finally joins the society of the Roundtable he is assigned the very seat once occupied by Marhaus, whom he slew in his role as defender of Cornwall.[24] That is a major structural shift from one paradigm to another! Isoud's domestication as exemplary lady in the Arthurian mold reaches a fine pitch in that final scene at Joyous Gard. Like Chrestien's and Hartmann's Enit, Isoud worries that her champion has become too much of a homebody, no longer intent on "worship" (renown, honor). But unlike Enit, she confronts him head-on:

> What shalle be said amonge all knyghtes? See how Sire Tristram hunteth and hawketh and coureth within a castel with his lady and forsaketh your worshyp. Allas, shalle some say, hit is pyte that euer he was made knyght or that euer he shold haue the loue of a lady. Also what shal quenes and ladyes saye of me? (*Caxton's Malory,* 1:423)

Imagine Gottfried's Isolde talking like that! These characters have settled down into new roles. Adultery is hardly an issue anymore, and heroic love has been converted into social virtue.[25] Even the Saracene Sir Palomydes, Isoud's first suitor and Tristram's perennial rival, is finally baptized (1:426). Clearly Malory felt that he had brought this story to a satisfactory conclusion and could turn his attention elsewhere.[26] Accordingly we are not informed of the couple's ultimate fate until much later and in brief parenthetical announcements. And what they tell us is quite different from the traditional ending. When Launcelot takes possession again of Joyous Gard, his tenants having returned to Cornwall after almost three years, he reminds his friends that "that fals traitour Kyng Marke" murdered Tristram with a spear from behind (1:562). And "La Beale Isoud," we learn elsewhere (and equally parenthetically), "dyed swounyng vpon the cross [i.e., corpse] of Syr Tristram" (1:552).

IV

It was no easy feat of the imagination to extricate from all this something resembling the fatal attraction of yore. But that is exactly what Algernon Swinburne did in *Tristram of Lyonesse,* a poem of five thousand

luxuriant lines in heroic couplets, arranged in nine cantos and a prelude and published in 1882, although begun many years earlier.[27] The
enlightened eighteenth century had neglected Caxton's Malory, but
Robert Southey's edition of 1817 brought it back, and by midcentury,
as one critic remarked, "Malory's *King Arthur* has become once again
a favorite pocket volume."[28] Apparently even schoolboys were deeply
immersed in Malory's Arthurian world. In the words of another contemporary observer, "The style of these romances recommends itself
at once to the schoolboy mind, healthfully active and energetic; with
very little love-making, few of the finer flights of fancy, and no moral
reflections, there are plenty of terrific encounters and hard blows."[29]
This is how Swinburne's contemporaries and their literary and artistic predecessors in the Pre-Raphaelite movement came by their basic
knowledge of medieval romance, and they judged each other against
this background. Hence Swinburne's objection to what Tennyson, the
poet laureate, had done with Arthur and Guinevere in *Idylls of the
King*: "Treated as he has treated it, the story is rather a case for the
divorce-court than for poetry."[30]

Swinburne himself had more to draw on. He had been familiar
since childhood with the Middle English stanzaic poem *Sir Tristrem,*
which presents, in some 3,500 verses, a cruelly abridged and coarsened
offshoot of Thomas of Britain's version and which had been published
by Walter Scott in 1804.[31] Fluent in French, Swinburne was in general
an avid student of medieval sources in early editions and translations.
Sir Walter's *Sir Tristrem,* to which the editor himself had provided
the conclusion, which is missing in the only surviving manuscript, was
accompanied by extensive notes and commentary, as was Francisque
Michel's first edition of much of the Old French verse poetry dealing
with Tristan and Iseult.[32] The poet also had at his disposal the great
library of his uncle, the earl of Ashburnham, which housed, among
many others, quite a few codices stolen from French libraries.[33] All this
explains why the often-quoted retrospective comments Swinburne
published in 1904 begin in the best Tristan tradition: "My aim was
simply to present that story, not diluted and debased as it had been in
our own time by other hands." By the same token, the conclusion nevertheless stakes out new ground: "not in the epic or romantic form of sus-

tained or continuous narrative, but mainly through a succession of dramatic scenes or pictures with descriptive settings or backgrounds, the scenes being of the simplest construction, duologue or monologue" (*Poems,* 1:xvii–xviii).

In other words, Mr. Swinburne wanted to have his cake and eat it, too. And that is why his *Tristan* opens, like Wagner's, with the voyage of the couple from Ireland to Cornwall. Using *Sir Tristrem* as his guide, Swinburne retained enough of the plot to establish the fateful union and to prepare for the inevitable denouement in Brittany, but mostly he inverted Malory's procedure and relegated the story to the far background: the Tristania in flashbacks and the Arthuriana as topics of conversation among the protagonists. The first lines of the *Prelude* announce all-encompassing love as the theme that will occupy the foreground of this canvas: "Love, that is first and last of all things made, / The light that has the living world for shade" (*Poems,* 4:5).[34]

What unites Tristram and Iseult is deeply sensual love that may be contested in societal terms but is in complete harmony with nature, especially the ever-present sea, Swinburne's other great theme from the Tristan past. Their love is fateful in the original sense: "No choice of will, but chance and sorcerous art" (*Poems,* 4:150). But this poet now achieves closure: fate and the vengeful fury of the "other" Iseult eventually lead to oblivion in the ebb and flow of tide and time.[35] There is no apotheosis, and tomb and chapel, the memorial structures erected for the couple by King Mark, sink into the sea:

Nor where they sleep shall moon or sunlight shine
Nor man look down for ever: none shall say,
Here once, or here, Tristram and Iseult lay:
But peace they have that none may gain who live,
And rest about them that no love can give,
And over them, while death and life shall be,
The light and sound and darkness of the sea.
(*Poems,* 4:151)

Someone wrote not long ago that there are "thirteen ways of looking at *Tristram of Lyonesse.*"[36] This then is the fourteenth: with these final lines the poet lays the couple to rest where he has found them and saved them, if only for the moment, through his art. As he puts it in the *Prelude*:

> Some yet are good, if aught be good, to save
> Some while from washing wreck and wrecking wave.
> Was such not theirs, the twain I take, and give
> Out of my life to make their dead life live
> Some days of mine, and blow my living breath
> Between dead lips forgotten even of death.
>
> (*Poems,* 4:12)[37]

Life-giving lips on dead lips: the poet's corporeal identification with his charges is about language. At the same time, those conceits inaugurate the imagery that will accompany them throughout the poem, beginning with "The touch of four lips on the beaker's edge" (4:36) from which "their four lips became one burning mouth" (4:38) and ending with the antiphonal response in the couple's final embrace when "their four lips became one silent mouth" (4:148).

Only the poet can resurrect them. Ultimately Swinburn's *Tristan,* surely the most convincing and rewarding modern version, is about poetry and the poet's role as the guardian of myth, and in that sense it brings us back to the twelfth century where we began.[38]

Notes

1. See Joan Tasker Grimbert, ed., *Tristan and Isolde: A Casebook* (New York: Garland, 1995). This collection of essays provides a useful introduction in some respects but suffers from the customary piecemeal treatment of the subject. Michael Dallapiazza, ed., *Tristano e Isotta: La fortuna di un mito europeo* (Trieste: Parnaso, 2003), is a serviceable handbook that concentrates on the continued reworkings of the subject up to the twentieth century and on the state of research in these areas.

2. *Mythus* is, of course, Richard Wagner's term, which might be considered reason enough to avoid it. But apart from that the term has been used variously and mostly quite loosely in Anglo-Saxon, Italian, French, and, less

conspicuously, German scholarship to describe the sum total of what the Middle Ages created on the subject. See Alois Wolf, *Gottfried von Straßburg und die Mythe von Tristan und Isolde* (Darmstadt: Wissenschaftliche Buchgesellschaft, 1989), 1: with this story "hat das Mittelalter es vermocht, seine vielfältigen Probleme, die es mit dem Eros hatte, zu einer Mythe zu verdichten" (the Middle Ages was able to consolidate into a myth the many problems it had with the erotic). I am inclined to reserve the term for what existed before all codification; perhaps *legend* would have been better. A somewhat different approach is exemplified, as her title suggests, by the work of Jacqueline T. Schaefer, "Mythocriticism, Computer-Based Mythanalysis, and the Case of 'Tristan,'" in *Littérature générale/Littérature comparée,* ed. Paul Chavy and György M. Vajda (Bern: Peter Lang, 1992), 135–42.

3. *Tristan et Iseut: Les poèmes français, La saga norroise,* ed. and trans. Daniel Lacroix and Philippe Walter (Paris: Librairie Générale Française, 1989), 434: Fragment Douce, 843–45. The notion that others have not done justice to the story is by no means confined to the Tristan literature, but it is more frequent as well as more specific there. On the general framework for these references, see Michael Curschmann, "Der Erzähler auf dem Weg zur Literatur," *Wolfram-Studien* 18 (2004): 11–32.

4. The idea, advanced most prominently by Joseph Bédier, that the early written versions are rooted in one lost *Ur-Tristan* is pretty much a thing of the past, but no new concept has as yet been articulated. See Fabrizio Cigni, "Tristano e Isotta nelle letterature francese e italiane," in Dallapiazza, *Tristano e Isotta,* 31–32; and Arianna Punzi, *Tristano: Storia di un mito* (Roma: Carocci, 2005), 9–20.

5. Some of the literature on the tensions between these two paradigms is discussed by William C. McDonald, *Arthur and Tristan: On the Intersection of Legends in German Medieval Literature* (Lewiston, NY: Edwin Mellen Press, 1991), esp. 1–22. More specifically, see Walter Haug, "Der *Tristan* — eine interarthurische Lektüre," in Walter Haug, *Brechungen auf dem Weg zur Individualität: Kleine Schriften zur Literatur des Mittelalters* (Tübingen: Niemeyer, 1995), 184–96; and Volker Mertens, "Der arthurische Tristan—*die fabelen, die hier under sint, / die sol ich werfen an den wint,*" in *Tristan–Tristrant: Mélanges en l'honneur de Danielle Buschinger à l'occasion de son 60ème anniversaire,* ed. André Crépin and Wolfgang Spiewok (Greifswald: Reinecke-Verlag, 1999), 365–79.

6. There were more of these compositions than have survived, as the troubadour Raimbaut de Vaqueiras attests; he speaks, around 1200, of an episode for which Tristan disguised himself as a watchman *(guaita).* See

Joseph Linskill, ed., *The Poems of the Troubadour Raimbaut de Vaqueiras* (The Hague: Mouton, 1964), XVII. 6. 201. "Entre ses braz tient la raïne" is the concluding line of the *Folie Tristan de Berne*; see *Tristan et Iseut,* ed. Lacroix and Walter, 310. Variations of this phrase act as a kind refrain to several of these episodes. Compare, for example, the variations in the *Folie Tristan d'Oxford* (ed. Lacroix and Walter, 280), line 988; or at the beginning of the Cambridge fragment of Thomas's work (ed. Lacroix and Walter, 336). I would like to think that that is what the famous lines in *Minnesangs Frühling* associate—"daz [diu chunigin] von Engellant / laege an minem arme" (if the queen of England were to lie in my arms) (*Des Minnesangs Frühling,* ed. Hugo Moser and Helmut Tervooren [Stuttgart: Hirzel, 1988], 21; IX, 1, 4–5). Such verse compositions would in turn be converted into oral prose for the purpose of informal entertainment, as attested, for example, in the *Vita* of Alpais of Cudot, written before the end of the twelfth century. See Peter Dinzelbacher, "Eine unbeachtete Erwähnung des 'Romanus de Tristan' aus dem 12. Jahrhundert," *Tristania* 18 (1998): 37–41 (Dinzelbacher imagines an actual recital, but the verbs used to describe the procedure, *explicere* and *disserere,* do not support that).

7. See Peter F. Ganz, ed., *Tristan,* Deutsche Klassiker des Mittelalters, N. F. 4, 2 vols. (Wiesbaden: Brockhaus, 1978), 1: ix.

8. See Mathilda Tomarin Bruckner, "The Representation of the Lovers' Death: Thomas' *Tristan* as Open Text," *Tristania* 9 (1983–84): 49–61.

9. On this point, see Walter Haug, "Struktur und Geschichte: Ein literaturtheoretisches Experiment an mittelalterlichen Texten," in Walter Haug, *Strukturen als Schlüssel zur Welt: Kleine Schriften zur Erzählliteratur des Mittelalters* (Tübingen: Niemeyer, 1989), 247–50.

10. For *Sir Tristrem,* see below. There may have been a Dutch version relatively close to Thomas, but the small fragment of ca. 1250 that survives also deviates in significant detail, demonstrating once more "die schwindelerregende Vielfalt der Tristantradition" (the dizzying diversity of the Tristan tradition) (Bart Besamusca, "Tristan und Isolt in den Niederlanden," in *Tristan und Isolt im Spätmittelalter,* ed. Xenja von Ertzdorff and Rudolf Schulz [Amsterdam: Rodopi, 1999], 417).

11. Marie-José Heijkant, *La tradizione del "Tristan" in prosa in Italia e proposte di studio sul "Tristano Riccardiano"* (Enschede: Sneldruk, 1989); Sebastian Iragui, "The Southern Version of the *Prose Tristan*: The Italo-Iberian Translations and Their French Source," *Tristania* 17 (1996): 39–54; Enrique Andrés Ros Domingo, *Arthurische Literatur der Romania: Die iberoromanischen Fassungen des Tristanromans und ihre Beziehung zu den französischen und italienischen Versionen* (Bern: Peter Lang, 2001).

12. Anne Berthelot, "Le *Tristan en Prose*: Normalisation d'un myth," in *Tristan–Tristrant: Mélanges Danielle Buschinger,* 37–45.

13. For a discussion of this image and the older literature, see Michael Curschmann, "Images of Tristan," in *Gottfried von Strassburg and the Medieval Tristan Legend: Papers from an Anglo-North American Symposium,* ed. Adrian Stevens and Roy Wisbey, Publications of the Institute of Germanic Studies, University of London, 44 (Cambridge: D. S. Brewer, 1990) 7–17; reprinted in Michael Curschmann, *Wort–Bild–Text: Studien zur Medialität des Literarischen in Hochmittelalter und früher Neuzeit,* 2 vols. (Baden-Baden: Valentin Koerner, 2007), 1:227–51. My examples come from this earlier article, but I have changed the thrust of my argument. In her recent paper on this topic, Melissa Furrow, "Artists Reading Romance: The Tryst beneath the Tree," *Dalhousie Review* 82 (2002): 11–31, deals only with a small segment of the material and ignores most of the earlier scholarship. Some potentially interesting observations are marred by curious misreadings of the pictorial evidence. The most recent commentary on the independent tryst representations can be found in Norbert H. Ott, "'Freisetzung' und 'Ritualisierung': Zu Struktur und Funktion von Einzelmotiven und Handlungsmomenten in literarischen Bildzeugnissen," in *Literatur und Wandmalerei II: Konventionalität und Konversation,* ed. Eckart Conrad Lutz et al. (Tübingen: Niemeyer, 2005), 254–60, 272.

14. Two scholarly editions of this prose work still await completion. For the Tristan story by itself, see *Le Roman de Tristan en prose: Les deux captivités de Tristan,* ed. Joël Blanchard (Paris: Klincksieck, 1976), 57–61. Since, however, the editor begins this major excerpt with the scene in the garden, quite the wrong impression is created as to its position in this composition as a whole. As far as the details are concerned, several important changes occur: Tristan comes lightly armed, and both lovers notice Mark sitting in the tree instead of his shadow or reflection. There is in fact no water. The Italian version, Filippo-Luigi Polidori, ed., *La Tavola Ritonda o l'Istoria di Tristano,* vol. 1 (Bologna: G. Romagnoli, 1894), chap. 63, has no water here either, and Mark's shadow on the ground alerts both lovers at the same time. It is not surprising, therefore, that, as Alison Stones shows elsewhere in this volume, none of the illustrated manuscripts of the *Tristan en prose* in fact even attempt to depict the tryst.

15. The speech scrolls read: "[Iseut:] tristram gardee de dire vilane por la pisson de la fonteine." "[Tristram:] dame ie voroi per ma foi qui fv ave nos monsignor le roi." "[Mark:] de dev sot il condona qui dementi la dame loial." ([Iseut:] Tristram, guard yourself against speaking discourteously. There is a fish [poison] in the fountain. [Tristram:] Lady, I wish by my faith my lord

the king were with us. [Mark:] By God, may the man who spoke badly of this loyal lady be condemned.)

16. See Luyster, this volume. Iseult's words also appear, in part, in Dirc Potter's description, *Der minnen loep,* ed. P. Leendertz (Leiden, 1845), bk. 2, lines 3613–36; and on one of the fourteenth-century slippers that have been excavated in Holland (Besamusca, "Tristan und Isolt," 427–28).

17. The most recent study of one of these "romance caskets," the copy in the Metropolitan Museum in New York, by Paula Mae Carns, "*Compilatio* in Ivory: The Composite Casket in the Metropolitan Museum," *Gesta* 44 (2005): esp. 73–75, lacks the methodological sophistication to deal with the often complex relationships between word and image, not least so in the case of the tryst. The common generic motif of a couple playing chess is occasionally paired with or placed next to the tryst scene, but that does not mean that the couple is here meant to represent Tristan and Iseult, as Olivia Remie Constable has proposed recently in "Chess and Courtly Culture in Medieval Castile: The *Libro de ajedrez* of Alfonso X, el Sabio," *Speculum* 82 (2007): 324–27. For that scene to carry this particular literary connotation it would have to include some detail that places it on a ship, where in fact it occurs in the *Tristan en prose.* The classic example is the so-called Burghley Nef (1482–83), a saltcellar in the form of a ship that shows the couple playing chess while holding hands under the main mast. See Charles Oman, *Medieval Silver Nefs* (London: Her Majesty's Stationery Office, 1963), fig. 9 and pls. 8–10.

18. On the terminological difference between image and picture, see Michael Curschmann, "Epistemological Perspectives at the Juncture of Word and Image in Medieval Books before 1300," in *Multi-Media Compositions from the Middle Ages to the Early Modern Period,* ed. Margriet Hoogvliet (Leuven: Peeters, 2004; *recte* 2005), 1–2; and Michael Curschmann, "Epistemologisches am Schnittpunkt von Wort und Bild," in Curschmann, *Wort–Bild–Text,* 1:21–22.

19. Dirc Potter, *Der minnen loep,* bk. 2, lines 3613–36. Potter's description is clearly derived from the kind of image realized on the wooden comb from the Rhinelands, for example, and makes his comment categorically different from the usual words of caution or condemnation that follow the textual tradition. That a pictorial tradition is the source of Potter's quote of Isolde's warning words in the picture (and, it should be added, Tristan's response) is also the opinion of Besamusca, "Tristan und Isolt," 426. The article by Bob Duijvestijn, "Tristan und Isolde in den Niederlanden," in *Tristan–Tristrant: Mélanges Danielle Buschinger,* 129–35, is methodologically obsolete (see esp. 132–34).

20. There were eight printings in the fifteenth and sixteenth centuries and two *rifacimenti*. See Eckhard Höfner, "*Tristan*-Fassungen in literarischer Umbruchszeit: Pierre Sala (um 1520–29) und Jean Maugin (1554)," in *Tristan–Tristrant: Mélanges Danielle Buschinger*, 243–63. The subsequent reception of the material in France is described briefly by Brigitte Linden, "La réception du roman de Tristan en France de la fin du 18e jusqu'au commencement du 20e siècle," *Tristania* 15 (1994): 33–56.

21. I have used Spisak's critical edition, *Caxton's Malory* (William Caxton, *Caxton's Malory*, ed. James W. Spisak, 2 vols. [Berkeley: University of California Press, 1983]). Since it is the printed version that eventually reached the nineteenth century, I am not concerned here with the unique Winchester manuscript and the scholarly discussion surrounding it, including its poetics.

22. Maureen Fries, "Indiscreet Objects of Desire: Malory's 'Tristram' and the Necessity of Deceit," in *Studies in Malory*, ed. James W. Spisak (Kalamazoo: Medieval Institute Publications, Western Michigan University), 87–107, has recorded some of the more important changes and realignments that occur in the French prose and in Malory. Heinz Bergner, "Die mittelenglischen Bearbeitungen des Tristanstoffes in *Sir Tristrem* und Sir Thomas Malorys *Morte Darthur*," in Ertzdorff and Schulz, *Tristan und Isolt im Spätmittelalter*, 397–412, offers mainly descriptions.

23. Of course this integration also includes reinterpretation of the Tristan material in this new context. For a brief plea in favor of a fair amount of cohesion in the context of Malory, see Nancy H. Owen and Lewis J. Owen, "The Structure and Function of the *Tristram* in Malory's *Morte Darthur*," *Tristania* 3 (1975): 3–21. Another aspect of the matter is treated by Charles Pastoor, "Mark and Tristram as Parody in Thomas Malory's *Book of Sir Tristram De Lyones*," *Tristania* 17 (1996): 55–70. On the trickster Tristan becoming a knight errant, see Hélène Dauby, "Le *Tristan* de Malory," in *Tristan–Tristrant: Mélanges Danielle Buschinger*, 109–15.

24. An inscription on Marhaus's former seat suddenly reads, "This is the syege of the noble knyght Sir Tristram" (*Caxton's Malory*, ed. Spisak, 1:300).

25. I agree with Dhira B. Mahoney, "Malory's 'Tale of Sir Tristrem': Source and Setting Reconsidered," in Grimbert, *Tristan and Isolde: A Casebook*, 238, that adultery is hardly a concern here.

26. In fact, speaking of his source, he states categorically that the last book of Tristram will not be adduced: "Here endeth the second book of Syr Tristram that was drawen oute of Frensshe into Englysshe, but here is no rehersal of the thyrd book" (*Caxton's Malory*, 1:426).

27. Of the copious scholarly literature on Swinburne and his *Tristram* in particular, I have found most useful two articles by Rikky Rooksby, "A Century of Swinburne," in *The Whole Music of Passion: New Essays on Swinburne,* ed. Rikky Rooksby and Nicholas Shrimpton (Aldershot: Scolar Press, 1993), 1–21; and "The Algernonicon, or Thirteen Ways of Looking at *Tristram of Lyonesse,*" 73–91. I quote from *The Poems of Algernon Charles Swinburne,* vol. 4 (New York: Harper and Brothers, 1904), by page numbers (there is no line count). The text can also be found in James P. Carley, ed., *Algernon Charles Swinburne,* Arthurian Poets (Woodbridge: Boydell Press, 1990), 14–159. It is worth mentioning at least that William Morris and Co. had preceded Swinburne with their stained-glass compositions for Harden Grange in 1862. Brief comments on this series can be found in Christine Poulson, "'The Most Beautiful Dreams': Tristram and Isoud in British Art of the Nineteenth and Early Twentieth Centuries," in Grimbert, *Tristan and Isolde: A Casebook,* 338–41.

28. David Masson, *British Novelists and Their Styles* (1859), quoted in *Malory: The Critical Heritage,* ed. Marylyn Jackson Parins (London: Routledge, 1988), 119.

29. Anonymous review of Thomas Wright's edition, in *Blackwood's Magazine* 88 (1860), quoted in Parins, *Malory: The Critical Heritage,* 122.

30. In A. C. Swinburne, *Under the Microscope* (1872), quoted in Parins, *Malory: The Critical Heritage,* 190.

31. The latest edition in the United States is Alan Lupack, ed., *Lancelot of the Laik and Sir Tristrem* (Kalamazoo: Medieval Institute Publications, University of Western Michigan, 1994). The volume by Claire Fennell, ed., *Sir Tristrem: La storia di Tristano in Inghilterra* (Milano: Luni, 2000), includes an Italian translation and an extensive introduction with bibliography.

32. Francisque Michel, ed., *Tristan: Recueil de ce qui reste des poèmes relatifs à ses aventures, composés en françois en anglo-normand et en grec dans les XII et XIIIe siècles,* 3 vols. (London: G. Pickering; Paris: Techener, 1835–39).

33. The story of one of the many that had disappeared from the Bibliothèque nationale is told by Léopold Delisle, *Les manuscrits du Comte d'Ashburnham* (Paris: H. Champion, 1883), 101–4. The scholarly literature on Swinburne's medievalism suggests that it could be studied more thoroughly, especially where its factual basis is concerned. Ludwig Richter, *Swinburne's* [*sic*] *Verhältnis zu Frankreich und Italien* (Leipzig: A. Deichert, 1911), treats only direct adaptations or translations of French or Italian models and does not even mention *Tristram.* Mary Byrd Davis, "Swinburne's Use of His Sources in *Tristram of Lyonesse,*" *Philological Quarterly* 55 (1976): 96–112, and others merely identify a few possible borrowings beyond Malory and *Sir Tristrem.*

Antony H. Harrison, *Swinburne's Medievalism: A Study in Victorian Love Poetry* (Baton Rouge: Louisiana State University Press, 1988), gives a general introduction but lacks specifics and the requisite knowledge of the actual medieval heritage; hence, among other things, the faulty assumptions as to what might have been available in Ashburnham's library (80). As I will just note in passing, that library did include at least one illustrated copy of the *Tristan en prose,* now in Florence, Biblioteca Laurentiana, MS Ashburnham 123 (Libri 50). See Bernhard Degenhart and Annegrit Schmitt, "Frühe angiovinische Buchkunst in Neapel: Die Illustrierung französischer Unterhaltungsprosa in neapolitanischen Scriptorien zwischen 1290 und 1320," in *Festschrift Wolfgang Braunfels,* ed. Friedrich Piel and Jörg Träger (Tübingen: Wasmuth, 1977), 89 n. 8.

34. As has been remarked more than once, these words and cadences are deliberately reminiscent of Francesca's in Dante's *Inferno* (5, 97 ff.).

35. The second (White) Iseult's role has been greatly enhanced by Swinburne, creating a negative counterpoint to the passionate love that drives the couple. The central cantos of the poem (IV–VII) are arranged in two opposing pairs in chiastic order to thematize the resulting tension. While in canto IV Tristram's wedding night occurs in Brittany, La belle Iseult spends the same night sleepless at Tintagel in anguished prayer and longing. And subsequently, in cantos VI and VII, blissful union of the couple in Joyous Gard is overshadowed by the White Iseult's monologue, replete with murderous thoughts.

36. Rooksby, "The Algernonicon."

37. It is because of this particular connection between the *Prelude* and the conclusion that I side here with the "annihilist position" identified by Rooksby, "The Algernonicon," 84. It is worth remembering in addition that the lines quoted above serve as a programmatic projection of what is yet to be accomplished: the *Prelude* was published separately in 1869.

38. I agree with David G. Riede, *Swinburne: A Study of Romantic Mythmaking* (Charlottesville: University Press of Virginia, 1978), 190, that Swinburne's poem is "by far the best modern rendering of the Tristram legend"; see also 190–93. Note the more general conclusion by Rebecca Cochran, "An Assessment of Swinburne's Arthuriana," in *King Arthur through the Ages,* ed. Valerie M. Lagorio and Mildred Leake Day, 2 vols. (New York: Garland, 1990), 2:70: "[The couple] are resurrected when their stories are transmitted through the songs of poet-lovers (e.g. Dante, Swinburne) throughout the ages."

CHAPTER SIX

Framing Tristan—Taming Tristan?

The Materiality of Text and Body in Hans Sachs's *Tragedia*

ELKE KOCH

Turning the Story into Drama

The merit of Hans Sachs's contribution to the tradition of the Tristan story is usually seen in his introduction of two new genres to it: *Meistersang* and drama.[1] Yet a comparison with the literary achievements of the medieval narrative tradition cannot fail to be to Sachs's disadvantage, especially as far as his dramatic adaptation is concerned. His verse *Tragedia mit 23 personen, von der strengen lieb herr Tristrant mit der schönen königin Isalden* exemplifies the late medieval tendency to moralize material from the literary tradition while reducing the rhetorical and structural complexity.[2]

Sachs's *Tragedia* begins with a prologue and ends with an epilogue delivered by a herald.[3] It is divided into seven acts. The first contains the Morholdt episodes and the second Tristrant's travels to Ireland. In the third act, the bond between the lovers is forged by Isalde becoming King Marx's bride and by drinking the love potion. The wedding is dealt with only briefly in the fourth act, and King Marx then watches his wife and nephew embrace and separates them, and the situation is resolved in the orchard episode. The fifth act contains the exile in the woods and Isalde's return to court. In the sixth act, Tristrant secretly visits the queen, first disguised as pilgrim and then as fool. The seventh and last act shows the death of the lovers and ends with the lament of Tristrant's wife.

Sachs's dramatic version might seem to some hardly worth a second look, especially with regard to his treatment of the famous "Tristan love."[4] Whereas his source, the prose *Tristrant,* exemplifies the tendency of late medieval romances to construct coherence through psychological motivation, Sachs's adaptation is regarded as reducing love to the sexual drive, which has to be domesticated by marriage.[5] Sachs's drama is embedded in a discursive background constituted by a vast body of late medieval didactic literature on the individual, the family, and gender relations that promotes and polices marriage as a fundamental element of social order and as the exclusive sphere of sexuality. No close reading of the text would unearth previously undiscovered subtleties of emotional nuance. Sachs's moralizing is evident, and in several instances love is explicitly equated with or at least linked to a "drive."[6]

Studies on the dramatic work of Sachs have pointed out that it is characterized by the didactic treatment of emotion—meaning above all love. Helmut Krause posits that control over the affects is one of Sachs's central themes.[7] He links this to a reception of Stoic concepts in the humanist tradition. Dorothea Klein discusses Sachs's concern with control over the passions against the backdrop of Protestant ethics and of the social conditions of the artisan population in late medieval cities.[8] Scholars sometimes refer to Norbert Elias's theory of the civilizing process to support the notion that Sachs's writing reflects and constitutes a heightened effort to control the affects.[9] Maria E. Müller, for example, understands Sachs's work as a literary project aimed at shaping rational, economical subjects.[10] The repression of drives is inherent to this development, which she regards as being related to social changes following the dissolution of feudal social structures.

The literary and social conditions of Sachs's didacticism and his relation to a normative discourse on sex and marriage are well researched, but his aesthetic devices have not yet been fully explored.[11] It is a scholarly commonplace that Sachs's dramatic work cannot be approached with categories drawn from the classical poetics of drama.

Studies on Sachs's dramatic technique tend instead to be situated in conceptual frameworks developed for modern drama.[12] Yet neither framework is sufficient or adequate; the heuristic tools needed to analyze Sachs's dramatic work are not yet fully developed. Turning instead to the concept of materiality is especially promising, because it opens up a view in which Sachs's didactic treatment of emotion can be considered with regard to the materiality of the body on the one hand and the materiality of the text within the literary tradition on the other. This chapter discusses these two dimensions of materiality as a key to analyzing the aesthetic strategies Sachs employs to represent love in drama, in the media of performance and print. The materiality of the body also needs to be considered on both the conceptual level and the semiotic level, in order to explore the ways in which Sachs's strategies are related to his concept of love.

Sachs's choice of genre should not be understood primarily as an aesthetic one. It is also related to what might be called Sachs's emotional pedagogy. The term *pedagogy* takes up a clue given by Sachs in the prefaces to his handwritten anthology, the *Spruchbücher* (didactic poetry books).[13] There, he announces his dramatic work as providing examples of virtues and vices for the young, although his efforts in moral education are of course addressed to a wider, heterogeneous audience.[14] The dominance of performance-related genres in Sachs's oeuvre has recently been discussed from the perspective of the history of media. Cornelia Epping-Jäger has described Sachs as representative of a situation in which modes of cultural production and reception characteristic of print culture and literacy are becoming operative but are not yet habitualized.[15] In his dramatic work, the writer functions as a mediator, exploring the archives of cultural tradition and reworking his material in a form that can be delivered in performance to a semi-literate or illiterate audience.[16]

Sachs's source has been identified as the 1549/50 Worms print of the prose *Tristrant and Isalde,* which is based on Eilhart's version.[17] Before Sachs wrote his *Tragedia* in 1553, he adapted the Tristan story for *Meistersang,* composing five songs in 1551. A sixth was written after finishing the Tristan *Tragedia.*[18] No manuscript of it has survived. The eighth *Spruchbuch,* which contained the drama, is lost, and no manuscripts used in a production of the play exist. The edition of the Tristan *Tragedia* by Adalbert von Keller is based on the print version that first appeared in 1561, in the third volume of the folio edition of Sachs's works.

This situation determines the materiality of the text. In printed form, the play can be read individually or out loud to others, and it can be excerpted for staging. Nevertheless, based on the records of Sachs's theatrical activities in Nuremberg, it is generally assumed that his dramatic works were originally written for performance. Given these circumstances, it does not make sense to analyze the materiality of the text as proceeding from manuscript to performance to printed book. Rather, this inquiry begins with an excursus on the book, moves from there to a discussion of the ways in which the text in this form presupposes performance, and then proceeds to a discussion of materiality on the level of the representation of emotion.[19] This dimension of materiality is defined by the role the body plays conceptually and semiotically in the representation of love.

A wide range of differences between Sachs and his source result from the change of genre. One such change is especially relevant to the representation of emotion and the question of materiality, namely, the transformation of the narrator. This analysis focuses on the monologues of the theater herald and on the potion scene, which are most significant in this context.

The Materiality of the Text

Concerning the relationship between the materiality of the text and its dramatic structure, the form and arrangement of the stage directions are of special interest. On the one hand, the *mise-en-page* indicates the dramatic structure by separating stage directions and monologue.[20] On the other hand, the typography of the stage directions assimilates the layout to that of nondramatic printed texts. The stage directions resemble captions or beginnings of chapters in narrative or nonfictional prose texts in which the first line is printed in larger letters than the following lines. Further, the speakers' names are not set apart.

The assimilation of the *mise-en-page* to nondramatic printed text is reflected in the linguistic forms of the stage directions. Whereas in other plays Sachs sometimes indicates special effects or miming, the printed text of his *Tragedia* shows no linguistic trace of the virtuality of the action.[21] This is especially evident in the few references to emotional expression: Marx exits angrily, not "as if he was angry" ("Der König geht zornig ab") (*Tragedia,* 15). The stage directions serve as narrative links between the monologues, making the drama readable as a story. Nevertheless, this tendency does not interfere with the dramatic function of the stage directions, which are in the present tense and contain only information relevant and easily adaptable to staging the drama.

The resulting visual and textual form oscillates between a "making present" of the action similar to the use of narrative perspective and a "distancing" of the action as theatrical play. This oscillation is especially evident in the scene of Tristrant's death. For obvious reasons, theatrical death matters for the question of virtuality. The stage directions indicate Tristrant's death as follows: "Er streckt sich unnd stirbt / man tregt in auff dem Sessel ab / und tregt ein verdeckte todenbar ein" (He stretches out and dies, he is carried off on a seat and a covered bier is carried in) (*Tragedia,* 26). The virtuality of the death is not marked. Tristrant does not act as if he dies; he does die. Yet the stage direction presupposes the virtuality of the action. On the level of language, Tristrant's body is transformed into a corpse. But this corpse is treated in a way that presupposes its embodiment by the living body of an actor. It is removed from sight and replaced by a lifeless object. In a sense, the stage direction doubles representation: The story is represented in the text as being represented on a stage. When analyzing the representation of emotion, this complex relationship between the materiality of the body and the materiality of the text must be taken into account.

The Materiality of the Body I: Setting the Frame

The roles played by the body in the concept of love and in the representation of this emotion are interrelated. The representation of emotion is not simply shaped by a preexisting concept; rather, this concept is reconstituted and shaped by the modes in which emotion is represented. In Sachs's *Tragedia,* the mode of representation is conditioned by the dramatic structure of the text. A comparison of Sachs's strategies of representation with those of his source, the prose *Tristrant,* shows that his change of genre correlates with shifts in the significance of the body on both the conceptual and semiotic levels.[22]

One aspect of the change of genre, which has important consequences for the representation of emotion, concerns the device of the narrator. Some of the functions of the narrator are taken over by the herald, who in narrator-like fashion comments on the story and provides an explicitly moral view.[23] But whereas in the prose *Tristrant* the narrator addresses the audience throughout the story, the *Tragedia* shows a different pattern. Here, his addresses to the audience are restricted to the prologue and epilogue, although he does appear several times as a figure within the play to report to other figures events taking place elsewhere (*Werke,* 12:149, 21–30). In this way the herald's speeches constitute a narrative and didactic frame for the dramatic action, which unfolds without comment. Commentary is suspended within the frame, its didactic impetus reinforced in the epilogue's elaborate warning against the dangers of love. The didactic dimension supports the argument that the narrative function is especially evident in the epilogue, where the herald also refers to other literary authorities on the matter of love, thus introducing intertextuality on the level of comment.

This narrative frame explicitly presents a distinct concept of love. In both the prologue and the epilogue, the love of Tristrant and Isalde is referred to as a violent drive. The prologue portrays the love that results from the potion as lovesickness, unextinguishable or inflamed desire *(brunst)* and pain (*Werke,* 12:143, 2–4). The prologue imposes an unambiguously negative view of love, which is manifested further in unpleasant physical sensations. In the epilogue, however, the picture of love becomes more complex. The herald begins with an extended reflection on the unruly love encountered in the story, which is explicated as possessing a strong and overruling force, as bringing fear, pain, and turmoil to the heart, as perverting mind, reason, and feelings, as inducing damage to honor and property and corruption to body and soul, finally resulting in the loss of God's grace (12:184, 31–185, 6; 185, 11–20). Still, the ambivalence of love is cautiously introduced into the discourse. Diogenes and Petrarca are quoted describing love as "poisonous honey" and "golden fetters" (12:185, 7–10). After this elaborate representation of love as a terrible danger, the tone shifts, and love is linked with marriage. Married love is appreciated by God and by society and will receive the blessing of prosperity (12:185, 21–28). So although the denigration of love takes up the larger part of the epilogue, the emotion is not wholly condemned. It should even be fostered in matrimony, in accordance with late medieval teachings on marriage and indeed ideas about marital love with a long tradition in the Middle Ages.[24] Thus love is characterized as an affect that is dangerous and desirable at the same time.

In a number of studies on Sachs's tragedy, researchers have argued that the play's dramatic action is not coherent with the moral in the epilogue.[25] This argument does not hold with regard to the representation of love. The *Tragedia* shows the dangerous consequences of illicit love. Hardly a single opportunity is missed to stress the constant mortal danger in which the lovers find themselves.[26] At the same time, their actions demonstrate the binding force of love, so that it can be inferred that love would have brought about stability and fertility had it been contained within marriage.

The concept of love as a dangerous drive is reflected in the expression (or lack of it) of love within the dramatic action as well. The stage directions in very few instances explicitly call for the expression of emotion (joy, sorrow, anger). Apart from two embraces, there is only one gesture that has direct significance for the representation of love. This gesture is a gaze that expresses love *as* desire. When Tristrant is asked by Isalde's father whether he desires her as a bride, he takes a look at Isalde and answers, "Ja, von hertzen ich ihr beger" (Yes, I desire her with all my heart) (12:155, 21), but then explains that he will step back in favor of his uncle, who is a much nobler match for her. Mentioning the gaze is an example of heightened emphasis. There is only one other stage direction noting a gaze, and here it does not emphasize but rather clarifies. In a burlesque scene in which Tristrant returns to Marx's court disguised as a fool, indicating the direction of the gaze is necessary to make clear the addressee of the figure's speech. In the case of Tristrant's glance at Isalde, no misunderstanding is possible.[27]

Although the dramatic dialogue gives no hint of any attraction between Isalde and Tristrant up to this point, it is made clear that Tristrant's desire for Isalde is not brought about by the potion. Rather, the potion works as an aphrodisiac. "Tristan love" is marked not as something unique, but as common desire magically reinforced. This representation is in accordance with Sachs's source. In the prose *Tristrant* the love of Tristrant and Isalde is neither paradigmatic nor unique. Nevertheless, Sachs differs from his source in important respects, one of which is that he dispenses with his source's careful motivation of love. *Tristrant* explains love's intensity and its overruling potency with the force of the potion but draws a distinct line between love under the spell of magic, which lasts for four years, and love that comes from habituation. While under the influence of the potion, the lovers go to any extreme to be together, culminating in the poverty and degradation of their exile in the woods. It is only when the effect of the potion has ended that the couple is able to leave the wilderness and face the risk of separation (*Tristrant,* 100, 2579–85). The lasting attraction of the lovers beyond this limit is explained by the influence of habit on the affects. Because the lovers are so close for an extended time, their love continues as a "natural" habituated love, which has become unusually strong (100, 2585–87).[28] In Sachs's dramatization, the four-year period is mentioned when Isalde's mother describes the working of the potion (*Werke,* 12:156, 20–25), but its implications are not elaborated there or later in the play.

In comparison with the prose *Tristrant* and especially with its medieval predecessors, the potion scene in Sachs's dramatic adaptation is so reduced as to appear inadvertently comical. Tristrant expresses the effect of the drink in eight lines, Isalde in four. These are very short speeches, even when compared to others in the play. Sachs's characteristic treatment of emotion becomes most clear when compared to his source. After Tristrant and Isalde have drunk the potion, the prose *Tristrant* narrates how they are inflamed with love, how they desire one another, wish to express their feelings and at the same time conceal them (*Tristrant,* 43–49). They experience conflicting states and impulses, represented by the traditional repertoire of physical sensations accompanying the onset of love: the rapid succession of feeling hot and cold, of blushing and becoming pale. Overwhelmed by this emotion, both are primarily concerned with the fear that the other might detect their state, and finally they separate, going to bed without having revealed themselves to one another. A long monologue by Isalde reflecting on her feelings follows. The growing pains of lovesickness are depicted in the physical changes of the two protagonists, and the narrator comments on their inner turmoil as well.

Lacking the device of the narrator as a mediator, Sachs's Tristrant and Isalde must express their feelings either verbally or nonverbally in the dramatic text. As already mentioned, in other scenes the stage directions indicate emotions. In the potion scene, no hint is given by gesture or posture of any expression of feeling, which is solely articulated through monologue and dialogue. I quote the passage in full:

> *Herr Tristrant trinckt und gibt es Isalden, die trincket auch*
> *und Tristrant spricht:*
> Was ist das gewest für ein wein?
> Wie springt und tobt das hertze mein?
> Mein gmüt ist in gantzer unrhu
> Und setzt mir lenger herter zu.
> Ich bin mit schmertzen gros umbfangen,
> Samb hab ein pfeil mein hertz durchgangen.
> *Isald spricht:*
> Es ist mir warlich auch nit recht.
> Mein hertz jamert und seuftzet schlecht
> Und all mein kreft thun sich bewegen.
> Ich will ein weil zu rhu mich legen.
> *Isald gehet auß. Herr Tristrant spricht:*
> Ich will auch gehn in mein gemach.
> Bin gleich vor lieb und senen schwach.
> (Werke, 12:157, 30–158, 10)

———

[*Tristrant drinks and gives it to Isalde; she also drinks and Tristrant says:* What kind of wine was that? How my heart jumps and

raves, my feelings are in turmoil and ail me more and more.
I am enclosed in heavy pain as if an arrow had pierced my heart.
Isalde says: I do not feel well either. My heart is deeply sorrowful
and sobbing and all my spirits are moving. I need to go lie down
for a while. *Isalde exits and Tristrant says:* I, too, will withdraw to
my chamber, I am likewise weak with love and longing.]

The protagonists give the audience insight into their inner feelings,
which are articulated as bodily sensations and as a general upsetting of
the soul. Love appears as turmoil, as disorder and pain; it is felt as sickness from the beginning. This expression translates the description of
love presented in the prologue into dramatic action. There is no ambivalence associated with love. It is experienced as a negative sensation.

Even this limited representation of love shows traces of a concept
of the affects that stands in the Augustinian tradition of medieval
Christian anthropology, which distinguishes between affects of the
soul *(affectus sensitivus)* and affects of the flesh *(affectus carnis)*, which
were seen as the source of sin and of perverse appetites.[29] In Tristrant's
and Isalde's monologues, the carnality of their affect is marked by its
association with weakness and inner disorder. But while the emotion
is thus closely linked to the material body, it is expressed exclusively
through language. In contrast to the visible symptoms of love that we
encounter in every narrative version of the *Tristan* story, the affect of
love remains invisible in the drama. It is hidden inside the body, raging in its interior, an energy that consumes the body or propels it into
action but does not communicate itself immediately through the body.
In terms of emotional pedagogy, this representation can be understood
as a means of distancing the affect of love, of avoiding contact with its
force. Representing emotion or affect as something that is held within
the body and therefore can be held back in it can be called a strategy of
containment.

Not only the physiognomy of love but also traditional symptoms
and sensational signs, especially the alternation of hot and cold, are
omitted. In *Tristrant,* the metaphor of fire is the most dominant motive
in this scene. In the *Tragedia* — and here again Sachs might seem unin-
tentionally comical, but what he does with the motif is interesting with

regard to the conception of emotion—love is described as a flaming or hot *brunst* (desire; heat in animals) in the prologue and by Brangel (Brangaene) (*Werke,* 12:143, 4; 159, 4). The lovers, however, refer to heat only *before* drinking the potion. The heat of the sun is mentioned twice as the reason for Tristrant's and Isalde's thirst (12:157, 18, 21).[30] Like the feeling of love, thirst is described as being painful. The close association of painful thirst and love situates these two experiences on the same level. Neither in contemporary concepts of emotions nor in modern emotion theory are thirst and love considered to belong to the same category of affective phenomena.[31] Sachs's association of thirst and love reconceptualizes love as an impulse of the flesh, removing it even further from the realm of the rational. The reshaping of love in Sachs's adaptation can therefore be described as a derationalization of the emotion.

Another instance of this derationalization is the omission of Isalde's reflections on her feelings after drinking the potion. The Isolde figure has a monologue on this topic in Sachs's source and in other versions, and although such a monologue is easily adaptable for drama, Sachs does not use this device. Instead reflection on love is restricted to the epilogue, and love is discussed only by the herald, a figure in the play whom it does not affect. Thus the self-reflexive element of love is completely eliminated. Distributing the reflection on emotion in this manner is a strategy of emotional pedagogy. It arranges rational and affective appeals in different modes. The herald's wordy warning against love aims at evoking in the imagination of the recipient fear and sorrow, as well as the attraction associated with love, but this evocation is contained within rational discourse. In contrast, the figures in the play express love without recourse to a discourse of rationality. This expression does not invite empathy, as the visual and the verbal information on emotion are very much diminished, and affect is held at a distance by the strategy of containment.[32]

The Materiality of the Body II: Staging Emotion

Up to this point I have discussed the dramatic representation of love as purely textual evidence, treating the materiality of the text as printed reading material that is indifferent to the potential of its performance. The conclusion suggests possible implications that the materiality of the body in performance could have for Sachs's aesthetic strategy of containment.

Usually the presence of the material body in performance is understood to be closely linked to emotional appeal. Traditional rhetoric ascribes the arousal of affect in the listener to the presence of the body of the actor or speaker who shows signs of these affects in his gestures.[33] Current performance theory highlights the affective dimension of the phenomenal body of the actor per se.[34] Transferring these premises to Sachs's representation of emotion has the disadvantage of deduction, but for the sake of argument this line of thought will be pursued. These concepts hint at the possibility that a performance of the play could counteract its tendency to distance affect, or at least create tension between the distancing of affect by textual strategies and the evoking of affect by strategies of staging. However, under the conditions of Sachs's theatrical production, the presence of material bodies opens up a different possibility. The materiality of the body onstage could also be employed to support the strategy of containment and avoid contact with the dangerous energy of desire.

As I previously argued with regard to Tristrant's death scene, the material body of an actor does not simply represent the textual body constituted by linguistic means. These two bodies can also present a perceivable contrast, as in the case of the living body and the textual corpse. With regard to the representation of desire, the difference between the material body and the textual body enhances the strategy of containment. The desire verbally expressed by an actor is contained within the textual body, and it is further excluded from becoming present because it is represented by a material body unaffected by desire.

The difference between the textual and the material body is an aspect of the virtuality of theatrical performance and must be taken into consideration when discussing the conditions of Sachs's theatrical practice. Not much is known about the mode of acting, but it is clear that Sachs's theater was not illusionistic.[35] The stage was created by separating a space in a church choir with curtains; there were costumes but no scenery; and female roles were played by men. Sachs's plays were performed by lay actors, *gesellen,* presumably members of the *Meistersingerschulen*. The fact that the actors were recognizable as members of the city community can be taken as further evidence for a performance that would display its own virtuality in full view. Under these conditions, the difference between material and textual bodies could have been perceptible throughout.

The potential of implementing the strategy of containment in performance can also be posited with regard to space. The prose *Tristrant* makes use of the device of the narrator to open up a third space, beyond the world of the protagonists and the world of the recipient. As Tristrant is given free access to Isalde's chamber after the orchard episode, the narrator imagines himself in the situation of Tristrant and explains that he would likewise have done everything to which his passions led him (*Tristrant,* 76, 1964–77, 1978). This comment constitutes a sphere in which identification is removed from the protagonists and exemplified by means of a new object, the narrator, who is not marked by differences of status and situation. In Sachs's dramatic adaptation of the text, the sphere of the protagonists is framed and safeguarded by the herald. He alone trespasses the boundary. In performance, then, the sphere of the protagonists is materialized by the space of the stage. Its boundaries are visible, helping to keep dangerous desire at bay.

Taming the Drive?

As an aesthetic strategy, containment is facilitated by structural features of the dramatic genre that can be supported by the materiality of performance. As a strategy of emotional pedagogy, containment is related to a concept of love as carnal affect. It might well be understood as a discourse concerned with control of the affects. The analysis presented here would fit well with views influenced by Norbert Elias and with earlier scholarship on Sachs that has described late medieval culture as being engaged in the process of civilization. But my argument here takes a different route. Sachs's emotional pedagogy prepares the ground for a repressive discipline of emotion by reinforcing an understanding of love as dangerous energy and therefore, eventually, as a drive. By constituting love as a drive, Sachs draws on earlier concepts of the emotion of love, but he also participates in shaping a concept of emotion that echoes in Elias's understanding of civilization and its history by equating love and desire, by derationalizing love, and by separating it from the body as a means of communication while at the same time planting it firmly within the body. For the project of writing a literary history of emotion, rather than reading late medieval literature with Elias's concept on our minds, we might instead read Elias against the backdrop of Sachs and his contemporaries.

Notes

1. Alexander Schwarz stresses Sachs's innovation in expanding the genre against the prevailing scholarly view of his work as trivializing; see "The Shoemaker's Tristans," *Tristania* 11.1–2 (1985–86): 21–28, 21.

2. Sachs encountered the Tristan story through the prose *Tristrant*, which is itself involved in the adaptation and transformation of the medieval tradition. See Bernward Plate, "Verstehensprinzipien im Prosa-Tristrant von 1448," in *Literatur—Publikum—historischer Kontext,* ed. Gert Kaiser, Beiträge zur älteren Deutschen Literaturgeschichte 1 (Bern: Peter Lang, 1977), 79–89; for a general discussion, see Jan-Dirk Müller, "Volksbuch/Prosaroman im 15./16. Jahrhundert—Perspektiven der Forschung," in *Internationales Archiv für Sozialgeschichte der deutschen Literatur, 1: Sonderheft Forschungsreferate,* ed. Wolfgang Frühwald, Georg Jäger, and Alberto Martino (Tübingen: Max Niemeyer, 1985), 1–128.

3. On the terminology, see Barbara Könneker, *Hans Sachs,* Sammlung Metzler 94 (Stuttgart: Metzler, 1971), 50–51.

4. Danielle Buschinger, "Zur Rezeption des Tristan-Stoffes in der deutschen Literatur des Mittelalters nach 1250," in *Studien zur deutschen Literatur des Mittelalters,* Wodan 53 (Greifswald: Reineke-Verlag, 1995), 70–80, describes the Tristan tradition from Gottfried onward as a process in which the "revolutionary" potential of Tristan love is continually diminished. Sachs's drama, which is only briefly mentioned, represents the final stage in this perspective. Albrecht Classen, "Mittelalterliche Chronistik und Literatur im Werk von Hans Sachs: Rezeptionshistorische Perspektiven im 16. Jahrhundert," *Colloquia Germanica: Internationale Zeitschrift für Germanistik* 37.1

(2004): 1–25, holds the view that Sachs radically undermines the principles of the literary material he himself has chosen, "insoweit als der *Tristan*-Stoff ihm bloß zur Abschreckung vor verkehrter Liebe dient" (18) (insofar as Sachs uses the *Tristan* material only as a deterrent against perverted love).

    5. See Müller, "Volksbuch / Prosaroman," 88–92; Dorothea Klein, *Bildung und Belehrung: Untersuchungen zum Dramenwerk des Hans Sachs,* Stuttgarter Arbeiten zur Germanistik 197 (Stuttgart: Hans Dieter Heinz Akademischer Verlag, 1988), 186–88.

    6. Hans Sachs, *Tragedia mit 23 personen, von der strengen lieb herr Tristrant mit der schönen königin Isalden, unnd hat 7 actus,* in *Werke,* ed. Adelbert von Keller and Edmund Goetze, 26 vols. (Stuttgart: Bibliothek des Literarischen Vereins, 1870–1908; reprint, Hildesheim: Georg Olms, 1964), 12:142, 24; 156, 23; 184, 34. The three references are all part of a *lieb-trieb* (love / drive) rhyme. Citations of Keller's edition of the *Tragedia* are to *Werke,* by volume, page, and line numbers. Translations are my own.

    7. Helmut Krause, *Die Dramen des Hans Sachs: Untersuchungen zur Lehre und Technik* (Berlin: Hofgarten, 1979), 61–72.

    8. Klein, *Bildung und Belehrung,* 188–203.

    9. Norbert Elias, *Über den Prozeß der Zivilisation: Soziogenetische und psychogenetische Untersuchungen,* 2 vols., Suhrkamp Taschenbuch Wissenschaft 158 (Frankfurt am Main: Suhrkamp, 1997).

    10. Maria E. Müller, *Der Poet der Moralität: Untersuchungen zu Hans Sachs,* Arbeiten zur mittleren Deutschen Literatur und Sprache 15 (Bern: Peter Lang, 1985), 213–22, 250–54, 268–84.

    11. On earlier research, see Niklas Holzberg, "Die Tragedis und Comedis des Hans Sachs: Forschungssituation—Forschungsperspektiven," in *Hans Sachs und Nürnberg: Bedingungen und Probleme reichsstädtischer Literatur; Hans Sachs zum 400. Todestag am 19. Januar 1976,* ed. Horst Brunner, Gerhard Hirschmann, and Fritz Schnelbögl (Nürnberg: Selbstverlag des Vereins für Geschichte der Stadt Nürnberg, 1976), 105–36.

    12. See Brigitte Stuplich, *Zur Dramentechnik des Hans Sachs* (Stuttgart: Frommann-Holzboog, 1998).

    13. Hans Sachs, *Spruchbücher,* in *Werke,* 23:575. See also Johannes Rettelbach, "Gattung, Buch und Performanz bei Hans Sachs nach dem Zeugnis der Vorreden," in *Literarisches Leben in Zwickau im Mittelalter und in der Frühen Neuzeit: Vorträge eines Symposiums anläßlich des 500-jährigen Jubiläums der Ratsschulbibliothek Zwickau am 17. und 18. Februar 1998,* ed. Margarethe Hubrath and Rüdiger Krohn, Göppinger Arbeiten zur Germanistik 686 (Göppingen: Kümmerle, 2001), 55–77, 66–67.

    14. Könneker, *Hans Sachs,* 51.

15. Cornelia Epping-Jäger, *Die Inszenierung der Schrift: Der Literalisierungsprozeß und die Entstehungsgeschichte des Dramas* (Stuttgart: M&P, 1996).

16. Whereas Epping-Jäger's work is situated in the context of an advanced theoretical and methodological debate on media and media history, a more traditional sociohistorical approach is taken by Ingeborg Spriewald, *Literatur zwischen Hören und Lesen: Wandel von Funktion und Rezeption im späten Mittelalter; Fallstudien zu Beheim, Folz und Sachs* (Berlin: Aufbau, 1990). Earlier research has already stressed the importance of media in Sachs's oeuvre; see Ingeborg Glier, "Die 'Dramen' des Hans Sachs: Wandlungen des frühen deutschen Theaters," in *Dichtung, Sprache, Gesellschaft: Akten des IV. Internationalen Germanisten-Kongresses 1970 in Princeton,* ed. Victor Lange and Hans-Gert Roloff (Frankfurt am Main: Athenäum, 1971), 235–42, esp. 238.

17. See Eduard Walther, *Hans Sachsens Tragödie Tristrant und Isalde in ihrem Verhältnis zur Quelle: Eine literarhistorische Untersuchung, Beilage zum 11. Jahresbericht der Kgl. Luitpold-Kreisrealschule* (München: C. Wolf und Sohn, 1902). Danielle Buschinger, "Die Mittelalter-Rezeption bei Hans Sachs," in *Studien zur deutschen Literatur des Mittelalters,* shows that Sachs must already have known the story from an earlier edition (379).

18. On the *Meisterlieder,* see Eli Sobel, *The Tristan Romance in the Meisterlieder of Hans Sachs,* University of California Publications in Modern Philology 40, no. 2 (Berkeley: University of California Press, 1963); Johannes Rettelbach, "Liebe—Drama—Meistergesang: Die Tristan-Lieder des Hans Sachs," in *Tristan–Tristrant: Mélanges en l'honneur de Danielle Buschinger à l'occasion de son 60ème anniversaire,* ed. André Crépin and Wolfgang Spiewok, Wodan 66 (Greifswald: Reineke-Verlag, 1996), 431–40.

19. The fascimile edition of the Tristan *Tragedia* is cited below as *Tragedia,* following the editors' page numbering: Hans Sachs, *Tragedia mit 23 Personen von der strengen Lieb Herr Tristrant mit der schönen Königin Isalden: Faksimileausgabe nach dem ältesten Druck aus dem Jahre 1561, erschienen in Nürnberg,* ed. Danielle Buschinger and Wolfgang Spiewok, Wodan 29 (Greifswald: Reineke-Verlag, 1993). Translations of Sachs's work are my own.

20. On the development of a dramatic *mise-en-page* in sixteenth-century print, see Julie Stone Peters, *Theatre of the Book, 1480–1880: Print, Text, and Performance in Europe* (Oxford: Oxford University Press, 2000), 15–31.

21. For example, in the *Hörnen Seuffriedt,* the stage directions indicate how smoke should be produced to signify the fight with the dragon, which takes place "offstage" (*Werke,* 13:341, 20–24). By contrast, there are no comparable clues concerning Tristrant's fight with the dragon in the *Tragedia.*

22. For Sachs's source, I cite *Tristrant und Isalde: Prosaroman; Nach dem ältesten Druck aus Augsburg vom Jahre 1484, versehen mit den Lesarten des*

zweiten Augsburger Druckes aus dem Jahre 1498 und eines Wormser Druckes unbekannten Datums, ed. Alois Brandstetter, ATB Ergänzungsreihe 3 (Tübingen: Max Niemeyer, 1966); further citations are to *Tristrant,* by page and line numbers. See Elisabeth Schmid, "Tristrant und Isalde," in *Die deutsche Literatur des Mittelalters: Verfasserlexikon,* vol. 9.2, rev. ed., ed. Kurt Ruh et al. (Berlin: de Gruyter, 1995), 1065–68.

23. On the herald figure replacing a narrator, see Michael Schilling, "Zur Dramatisierung des 'Wilhelm von Österreich' durch Hans Sachs," in *Zur deutschen Literatur und Sprache des 14. Jahrhunderts: Dubliner Colloquium 1981,* ed. Walter Haug, Timothy R. Jackson, and Johannes Janota, Reihe Siegen, Beiträge zur Literatur- und Sprachwissenschaft 45 (Heidelberg: Carl Winter, 1983), 262–77. The narrative structure of the prose *Tristrant* cannot be analyzed here. For the sake of contrast, I use a rather traditional concept of narrator as a personalized subject who tells the story as well as comments on it, the latter function of which is delegated to the herald.

24. Rüdiger Schnell, *Sexualität und Emotionalität in der vormodernen Ehe* (Köln: Böhlau, 2002).

25. See Holzberg, "Die Tragedis und Comedis des Hans Sachs," 126; Klein, *Bildung und Belehrung,* 172–73, 177; Rettelbach, "Liebe—Drama— Meistergesang," 430–40. The argument relies on the finding that Tristrant and Isalde are never overtly criticized but that their adversaries at King Marx's court are characterized by negative attributes. Also, the ambivalence is attributed to Sachs's source. A number of explanations for this incongruence have been put forth. Schwarz, "The Shoemaker's Tristans," 26, argues that the story of Tristan love possesses an inherent ambivalence that defies Sachs's didactic efforts and that it fascinated Sachs in spite of himself, which means that his choice of the subject is marked by contradictory impulses in the first place. More convincing is the explanation offered by Schilling, "Zur Dramatisierung des 'Wilhelm von Österreich,'" that Sachs's didactic ambition itself implies different aims and needs that may interfere with one another: the aim of conveying social norms and the project of giving a literary education to a broader public of city artisans, the intention to instruct, and the need to engage the attention and involvement of an audience. My argument is that ambivalence is already built into the concept of love as a drive that has the potential to constitute a powerful social bond as well as the risk of social disruption if not channeled into the correct social institution, i.e., marriage.

26. This danger is evoked either as a consequence of lovesickness or as caused by Marx's anger; *Werke,* 12:159, 7–9; 163, 33–34; 163, 15–18; 169, 35–170, 6; 170, 20–21; 172, 25; 173, 1–2; 175, 8–9; 176, 20; 179, 9–10; 180, 9–10; 180, 19–20.

27. Marx leaves the queen with her entertainer, and Tristrant calls after the king, "wie steht dir dein rock hindn so wol" (How well your frock becomes you from behind) (*Werke,* 12:178, 26). In this case, the indication of the glance ensures that the joke is properly understood.

28. On nature as a concept in the motivation of love, see Plate, "Verstehensprinzipien im Prosatristrant."

29. See Karl Heinz Zur Mühlen, "Die Affektenlehre im Spätmittelalter und in der Reformationszeit," *Archiv für Begriffsgeschichte* 35 (1992): 93–114.

30. The motif of thirst appears in the prose *Tristrant,* where it is caused by extended talking: "vnd lang stund vertreib in dem reden ward in ser dürsten" (and because of long hours spent talking they became very thirsty) (44, 1115). Cora Dietl, "'Höfische Minne' auf der Meistersängerbühne: Zur Dramatisierung höfischer Liebesromane durch Hans Sachs," in *The Court Reconvenes: Courtly Literature across the Disciplines; Selected Papers of the International Courtly Literature Society,* ed. Barbara K. Altmann and Carleton W. Caroll (Woodbridge: D. S. Brewer, 2003), 345–56, reads the potion scene as modeled on the Fall of Adam and Eve. She interprets the potion accordingly as "verbotene Köstlichkeit" (forbidden delight) (351) and leaves the motif of thirst aside.

31. Medieval theories of the affects draw on ancient Greek concepts of the soul. The status of affects in relation to reason is open to discussion, whereas hunger and thirst are understood as having no relation to reason at all. See the overview by Anja Kühne, *Vom Affekt zum Gefühl: Konvergenzen von Theorie und Literatur im Mittelalter am Beispiel von Konrads von Würzburg "Partonopier und Meliur,"* Göppinger Arbeiten zur Germanistik 713 (Göppingen: Kümmerle, 2004), 70, 73, 79, 84. In modern emotion theories, hunger and thirst are typically referred to as bodily states from which emotions differ in various ways. For example, Agnes Heller, *Theorie der Gefühle* (Hamburg: VSA-Verlag, 1980), draws a terminological line between hunger and thirst as "drives" (91–98) on the one hand and affects and emotions on the other.

32. On strategies of avoiding emotion ("Affektvermeidung"), see also Helmut Krause, *Die Dramen des Hans Sachs: Untersuchungen zur Lehre und Technik* (Berlin: Hofgarten, 1979), 147–52.

33. The classic reference for this is Marcus Fabius Quintilianus, *Institutio Orationis,* in *Ausbildung des Redners,* ed. and trans. Helmut Rahn, vol. 1 (Darmstadt: Wissenschaftliche Buchgesellschaft, 1995), VI, 26–36.

34. Erika Fischer-Lichte, *Ästhetik des Performativen,* Edition Suhrkamp 2373 (Frankfurt am Main: Suhrkamp, 2004), 58–126.

35. See Könneker, *Hans Sachs,* 58–60.

CHAPTER SEVEN

Time, Space, and Mind

Tristan in Three Dimensions in Fourteenth-Century France

AMANDA LUYSTER

In the Lancelot-Grail cycle, Lancelot, imprisoned, paints the tale of his illicit love for Queen Guinevere on the walls of his prison.[1] King Arthur later discovers these paintings, as is depicted in a fifteenth-century manuscript (fig. 7.1). Although Arthur has not been convinced by court gossip of the infidelity of his queen, he is convinced by the seeming reality of these images. For King Arthur it is as if he has come across the actual adulterous couple. The images act as if they were reality; upon seeing them, he is shocked and heartbroken. Unlike speech, the image here has the power and presence of reality. The power of the image to evoke reality has also been explored by scholars such as David Freedberg, who suggests that the differences between represented reality and reality are not so great as they have been made to seem.[2] Recent neuroscience confirms this hypothesis: many of the same neurons fire whether a subject is engaged in a particular activity or watching an image of someone else engaged in that activity.[3] Viewers can—in some ways, at least—experience the image, that is, represented reality, as if it is reality.

The Arthurian wall paintings at the château of Saint-Floret in Auvergne (ca. 1350–60) also re-create time and space and a full-body experience, an experience like that of reality. By means of the cycle's

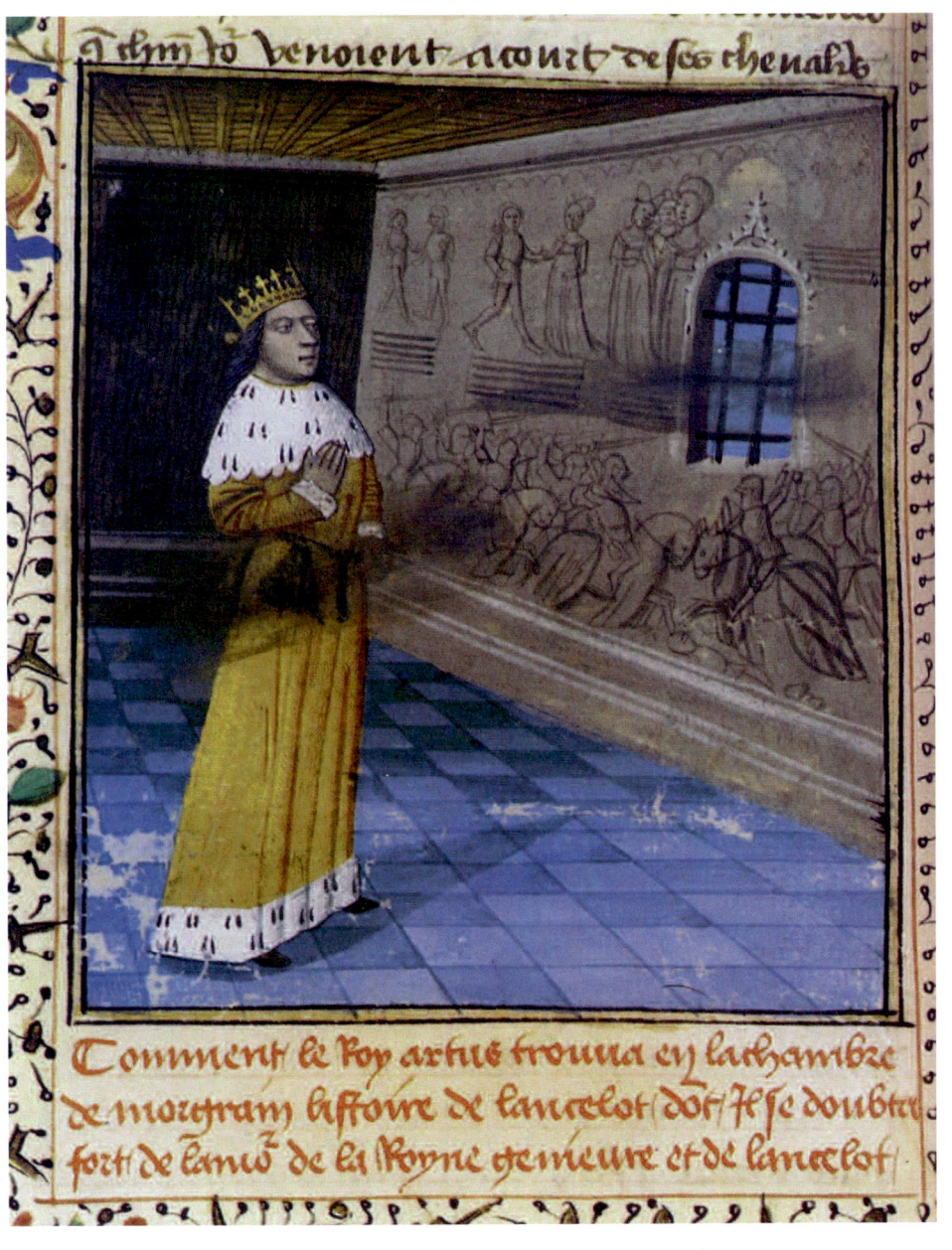

Figure 7.1. Arthur views paintings revealing Lancelot's love for Guinevere.
ca. 1470. Paris, Bibliothèque Nationale, Ms. Fr. 112, vol. III, fol. 193v.
Image courtesy of Bibliothèque Nationale de France.

(visual) painted appearance and (material) existence within an architectural space, the world at Saint-Floret appears as if it had three dimensions, height and depth and breadth. More metaphorically, the world at Saint-Floret seems to exist within time, space, and mind. By this I mean that the created world at Saint-Floret is granted space, in which motion occurs, and time, in which action occurs, and yet all this motion and action and spatial landscape is finally brought to life only in the mind of the beholder. It is by means of the material of paint and stone that the visual effect is achieved; it is by means of the visual that this apparently material world is brought into existence in the mind of the beholder. The unusual complexity and focus on re-creating movement through time and space at Saint-Floret should be related to religious wall paintings of the fourteenth century. After 1300, as Hans Belting and others have noted, religious painting becomes increasingly narrative and places more emphasis on depicting emotion and physical sensation.[4] Unusually, at Saint-Floret the focus on the re-creation of actual lived experience is transferred to the secular realm. The comparison to religious cycles is particularly apt for the Saint-Floret paintings because they exhibit many formal similarities to religious paintings at Avignon.[5] Saint-Floret's designer and artists probably had experience in Avignon; certainly its patron did.

The murals at Saint-Floret provide the most extensive depiction of romance in surviving medieval French wall painting. Life-size images of jousts and lovers' meetings cover the walls of the château's large hall, depicting the romance of Tristan and Yseut as retold in the *Meliadus* of Rusticien de Pise (written ca. 1271). These images are also accompanied by substantial extracts of painted text, which is rare in secular imagery (figs. 7.2–7.10). Little scholarship has been dedicated to these images, and that which exists is largely devoted to identifying the text that the images depict.[6] Yet this cycle contains much more sophisticated play that deserves recognition. I examine the visual rhetoric of the cycle, first articulating its unique spatial narrative and then identifying the narrative traditions to which its structure relates.

The cycle is primarily based on the *Meliadus* of Rusticien de Pise (or Rusticiano da Pisa, as he was an Italian writing in French), a compilation containing episodes from the French prose *Tristan* and the

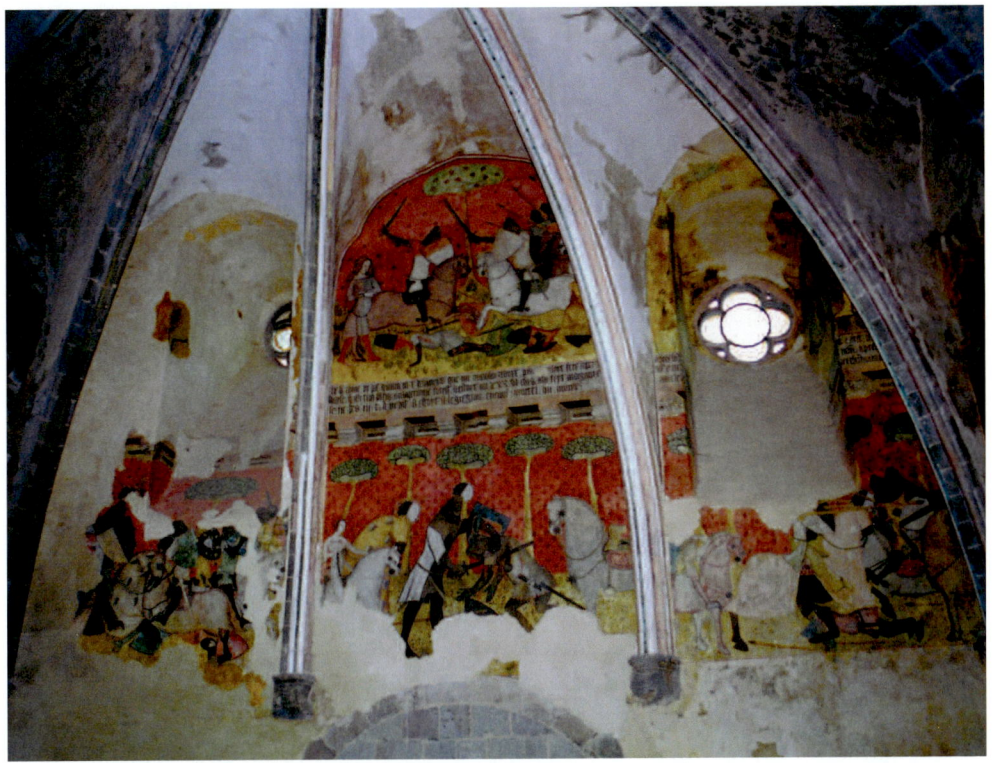

Figure 7.2. North wall. Hall, Château of Saint-Floret (Auvergne), France. Paintings ca. 1350–60. Photo by the author.

prose *Palamedes* as well as other accounts.[7] Rusticien's *Meliadus* was a relatively obscure text, compared at least to the prose *Tristan,* with only ten known copies surviving, six of which date from the fourteenth century (the prose *Tristan* survives in some eighty manuscripts).[8] Saint-Floret's images do not relate closely to the illustration program of any manuscript of Rusticien's text, with, at greatest, only approximately 25 percent overlap with any manuscript's illustrations.[9] There is also one image at Saint-Floret that is not included in any extant text of the *Meliadus*: a representation of the orchard scene or the tryst under the tree (figs. 7.3, 7.4). This is the most frequently represented single image of Tristan and Yseut, partly because it manages to suggest the

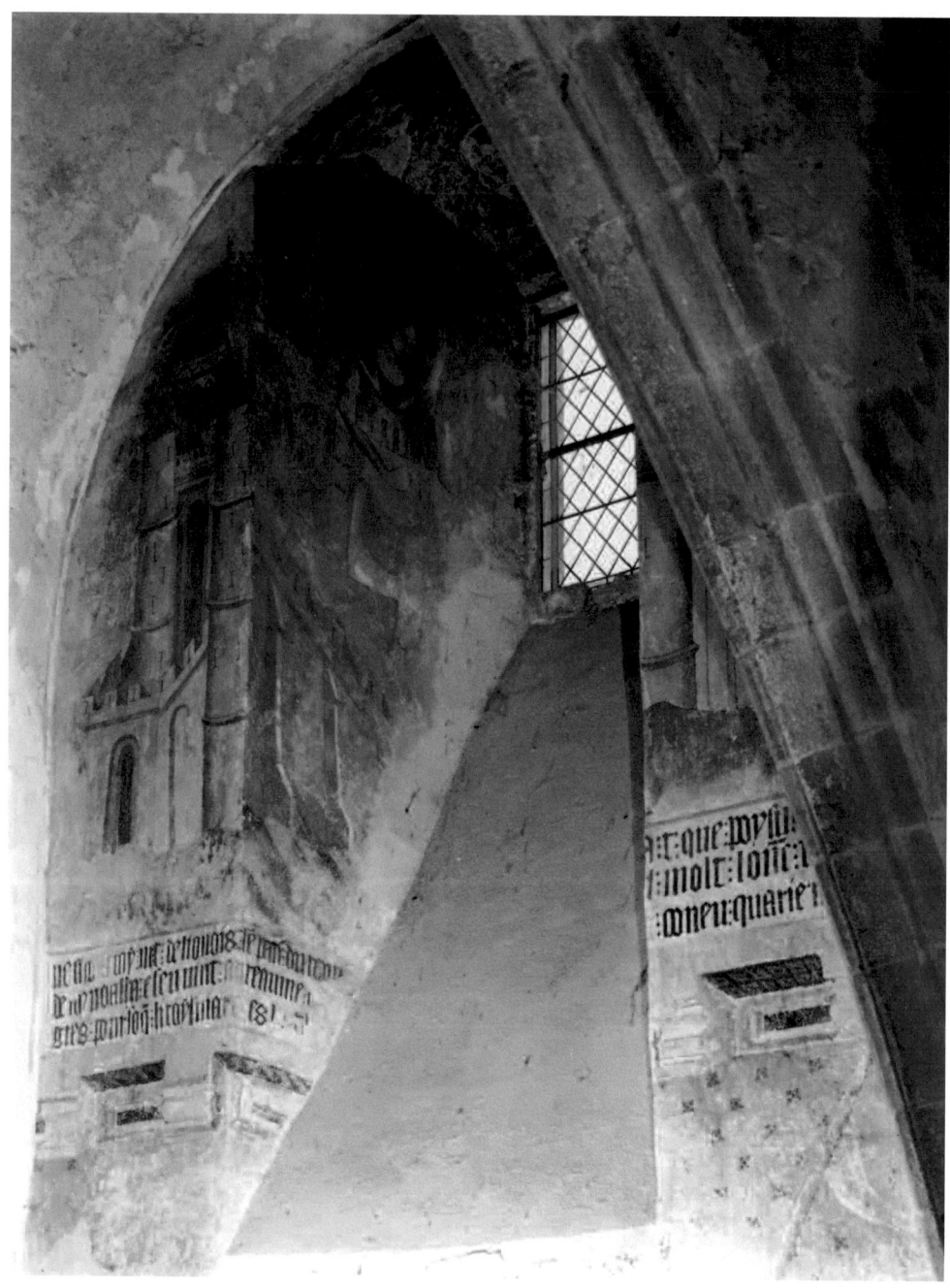

Figure 7.3. Tryst under the Tree; Tristan (left). South wall. Hall, Château of Saint-Floret (Auvergne), France. Paintings ca. 1350–60. Image courtesy of Service regional de l'Inventaire/ADAGP. Cliché Rober Choplain, Roland Maston.

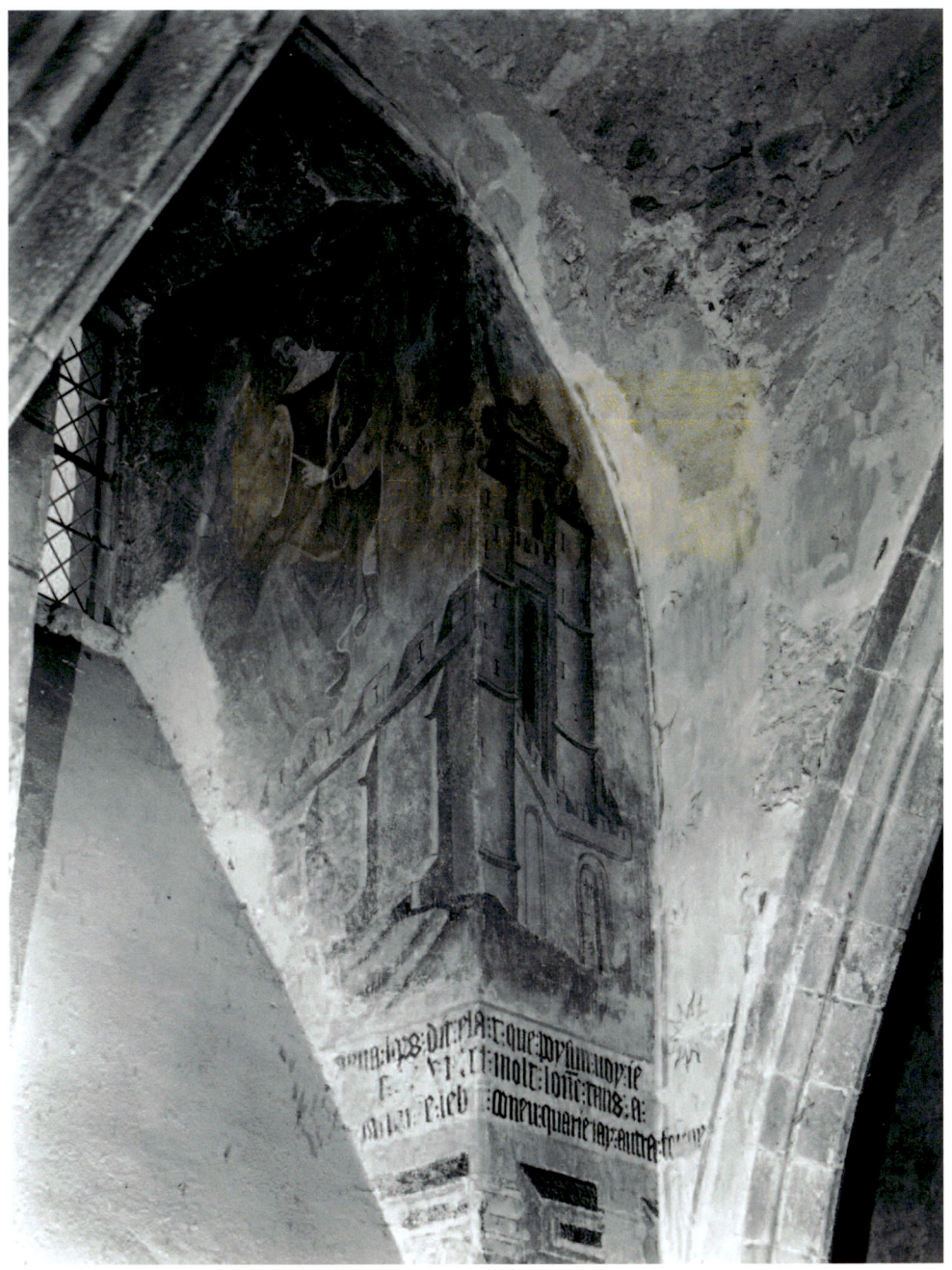

Figure 7.4. Tryst under the Tree; Yseut (right). South wall. Hall, Château of Saint-Floret (Auvergne), France. Paintings ca. 1350–60. Image courtesy of Service regional de l'Inventaire/ADAGP. Cliché Rober Choplain, Roland Maston.

complicated triangular relationship between the lovers and the cuckolded husband.[10] The scene depicts an assignation in the orchard between Tristan and Yseut, who, alerted to Mark's presence (hidden in
the tree above) when they catch sight of his head reflected in a pool of
water, conduct a conversation intended to suggest their innocence.
The tryst is not included in any extant version of Rusticien's *Meliadus*
but is included in the prose *Tristan* as well as many other textual and
visual iterations of the tale. This painted window embrasure displays
Tristan at the left side, Yseut to the right, and King Mark, hiding
in the tree, above. The designer of the cycle was careful to provide
a logical connection between the orchard scene and the *Meliadus*'s narrative by means of an inscription that uses the orchard scene as a jus-
tification for Tristan's departure into the forest of Logres, the next
scene in the *Meliadus*.[11]

In the orchard scene at Saint-Floret, an inscription also mentions a
"fish" to direct Tristan's attention to Mark's reflection in the water:
"'Tristan, what fish do I see? I have not seen such for a very long time';
'Lady, I recognized it well, for I have seen it before.'" The motif of the
fish is found earlier and more frequently in visual media, suggesting
that the cycle's designer may have been familiar with both the tryst and
the fish motif from their circulation in oral or visual media.[12] The designer, then, seems to have been familiar not only with the *Meliadus* but
also with other Tristan material. Indeed, the images of the tryst and
other scenes relating to the French prose tradition would probably also
have been recognizable at least to a certain portion of the population.
The *Meliadus*'s story of the aged knight Branor, however, which is an
important part of the cycle at Saint-Floret (fig. 7.5), is not part of the
prose *Tristan* and hence is much less common. The images of Branor
and his adventures at Saint-Floret would have been recognized as unusual. Therefore the ensemble at Saint-Floret could have been recognized as, in part, a rehearsal of a well-known story, that of the prose
Tristan, but with an unusual and probably not well-known beginning.

The images painted on the walls at Saint-Floret are framed but are
not always flat, as on the page. The picture surface may wrap around
corners and into window embrasures, suggesting a plasticity of form
and thickness of space that are not entirely alien to those the viewer's
body also occupies. The format and placement of the images allows the

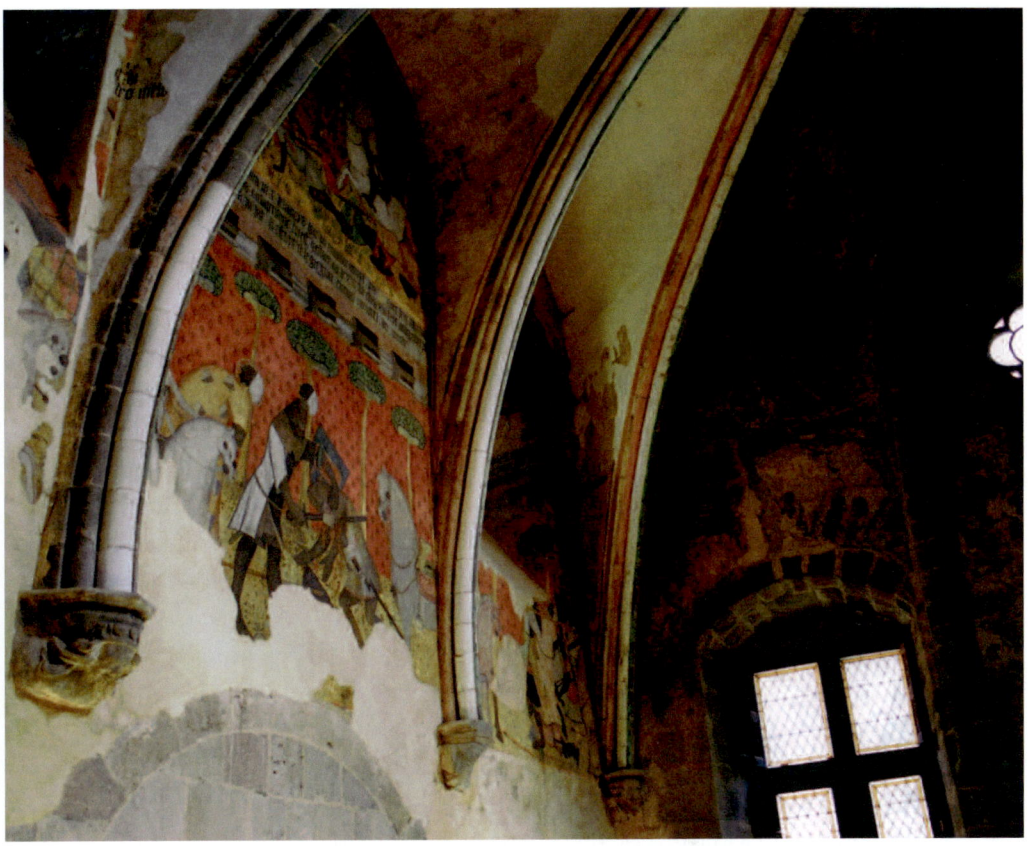

Figure 7.5. Branor slays Caracados. North wall. Hall, Château of Saint-Floret (Auvergne), France. Paintings ca. 1350–60. Photo by the author.

viewer's journey around the room, stopping at each wall, to mimic the journey of Tristan and his comrades through the châteaux and forests of legend. The viewer must move through space and must take time to view the cycle. That experience that the viewer has, moving through time, makes it easy to attribute movement and change to the figures that the viewer serially examines, as illustrated in figure 7.11. This process heightens the realism of the representation, since the narrative occupies a span of the viewer's time ("real" time) and is discovered through the viewer's movements in "real" space. It also increases the viewer's sense of involvement in the narrative world.[13]

The painted text included at Saint-Floret also allows the eruption of the characters and events into speech, and viewers can use that text as a jumping-off point to show off their knowledge of the Arthurian world and their own skills in rendering narrative. However, the text also helps to articulate the cycle's presentation of time and space. The interaction of text and image is the focus of the remainder of this chapter.

As Herbert Kessler neatly summarizes, "accompanying texts anchored pictures, verified and explained them; while pictures served words in much the same fashion, validating them through the special authority attached to sight, and revealing their significance."[14] Texts help to define and explain pictures, while pictures validate texts and make them comprehensible (imaginable). Kessler is primarily concerned with religious images, and he emphasizes the role pictures play in interpreting texts, providing a visual exegesis for written accounts. The inscriptions at Saint-Floret also serve to anchor and explain the images they accompany, just as the pictures clarify and validate the text that accompanies them. There is also, however, a certain amount of slippage at Saint-Floret between what is represented pictorially and what the accompanying text suggests.

Sometimes the texts explicitly state that they show a series of events ("This is how . . . "), but only one of those events is depicted. These texts mark out a span of time within which the moment of the image takes place. The text still explains the image, and the image makes the text concrete, but the overlap between the two is not exact. Therefore the relation is not one-to-one, whereby the text and image move in lockstep, but the mismatch generates a creative dissonance, a generative difference. Text and image rub against each other, they open up spaces in between, and another dimension is born (from the tiny holes, the new dimension emerges and slowly expands). From the friction, from the slippage, a new *space* of narrative is born, neither linear like text nor two-dimensional like a flat picture, but looming large in three dimensions.[15] This spatial image is richer and more compelling, less rigid, than either text or picture alone, and it quivers with the movement of life.

An example will clarify my meaning. The rightmost south wall shows two sides of a single embrasure (fig. 7.6). The inscription reading,

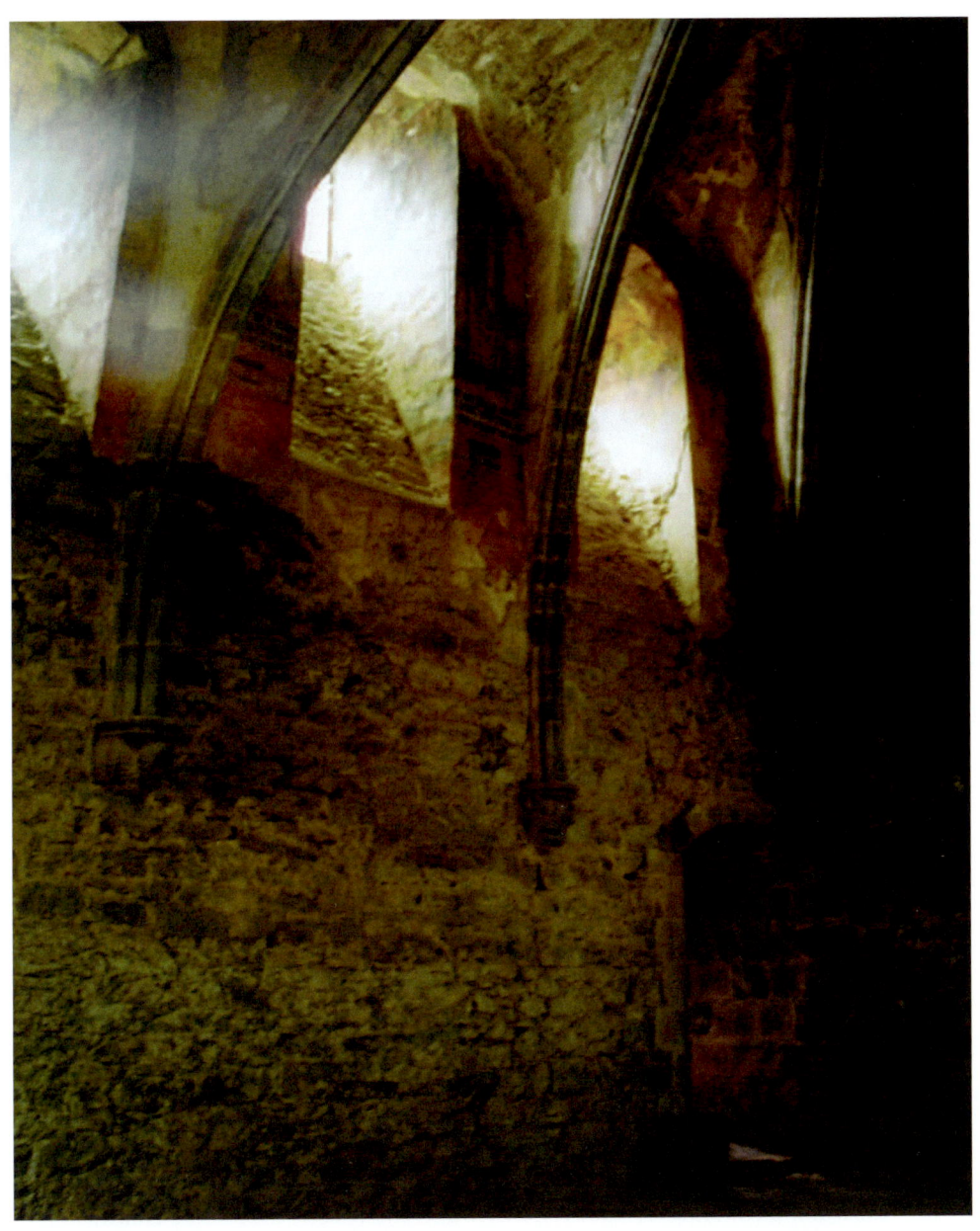

Figure 7.6. Palamedes visible in rightmost embrasure. South wall. Hall, Château of Saint-Floret (Auvergne), France. Paintings ca. 1350–60. Photo by the author.

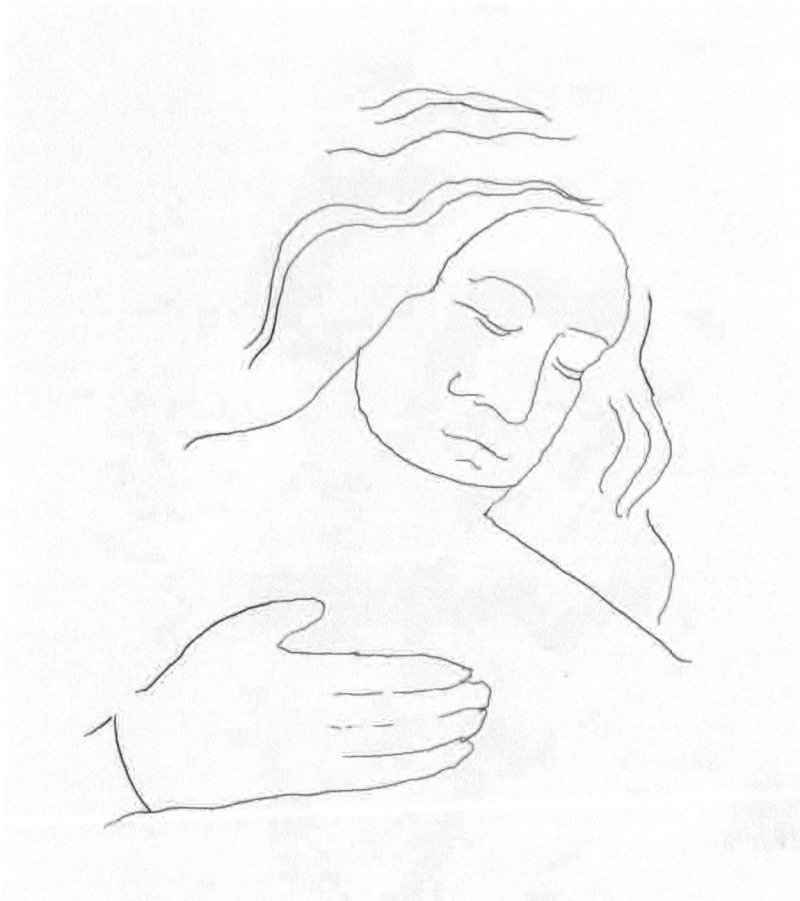

Figure 7.7. Line drawing by author of a detail of Tristan sleeping. South wall. Hall, Château of Saint-Floret (Auvergne), France. Paintings ca. 1350–60.

"This is how Sir Tristan rode through the realm of Logres seeking adventure, and came [toward nightfall] . . . ," is located under an image of Tristan sleeping (fig. 7.7). The image above the inscription does *not* show how Tristan rode through the forest, despite its claim. It shows what happened after Tristan rode through the forest. The inscription on the other side of the embrasure (fig. 7.8) describes Tristan falling asleep and then the arrival of Tristan's enemy, Palamedes.

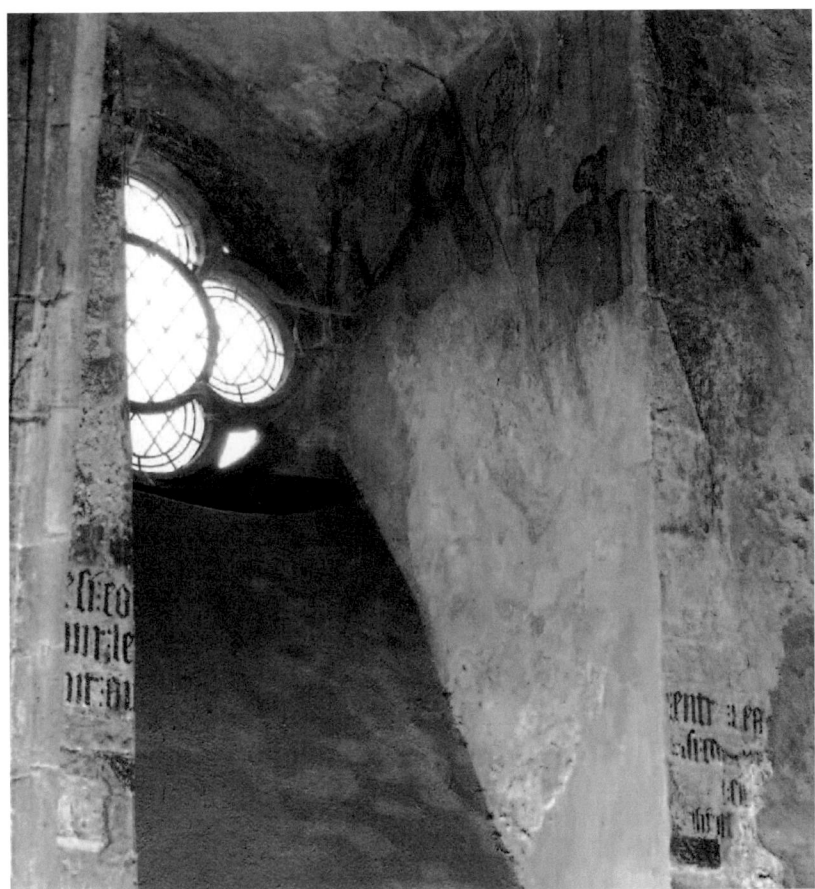

Figure 7.8. Detail of Palamedes wakeful. South wall. Hall, Château of Saint-Floret (Auvergne), France. Paintings ca. 1350–60. Image courtesy of Service regional de l'Inventaire/ADAGP. Cliché Rober Choplain, Roland Maston.

Palamedes comes along later to the same spot, after Tristan has already fallen asleep: "Here he lay down in the forest between fair trees and slept on his shield and it happened by chance . . . [his] mortal enemy lay down and lamented." Palamedes remains wakeful, as is apparent from his open eyes. Neither sees the other until daylight.

The inscriptions together tell a narrative that continues through time, including the following events: Tristan riding through the forest,

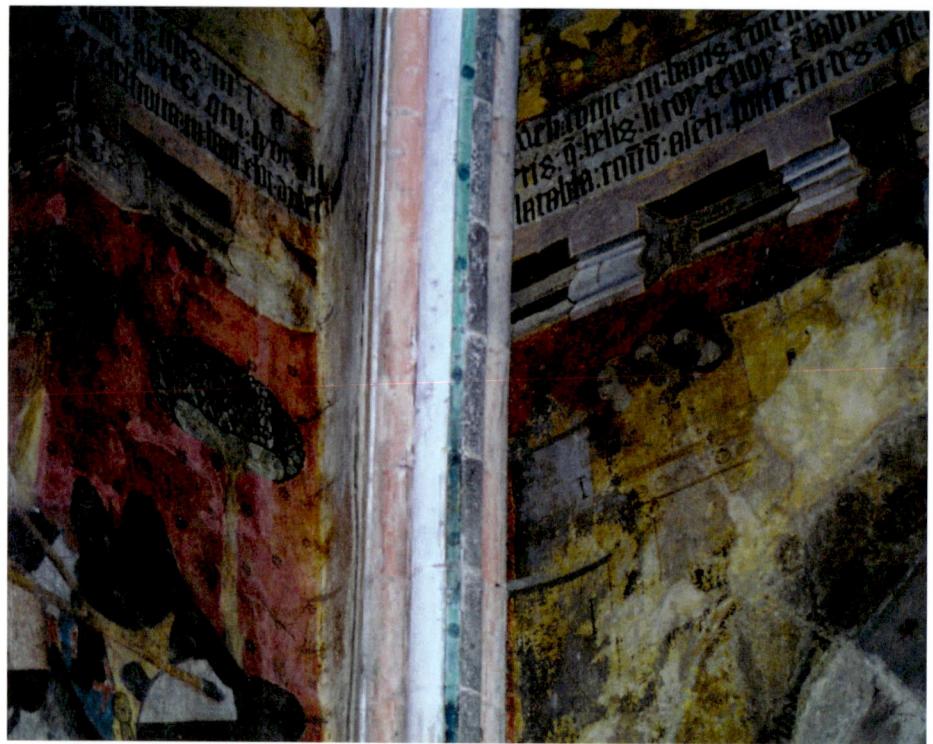

Figure 7.9. Branor delivers captive knight. Guinevere and ladies receive message. Northeast corner. Hall, Château of Saint-Floret (Auvergne), France. Paintings ca. 1350–60. Photo by the author.

Tristan falling asleep on his shield, Palamedes arriving, Palamedes lying down but unable to sleep, lamenting. The images do not show all those events, despite the insistence of the inscriptions, "this is how" (voici come). The images show only two events: Tristan sleeping and Palamedes remaining wakeful. Yet the combination of inscription and image come together to generate a remarkable illusion of time and space. For through the union of both the viewer has been made aware of the passage of time in a particular space — that here, in this spot in the forest, Tristan arrived and dismounted and fell asleep, and also, at this adjacent spot in the forest, Palamedes too arrived and dismounted and then lay awake.

The effectiveness of this composition becomes clearer after considering the choice that the designer did not make. Let us imagine that the designer had in fact selected an image of Tristan riding for the left side and an image of Palamedes lying awake on the right. The image on the left would then be definitively before the image on the right. This option was not selected, and I suggest it is because the designer wanted to present the embrasure as unified in space and time, as in the tryst. The depiction of two different moments, even if taking place at the same location, would have broken the organic wholeness of the space of the embrasure. The image of Tristan sleeping, by contrast, functions to unite the space because it is an ambiguous image, one that could refer to the moment of Tristan's falling asleep or the continuous sleeping of Tristan while Palamedes arrived. Tristan fell asleep, and then he remained sleeping, all the while that the inscription tells us that Palamedes arrived and lay down and started his lamenting.

The choice to depict an ambiguous moment, which then appears to reflect two or three separate moments (when Tristan fell asleep and his being asleep later, when Palamedes arrives and lies wakeful), means that the pictorial space remains unified while the accompanying texts refer to a longer stretch of narrative time during which other things happened. The passage of time within this space, then, is suggested both by the verbal recapitulation in the inscriptions and by the careful selection of imagery that implies more than one moment in time. The image of Tristan sleeping gains a surprising realism: it appears to endure in time, as if Tristan slept on and on, all through the night.

Not only does the viewer see the two men resting, but he or she has also been made aware of Tristan's earlier ride across the forest and Palamedes's more recent arrival. Though neither of the latter two events is pictured, their visual presence is alluded to by means of the placement of the inscriptions and the dual system of text and image. The inscriptions run through time, whereas the images mark out a certain space within that time. A certain depicted space can then be marked by other events that happened earlier or later in the same place. The illusion of both space and time passing within that location has been created.

Another example will amplify my meaning. A speech scroll painted on the east wall reads, "Sir King, the knight who overthrew so many of your [knights] the day of Pentecost . . ." This event at Pentecost is no longer conserved at Saint-Floret, although the speech scroll refers to the knight Branor, who is present in repeated images on the lower register (fig. 7.5). The speech scroll derives from a messenger (now fragmentary) who was sent by Branor to the court. While the messenger is speaking, however, Queen Guinevere and her ladies do not appear attentive (fig. 7.9); their interest has been drawn elsewhere. The direction of their gaze suggests that the ladies, while hearing of the deeds of Branor, are watching those same deeds take place on the adjacent wall. Guinevere was not present at those events, but it seems that as she listens to and imagines them, she "sees" Branor's past victories. The well-known lines from Richard de Fournival's late-thirteenth-century *Bestiaire d'Amour* explain what is happening:

> For when one sees an illustrated story *(histoire painte),* whether about Troy or something else, one sees the actions of brave men which were in the past as if they were present. The same thing with words. For when one reads a story *(romans),* one listens to the adventures as if one saw them happening in the present.[16]

Guinevere, listening to the messenger's recitation of Branor's actions, which were in the past, sees them "as if they were present." This is represented in her rapt gaze toward the scenes on the north wall. The viewer at Saint-Floret, in turn, who "reads the story," also "listens" to the adventures as narrated in the texts and "sees" its events in the present. The images, inscriptions, and speech scroll at Saint-Floret can also be seen as speaking and staging the represented events.[17]

For the viewer, the movement of body and gaze from the north wall to the east brings an irrevocable shift in narrative time. The viewer first saw Branor's battles (on the north wall) as they occurred, in the present moment; now the viewer, after reading the speech scroll (on the east wall), has been swept along with the narrative and can only see Branor's deeds as having already occurred, as now being evoked as the past—although "seen" as if in the present—from a new present, that at the court at Camelot.

Other inscriptions establish temporal or causal connections between depicted scenes. One of the inscriptions below the tryst, "This is why Sir Tristan of Lionois departed from the realm of Cornwall and came to the realm of Logres, because King Mark . . . ," links the tryst with the image of Tristan in the forest of Logres that follows. Another inscription, located beneath a single image on the north wall (see figs. 7.2, 7.10), makes reference to a series of other events, some of which are depicted elsewhere. Thereby it links a set of separate images into a single narrative and uses causality to drive the narrative.

> This is how Sir Palamedes delivered Sir Tristan of Lionois, whom a vavasour held as prisoner and wished to have his head cut off, because he had slain his son in the Perilous Forest, who was one of twenty-six knights of Morgain la Fey; and because of this Sir Tristan made peace with Sir Palamedes; yet he was his greatest mortal enemy in the world.

The image only shows Palamedes rescuing Tristan from a party of mounted knights; Morgan la Fey and the vavasour's son are not present. The function of the inscription is that it links the image to others that narratively precede and follow it. The embrasure to the left (see fig. 7.2) depicts Tristan's adventures in the Perilous Forest, presumably having to do with the son, who was a knight of Morgan la Fey (the Perilous Forest and "la Fey" are mentioned in the inscription there); that to the right continues Tristan's adventures with Palamedes. The depicted rescue unites the two knights in friendship, and later they are shown together in the mounted battle against Galahad.

If these images appeared without inscriptions, they might seem to present only a series of disparate instants. The designer uses the text, however, to link the scenes into a single program. The inscriptions, inspired by but quite different from the text of the *Meliadus,* often explicitly link one scene to the one that follows or precedes it, either by using chronological connectors, like "after . . . ," or causal ones, like "because . . . " The connectors also bring to mind other events before and after that may or may not be explicitly included in the program. In the interaction between the images and inscriptions, a narrative thread is woven, and a narrative universe is born.

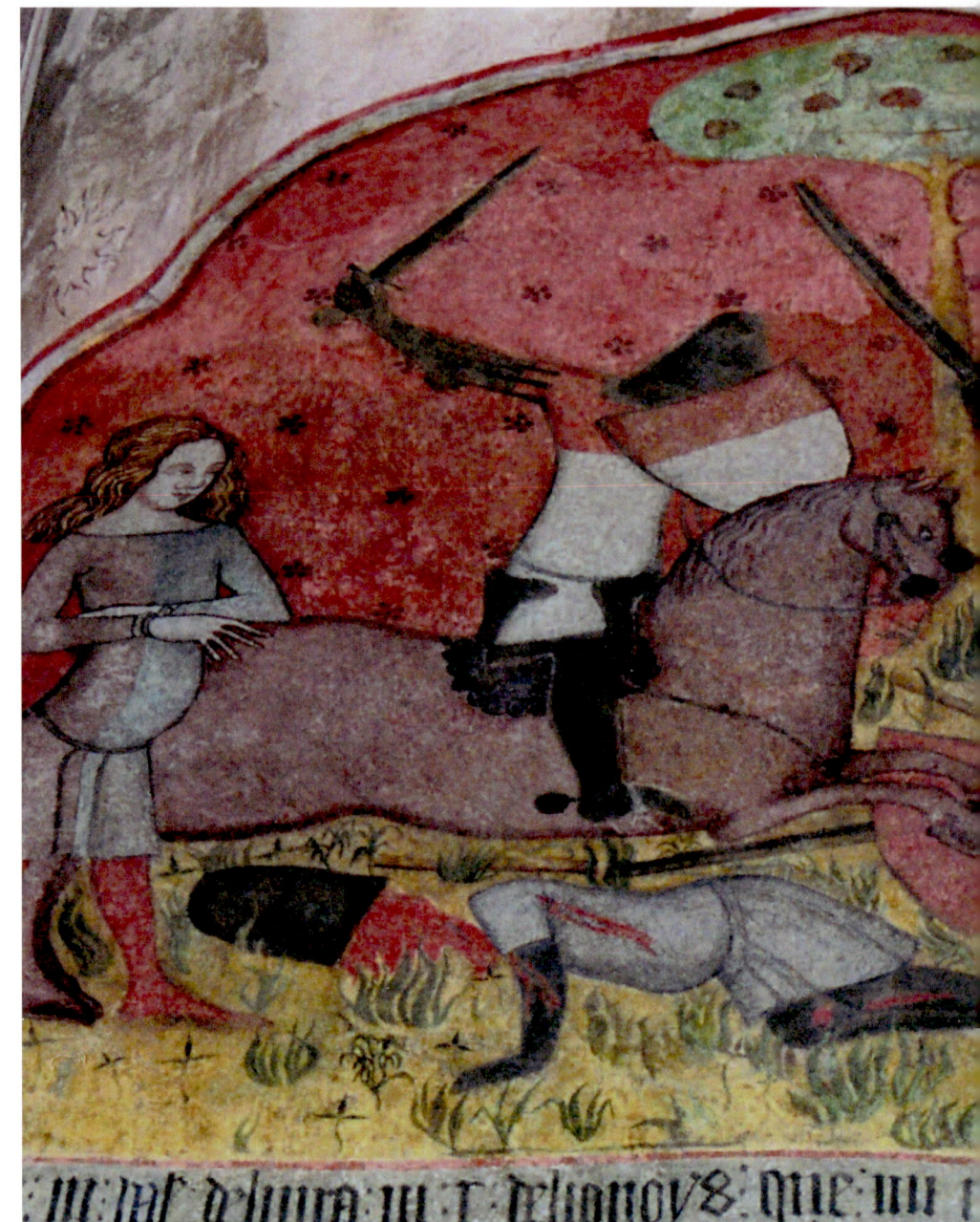

: iii· pat· dclittra· iii· t· dchonoys· que· iiii· c
tua· lõñs· anlacailhuc· foreſt· ą·eſtop
iii· t· ā·iii·pat· ſi·eſtopt· il· legicgu

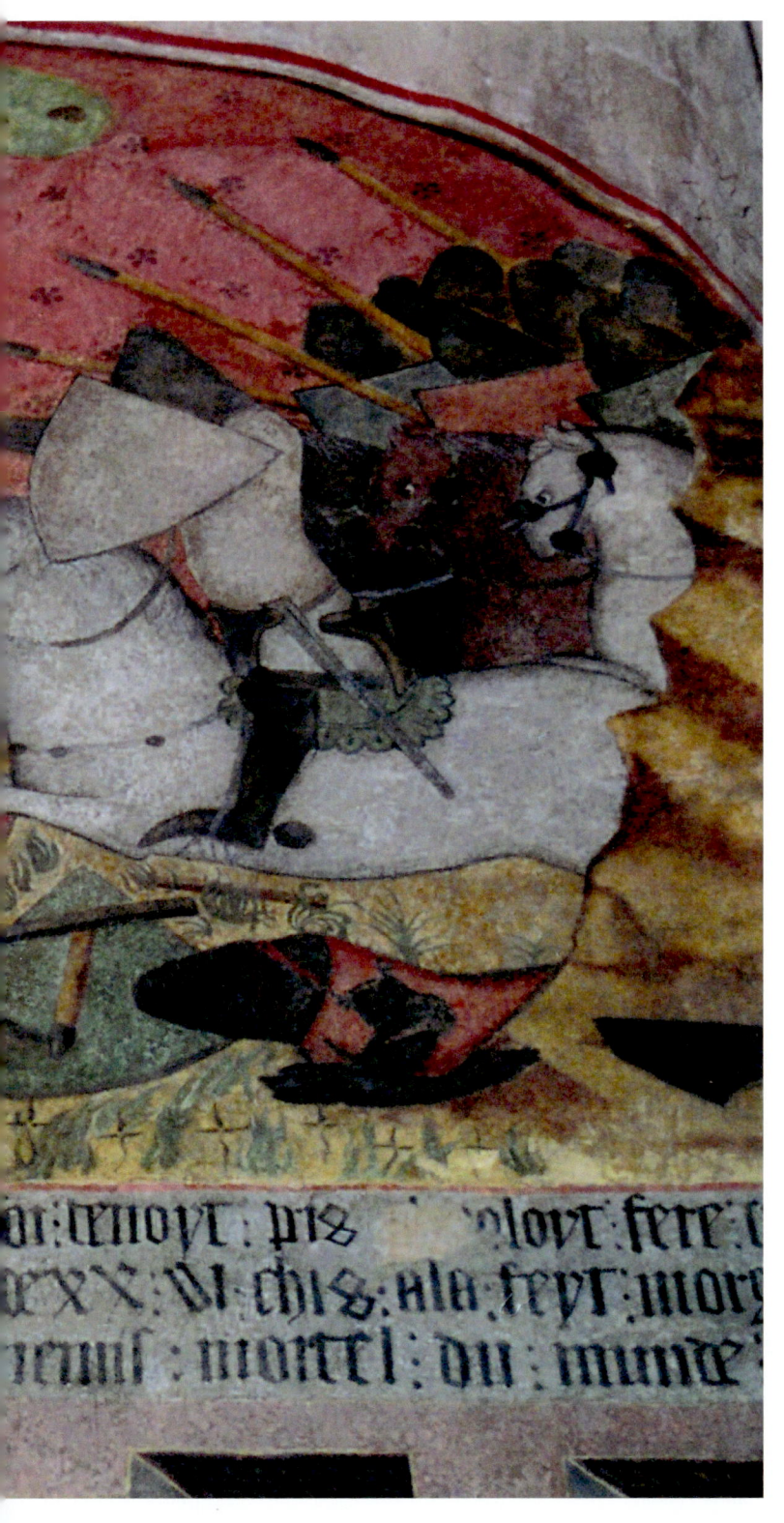

Figure 7.10.
Rescue of Tristan
by Palamedes.
North wall. Hall,
Château of Saint-
Floret (Auvergne),
France. Paintings
ca. 1350–60. Photo
by the author.

Not only time and space, joined into narrative, but also movement is re-created in these images. As one moves to the right to examine the image after the tryst, one imagines that Tristan, too, rode toward the right, from the tryst (in the center of the south wall) to the forest of Logres (on the right side of the south wall), where he sleeps (figs. 7.6, 7.7). Tristan's motion toward the right, just like Branor's on the lower register, accompanies and strengthens the sense of narrative motion, of movement through time accompanying movement through space. Figures who are less important to the story line, like Branor's opponents, may move leftward without disrupting the general flow. Palamedes, too, when he is first introduced into the narrative, arrives moving leftward (he has apparently come in from the right side), before he settles down in the forest to sleep. When he next appears, in the scene of Tristan's rescue, however, both he and Tristan are moving with the narrative flow to the right. The overall left to right motion of the program, then, is also carried through in each individual image, where the character in focus literally carries the narrative from his entrance on the left side of the image toward the right. The direction of flow from left to right should be seen in relation to the influential manuscript tradition, in which text and images also move in the same left-right direction.

Unlike manuscripts, however, at Saint-Floret there may also be some sense of moving place as the narrative flows around the walls. Elizabeth Rodini's work in narrative at San Marco suggests that those who designed and viewed medieval cycles could have a keen sense of space; her analysis shows how a mosaic cycle at San Marco has been laid out in the reverse direction of usual reading: instead of left to right, it reads right to left.[18] This program shows the journey of the saint's body from the east to the west as if drawn on a map. Such a cycle shows how important a sense of place may be in structuring medieval pictorial programs. This emphasis on the role of location to structure narrative was not limited to this piece; its roots went much further back. Jocelyn Penny Small's examination of narrative in classical art suggests the determinative role of place in some Greek visual production: figures and events could be laid out not in the temporal order with which modern viewers are familiar but instead according to the place in which they occurred.[19]

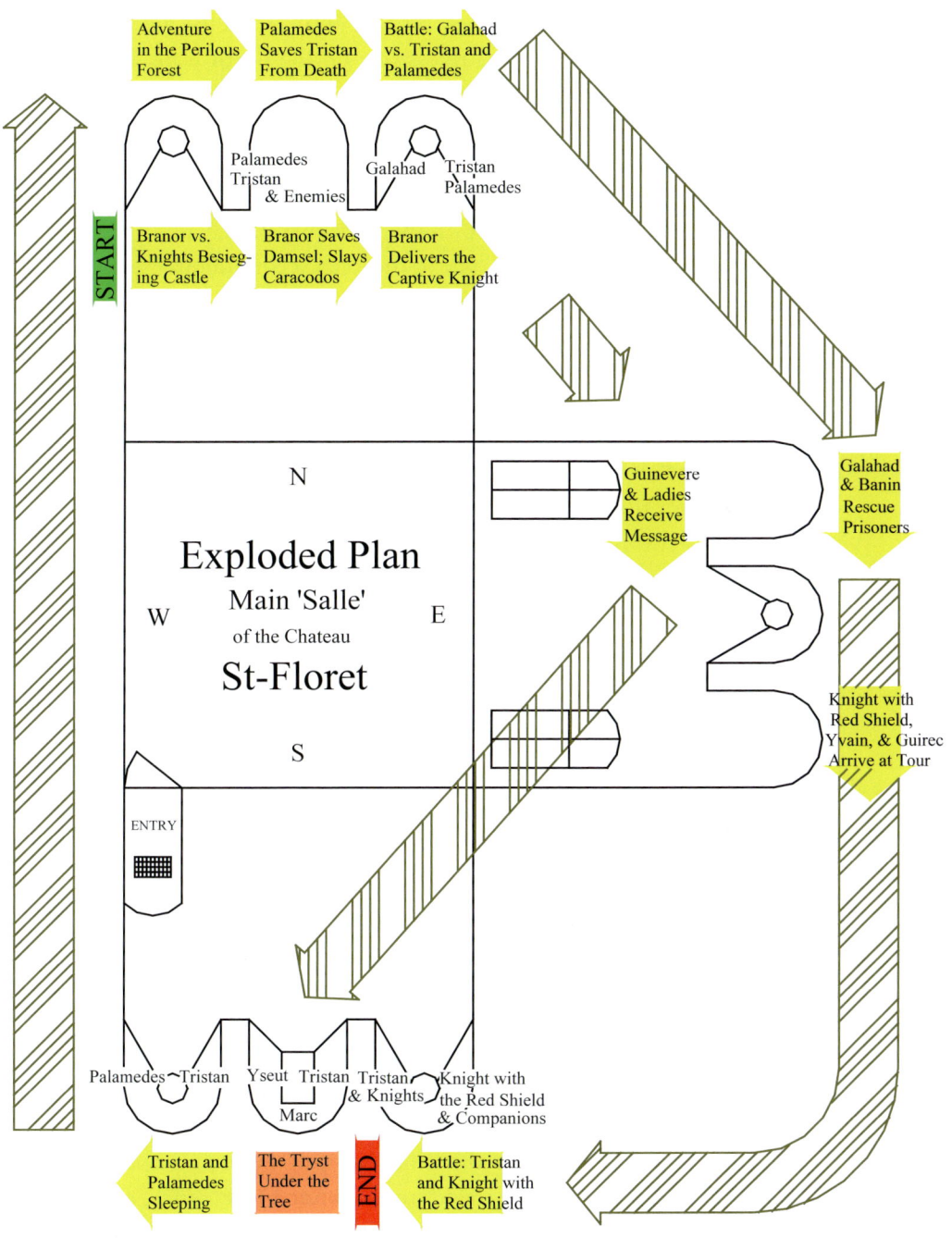

Adventure in the Perilous Forest

Palamedes Saves Tristan From Death

Battle: Galahad vs. Tristan and Palamedes

Palamedes Tristan & Enemies

Galahad

Tristan Palamedes

START

Branor vs. Knights Besieging Castle

Branor Saves Damsel; Slays Caracodos

Branor Delivers the Captive Knight

N

Guinevere & Ladies Receive Message

Galahad & Banin Rescue Prisoners

Exploded Plan

Main 'Salle'

of the Chateau

St-Floret

W

E

S

ENTRY

Knight with Red Shield, Yvain, & Guirec Arrive at Tour

Palamedes Tristan

Yseut Tristan

Marc

Tristan & Knights

Knight with the Red Shield & Companions

Tristan and Palamedes Sleeping

The Tryst Under the Tree

END

Battle: Tristan and Knight with the Red Shield

Figure 7.11. Plan of the wall paintings at Saint-Floret. By the author.

At Saint-Floret, a grouping of events that occurred in the wilderness (Branor's deeds) are shown successively on the north wall. The change in the location of the narrative, from the wilderness to Arthur's court, accompanies a shift to a different wall. Moreover, that new wall also seems to consistently represent a single place: the towers painted at both ends of the east wall suggest that its entire lower register is unified in representing Arthur's court. In the narrative stretch along the lower north to the lower east wall, one of the longest continuous extant stretches of painting, some care has been taken to map the shift from one place to another to the transition from one wall to another. Not all of the registers were treated as geographic units, since the tryst, which takes place at King Mark's castle, is located in a different place than the events that take place to either side. But at least in some circumstances, the narrative at Saint-Floret suggests not only a journey through time but also a journey through different locales, some of which are visually associated with distinct segments of the room's architecture.

The viewer's journey around the room, stopping at each wall, mimics the journey of Branor, Tristan, and Palamedes through the châteaux and forests of legend, like a secular pilgrimage. The viewer must move through space and must take time to view the cycle; that experience makes it easy to attribute movement and change to the figures that the viewer serially examines. The images' size and existence in three-dimensional space, through which the viewer travels, makes the viewer's experience of the fictional universe not unlike his or her experience of the real.

Such a highly physical, enacted rendering of a secular narrative is distinctly unusual. However, it is somewhat more usual in religious cycles, particularly those of the later Middle Ages. Medieval images of religious narrative apparently possessed great powers to involve the viewer physically in the scenes presented. Such images appealed to the senses of touch and taste: the faithful were asked, for example, to imagine themselves present at the narrative of the Crucifixion, watching the nails being hammered through Christ's flesh and the sponge soaked in vinegar held to his cracked lips.[20] Such a comparison to religious painting is not irrelevant to Saint-Floret since, as I have argued elsewhere, both the designer and that artist likely had experience with the religious paintings in Avignon, the fourteenth-century papal capital.[21]

The complexity of the Saint-Floret image cycle and, in particular, its extensive use of text, had presented a certain mystery. How and why was such a high-quality, sophisticated production commissioned and completed in a location that had no known links to artistic centers? Documents at the Paris National Archives suggest that part of the reason lies in the close social links between the family that owned the château and a family that, although deriving from close by, had recently come into power in the papal capital of Avignon. The lord of Saint-Floret, the patron of the image cycle, had long been in the service of the la Tour family of Auvergne.[22] That family had, since the early fourteenth century, been among the most important in Avignon. The la Tour family provided numerous cardinals as well as a bride, in 1353, for the family of Pope Clement VI. I have found that this marriage was one that the lord of Saint-Floret attended in Avignon.[23]

In addition to this historical link between Saint-Floret and Avignon, striking formal parallels exist between these secular images and two cycles of religious wall paintings in the papal palace of Avignon (fig. 7.12). The chapels of Saint Martial and Saint John in Avignon (ca. 1344–46 and ca. 1346–48), which depict saints' lives, were commissioned by Pope Clement VI. Although these two cycles have been much discussed, no substantive connection to secular images has been previously proposed.[24] All three mural cycles, which include figural images and painted words, bear many similarities in their use of text and image to create a physical and emotional experience. In all three cases, life-size images occupy multiple registers and extend into window embrasures, creating the illusion of a three-dimensional architectural setting. Moreover, both at Saint-Floret and in Avignon, figures who are intended to be understood as behind other figures are painted around the corner of a wall, suggesting that walls are not flat surfaces but rather windows behind which a three-dimensional space is suggested. Other similarities in figure style and the use of false architectural motifs also exist, but this is not the place for a close stylistic comparison. Yet, in sum, these similarly complex wall paintings also convey the dimensions of time and space to a viewer who, in walking and

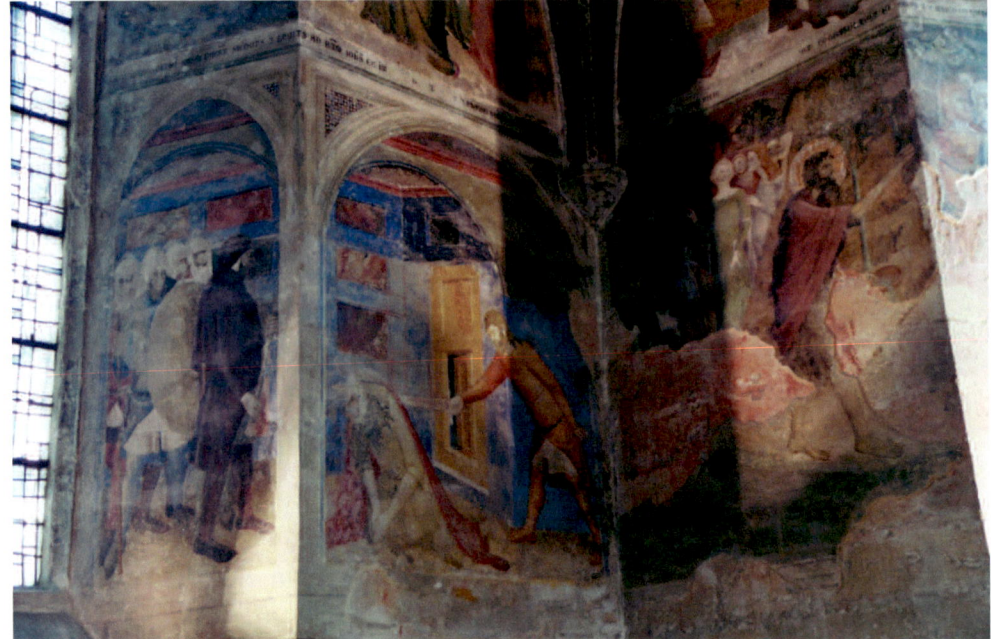

Figure 7.12. Chapel of St. John (or du Consistoire), papal palace, Avignon. Matteo Giovanetti, 1346–48. Photo by the author.

changing position to take in each individual scene, experiences the time and space of the story from the vantage point of his or her own body.

In conclusion, the Saint-Floret murals stand as a rare surviving instance of a high-quality and intellectually sophisticated secular production, commissioned and executed at a small and heretofore practically unnoticed site. The murals represent space in which time passes, such as the forest in which Tristan sleeps and Palamedes arrives, and space that is identified with certain locales like the wilderness or King Arthur's court. They also represent important characters moving through space, as in Branor's movement from left to right, thereby directing the viewer's steps as if in a reflected image of the hero, across the "mirror" surface of the painted wall. The cycle also suggests the passage of time and its sudden shift from present to past, as the deeds of Branor that the viewer witnesses are suddenly transformed into imagined

deeds of the past, retold as history by the messenger to Queen Guinevere, now visible only as imaginings. Such evocative renderings seem
to blur the boundaries between material and visual, creating memo-
ries painted, as it were, on the walls of the mind. I suggest that such
unusually physical renderings, very like those experienced in real life,
may have been derived from the designer's familiarity with religious
cycles at Avignon and with the increasing tendency in religious painting of the fourteenth century to focus on immediacy and physical presence. The cycle at Saint-Floret does not simply manifest the linear dimension of text, or the two dimensions of the flat picture; rather, it
uses both of these to create a three-dimensional shell within which life
can exist, to create the crumbling material boundaries within which
we can move, breathe, consider, and love.

Appendix: Selected Extant and Recorded Inscriptions at Saint-Floret

I list the relevant inscriptions below, following the narrative order of
the *Meliadus,* and include a reference to their location and to the image
beneath which they are placed (if one remains).[25] I begin with the inscription on the lower left of the east wall, which marks the earliest
point in the extant textual narrative (although the visual narrative
contains earlier events).

East, lower left
Three women on castle ramparts.
sire roi, le chevalier qui abati tant de votres le iour de la pantecoste . . .
"Sir King, the knight who overthrew so many of your (knights) the
day of Pentecost . . ."

South, middle embrasure, left jamb
Young man behind castle wall.
*uesi pourcoy monseignor tristan de lionois sen parti du reaume de cornoalha
e sen uint au reaume de logres poursequ li roys mar . . . es point lieu(?)*
"This is why Sir Tristan de Lionois departed from the realm of
Cornwall and came to the realm of Logres, because King Mark . . ."

South, middle embrasure, top
Tree and the head of an older man with a crown.
(No inscription.)

South, middle embrasure, right jamb
Young woman behind the castle wall.
*dit ela: tristran, que poyson uoy ie? ie ne ui tel molt lonc tans. a. dama, ie le
bien coneu quar ie lay autrefois ueu.*
"'Tristan, what fish do I see? I have not seen such for a very long time.'
'Lady, I recognized it well, for I have seen it before.'"

South, right embrasure, left jamb
Young man sleeping in the forest.
*uesi come monseignor tristan chiuachoyt pour le reaume de logres quetant
auanture, e uint [uers la nuit]*
"This is how Sir Tristan rode through the realm of Logres seeking
adventure, and came [toward nightfall] . . ."

South, right embrasure, right jamb
Another young man sleeping in the forest.
*uesi se cocha en la forest entre [beaus] a[rbres e dor]mi sur sun ecut,
e auint ansi com auanture . . . enemi mortel se cocha e se co[m]ple[int] . . .
e pourquoy se cocha si . . . si fort qant . . .*
"Here he lay down in the forest between fair trees and slept on his
shield and it happened by chance . . . mortal enemy lay down and
lamented . . . why he lay down so . . . so much[26] when . . ."

North, left embrasure, right jamb
Fragments of a horse.
*. . . [con]pagnon de la tabala . . . [ica eleh?] . . . [nin?] an la perilluse
[for]est uii iors apres quil fu pa(r)tis de camelot.*
". . . companion of the table . . . (?) . . . in the Perilous Forest seven
days after he had departed from Camelot."

North, left embrasure, left jamb
No image remains.
*[tristan de liono]is deliura dina[dan] . . . [e]stoyent a la fey . . . i auantura
que . . .*

"Tristan de Lionois delivered Dinadan . . . belonged to the Fay . . .
it happened that. . ."[27]

North, upper register, central image
Battle between two knights, one accompanied by the unarmed man.
*uesi come monseignor palamedes deliura monseigneor tristan de lionois que
un uauasor tenoyt pris et li uoloyt fere coper la teta pourse que il li tua sun
fis an la perilhue forest qui estoyt un de xxvi cheualiers a la fey morgain;
e por se fit pes monseignor tristan a monseignor palamedes; si estoyt il le
gregnor enemis mortel du munde*
"This is[28] how Sir Palamedes delivered Sir Tristan of Lionois, whom a
vavasour held as prisoner and wished to have his head cut off, because
he had slain his son in the Perilous Forest, who was one of twenty-six
knights of Morgain la Fey; and because of this Sir Tristan made peace
with Sir Palamedes; yet he was his greatest mortal enemy in the world."

North, right embrasure, left jamb
The knight bearing the shield with the red cross.
*apres la deliueranse de monseignor tristan chiuauchoyent monseignor
palamedes e monseignor tristan ensenble e encontrerent monseignor galaaz
e le firent ioster ansi come [paur?]*
"After the deliverance of Sir Tristan Sir Palamedes and Sir Tristan rode
together and met Sir Galaad and made him joust as if [fear (?)] . . ."

Notes

1. This event takes place in the Vulgate or Lancelot-Grail cycle. See
H.O. Sommer, ed., *The Vulgate Version of the Arthurian Romances,* 7 vols.
(Washington, DC: Carnegie Institution, 1909–16), 5:217 ff.; and Muriel A.
Whitaker, *The Legends of King Arthur in Art,* Arthurian Studies 22 (Wood-
bridge: D.S. Brewer, 1990), 122–23.

2. David Freedberg, *The Power of Images: Studies in the History and
Theory of Response* (Chicago: University of Chicago Press, 1989), 436–38.

3. David Dobbs, "A Revealing Reflection: Mirror Neurons Are Providing Stunning Insights into Everything from How We Learn to Walk to
How We Empathize with Others," *Scientific American Mind* (April 2006):
22–27.

4. The role of devotional literature and the lives of saints in spurring visual production has been explored by many scholars. For a brief historiography, see Margaret Plant, "Fresco Painting in Avignon and Northern Italy: A Study of Some Fourteenth-Century Cycles of Saints Lives outside Tuscany" (Ph.D. diss., University of Melbourne, 1981), 34 ff. On the affective in particular, see Janet Robson, "Judas and the Franciscans: Perfidy Pictured in Lorenzetti's Passion Cycle at Assisi," *Art Bulletin* 86.1 (2004): 31. Selected other examples include — on narrative imagery — Hans Belting, "The New Role of Narrative in Public Painting of the Trecento: Historia and Allegory," in *Pictorial Narrative in Antiquity and the Middle Ages,* ed. Herbert L. Kessler and Marianna Shreve Simpson (Hanover, NH: University Press of New England, 1985), 152. On devotional imagery, see Jeffrey F. Hamburger, "The Use of Images in the Pastoral Care of Nuns: The Case of Heinrich Suso and the Dominicans," *Art Bulletin* 71.1 (March 1989): 45. For a brief suggestion of the importance of these findings in secular material, see M. A. Michael, review of *Narrative and Experience: Innovations in Thirteenth-Century Picture Books,* by Kumiko Maekawa, *Speculum* 78 (2003): 1340–41.

5. Much of the data, although not all the conclusions, relevant to Saint-Floret in the present chapter can be found in my dissertation, Amanda Luyster, "Courtly Images Far from Court: The Family St. Floret, Representation, and Romance" (Ph.D. diss., Harvard University, 2003). Stylistic analysis of the paintings and their relationship to Avignon can also be found in Amanda Luyster, "Avignon's Courtly Style Far from Court: The Murals at Saint-Floret," in *Petrarch's Babylon: Cultural Exchange in Papal Avignon,* ed. Susan Noakes (Minneapolis: University of Minnesota Press, forthcoming).

6. These paintings have been included in various surveys but have been examined in depth only in Luyster, "Courtly Images Far from Court" and "Avignon's Courtly Style"; and Roger Sherman Loomis and Laura Hibbard Loomis, *Arthurian Legends in Medieval Art,* Modern Language Association of America Monograph Series (New York: Modern Language Association of America, 1938), 57–60.

7. For Rusticien's text, see the abridged version (following BN fr. 340, with other manuscripts as comparandi) published as an appendix to the prose *Tristan* in Eilert Löseth, *Le roman en prose de Tristan: Le roman de Palamède et la compilation de Rusticien de Pise; analyse critique d'après les manuscrits de Paris* (Paris: É. Bouillon, 1890; reprint, Genève: Slatkine Reprints, 1974), 423–73. See also extracts in Loomis and Loomis, *Arthurian Legends,* 58–61.

8. For full details regarding the manuscripts of Rusticien's *Meliadus,* see Luyster, "Courtly Images Far from Court," 166. See also Brian Woledge,

Bibliographie des romans et nouvelles en prose française antérieurs à 1500 (Genève: Droz, 1954), no. 152. For illustrated versions of Rusticien's text, see Patricia M. Gathercole, "Illustrations on the Manuscripts of Rusticien de Pise," *Italica* 44 (1967): 400–408. For a useful overview of the prose *Tristan,* see Norris J. Lacy, "The Evolution and Legacy of French Prose Romance," in *The Cambridge Companion to Medieval Romance,* ed. Roberta L. Krueger (Cambridge: Cambridge University Press, 2000), 174–77.

    9. Luyster, "Courtly Images Far from Court," 170.

    10. Visual depictions of the tryst appear in many contexts and have been read in many ways. For a good overview, see Julia Caroline Walworth, "Tristan in Medieval Art," in *Tristan and Isolde: A Casebook,* ed. Joan Tasker Grimbert, Arthurian Characters and Themes 2 (New York: Garland, 1995), 279–83. See also Michael Curschmann, "Images of Tristan," in *Gottfried von Strassburg and the Medieval Tristan Legend: Papers from an Anglo-North American Symposium,* ed. Adrian Stevens and Roy Wisbey, Publications of the Institute of Germanic Studies, University of London 44 (Cambridge: D. S. Brewer, 1990), 9–12; reprinted in Michael Curschmann, *Wort–Bild–Text: Studien zur Medialität des Literarischen in Hochmittelalter und früher Neuzeit,* 2 vols. (Baden-Baden: Valentin Koerner, 2007), 1:227–51. An important survey of Tristan imagery, including the tryst, is Hella Frühmorgen-Voss, "Tristan und Isolde in mittelalterlichen Bildzeugnissen," *Deutsche Vierteljahrsschrift* 47 (1973): 645–63; reprinted in Hella Frühmorgen-Voss, *Text und Illustration im Mittelalter: Aufsätze zu den Wechselbeziehungen zwischen Literatur und bildender Kunst,* ed. Norbert H. Ott, Münchener Texte und Untersuchungen zur deutschen Literatur des Mittelalters 50 (München: Beck, 1975), 119–39. Also see the useful catalog of Tristan imagery in Norbert H. Ott, "Katalog der Tristan-Bildzeugnisse," in Frühmorgen-Voss, *Text und Illustration im Mittelalter,* 140–71.

    11. For transcriptions of all the inscriptions at Saint-Floret, with translations, see the appendix.

    12. The motif of the fish has been found in conjunction with pictorial representations of Tristan and Yseut, including a Rhenish wooden comb, ca. 1410, now in Bamberg, and a fifteenth-century leather slipper, found in a well at Mechelin, with an inscription in Middle Dutch. For the motif of the fish and the comb, see Loomis and Loomis, *Arthurian Legends,* 59, 68. For the slipper, see Martine Meuwese, "Arthurian Illuminations in Middle Dutch Manuscripts," in *Word and Image in Arthurian Literature,* ed. Keith Busby (New York: Garland, 1996), 159. For the motif of the fish in a Netherlandish text, *Der minne loep,* by Dirc Potter, see Frühmorgen-Voss, "Tristan und Isolde in mittelalterlichen Bildzeugnissen," 129.

13. Plant, "Fresco Painting in Avignon and Northern Italy," 15, similarly argues for the role of time in exploring a fresco cycle.

14. Herbert L. Kessler, "Reading Ancient and Medieval Art," *Word & Image* 5.1 (1988): 1.

15. The term *slippage* is derived from Saussurian linguistics. In that context, slippage is generally used to refer to the changing relationship between a signifier and the signified; I use it here to suggest a changing relationship between two different kinds of signifiers, word and image.

16. Helen Solterer, "Letter Writing and Picture Reading: Medieval Textuality and the *Bestiaire d'Amour,*" *Word & Image* 5.1 (1989): 131.

17. Sylvia Jean Huot, *From Song to Book: The Poetics of Writing in Old French Lyrics and Lyrical Narrative Poetry* (Ithaca, NY: Cornell University Press, 1987), suggests that even in the late fourteenth century "writing retained a certain dimension of orality, being understood as the representation of speech."

18. Elizabeth Rodini, "Mapping Narrative at the Church of San Marco: A Study in Visual Storying," *Word & Image* 14.4 (1998): 387–96.

19. Jocelyn Penny Small, "Time *in* Space: Narrative in Classical Art," *Art Bulletin* 71.4 (1999): 562–75.

20. See Plant, "Fresco Painting in Avignon and Northern Italy"; Robson, "Judas and the Franciscans"; Belting, "New Role of Narrative in Public Painting of the Trecento"; Hamburger, "Use of Images in the Pastoral Care of Nuns."

21. Luyster, "Avignon's Courtly Style."

22. For a published summary of many of the documents relevant to the Saint-Floret family, see Henri Du Ranquet, "Généalogie des de Saint-Floret et des de Jehan de Saint-Floret," *Le Moyen âge,* 2nd ser., 24 (May–August 1922): 171–78. For full details, see Luyster, "Courtly Images Far from Court," esp. appendixes A and B.

23. Etienne Baluze, *Histoire généalogique de la maison d'Auvergne,* 2 vols. (Paris: Chez Antoine Dezallier, 1708), 615.

24. See Enrico Castelnuovo, *Un pittore italiano alla corte di Avignone: Matteo Giovanetti et la pittura in Provenza nel secolo XIV* (Turino: Einaudi, 1962); Enrico Castelnuovo, Simone Darses, and Sylvie Girard, *Un peintre italien à la cour d'Avignon* (Paris: G. Monfort, 1996). For diagrams and inscriptions of the Avignon cycles, see F. Enaud, "Les fresques du palais des Papes d'Avignon," *Les Monuments Historiques de la France* 17.2–3 (1971): 1–139. Also useful is R. Lentsch, "Les grands thèmes religieux des fresques du palais des Papes," in *Le décor des églises en France méridionale (XIIe–milieu XVe s.),*

(Toulouse: Privat, 1993), 291–312. For more attention to theoretical considerations, see Plant, "Fresco Painting in Avignon and Northern Italy," 49–77.

25. The original transcription of the inscriptions was made by Dauvergne but carefully reedited by R. S. Loomis in the 1940s. I give Loomis's transcription alongside a slightly emended version of Loomis's English translation (Roger Sherman Loomis and Laura Hibbard Loomis, *Arthurian Legends in Medieval Art,* Modern Language Association of America Monograph Series [New York: Modern Language Association of America, 1938], 59–61).

26. Loomis: "mighty." My thanks to Virginie Greene of Harvard University for her suggestions.

27. Loomis: "an adventure which."

28. Loomis: "See."

CHAPTER EIGHT

Tristan Love

Elite Self-Fashioning in Italian Frescoes of
the Thirteenth and Fourteenth Centuries

KLAUS KRÜGER

Tristan will not play much of a role in this chapter—nor will Isolde. To be sure, their medieval epic will be encountered here and there in the discussion of public and private representational imagery in the Italian Duecento and Trecento. However, in this Italian material their appearance is minimal, to say the least.

Nevertheless, according to some researchers, there is one rare instance where the epic does make an appearance. In the early twentieth century art historians were convinced that they had identified this narrative of fated love in several fresco fragments from the former residence of the Teri family in Florence (fig. 8.1). The seven fragmentary pictorial fields, which originated in the late Trecento, did not survive the late-nineteenth-century demolition of this private house on the Via dei Pescioni, where they were originally located in one of the living rooms on the first upper floor; however, they were preserved in drawings and watercolor copies executed shortly before the demolition.[1] The lozenge-shaped pictorial fields were arrayed in horizontal registers one above the other. Along with stags, bulls and bears, and a series of mainly exotic birds, including pelicans, flamingos, pheas-

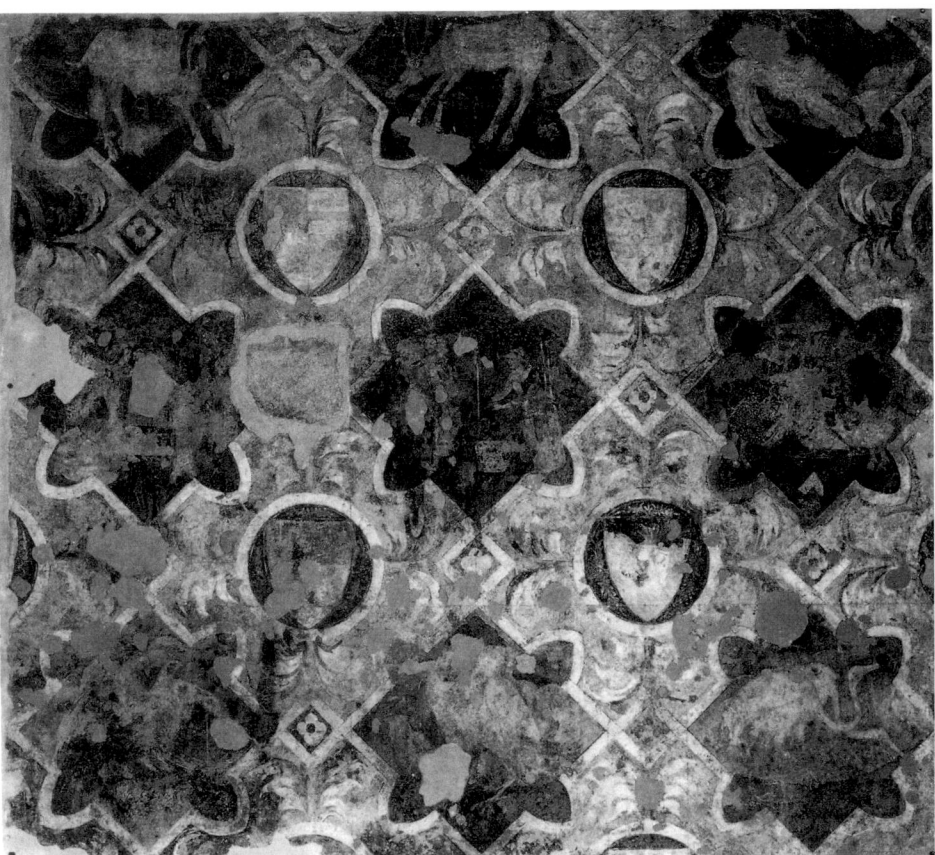

Figure 8.1. Fragment of interior decoration, originally from a house in Via dei Pescioni, Florence, Palazzo Davanzati, end of 14th century–early 15th century. *This and all subsequent photos in chapter 8 by the author.*

ants, and aquatic birds (fig. 8.2), the middle register displays a series of relatively small-scale scenes whose common theme is no longer identifiable. What we can identify are small groups of human figures who are turned toward one another. In the scenes we see, variously, a female figure, sometimes carrying a fruit basket and standing next to a tree facing two men; jousting scenes with two mounted knights rushing violently toward one another, riding horses attired in elaborate caparisons; a woman carrying a banner in her right hand while

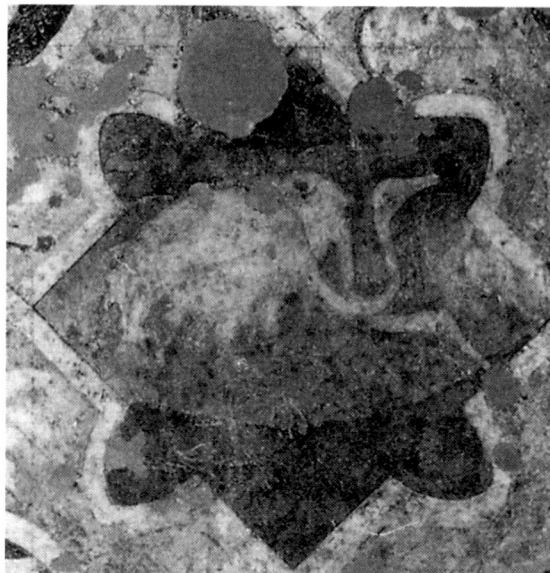

Figure 8.2. Detail of interior decoration from a house in the Via dei Pescioni, Florence, Palazzo Davanzati.

riding a horse that, like her, is outfitted with an elaborate costume (fig. 8.3); a small group of people in a tent, possibly a seated woman accompanied by a man on horseback who receives tribute from the knight who kneels before her; additional scenes of figures on horseback; and, finally, a scene showing elegantly attired men and women strolling gracefully in a garden or natural setting, suggested by the presence of trees.

Given the condition of these frescoes, it is hardly possible to identify an overarching or continuous narrative sequence. The depicted protagonists go about their business, moving in various directions in juxtaposed pictorial fields, yet the fields show no obvious sequential logic. The highly animated design of the framing system — based as it is on dominant square pictorial fields, set against a pale ground embellished by vegetal forms showing individual tondi with fictive coats of arms that include freely invented heraldic motifs — does not seem to have been conceived primarily for the sake of a visibly unified or integrated progression of continuous scenes. Like the depictions of animals above and below, the scenes in the central register seem rather to be independent of one another, each offering itself up to isolated con-

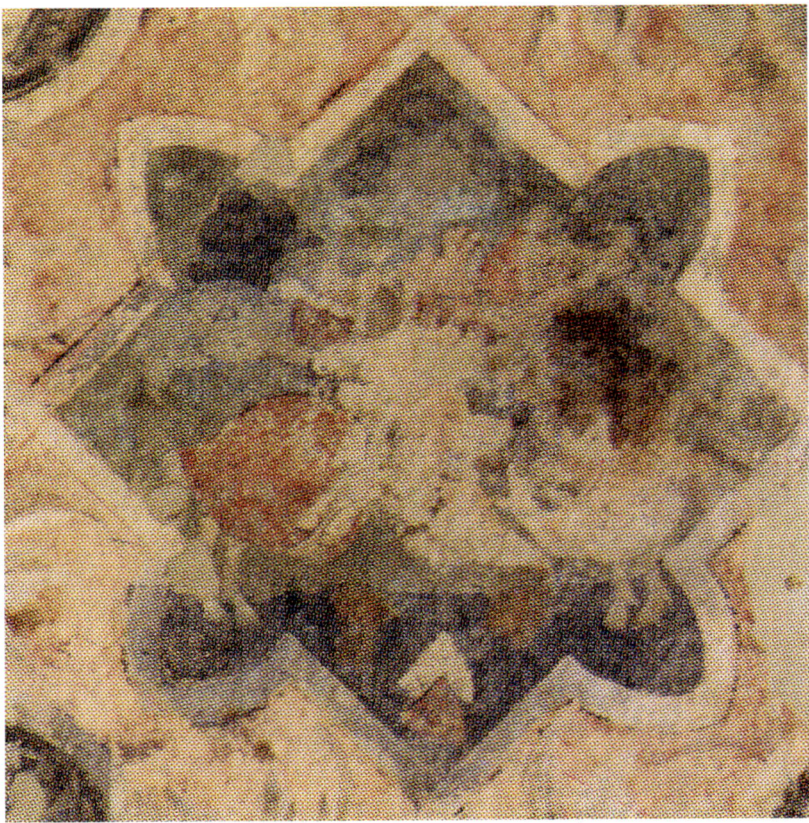

Figure 8.3. Detail of interior decoration from a house in the Via dei Pescioni, Florence, Palazzo Davanzati.

templation. Their thematic substrate appears to be incorporated into an overall decorative schema whose individual motifs are of courtly provenance: natural scenery as the setting for love ambitions, a chivalrous knightly tournament, and segments of untamed wilderness composed of forests and mountains and populated by exotic birds and wild beasts.

It is impossible, therefore, to confirm the early-twentieth-century proposals that identified these scenes specifically with the narrative of Tristan and Isolde.[2] Not only were these proposals offered in a cursory fashion and without the benefit of detailed analysis, but, more relevantly, if one searches, even just in Florence, for other monumental

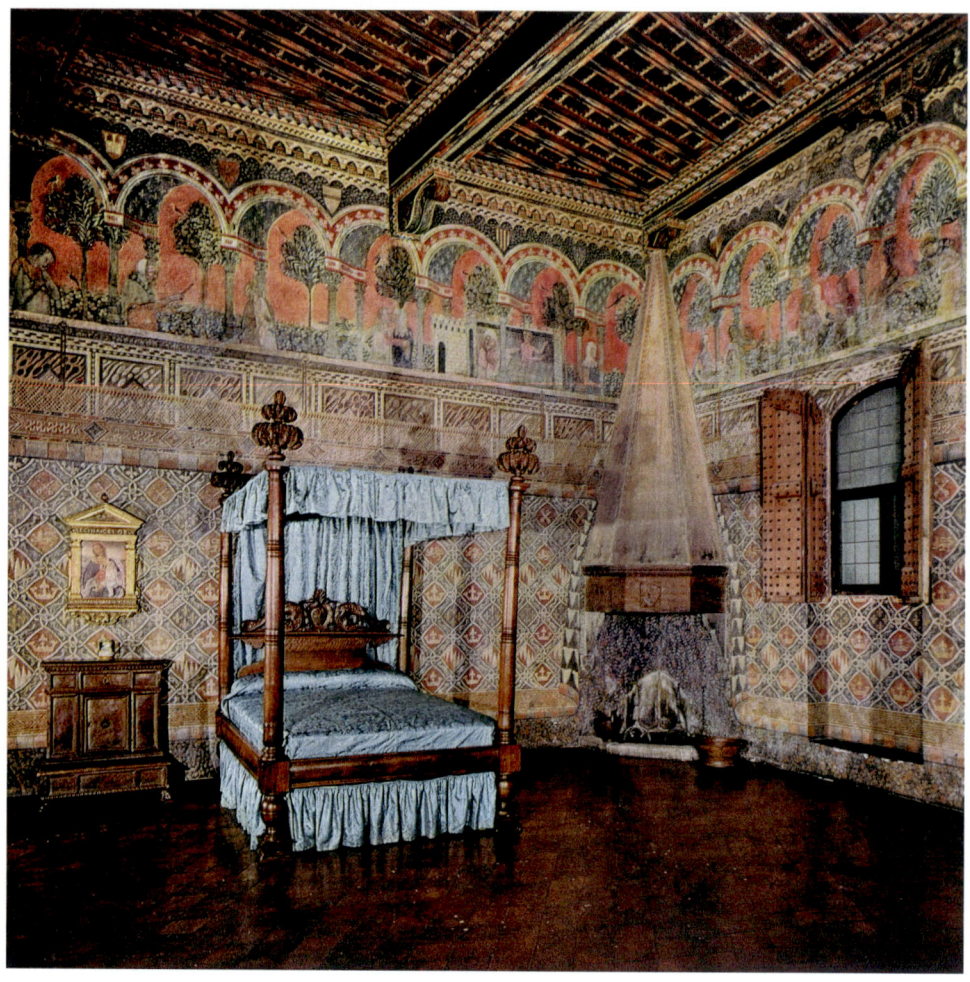

Figure 8.4. Mural in the Stanza della Castellana, Florence, Palazzo Davanzati, ca. 1395.

pictorial cycles containing verifiable references to specific literary models, one finds only the celebrated decorations of the so-called Stanza della Castellana in the second story of the Palazzo Davanzati (fig. 8.4). The scheme of this fresco cycle, which dates from circa 1395, encompasses a whole wall zone. A trompe l'oeil curtain hangs before simulated marble paneling, and above this, in the upper zone, a painted arcaded gallery running around all four walls has set into it twenty-two episodes from the tragic love story of the Châtelaine de Vergy, also known as the Castellana del Vergiu.[3] This pictorial narrative shows how the fulfilled but secret love affair between a patrician woman of Vergy (i.e., the Castellana) and a knight named Guillaume, alias Guglielmo, was progressively destroyed when the duchess of Burgundy fell in love with the same knight. When Guillaume rejected her without explanation, he set in motion a highly involved and tragic dramatic entanglement that essentially follows the biblical story of Joseph and Potiphar. The narrative leads from deception to disappointment, from disappointment to misunderstanding and betrayal, and, finally, to the Castellana's death from sheer despair, followed thereafter by the knight's suicide and the murder of the duchess by her enraged husband, the duke of Burgundy, after which he travels to Palestine as a Templar to do penance for his sins. This story, traceable to an early French courtly verse epic from circa 1250, enjoyed great popularity in the later Middle Ages and was disseminated in numerous French manuscripts. It also received Italian, German, and Dutch translations, variants, and modernizations.[4]

The Florentine murals represent the sole surviving Italian instance of a monumental fresco cycle based on this thematic material; other than that, one finds the story depicted with great frequency on ivory boxes and other small luxury objects.[5] Without analyzing the pictorial scheme of these murals in more detail, it can be said that the integration of the narrative into a decorative system based on standards wholly different from those of a monumental narrative cycle does little to ensure the legibility of the sequence of scenes and perhaps even seriously prevents its comprehension. The space of a small loggia, conceived in a unified stage and offering simulated views onto a gardenlike natural setting—showing green hedges, trees bearing various fruits, and numerous birds—evidently contradicts the action's internal narrative logic. For that logic unfolds not only in a variety of different locations and diverse temporal sequences but also through a complicated interlocking of desired and undesired encounters and spatiotemporally diverse communicative situations. This contradiction is immediately noticeable in the scene in which the duchess, shown in

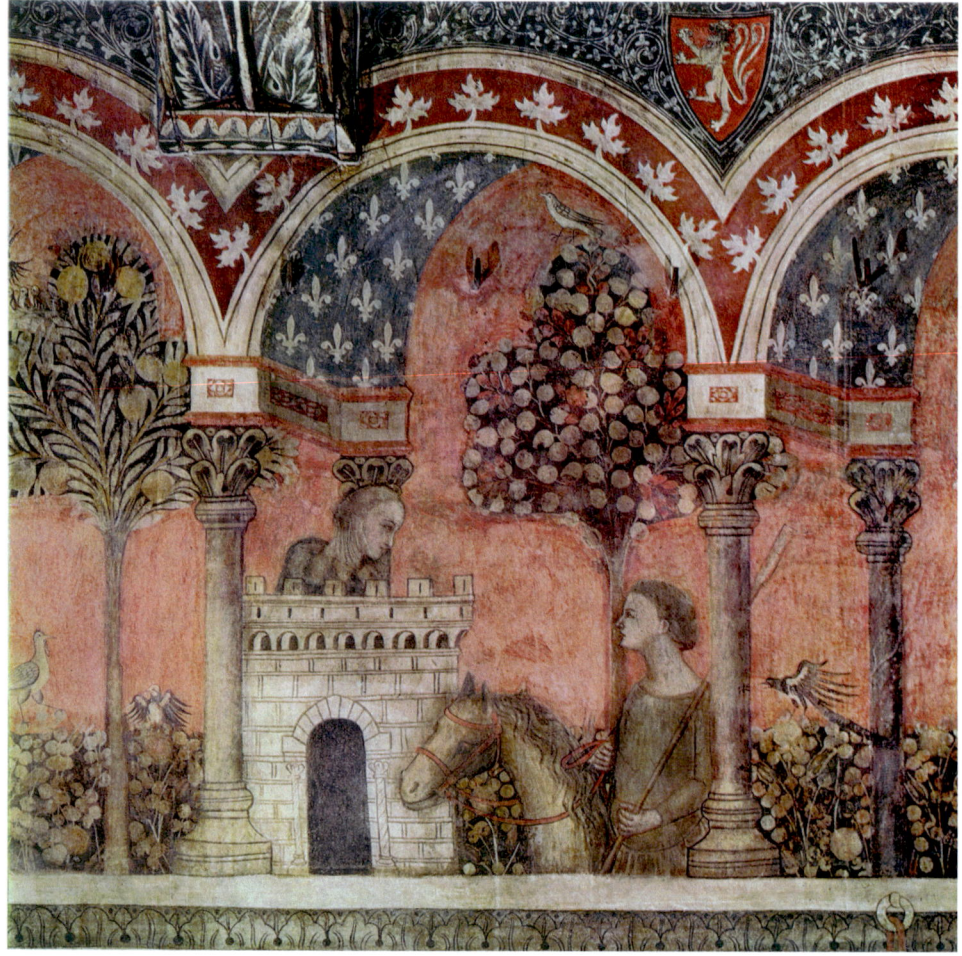

Figure 8.5. Detail of the Stanza della Castellana mural.

her crenellated tower, leans out to signal to her elected but resistant lover, the young knight seated on a horse (fig. 8.5). Or consider the scenario of the ducal bedchamber, in which the duchess refuses the sexual overtures of her husband the duke, in the hope that he will reveal to her the secrets of the Castellana and her knightly lover (fig. 8.6). In both examples (and there are others), the narrativistic logic of the scenes is not integrated into, or synchronized with, the narrow spatial structure and strictly repetitive sequence of the loggia.

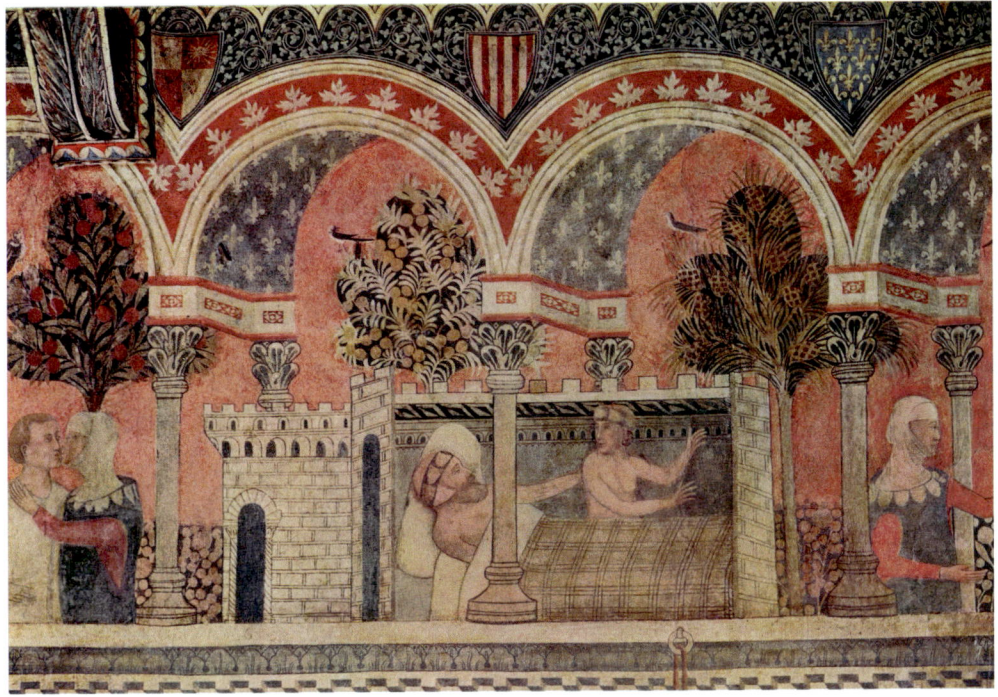

Figure 8.6. Detail of the Stanza della Castellana mural.

The decorative system of the room as a whole is traditional and, in this period, was widely disseminated. It coincides with decorative systems found among the standard repertoires of painters' workshops specializing in commissions to decorate the interiors of these private residences. Thus one may speak of a decorative system in which there is a limited and determinate range of standardized variables, all of which are common to fresco painting: for example, a painted and thus simulated patterned carpet set before a painted and thus simulated marble wall paneling, all of which covers the lower two-thirds of the walls, while the upper third is typically decorated with a simulated loggia decorated with coats of arms. This loggia was featured either as a columned arcade or as roofed with consoles projecting the illusion of a background natural setting of trees and exotic birds. Such stereotyped designs were produced in other rooms of the Palazzo Davanzati as well, for example, in the Stanza dei Papagalli, the Stanza dei

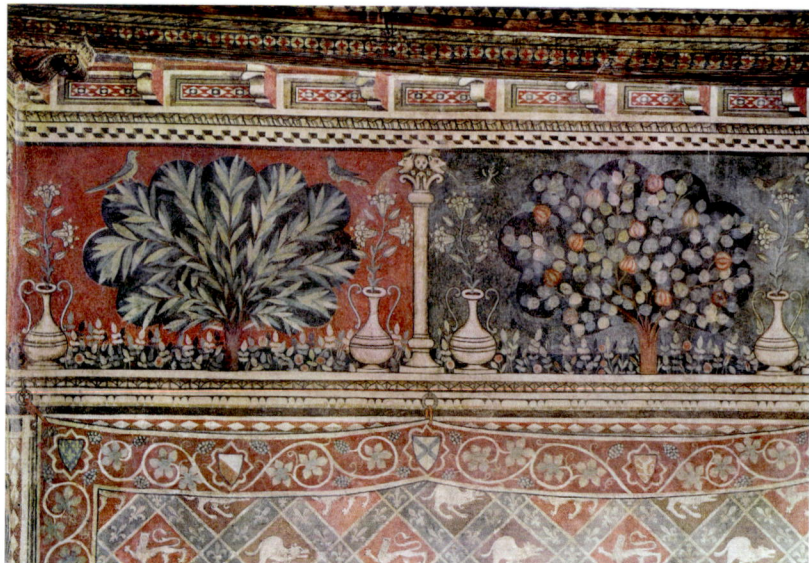

Figure 8.7. Sala Impannate, detail, Florence, Palazzo Davanzati.

Pavoni, and the Sala delle Impannate (fig. 8.7). Likewise we find similar designs in the Villa Tornabuoni-Lemmi to the north of Florence (Careggi; fig. 8.8) and in surviving remnants of the former decorations of the Casa dei Sassetti and the Casa dei Lamberti.[6] It is clear that adjusting the epic narrative cycle to suit a decorative schema already in place constituted a hybridization or, to be more precise, an importation of an element substantially alien to the decorative system that transformed its aesthetic logic.

In the Stanza della Castellana, the story of courtly love was apparently not adopted with the intention of providing a faithful visual or pictorial translation of a literary prototype, or with the intention of reconceptualization in a different media in order to provide the beholder with a moral narrative of internal psychological tension. Rather, what we see is an abstraction away from the narrative, away from its core intention of demonstrating ideal love produced through a conventional repertoire of references (to devotedness and fidelity, betrayal and deception, despair and penance, in fine: to virtue and love),

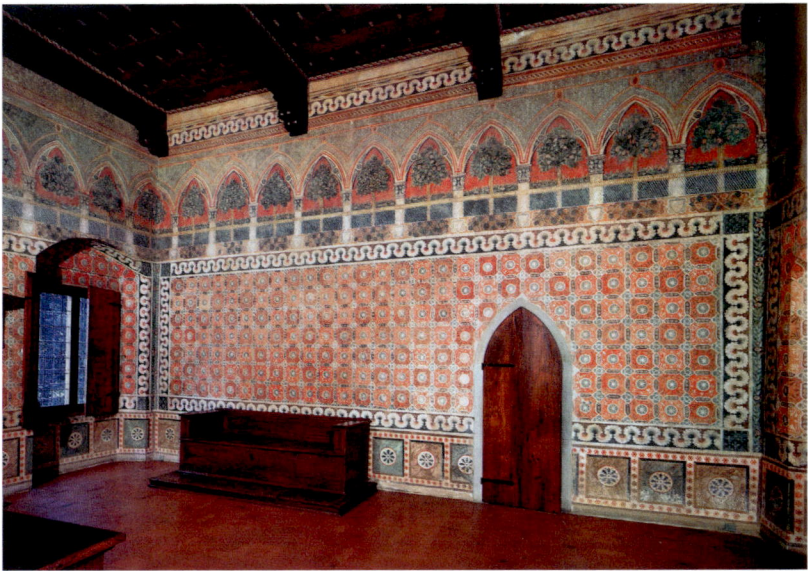

Figure 8.8. Interior decoration, Florence, Villa Tornabuoni-Lemmi di Careggi.

toward the creation of a metasystem of references produced by being incorporated into an already meaningful system of decorative signs. The significance of the representation does not lie in its transparent legibility but rather in its opacity. Nevertheless, this system of representation acquires cultural distinctiveness by becoming the product of its elite patrons' self-fashioning.

To make this argument clearer, let us consider the social significance of the aesthetic derived from this decorative system, which is widely used in communal residential buildings and might be described as an opaque medium of distinctiveness. These decorative programs were doubtless designed to evoke imaginary realms or ambiences of elegance and luxury. This was the point of showing gardens abundant with foliage and flowers, exotic animals and birds—a tranquil paradise detached from the hustle and bustle of everyday life, psychologically and physically removed from an urban environment. To create such imaginary realms within domestic interiors produced an obvious alterity to the dark and narrow streets outside; a spatial contrast to the crammed feel of the city, with its absence of park and landscaped areas; and a temporal contrast to exploited and hurried lives. These pictorial settings, which so obviously expressed a yearning for escape, aimed at approximating the residential interiors with their existing parameters of cultural habits and elite self-conceptions found in the literary discourse of, for example, Boccaccio's *Decameron,* in which members of a wealthy urban society escape into a safe and unspoiled *locus amoenus* with its "lush greenery, singing birds and open skies in place of the depressing view of the blank walls of the town," and into the luxurious pleasures of commodious country houses "with their richly outfitted, spacious rooms and in particular with the embellishments of their cheerful paintings *(liete dipinture)*."[7]

At first view, therefore, the combination of these motifs and the whole pictorial setting found in the decorative schemes may be interpreted as attempts to transform or to metamorphose domestic interiors into refuges or imaginary realms offering refreshing and spacious access to the natural world. But, at the same time, this natural world was more than simply natural. It was encoded also with social habits and cultural signs. To the extent that the images mirrored more truthful forms of virtue and love, the natural world could be interpreted as establishing a horizon over which the proprietor's self-image was elevated and idealized. Implicit in this interpretation is the idea that the significance of the specific motivic references was not made explicit. Foregrounded in the decorations instead was cultural practice as determined by the social conventions embedded in the iconography. The meanings may be elucidated by referring to conventions of social behavior.

These schemas recapitulated visual models found in the collective imaginary and the self-conceptions of the society they served. Consider the artistic paradigm associated with the Florentine chancellor and humanist Brunetto Latini as early as 1260 in his widely known encyclopedia, *Li livres dou Trésor.* In this text Latini asserts that thus far the Italians had only known how to wage war against one another and accordingly preferred to erect plain towers and stone buildings, in contrast to the French who, enjoying themselves without warfare, noise, or commotion, preferred to award themselves imposing, spacious, and well-decorated residences.[8] Latini's model was both cultural and social: a model in which the interior decorative scheme confirmed both the proprietor's cultivated lifestyle and his desire for peaceful and prosperous circumstances.

In the Florentine Trecento, the painted decorative schemes found in private residential rooms served also as *opaque* media of cultural and social distinction. They manifested specific qualities and levels of style indicative of an owner's social standing and self-assertions whose significance went far beyond the surface of iconographic codes. No longer did social equals contend on the battlefield. Rather, they sought to surpass their opponents by advertising their prosperity and the distinctiveness of their cultural deportment. Put differently: contests between social actors were enacted through artistic means in the domain of symbolic communication. However, this claim must be qualified, given how much the decorative schemes, as I stressed earlier, were already highly standardized and executed by highly specialized painters of domestic interiors *(dipintori di camere)*. Down to the very last details of their artistic work, these painters tended to display all the trademarks of serial execution and division of labor prevailing in their workshops, procedures that were designed to optimize efficiency. Subject, that is to say, to conditions of production and of marketing, they were left with little freedom significantly to modify or vary the painted settings or to introduce distinctions of quality.

The stereotypical patterns of production tended to rule out, therefore, the introduction of motivically or thematically individualized iconographic programs. In his novellas that appeared roughly at the same time that the paintings originally contained in the Palazzo Davanzati or the Casa dei Teri were produced, the humanist man of letters, Franco Sacchetti, made repeated and ironic reference to this very state of affairs. He comments, for example, on how one Bartolo Gioggi, who specialized in private interior paintings, was commissioned to decorate a private residential chamber for his client Pino Brunelleschi with frescoes showing "numerous birds among the trees."[9] When Bartolo completed his work, however, Brunelleschi charged him with having painted far too few birds, to which Bartolo replied with this laconic remark: "It is true that I didn't paint very many. Unfortunately, one of your servants left the window open, and most of them escaped through it and flew away."[10] This anecdote shows the ironic reaction to contemporary demands for depictions of nature, depictions that were increasingly drained of symbolic or narrative significance the more completely conventionalized or standardized they became. In these terms, the conventionalizations themselves came to determine the reference, function, and significance of the signs and representational motifs themselves. The birds—but implicitly also the trees, their foliage, fruit, and all other natural motifs—were, although carrying illusory significance, deprived of their potency. One might even say they were desubstantialized. Consequently, their continuing significance resided far less in their depictive reference and far more in the spectacular value qua representations. Such works cannot be evaluated solely according to their artistic quality but must be assessed according to the quantifiable or professional standards they maintained in this highly competitive setting of social relations. Regarded as both media of distinction and egalitarian media, determined according to economic criteria, the works become vivid mirrors of contemporary Florentine society. This said, however, one should not ignore how the dissemination of the symbol system and the greater accessibility to its signs led to an impoverishment of meaning overall.

This thesis, that the decorative programs are interpreted as opaque media of social and cultural distinction, can be further corroborated. An examination of the surviving interior decorations of Florentine private residences shows us that the numerous coats of arms embellishing the frescoes were often derived from freely invented heraldic figurations bearing no connection whatsoever to specific families or noble houses. Even where the individual emblems are more or less identifiable as self-representations of specific patrons and of their broader familial or sociopolitical networks, there was a simultaneous proliferation of nondeterminate and largely unverifiable references that seemed to connect the patron's family to noble houses or dynasties from the remotest provenances. In this way, these decorations produced imaginary elitist communities as projections of patrons promoting their own social and cultural status. The opaque symbol system testifies to layers of reference upon reference extending far beyond the only apparently transparent or concrete narrativized scenes.

Franco Sacchetti showed us the extent to which contemporaries were fully aware of this opacity. In his novellas he repeatedly ironized the arbitrary status of the heraldic emblems evidenced in the painted coats of arms, and also the ways in which social distinctions were constructed with little consideration of the facts of family genealogy and far more by reference to financial influence and success: a construction that contributed, as we know, to the formation of a *nouveau riche* nobility. Sacchetti shows how the coats of arms were freely invented artistic inventions bearing little relation to any socially binding or legitimate substance. The Florentine painter Luchino, so Sacchetti tells, produced coats of arms and devices for his clients according only to their ability to pay, as though these were "the loveliest accidents in the world."[11] In another novel he recounts that when the celebrated painter Buffalmacco was commissioned to paint the coat of arms of Bishop Guido Tarlati of Arezzo in the bishop's private palazzo, he inverted the prescribed figuration that should have shown an eagle rending a lion and painted instead a lion tearing the eagle apart.[12] To renaturalize the conventionalized language of signs in this ironic way subtly points to the loss that had befallen the domain of symbolic communication and its significations, which were once authentic and binding.

This loss testified to broader political, economic, and social upheavals. It is well known that the transformation of the Florentine community into a republic of the guilds ushered in a far-reaching disempowerment of the nobility and the magnates holding large estates by dramatically curtailing their political and legal claims.[13] In the formation of a new collective identity, the bourgeoisie and *popolo* who rose now to political power and assumed legal authority sought to disempower and quite radically to displace in the public sphere the former modes of self-fashioning favored by the nobility: for example, by the strict interdiction of painted coats of arms or even of portraits of officials on governmental or administrative buildings. In the private sphere, however, the new rulers oriented themselves to the very modes they disapproved of so vigorously in public. There was a marked transition, therefore, from representative staging in the *public* and now depersonalized realm to representative self-staging in the *private* domestic realm. The former implicitly critiqued the values associated with the latter: the noble way of life, the aristocratic self-understanding, the projections of elite community. This appropriation of symbolic codes in the establishment of the new bourgeoisie was inevitably contradictory and led to further draining of meaning from the codes.

The contradiction may be seen in both private and public pictorial programs found in the communal context. The Cerchi family,
for example, many of whose members became active in the Republi-
can government, commissioned a set of frescoes (now almost entirely
destroyed) to be painted in the second upper story of their palazzo,
erected during the later thirteenth century in immediate proximity to
the seat of government at the Palazzo dei Priori.[14] The frescoes show
courtly hunting scenes (fig. 8.9) and a splendid jousting tournament
(fig. 8.10). The horses of the well-attired knights are equally well
clothed with elaborate banners and textiles, showing coats of arms
whose heraldry identifies them as representatives of the French
and English royal houses. If the account of Enrica Neri Lusanna is
correct (the first account of this recently discovered fresco cycle)—
according to which representatives of other great families or ruling
houses figure in the decorative scheme alongside the two knights—
then it is clear that the Cerchi family's motivation for including them
may be read as this family's imaginary self-positioning of themselves
on the stage of international relations.[15] If we remember that the social and political influence of the Cerchi was falling at just this time
(ca. 1320–30), their frescoes may be read as testifying to the displaced
or compensatory character of their claims to power.

In other contexts of comparable subject matter, it is possible to
clearly identify the instrumental and compensatory core of topically
determined references inherent in the pictorial schemes, undercut-
ting and even contradicting interpretations of these images that find
in them visually concretized poetry, courtly modes of deportment,
chivalrous ideals, or tales of courtly love. Consider another example,
from the celebrated fresco program of the Camposanto in Pisa, dating
from circa 1335.[16] Appearing in the monumental mural showing the
Trionfo della morte, and surrounded by scenes manifesting the hor-
rors of death, a company of young nobles is shown, amid shrubs and
orange trees, seated on a colorful, checkered bench amply decorated by
references to courtly values (fig. 8.11). This particular pictorial segment, with its green arbor and its intimate group of young people playing music and engaging in amorous intrigues, creates the impression
of a genuine citation, displaying in condensed form topical visions of
courtly love, falconry, musical amusements, and aristocratic idleness

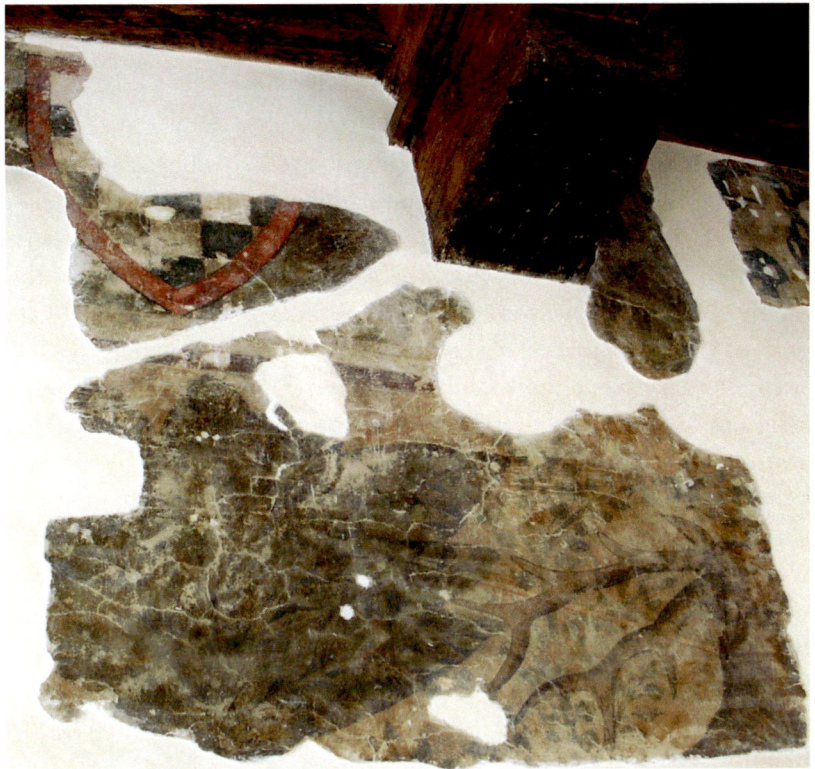

Figure 8.9. Hunting scene, Florence, Palazzo dei Cerchi, first half of the 14th century.

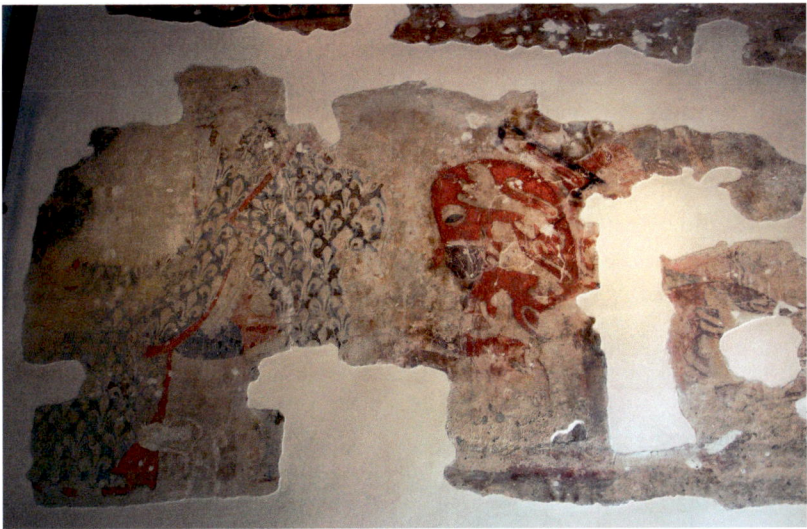

Figure 8.10. Tournament scene, Florence, Palazzo dei Cerchi, first half of the 14th century.

on the part of ladies of wealth, sitting with their lap dogs, and so on. It is well known that especially in the realm of handcrafted objects — whether jewelry boxes, ivory caskets, or mirror cases (as we have seen already in the case of the *Castellana di Vergiu*) — such images of the theme Garden of Love were widely disseminated as representing gardens of paradise, places of carefree joy, and are thus generally considered to be emblematic of chivalric and noble virtues.[17] The images assumed fixed topoi both in courtly love poetry and in allegorical literature. In the Camposanto, the formal structure of the image evidences a citation of just such a topos through its frieze style and nearly isocephalic arrangement of the figures on the surface of the picture plane. The motif is not developed as an argument; it is not thematically individualized, nor is it notably specific regarding its content. It is, instead, semantically inverted in relation to the composition as a whole, so as to become a negative image of the "vita oziosa," of a life dedicated to love and consecrated to death. As such, it contradicts the larger panoramic image of the Thebaid, painted next to the *Trionfo della morte,* an image that confronts the viewer with the monastic and hermetic life of the early desert monks as an ideal paradigm of a Christian and pious paradise lived out here on earth (fig. 8.12). In a manner consistent with the pictorial program in Pisa, this topos reappears later in Florence in the complex decorative program of the chapter room of S. Maria Novella (ca. 1365). Here, too, one sees the Garden of Love with its music-making nobility showing a time and place either prior to or beyond paradise and from which no direct path is offered that would lead to the gate of heaven guarded by Saint Peter (fig. 8.13).

I could mention many other examples, say, the well-known *camera* in the tower building of the Palazzo Communale in San Gimignano, which might have been among the semiprivate spaces of the *Podestà* (fig. 8.14).[18] Most interpretations of these murals are shrouded by aporias and uncertainties. Alongside the story of Aristotle and Phyllis and that of the Prodigal Son, the scenes include an unidentified narrative involving the dangers faced by a young man who (not unlike the Prodigal Son), so tempted by love, forgets the tasks assigned to him. As Jean Campbell has stressed, in the apparently intimate imagery there is no direct or personal connection to the Podestà, whose office rotated at

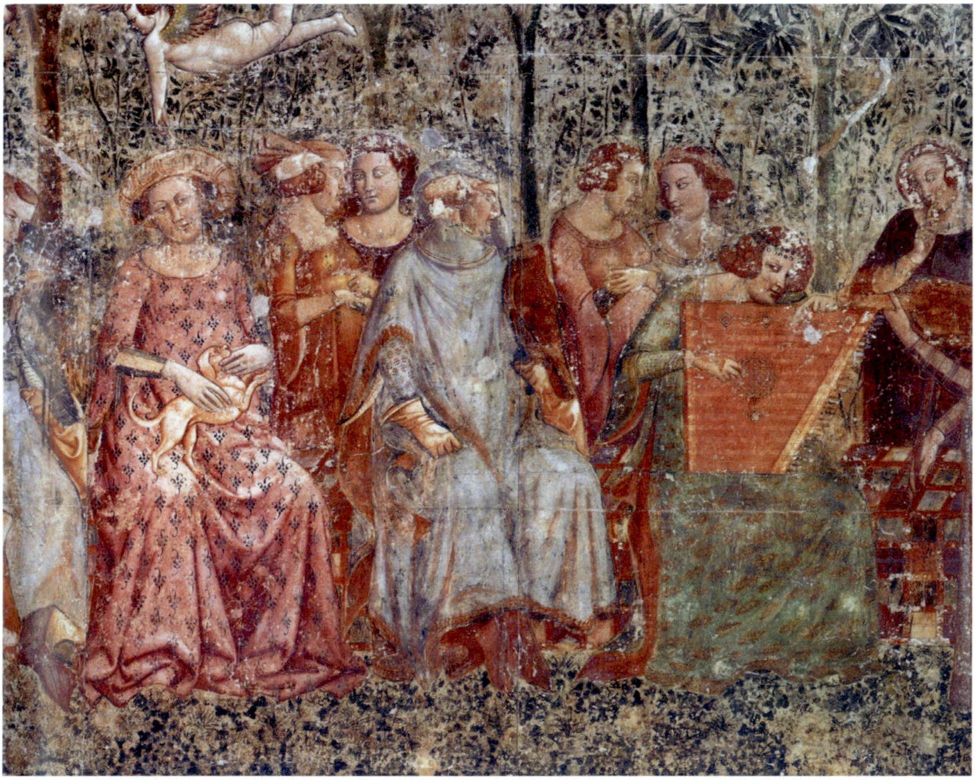

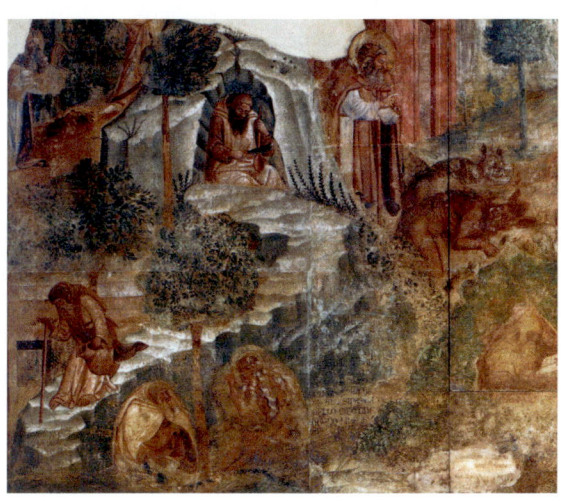

Figure 8.11. Buffalmacco, Triumph of Death, detail, Pisa, Camposanto, ca. 1335.

Figure 8.12.
Buffalmacco,
Thebaid, detail, Pisa,
Camposanto, ca. 1335.

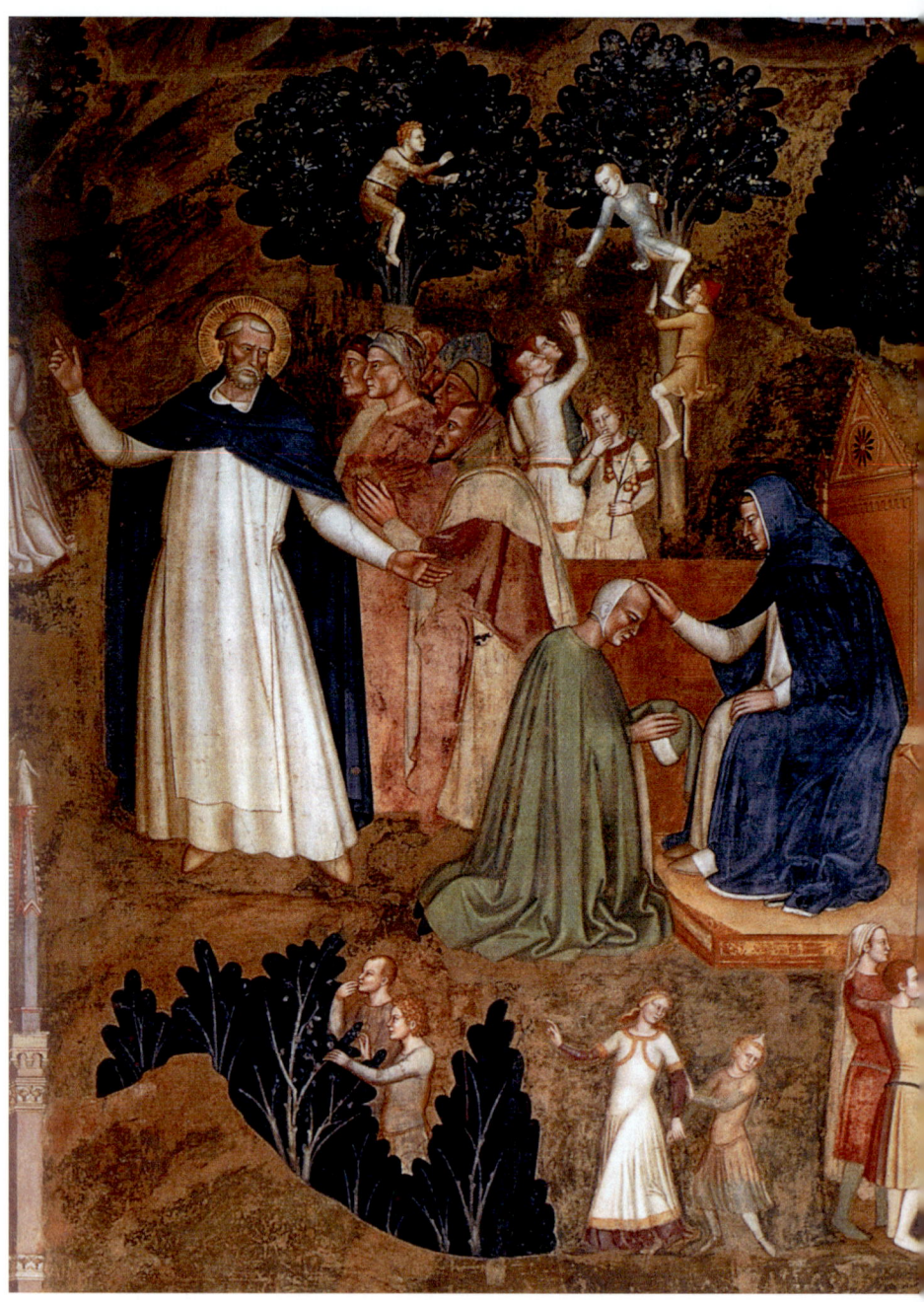

Figure 8.13. Andrea di Bonaiuto, Via Veritatis, detail, Florence, S. Maria Novella, Spanish Chapel, ca. 1365.

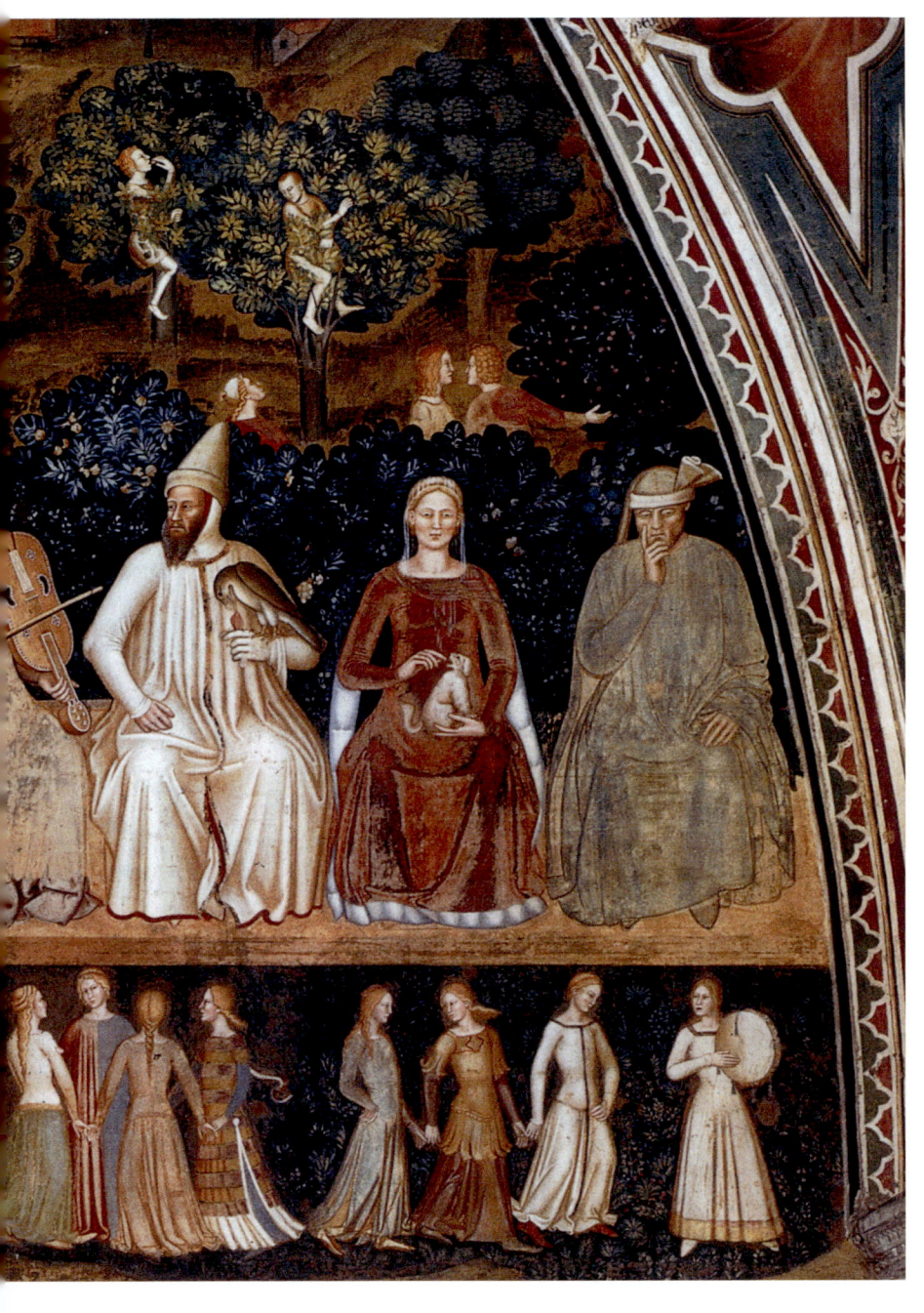

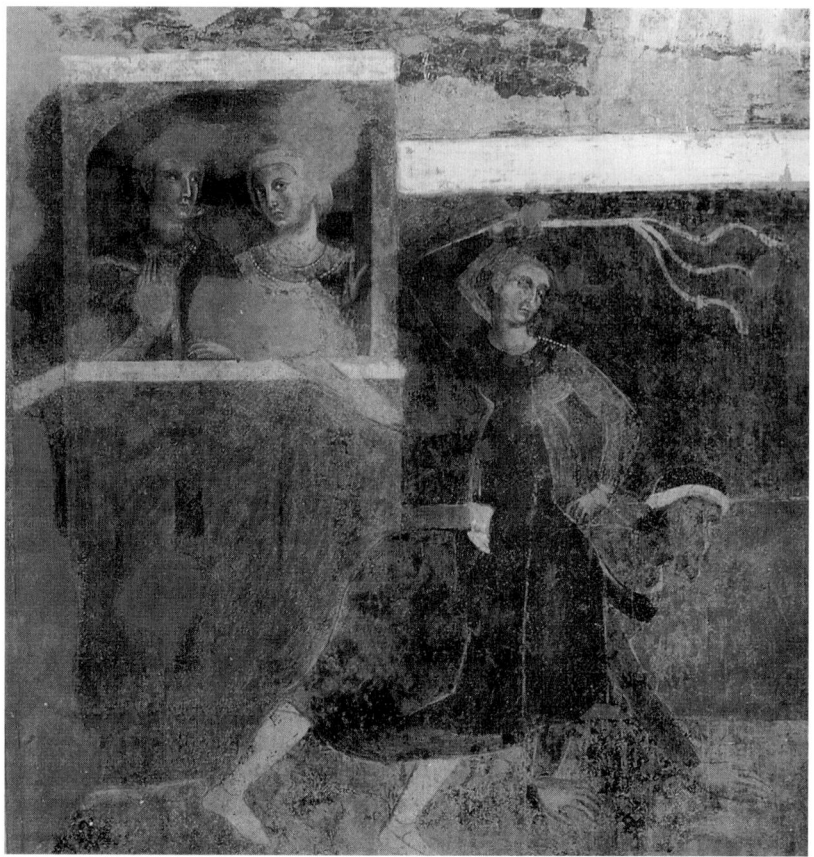

Figure 8.14. Memmo di Filippuccio (attr.), Aristotle and Phyllis,
San Gimignano, Palazzo Communale, ca. 1305–15.

six-month intervals. It is conceivable that the rather banal representation of the *curialitas,* suggesting a more moderate or circumspect approach to love, was intended, as Campbell writes, to show a generalized
"code of civilized behavior, rather than anything specifically chivalric or courteous."[19] If this is correct, then the imagery is consistent with
the distinctive institutionalized topoi relating to the deportment and
maxims of conduct in the rhetorical texts and educational writings
of Brunetto Latini and others. Both ethically and socially, the historical
context was thus conditioned by a social contradiction: while the Podestà and the dominant classes of the commune pursued their politic

stratagems in direct opposition to the nobility's specific cultural practices, they appropriated the nobility's images and ideals of chivalrous love and virtue for the sake of their own self-fashioning. As I argued above, these appropriative practices gave the images second-order meanings or new levels of reference liberated from older meanings while simultaneously untethering those images from the substantial or authoritative meanings they once had.

None of the clients who commissioned such pictorial programs, and certainly not the Podestà of San Gimignano, would therefore have thought to interpret the story of the young Tristan (kidnapped by Norwegian merchants while preoccupied by a game of chess) in terms of maxims of noble comportment, even if, and this has been my point all along, what we *seem* to be shown is a knight or nobleman, setting out on a hunt, only to become emotionally entangled on the way with an enticing young maiden.

Notes

This article is based on a conference paper. Only the most indispensable references have therefore been inserted in the notes. The manuscript was completed in 2007; subsequent publications on the subject have not been considered.

1. Attilio Schiaparelli, *La casa fiorentina e i suoi arredi nei secoli XIV e XV,* ed. Maria Sframeli and Laura Pagnaotta (Firenze, 1908; reprint, Firenze: Le Lettere, 1983), 157–59; Maria Sframeli, *Il centro di Firenze restituito: Affreschi e frammenti lapidei nel Museo di San Marco* (Firenze: Bruschi, 1989), 164, cat. 10 (with citations of the literature).

2. See Sframelli, *Centro di Firenze restituito,* 164, cat. 10.

3. Maribel Königer, "Die profanen Fresken des Palazzo Davanzati in Florenz: Private Repräsentation zur Zeit der internationalen Gotik," *Mitteilungen des Kunsthistorischen Instituts in Florenz* 34 (1990): 245–78.

4. Ibid., 249–51.

5. Walter Bombe, "Die Versnovelle der Kastellanin von Vergi in Elfenbein-Schnitzereien des Florentiner Museo Nazionale," *Monatshefte für Kunstwissenschaft* 7.2 (1914): 61–66; Beate Schmolke-Hasselmann, "La Châtelaine de Vergi auf Pariser Elfenbein-Kästchen des 14. Jahrhunderts: Zum Problem der Interpretation literarischer Texte anhand von Bildzeugnissen," *Romanisches Jahrbuch* 27 (1976): 52–76.

6. See Monika Dachs, "Zur ornamentalen Freskendekoration des Florentiner Wohnhauses im späten 14 Jahrhundert," *Mitteilungen des Kunsthistorischen Instituts in Florenz* 37 (1993): 71–129, passim.

7. Giovanni Boccaccio, *Il Decamerone,* ed. Vittore Branca (Milano: A. Mondadori, 1985), 20: "s'odono gli uccelletti cantare, veggionvisi verdeggiare i colli e le pianure . . . il cielo più apertemente . . . le quali molto più belle sono a riguardare che le mura vòte della nostra città." *Decamerone,* 23: "e con logge e con sale e con camere, tutte ciascuna verso di sé bellissima e di liete dipinture ragguardevole ed ornata." The translations in the text are my own.

8. Brunetto Latini, *Li livres dou Trésor,* ed. Spurgeon Baldwin and Paul Barrette (Tempe: Arizona Center for Medieval and Renaissance Studies, 2003), I, 129: "de fere tor & autres maisons de pierres"; "font maisons grant & pleinieres & peint"; and "por avoir joie & delit sans guerre & sans noise."

9. Franco Sacchetti, *Il Trecentonovelle,* ed. Valerio Marucci (Roma: Salerno, 1996), 568 (Novella CLXX): "che tra gli alberi di sopra dipignessi molti uccelli."

10. Ibid.: "Messere, io ce ne dipinsi molti piú; ma questa vostra famiglia ha tenute le finestre aperte, onde se ne sono usciti e volati fuori maggior parte."

11. Ibid., 474 (Novella CL): "la più bella ventura del mondo."

12. Ibid., 533–38 (Novella CLXI).

13. Marvin Becker, *Florence in Transition,* 2 vols. (Baltimore, MD: Johns Hopkins University Press, 1967–68); Gene Adam Brucker, *The Civic World of Early Renaissance Florence* (Princeton, NJ: Princeton University Press, 1977).

14. Brenda Preyer, "Two Cerchi Palaces in Florence," *Villa I Tatti* (1985): 613–30; Enrica Neri Lusanna, "Interni Fiorentini e pittura profana tra Duecento e Trecento: Cacce e giostre a palazzo dei Cerchi," *Opere e giorni: Studi su mille anni di arte europea,* ed. Klaus Bergdolt and Giorgio Bonsanti (Venezia: Marsilio, 2001), 123–30.

15. For the account of this fresco cycle, see Neri Lusanna, "Interni Fiorentini e pittura profana."

16. Friederike Wille, *Die Todesallegorie im Camposanto in Pisa: Genese und Rezeption eines berühmten Bildes* (München: Allitera, 2002).

17. Paul F. Watson, *The Garden of Love in Tuscan Art of the Early Renaissance* (Philadelphia: Art Alliance Press, 1979).

18. C. Jean Campbell, *The Game of Courting and the Art of the Commune of San Gimignano, 1290–1320* (Princeton, NJ: Princeton University Press, 1999), esp. 107–90.

19. Ibid., 112.

PART III

The Visual Culture of *Tristan*

CHAPTER NINE

Discourses of Curiosity

The Materiality of Meaning in Edition Studies
and Cultural Studies

MARTIN BAISCH

This study is an experiment. It is an attempt to use the term *materiality* in the context of Gottfried von Strassburg's *Tristan* in two ways and to link them. The first definition of the category *materiality* is self-evident, given the known conditions of production, reception, and distribution of medieval literature. Materiality means here the actual transmission of the text as an artifact in its tactile, haptic, visual, and sometimes ol-factory dimensions. Discussed by scholars under the rubric of mate-rial philology, the materiality of the transmission of medieval litera-ture should also be regarded as a starting point in the current debate about the *rephilologization* of literary studies.[1] This methodological orientation enables both conceptualizing the philology of manuscript culture and conceptualizing manuscript culture as a specific topic of philology.[2] In this way, scholars are working toward a deeper under-standing of medieval textuality and of premodern models of texts. As well, a renewed interest in philology has brought new energy to edi-torial work on Gottfried's *Tristan and Isolde,* a scholarly enterprise that had been stagnant for years.

    The second definition of the term *materiality* refers not to the trans-mitted manuscripts and their materiality but rather to the materiality of meaning itself. This understanding turns the relationship between text and materiality on its head. The importance given by editors to the materiality of (transmitted) texts must be seen in the context of a general turn in literary studies in the 1960s. Critics began to concentrate more and more on the material aspects of works of art. This *turn to materiality* was related to a strongly anti-hermeneutic approach then current in many fields of theoretical inquiry, where it took a more complex form than in editorial work.[3] According to Roger Lüdeke, the material attributes of the storage medium—the book, for example—lose their secondary status as simple carriers of meaning when research focuses on the influence of the media itself, on the meaning of the text, and on the conditions of transfer. This kind of criticism concentrates on the *medium, body,* and physical *carrier* of literary texts.[4]

According to this perspective, materiality belongs to a research context that investigates the "non-representational moment(s) of representation" and that has intensely discussed such factors as *appearance, aura,* or *presence*.[5] It also claims that media, for example, medieval manuscripts, do not serve, or do not serve well, for any kind of information transfer, creation of communication, or storage of knowledge. Rather, they are a realization of absence, a creation of aura, and a transfer of salvation.[6] For example, the material appearance of a codex can so dominate the text that the materiality of the medium excludes textuality. Further, textuality can be blocked and ignored, as Peter Strohschneider showed in his analyses of Wolfram's *Parzival* and the *Magnetberg* episode in *Reinfried von Braunschweig*. The phenomenal materiality of the manuscript thus dominates its discursive dimension.[7]

My aim here is to link both perceptions of materiality in one theory that integrates a philological analysis of transmitted materials into a more general investigation of culture. Discussions about the conditions and functions of materiality and presence in medieval culture are necessarily influenced by the concrete materiality of transmission. It is thus desirable to situate the epistemological and functional significance of textual criticism within cultural studies, for it can by no means be separated from them.

To illustrate this thesis I have selected as an example the poetic commentaries in Gottfried's *Tristan,* one of the most difficult yet central problems of this romance.[8] This example has been chosen because the insertion of these digressions into the narrative affects the scope of both kinds of materiality mentioned above. On the one hand, poetic commentaries as *material text* differ from manuscript to manuscript, from one means of transmission to another.[9] On the other hand, poetic commentaries, understood as *semiotic text,* are a means of producing and reflecting on presence and, as I discuss first, can also be seen as producing presence.[10] Next I briefly describe and analyze the beginning of the betrayal episodes in Gottfried's romance, taking into consideration the results of a textually critical analysis. I conclude by discussing editorial and philological problems of Gottfried's *Tristan* from the perspective of materiality.

Poetic Commentaries and the Materiality of Meaning

Commentaries are characteristic of the courtly romances of the twelfth and thirteenth centuries. Functioning as an excursus, they accompany the narrative and momentarily interrupt it, underscoring dimensions of meaning derived from the narrative level or constituting new dimensions of significance. As an aspect of formalized literature, commentaries are also portals through which widely shared, often objective knowledge is made available. To further explore the functions of commentary and excursus in Gottfried's *Tristan*, three features are discussed below: commentary as a mode of rational explanation, presence, and curiosity.

Commentaries are related to the mode of rational explanation that became increasingly popular in the courtly romance from the twelfth century.[11] Klaus Ridder understands specific modifications in the fabric of telling and reflection as *one* form of the literary mode of rational explanation. He discusses moments when two spheres confront one another in the texts: the commentary, the sphere in which the fictional narrator and the imagined listener interact; and the narration, the sphere in which the characters are the actors.[12] Authors of courtly romances integrated knowledge of diverse provenance into their excurses, in order to reflect on a general, abstract level about their narratives and to spread general knowledge throughout their romances.[13]

Authors who had received a clerical education adopted the form of Latin commentaries for their vernacular texts in order to incorporate such modalities of reflection into their narratives, enabling conversations about what they had read and heard.[14]

Yet Gottfried's *Tristan* makes use of poetic commentary in a way that is unlike any other courtly romance. Two hundred years of research has not managed to explain it entirely. Perhaps its most important function is to make the narrative ambiguous. This is facilitated by other means of expression in the work, for example, allegories and other narrative devices, which are strongly linked to the commentaries.[15] The commentaries, however, enable the production of and reflection on phenomena such as contemporarity, or presence.

Literary texts, even Gottfried's *Tristan,* produce effects of presence in many ways: through deictically indexed expressions, changes in verb tense (similar to Chrétien's *Cligès*), and turns of phrase that reflect oral speech.[16] They also employ figures belonging to the inventory of classical rhetoric, for example, personification, apostrophe, exclamations, and descriptions, of which Gottfried was a master (e.g., the entrance of Tristan and Isolde at the trial in Weisefort). At the end of the prologue Gottfried falls back on discursive models of memory and salvation in order to lend his protagonists an aura of the contemporary.[17] The presence effects there are created in analogy to the Eucharist. As Christian Kiening puts it:

> besteht dabei auch die Möglichkeit, mit dem, was als Gegenstand gegenwärtig wird, das vergegenwärtigende Medium der Schrift bzw. des Textes selbst hervortreten zu lassen: durch Anordnung und Hervorhebung, Reim und Rhythmus, Kursus und Figürlichkeit—all das, was den 'Glanz' von Schrift und Rede vermittelt; aber auch durch Reflexion und Digression, Kommentar und Exegese—all das, was Texte als Texte markiert

> ———

> [Using what is present in the object, it is also possible to emphasize those aspects of writing, of text, that are already available and that create the effect of presence: order and emphasis, rhyme and rhythm, cursus and figuration, all of which communicate

the glamour of writing and speech; and also reflection and digression, commentary and exegesis, which mark text as text.][18]

The first of the three great courtly love excursuses, which the text dubs "ein langiu rede von minne" (a long speech about courtly love), serves as a prominent example of the creation of presence effects. The first excursus is inserted into the text directly after Tristan and Isolde drink the love potion, reflect on the effects of the fatal event, and come together in love for the first time. The excursus is characterized by a deictically indexed manner of speech: the often anaphoric repetition of *we* summons the so-called penitent sermon tone of the excursus (*Tristan* 12217 ff., 12279 ff.), which suggests criticism of the contemporary way of life.[19] The narrator accuses himself as well as his contemporaries of sinning against love in words and deeds, of accepting love's "venality." The commentary alternates between conjuring the unusual power of unconditional love and criticizing contemporary fashions of courtly love. This alternation was marked in the younger manuscripts by varying initials and capital letters.[20] There are more episodes that produce effects of presence, for example, Mark's so-called *Maifest* (May Festival) or the *Petitcreiu* episode, which must be left for discussion elsewhere.

Curiosity as a narrative phenomenon seems to be closely linked to the insertion of a commentary level into the narrative. Gottfried often makes theoretical digressions after speaking about or visualizing specific objects, artifacts, or circumstances that provoke the curiosity and the astonishment of the figures and the audience.[21] Thus they steer the emotional responses to the narrative, and belong to striking and highly effective poetics that are among the most widely discussed topics concerning Gottfried's rhetorically charged romance.[22]

Mark's Doubt and the Poetic Commentaries

In the betrayal episodes of the romance, the curiosity of the reader or the audience is correlated to the doubts of the cuckolded king. More precisely, his doubts and suspicion keep the story going. The reader (or hearer) is curious not because he or she wants to know *whether* the king is being cuckolded but because he or she wants to know *how*. The fact that the reader knows more than the king does not make the latter ridiculous. Rather, the text enacts the pleasure of deceit, of misleading, which corresponds to the reader's curiosity about the manner in which Mark sets his traps and the couple escapes them.

In the betrayal episodes the rational capacities of the protagonists have to win out again and again in situations of moral danger. These episodes of adultery begin with a farcical scene, known in German as the *bettemaere* (bed story), which is set in the royal bedchamber.[23] The Eilhart version of *Tristan* does not contain this scene. The Munich *Tristan* manuscript (Munich, Bayerische Staatsbibliothek, Cgm 51) shows a redactor making many changes to this episode.[24] King Mark wonders about the gossip at the court, which he has learned about from Duke Marjodo, and he accepts the duke's advice that he interrogate Queen Isolde when they are alone at night. In the first round of questioning, Mark gains an advantage. Asked whom she would desire as protector during the absence of the king, who has (deceitfully) announced that he is going on pilgrimage, Isolde answers: Tristan. The answer saddens Mark, and he forwards it and his displeasure to Marjodo. The redactor of the Munich *Tristan* manuscript shortened Marjodo's reaction, eliminating his evaluative remarks that Isolde cannot hide her love for Tristan and his directive to Mark that it is absurd to allow Tristan to remain at court.[25] Thus in Cgm 51 Marjodo's answer is changed so that it does not provide Mark with guidelines or instructions for further action.

The happily unsuspecting queen tells her intimates about the dialogue with Mark. As Brangaene, who is versed in courtly intrigues, hears in whose custody Isolde wishes to be placed, she recognizes the deceit and knows that Marjodo is behind it (*Tristan* 13727–52). Brangaene's shocked, uncourtly exclamation—"â, tumbe" (you fool) she shouts at her lady—is downplayed in the text of Cgm 51, reduced to the more generic interjection "owe" (alas), which respects the queen's status.

After the dialogue between Isolde and Brangaene, the narrator turns again to the figure of Mark in order to reflect in an excursus upon Mark's doubts and suspicions. This episode, known as the "zwîvel unde arcwân" (doubt and suspicion) excursus, has been heavily abridged in Cgm 51.[26] Addressing the audience, the excursus begins with two rhetorical questions (*Tristan* 13781–84). In the initial part of the excursus, the narrator rejects the possibility that a true lover could be suspicious of his beloved:

> wan daz ez al div werlt tuot.
> so ist ez ein harte vnwiser muot.
> vnde ist ein michel tumpheit.
> daz man an liebe zwifel treit.
> wan niemen ist mit liebe wol.
> an dem er zwifel haben sol.
>   (Cgm 51, fol. 73ra; *Tristan* 13795–13800)

———

[Except that it is the way of the world; it is a very imprudent attitude and great folly to harbor suspicion in love: for none is at ease with a love of which he must needs be suspicious.]

Still more damage would develop, the narrator elaborates, if the suspecting lover attempted to transform his suspicious thoughts into objective knowledge: "daz ist im danne ein herzeleit. / vor allem herze leide" (The fact which he was at pains to track down becomes a grief surpassing all others) (Cgm 51, fol. 73ra; *Tristan* 13808–9). At this point the redactor of Cgm 51 interrupts the transcription of the excursus, thus omitting the original text's radical and surprising shift of argument in the evaluation of suspicion in love.

> Der Zweifel, als das geringere Übel, ist, an der Wahrheit gemessen, gut. Wo nämlich Übel schlimmeres Übel hervorbringt, ist das geringere von beiden gut. Der bedrückendste Zweifel ist also leichter zu ertragen als seine Bestätigung. Da der Zweifel nun einmal zur Liebe gehört, soll sie daran festhalten. Mit ihm nur kann sie sich bewahren, denn die Wahrheit ist das Ende der Liebe.[27]

———

[When measured again truth, doubt is good because it is the lesser evil. For when evil brings forth greater evil, the lesser of the two is good. The most oppressive doubt is easier to bear than corroboration. And since it is a fact that doubt and love belong together, love should hold fast to it. Only with doubt can love survive, for truth destroys love.]

By leaving out this additional theoretical elaboration of the question, which complicates the issue, the text in Cgm 51 is deprived of an elaborate thinking process. Cgm 51 lacks this positive evaluation of doubt and suspicion. Instead, in it, they remain malicious.

Given this context, it makes sense to inquire again into the function of the doubt and suspicion excursus in the unabridged text. Mark Chinca writes:

> This excursus recasts the initial narrative situation, that of Mark beset by doubt and suspicion, as an instance of the universal condition of lovers. The king, a definite person, has become a function of an indefinite type. Likewise the policy he subsequently adopts for finding out the truth is shown to be in accordance with love's habitual way of operating. The behavior of an individual is derived from general principles, which render it intelligible and enable one to predict its development and final outcome. . . . There remains, however, something in this digression that is surplus to the requirement of explaining the definite by derivation from the indefinite. Gottfried's reasoning implies advice.[28]

In talking about the universal condition of lovers, the excursus is producing effects of presence. The commentary also refers to Mark's jealousy, so the insertion that interrupts the narrative also serves to characterize the king. Mark's behavior is legitimized by the excursus: "To love is to doubt, it seems, and the lover inevitably progresses from doubt to certainty. Mark may be foolish, he may be embarked on a course that will end in certain grief and shatter his love for Isolde, but neither he nor any lover can act otherwise."[29]

Foolish Mark is no more stupid than the narrator who apparently possesses superior knowledge. Both reach the same aporia; even the dialectician knows no better. "The analytical excursus remains, in spite of its own pretensions, fully consonant, because Mark's foolishness is our foolishness as well, from which even the narrator does not escape."[30] Yet it is exactly this section of the unabridged "doubt and suspicion" excursus excusing Mark's actions that is missing from Cgm 51, so that in it the excursus is nothing less than unconcealed criticism of King Mark.[31] The end of the excursus leads once more to Mark, who wants to be freed of his suspicions by forcing the discovery of the truth.[32]

In the second round, another nocturnal dialogue between Mark and Isolde, Mark, advised by Marjodo (*Tristan* 13877–81), returns to announce his departure. First the king allows his body to speak. He hugs and kisses Isolde on the eyes and mouth in order to prove the authenticity of his love. Mark lies to find out the truth, and he makes use of the materiality and presence of his body. Such love sets traps. The narrator signals sympathy for Isolde: "diu gelêrte küniginne / si stiez sin wider sin" (The well-tutored Queen parried cunning with cunning) (*Tristan* 13882–83).[33] The queen pretends to have at first understood Mark's pilgrimage as a joke (a deception). Now, though, she pretends to recognize that Mark is serious. To eliminate Mark's suspicions, she too resorts to physical gestures and begins to cry. This tactic succeeds (13885–98). The narrator attaches a misogynistic commentary to Isolde's deceit; there is nothing untrue to be discovered in women, except for their ability to cry without reason and whenever they want (13899–906). Addressing the listeners directly, this excursus on Isolde's deceit presents a generalized view and produces effects of presence. Yet it, too, cannot be found in Cgm 51. Since this little commentary relates to Isolde's deception, we can conclude that the scribe objected to depicting the queen negatively on the commentary level. Further abridgements in this episode create a tendency to present the character of Isolde in a positive light.

Mark becomes angry, and he sinks into "zorngallen" (bitter anger) (*Tristan* 14150). Here the second nighttime conversation of mutual deception ends in Cgm 51. Missing in it is a further discussion between Isolde and Brangaene, as well as the fourth and final night of deception, in which Isolde takes the initiative. In the unabridged version, Isolde uses the materiality of her body (tears, hugs, and kisses) in order to deceive her husband and king (14151–238). She also speaks about her hatred of Tristan and proclaims her desire to be under

Marjodo's protection.[34] Mark is not able to resist this complex and richly deceptive behavior. Thus the writer of Cgm 51 destroys Gottfried's artfully constructed structure of four speeches, in which each team (Mark–Marjodo; Isolde–Brangaene) wins the battle of words twice. According to Gottfried, the whole episode ends in a draw. King Mark does not succeed. The conflict between the parties remains in a state of suspense. The second part of the doubt-suspicion excursus claims that such a state is easier to bear for all persons involved. But the redactor of Cgm 51 has omitted this part of the doubt-suspicion excursus. The content of the remaining excursus, which emphasizes the negative aspects of doubt, along with the changes to the text, the missing passages, and further reformulations, strongly influence the characterization of Mark, increasing the negativity of his character. In this way Cgm 51 does allow the reader or hearer to participate in the paradoxical experience that doubt and suspicion in love cannot be overcome.

The Inaccessibility of Culture and the Materiality of Transmission

In his recent book on Tristan, Tomas Tomasek voices the following opinion about Cgm 51 and about the tradition of Gottfried's text in general:

> M ist für die Forschung auch deshalb von Interesse, weil die Handschrift . . . signifikante Kürzungen aufweist, die sie über *BEbe an B und E (auch N) weitergegeben hat, so dass der Text von MBE in der Forschung gern als "Kurzfassung" des *Tristan* bezeichnet wird. Von einer Kurzfassung im Sinne einer eigenständigen, geplanten Gesamtredaktion kann hier allerdings kaum gesprochen werden, da es sich . . . um vom Schreiber nicht zuletzt aus Platzersparnisgründen während des Schreibvorgangs vorgenommene Straffungen handelt. . . . Von Gottfrieds Werk existieren keine Fassungen mit Originalitätsmerkmalen, denn die einzig abweichende MBE-Version trägt die Züge einer kürzenden, gegenüber dem Autortext sekundären Bearbeitung. . . . Angesichts

der vielfältigen Probleme, mit denen sich die Gottfried-Philologie bei der Deutung der Dichtung konfrontiert sieht, ist es hilfreich zu wissen, dass die Überlieferungszeugen des *Tristan* und— ungeachtet des editionsphilologischen Nachholbedarfs— die auf ihnen basierenden Ausgaben eine zumindest hinreichende Interpretationsgrundlage bieten.[35]

―――――――

[M (Munich) is also of interest to scholarship because it contains abbreviations of the narrative that were passed on to manuscripts B and E (also N) via a hypothetical manuscript group *BEbe. For this reason, scholarship has dubbed the text of MBE the short version of *Tristan*. In fact, it is erroneous to speak of a short version here if by that term is meant an independent, planned redaction of the entire work, since what we have is an abridgment arising mostly from a lack of space and carried out by the scribe during the writing process. . . . No version of Gottfried's work exists that shows any signs of being an original. The MBE version, the only one that differs from the others, has the characteristics of a secondary and abridged reworking of the author's text. . . . In view of the manifold problems confronting Gottfried scholarship when interpreting the poem, it is helpful to know that the manuscript witnesses for *Tristan* and the edition based on them offer an adequate foundation for interpretation (even if there is room for improvement from the perspective of philology and editing).]

In my opinion, something has gone wrong here, both terminologically and concerning the content of the argument. Tomasek seems to be working with a classical conception of authorship, which sees the author as a figure producing coherence and centering the discourse, a conception that ignores the contingency and materiality of the transmission of medieval texts. Yet in the past few decades, scholars have shown that to talk about courtly romances philologically means talking about versions of courtly romances.[36] Moreover, Tomasek fails to see the effects of this debate in textual criticism, which resulted in new research perspectives with regard to the poetry of the courtly romance under the keywords *retelling* and *rewording*.[37] Christian Kiening emphasizes that medieval texts "konstituieren sich nicht als Ausdruck dichterischer Originalität, sondern als Teilhabe an einem 'Überliefer-ungsgeschehen,' als Aufnahme, Abwandlung und Anverwandlung anderer Texte" (are not constituted as an expression of authorial origi-nality, but rather through participating in a process of transmission, as the inclusion, modification, and adaptation of other texts).[38] Toma-sek ignores also some fundamental insights of new literary theories, for example, Umberto Eco's differentiation between the author's in-tention and the *intentio operis.*

A *Tristan* philology influenced by cultural studies would pay more attention to the materiality of its object. Its task consists of a critical reprocessing of the forms of the text (which after all remained a frag-ment) found in manuscripts and of the various configurations of the text and the cycles of illustration. It should also reflect on the pos-sibilities of making a virtual manuscript (especially because there are so many variants), as the Basler *Parzival* project has impressively demonstrated.[39]

Traditional editing ignores the medium of literary transmission, the manuscript as manuscript (i.e., as a haptic object): "In the material medium of parchment and ink, the editing of the intelligible text has been developed as an art of the impossible—as the art of actually di-vorcing the undivorcable, namely text from its material support. Yet this art has been practiced, and has been practicable, ineluctably on the condition that the text divorced from its support of origin be rein-scribed onto a target material support."[40] We might consider how edit-ing might be able to do without the traditional hierarchical understand-ing of text first and document second. Hans Walter Gabler suggests that this hierarchy be inverted, from text and document to document and text. In this manner the text becomes a function of the document:

> It must be emphasized that we ought to question the validity
> of perpetuating the orthodoxy of viewing "text and document"
> in a hierarchical order. What I propose, instead, is a redefinition,
> by inverse ordering, of this hierarchy—an inversion applicable
> not merely to the explorative practice of electronic editions, but
> ultimately to our conceptualizing of "documents" and "texts"

throughout in scholarship and criticism. The document need no more be defined as a function of the text, as, implicitly or explicitly, in traditional editing. On the contrary, the text should be seen fundamentally as a function of the document. For, after all, it is documents that we have, and documents only. In all transmission and all editing, texts are (and, if properly recognized, have always been) constructs from documents. For to edit texts critically means precisely this: to construct them.[41]

Theoretically, the reversal of the hierarchy of text and document is an important and valid position. The consequences for the practice of editing, however, are defined by the specific conditions of a given tradition.

The unavailability of the medieval culture becomes especially clear when we consider the materiality of the available manuscripts. The changes in the deception dialogues in Cgm 51 show a programmatic distancing from Gottfried's version. The analysis of details in different versions of the text draws our attention to the ideologically and aesthetically transgressive potential of Gottfried's work. His contemporaries argue against it, correct it, criticize it. The meaning of materiality is based on the materiality of meaning.

Notes

1. Jan-Dirk Müller, "Neue Altgermanistik," *Jahrbuch der Schillergesellschaft* 39 (1995): 445–53; Stephen G. Nichols, "Introduction: Philology in a Manuscript Culture," *Speculum* 65 (1990): 1–10; Stephen G. Nichols, "On the Sociology of Medieval Manuscript Annotation," in *Annotation and Its Texts,* ed. Stephen A. Barney (New York: Oxford University Press, 1991), 43–73; Stephen G. Nichols, "Why Material Philology? Some Thoughts," in *Philologie als Textwissenschaft: Alte und neue Horizonte,* ed. Helmut Tervooren and Horst Wenzel, *Zeitschrift für deutsche Philologie, Sonderheft 116* (Berlin: Erich Schmidt, 1997), 10–30; Walter Erhart, ed., *Grenzen der Germanistik: Rephilologisierung oder Erweiterung?* Germanistische Symposien: Berichtsbände XXVI (Stuttgart: Metzler 2004); Ulrich Wyss, "Entphilologisierung: Aderlaß in der Mediävistik und Neubegründung durch den Auszug der Linguisten," in *Literaturwissenschaft und Linguistik von 1960 bis heute,* ed.

Ulrike Haß and Christoph König, Marbacher Wissenschaftsgeschichte 4 (Göttingen: Wallstein, 2003), 21–30.

2. Peter Strohschneider, "Innovative Philologie?," in *www.germanistik 2001.de: Vorträge des Erlanger Germanistentags,* ed. Hartmut Kugler and Friedrich M. Dimpel (Bielefeld: Aisthesis, 2003), 901–24.

3. Hans Ulrich Gumbrecht, ed., *Materialität der Kommunikation,* Suhrkamp Taschenbuch Wissenschaft 750 (Frankurt am Main: Suhrkamp, 1988).

4. Roger Lüdeke, "Materialität und Varianz: Zwei Herausforderungen eines textkritischen Bedeutungsbegriffs," in *Regeln der Bedeutung: Zur Theorie der Bedeutung literarischer Texte,* ed. Fotis Jannidis, Gerhard Lauer, Matías Martínez, and Simone Winko, Revisionen 1 (Berlin: de Gruyter, 2003), 459:

> Die materiellen Eigenschaften des Speichermediums verlieren ihren sekundären Status als einfache Bedeutungträger in dem Moment, in dem die spezifischen Bedeutungseffekte der materiellen Aufzeichnungs- und Vermittlungsbedingungen selbst in Zentrum des Forschungsinteresses gelangen: in Untersuchungen, deren Schwerpunkt sich verstärkt auf die 'Medien,' 'Körper' und physischen 'Träger' von Texten verlagert.

> ———

> [The material characteristics of the storage medium lose their secondary status as simple carriers of meaning at the moment when scholarship sets its sights on studying the specific effects that the material conditions of recording and communicating have on the creation of meaning, for example, in studies where the center of gravity has shifted toward studying media, the body, and the physical carriers of texts.]

5. Christian Kiening, "Gegenwärtigkeit: Historische Semantik und mittelalterliche Literatur," *Scientia Poetica* 10 (2006): 24:

> Das, was in Dingen, Phänomenen oder Situationen gegenwärtig wird, hat zwar Teil an den Ordnungen des Sagens und des Zeigens. Doch es ist zugleich deren Unverfügbares, Rückseite und Möglichkeitsbedingung: das, was in den Bedeutungen nicht aufgeht, sondern mit diesen einher und über diese hinausgeht. Dieses nicht-repräsentatorische Moment der Repräsentation hat in den letzten Jahren unter Stichworten wie 'Erscheinen,' 'Aura,' 'Materialität' oder eben 'Präsenz' verstärkt Aufmerksamkeit auf sich gezogen.

> ———

> [Whatever is present in objects, phenomena, or situations does participate in the arrangements of saying and showing. But there is also a part

that is not within reach, that turns its back, the conditions that create its possiblity, that part which transcends its meanings, coexisting with and exceeding them. This is representation's nonrepresentational side, and in recent years key terms such as *appearance, aura, materiality,* and *presence* demonstrate that it has attracted increased attention.]

And see Kiening's "Ästhetik des Liebestods: Am Beispiel von *Tristan* und *Herzmaere,*" in *Das fremde Schöne: Dimensionen des Ästhetischen in der Literatur des Mittelalters,* ed. Manuel Braun and Christopher Young, Trends in Medieval Philology 12 (Berlin: de Gruyter, 2007), 171–76.

6. Hans Ulrich Gumbrecht, *Diesseits der Hermeneutik: Die Produktion von Präsenz,* trans. Joachim Schulte (Frankfurt am Main: Suhrkamp, 2004); Martin Seel, "Über den kulturellen Sinn ästhetischer Gegenwart—mit Seitenblicken auf Descartes," *Merkur* 61.7 (2007): 619–26.

7. Peter Strohschneider, "Sternenschrift: Textkonzepte höfischen Erzählens," *Wolfram-Studien* 19 (2006): 34 ff.

8. See Christoph Huber, *Gottfried von Straßburg: Tristan,* Klassiker-Lektüren 3 (Berlin: Erich Schmidt, 2000; rev. ed., 2001), 112–19; Bernd Schirok, "Handlung und Exkurse in Gottfrieds Tristan: Textebenen als Interpretationsproblem," in *Texttyp, Sprechergruppe, Kommunikationsbereich: Studien zur deutschen Sprache in Geschichte und Gegenwart; Festschrift für Hugo Steger zum 65. Geburtstag,* ed. Heinrich Löffler (Berlin: de Gruyter, 1994), 33–51; Walter Haug, "Erzählung und Reflexion in Gottfrieds *Tristan,*" in *Der Tristan Gottfrieds von Straßburg: Symposion Santiago de Compostela, 5. bis 8. April 2000,* ed. Christoph Huber and Victor Millet (Tübingen: Niemeyer, 2002), 281–94.

9. Peter Shillingsburg, *Resisting Texts: Authority and Submission in Constructions of Meaning,* Editorial Theory and Literary Criticism (Ann Arbor: University of Michigan Press, 1997), 74: "A material text, any material text, is the reader's only access route to the work. A linguistic text cannot exist for anyone (who does not already hold it in memory) without a material medium; the linguistic text and its medium are the material text with all the implications of that union. Material texts are the production of utterance. The first material text (say the manuscript) is the first attempted union of the essayed version and a document."

10. Ibid., 71: "A semiotic text consists of the signs found recorded in a physical form of the work."

11. Klaus Ridder, "Rationalisierungsprozesse und höfischer Roman im 12. Jahrhundert," *Deutsche Vierteljahrsschrift für Literaturwissenschaft und Geistesgeschichte Sonderband* 78.2 (2004): 175–99; Christoph Huber, "Formen des

'poetischen Kommentars' in mittelalterlicher Literatur," in *Commentaries—Kommentare,* ed. Glenn W. Most, Aporemata 4 (Göttingen: Vandenhoeck and Ruprecht, 1999), 323–52.

12. Ridder, "Rationalisierungsprozesse und höfischer Roman," 186.

13. Ibid., 187.

14. Ibid., 187. See Schmitz, *Die Poetik der Adaptation: Literarische inventio im "Eneas" Heinrichs von Veldeke* (Tübingen: Niemeyer, 2007), 8–10.

15. Jan-Dirk Müller, "Gottfried von Straßburg: *Tristan*; Transgression und Ökonomie," in *Transgressionen: Literatur als Ethnographie,* ed. Gerhard Neumann and Rainer Warning, Litterae 98 (Freiburg: Rombach, 2003), 223:

> Narration, Allegorese, Kommentare und Exkurse treten füreinander ein und wirken, indem sie Euphorisches und Dysphorisches verschränken, in der Ambiguisierung der Minne zusammen. Die ineinander geschachtelten Schreibweisen sind mehr als unterschiedliche Annäherungsversuche an den Gegenstand, nämlich disparate Antworten auf seine Inkommensurabilität und Ambivalenz.

> ——————

> [Narration, allegory, commentary, and excurses stand in for one another and work together to make *Minne* ambiguous by means of interlocking euphoric and disphoric elements. . . . These ways of writing, which are folded into one another, are more than merely different attempts to approach the object of study (i.e., *Minne*). Rather, they are disparate answers to *Minne*'s incommensurability and its ambivalence.]

16. Karl Bertau, *Über Literaturgeschichte: Literarischer Kunstcharakter und Geschichte in der höfischen Epik um 1200* (München: C. H. Beck, 1983), 128, describes Gottfried's poetic technique as "Verklanglichung des Sinns" (meaning transformed into sound). See also Bertau, *Deutsche Literatur im Europäischen Mittelalter* (München: C. H. Beck, 1972), 929–33. According to Bruno Quast, "Gottfried von Straßburg und das Nichthermeneutische: Über Wortzauber als literarästhetisches Differenzkriterium," *Mitteilungen des Deutschen Germanistenverbandes* 51.3 (2004): 257, "entwickelt Gottfried die Vorstellung eines Wortzaubers, der auf Sinnevidenz nicht verzichten kann" (Gottfried develops a concept of word magic that cannot forego the evidence of the senses), to which Bertau has attested a transformation of significance into sound as a principle of form.

17. Kiening, "Ästhetik des Liebestods," 182–85.

18. Kiening, "Gegenwärtigkeit: Historische Semantik und mittelalterliche Literatur," 27 ff.; and see the excellent introduction by Christina Lech-

termann, *Berührt werden: Narrative Strategien der Präsenz in der höfischen Literatur um 1200,* Philologische Studien und Quellen 191 (Berlin: Erich Schmidt, 2005), 7–19. This and all other translations in the text and notes are by Ann Marie Rasmussen.

19. Citations are from *Tristan,* ed. Karl Marold, Friedrich Ranke, and Werner Schröder (Berlin: de Gruyter, 1977), given by line numbers; and translations are from *Tristan,* trans. Arthur T. Hatto (Harmondsworth: Penguin, 1960; reprint, London: Penguin, 2004).

20. Tomas Tomasek, *Gottfried von Straßburg,* Universal-Bibliothek 17665 (Stuttgart: P. Reclam, 2007), 153.

21. C. Stephen Jaeger, "Wunder und Staunen bei Wolfram und Gottfried," in *Inszenierungen von Subjektivität in der Literatur des Mittelalters,* ed. Martin Baisch et al. (Königstein: Ulrike Helmer, 2005), 122–39.

22. See Tomasek, *Gottfried von Straßburg,* 253 ff.: "Gottfrieds Rhetorik zielt zweifellos darauf, beim Publikum eine 'affektbetonte Vereindringlichung' . . . zu erzielen—u.a. durch die große Fülle von Wortfiguren, von denen . . . 'sinnliche Wirkungen' ausgehen, die aber zugleich auch ein hohes Maß an semantischer Differenzierung erzeugen" (Doubtless Gottfried's rhetoric is intended to create in its audience an emotionally charged intensification by means [among others] of the great number of rhetorical figures that give rise to sensory effects but that also aims for a high degree of semantic differentiation).

23. See Rainer Warning, "Die narrative Lust an der List: Norm und Transgression im Tristan," in Neumann and Warning, *Transgressionen: Literatur als Ethnographie,* 175–212, on the betrayal episodes.

24. Gottfried von Strassburg, *Tristan und Isolde: Mit der Fortsetzung Ulrichs von Türheim; Faksimile-Ausgabe des Cgm 51 der Bayerischen Staatsbibliothek München,* ed. Ulrich Montag and Paul Gichtel (Stuttgart: Müller und Schindler, 1979).

25. The scribe changes the rest of Marjodo's answer syntactically: "zware herre im ist also. daz muget ir merken wol hie bi. als liep iu wip und ere si. so dultes nimere" (In truth, my lord, that is how things are with him. You can tell, for however much he loves his wife and his honor, he will not tolerate this any longer) (Munich MS, fol. 72va; see *Tristan* 13712–19).

26. The first appearance of these terms is found in *Tristan* 13721; see the commentary by Rüdiger Krohn, ed. and trans., 3 vols. (Stuttgart: P. Reclam, 1993–95), 3:201 ff.

27. See Winfried Christ, *Rhetorik und Roman: Untersuchungen zu Gottfrieds von Straßburg Tristan und Isold,* Deutsche Studien 31 (Meisenheim am Glan: Anton Hain, 1977), 58.

28. Mark Chinca, ed., *Gottfried von Straßburg: Tristan,* Landmarks of World Literature (Cambridge: Cambridge University Press, 1997), 73 ff.

29. Ibid., 74. See *Tristan* 13827–30: "zwîvel sol an liebe wesen: / mit dem muoz liebe genesen; / die wîle sî den zwîvel hât, / die wîle mag ir werden rât" (doubt shall dwell with love and with love shall be healed, for as long as love has doubt she can find help).

30. Gert Hübner, *Erzählform im höfischen Roman: Studien zur Fokalisierung im Eneas, Iwein und im Tristan* (Tübingen: A. Francke, 2003), 333.

31. Chinca, *Gottfried von Straßburg: Tristan,* 74, emphasizes how limited the validity of the excursus is: "Although it is couched in the terms of quaestio infinita, the excursus has only intermittent validity. Its supposedly universal principles do not govern Mark's doubt for all of the time, and they are even contradicted by what Gottfried says in another excursus."

32. The scribe changes lines 13857 ff.: "Aber kam ez eines nahtes sô, / als er ez unde Marjodô . . . zu aber chom ez eines nahts so. / daz der chunch vnde Mariodo."

33. Peter Kern, "Sympathielenkung im *Tristan* Gottfrieds von Straßburg," in *Sammlung — Deutung — Wertung: Ergebnisse, Probleme, Tendenzen und Perspektiven philologischer Arbeit; Festschrift für W. Spiewok zum 60. Geburtstag,* ed. Danielle Buschinger (Stuttgart: Sprint-Druck, 1988), 215 ff., believes that the reader or the listener of the romance has a liking for Tristan and Isolde:

> Da ist zum einen der Stoff selber, das Sujet der schwankhaft getönten Geschichten vom übertölpelten Ehemann, ein in der ganzen Weltliteratur seit eh und je verbreitetes Genre, bei dem es geradezu zur literarischen Konvention gehört, dass das Herz des Lesers für die findigen Liebenden schlägt, der hintergangene Ehemann aber dem Spott preisgegeben ist. . . . Aus dem Minnesang kannte das damalige Publikum ja die huote (die Aufpassersituation), die merkaere und die nîdaere (die Aufpasser und Mißgünstigen); sie waren dort stets aus dem Blickwinkel der Liebenden gesehen und als Minnefeinde verurteilt, gescholten, verwünscht.

> ———

> [First, there is the story itself, the fabliau-like topic of the duped husband, a hoary genre of world literature. It is virtually a literary convention of this genre that the reader's heart beats higher for the clever lovers, while the betrayed husband is exposed to mockery. From the genre of courtly love poetry *(Minnesang),* the medieval audience was acquainted with the guardianship of women *(huote)* and the watchers

(merkaere) and the envious ones *(nîdaere),* which were always viewed from the perspective of the lovers and were judged, scolded, and cursed as the enemies of love.]

34. Commenting on the materiality of Isolde's body, James A. Schultz, "Bodies That Don't Matter: Heterosexuality before Heterosexuality in Gottfried's *Tristan,*" in *Constructing Medieval Sexuality,* ed. Karma Lochrie (Minneapolis: University of Minnesota Press, 1997), 94, notes: "Before 1200 they [breasts] do not figure in any description of beautiful women in MHG texts. In fact, Isold's embrace of Mark, mentioned earlier, and Jeschute's second encounter with the hero of Parzival represent the first references by MHG writers to women's breasts in erotic contexts." See Hartmut Semmler, *Listmotive in der mittelhochdeutschen Literatur: Zum Wandel ethischer Normen im Spiegel der Literatur,* Philologische Quellen und Studien 122 (Berlin: Erich Schmidt, 1991), 133: "Die Initiative geht diesmal allein von Isot aus. Zunächst setzt sie massiv nonverbale Mittel ein, um ihre Zuneigung zu bekunden. Dann folgt ein formal dicht durchstrukturierter Monolog Isots" (This time Isolde takes the initiative alone. First she employs nonverbal means to signal her affection. There then follows a monologue by Isolde that is tightly structured formally).

35. Tomasek, *Gottfried von Straßburg,* 57 ff., 66.

36. Joachim Bumke, *Die vier Fassungen der Nibelungenklage: Untersuchungen zur Überlieferungsgeschichte und Textkritik der höfischen Epik im 13. Jahrhundert,* Quellen und Forschungen zur Literatur- und Kulturgeschichte 8 (Berlin: de Gruyter, 1996); Nikolaus Henkel, "Kurzfassungen höfischer Erzähldichtung im 13./14. Jahrhundert: Überlegungen zum Verhältnis von Textgeschichte und literarischer Interessenbildung," in *Literarische Interessenbildung im Mittelalter: DFG-Symposion 1991,* ed. Joachim Heinzle, Germanistische Symposien 14 (Stuttgart: Metzler, 1993), 39–59; Peter Strohschneider, "Höfische Romane in Kurzfassungen: Stichworte zu einem unbeachteten Aufgabenfeld," *Zeitschrift für deutsches Altertum und deutsche Literatur* 120 (1991): 419–39.

37. See Joachim Bumke and Ursula Peters, eds., *Retextualisierung in der mittelalterlichen Literatur: Zeitschrift für deutsche Philologie,* Sonderheft 124 (Berlin: Erich Schmidt, 2005).

38. Christian Kiening, *Zwischen Körper und Schrift: Texte vor dem Zeitalter der Literatur* (Frankfurt am Main: Fischer, 2003), 25.

39. Michael Stolz, "Wolframs *Parzival* als unfester Text: Möglichkeiten einer überlieferungsgeschichtlichen Ausgabe im Spannungsfeld traditioneller Textkritik und elektronischer Darstellung," *Wolfram-Studien* 17 (2002):

294–321; Michael Stolz, "Computergestütztes Kollationieren—Ein Werk-stattbericht aus dem Basler *Parzival*-Projekt," in *Edieren in der elektronischen Ära,* ed. Gottfried Reeg and Martin J. Schubert, Informations-Technologie und Geisteswissenschaften—Schriften der Internationalen Tustep User Group 1 (Berlin: Weidler, 2004), 113–26.

40. Hans Walter Gabler, "The Primacy of the Document in Editing" (unpublished manuscript). German version at http://computerphilologie .tu-darmstadt.de/jg06/gabler.html (January 23, 2008).

41. Ibid.

CHAPTER TEN

Textual Worlds—Pictorial Worlds

Interpreting the Tristan Story in Illuminated Manuscripts

ELKE BRÜGGEN
and HANS-JOACHIM ZIEGELER

The relatively weak representation of the Tristan story in the German illuminated manuscripts of the Middle Ages contrasts with a multitude of text-independent pictorial witnesses realized in different media as either cyclical designs or singular depictions.[1] As Norbert H. Ott observes, with more than sixty pictorial representations, a text-independent iconography is highly characteristic for the Tristan material.[2] This observation retains its value even with the reservation, already considered by Ott, that a comparison of materials "which were illustrated in the scriptographic tradition with those for which separate images exist" would only achieve full significance if it also included illustrated manuscripts not belonging to German literature.[3] It is important to stress that only on the basis of such material evidence would it be possible to analyze whether the approaches to the material chosen in different media vary, and whether such variation can provide information about "specific interpretative intentions, attempts at identification, ideological models."[4]

Important preliminary research that could facilitate such comparisons has not yet been undertaken. Even the three main manuscripts in which text versions of the material evidence associated with the

names Gottfried von Strassburg and Ulrich von Türheim were combined with sequences of images have yet to be studied in depth with
regard to similarities and differences in their ways of visualizing the
material. Previous research has mainly focused on the early Munich
manuscript (Bayerische Staatsbibliothek, cgm 51). But the *Tristan*
manuscript in Cologne (Historisches Archiv der Stadt, W*kl.f°88)
and the one in Brussels (Bibliothèque Royale de Belgique, MS 14697)
await a thorough analysis; indeed, the Brussels manuscript has not
even been described in detail. Therefore, this chapter focuses on a specific thematic unit, namely, the story of Riwalin and Blanscheflur, Tristan's parents, and offers a comparative analysis of the diverse forms of
coexistence, cooperation, and conflict between text and image. This
analysis is preceded by two sections. As a means of orientation, we provide basic information concerning the three codices to be analyzed
here. This is followed by considerations of the different ways in which
each manuscript handles the cyclical method of illumination.

I

The earliest and—at least in terms of splendid book decorations—
most magnificent of these manuscripts is Cgm 51 of the Bayerische
Staatsbibliothek in Munich.[5] In two-column text, Gottfried's fragment is followed by the *Tristan* sequel by Ulrich, both in abridged
versions.[6] A dating of the manuscript earlier than the fifth decade of
the thirteenth century seems hardly reasonable.[7] Fifteen folios with
illustrations now remain. They were produced separately, not much
later than the written pages, and bound singly into or attached to the
fascicles.[8] With its full-page pictorial folios, divided into several registers and displaying about 118 scenes, the manuscript represents a type
of illumination completely different from that of the other two codices.
It was clearly influenced by the example of Latin scriptoria and became constitutive for German illuminated epic manuscripts in the thirteenth century.[9]

The text of the *Tristan* manuscript MS W*kl.f°88 from the Historisches Archiv der Stadt Köln is closely related to the text of the

Munich manuscript (and also to that of the manuscript of the Biblioteca Estense, MS Est. 57, in Modena).[10] The scribe, Willekin, finished working on it on August 23, 1323, as his entry on folio 263 tells us. Nine pen drawings decorated with a very limited range of colors accompany the text, seven of which belong to Gottfried's version of the Tristan story and two to the sequel by Ulrich.[11] They are included in a two-column text as framed single-column pictures. The manuscript represents a type of epic illustration mainly used in France, where it played an important role alongside historiated initials, rectangular pictures spread across several columns, and marginal illustrations.

The paper manuscript MS 14697 in the Bibliothèque Royale de Belgique in Brussels was produced by Diebold Lauber in Hagenau. Using criteria based on style and costume history, the art historian Lieselotte E. Saurma-Jeltsch has recently suggested a date for the manuscript of "around 1455."[12] No full or even completely correct description of this single-column manuscript exists, even though it was analyzed and described in the first critical edition of Gottfried's *Tristan* by Eberhard von Groote, and several descriptions have appeared since then.[13] Although we cannot make up for this here, it is important for our discussion that the manuscript's general layout be clear.

Originally, the Brussels manuscript seems to have been composed of exactly 600 sheets of paper. Now, there are only 597 left; two sheets are missing at the end, and one sheet has been torn out between folios 411 and 412. The manuscript comprises four entities, all set down in single columns of about twenty-one to twenty-four lines per page: first, a table of contents (fols. 1r–8v); second, Gottfried's *Tristan* (fols. 9v–510v); followed with virtually no indication of a change in text by the third text, namely, *Tristan als Mönch* (Tristan as a Monk) (fols. 511r–78v); without a marked transition the fourth text follows, namely, the final 875 lines of Ulrich's *Tristan* (lines 2855–3730 on fols. 578v–97v, respectively 600r). This amounts in total to about 23,000 lines with several smaller omissions. All three parts were considered to be one large *Tristan* unit, as is made clear by the table of contents, which names 182 chapters for the entire constellation of texts. The Brussels manuscript actually comprises 184 sections, called chapters, each of which has a prose heading briefly summing up the contents of the chapter.[14] The chapters are counted in roman numerals that precede the headings.

II

The Byzantinist K. Weitzmann, whose classic study *Illustrations in Roll and Codex* may be mentioned in this context, regarded cyclical (or sequential) representation as the way to reproduce literary contents in a pictorial medium that is closest to the text.[15] However, a study of the Munich, Cologne, and Brussels *Tristan* manuscripts already reveals huge differences. On the one hand, these result from the number of miniatures and the preference for monoscenic or polyscenic representations. Completely different frameworks for the pictorial *narration* and its relationship to the sequencing of the text are provided in the Cologne and Munich manuscripts, when in one case the decision is made to condense a story into nine monoscenic depictions (Cologne), while in the other the story is displayed in 118 (surviving) pictorial scenes on fifteen pictorial folios with a total of 84 registers (Munich). Differences can also result from the way in which the arrangement of the miniatures corresponds to the *mise-en-page* of the text. The relation between text and image may, in a strictly material sense, be more or less close, depending on the positioning of the miniatures. Thus single-column pictures can be integrated into the text so they are in immediate proximity to the lines to which they refer. Such a procedure was used in part in the Cologne manuscript, where the miniatures turn up in different places within the columns, in several cases directly following the lines to which they form a visual equivalent (images 1, 4, 7, and 9). In other cases additional text precedes the miniature in question, which can be explained by the fact that other goals were combined with the attempt to bring text and image as closely together as possible. One obvious goal was to mark textual units by placing the miniatures at the end of an episode. In addition, an attempt was clearly made to visualize the dramatic culminating points of the individual episodes. In those cases in which these culminating points do not coincide with the end of the episode, the structuring principle of dividing the material into episodes was apparently regarded as more important than the exact integration of the miniature into the text, and thus the direct connection between the miniature and the corresponding lines was lost.[16]

A far stricter separation of text and image is produced by the type of illumination chosen for the Munich manuscript. The concentration of the miniatures on separate folios leads to greater independence for the pictorial visualization of the Tristan story and seems to result in a more dynamic cooperation and confrontation between the textual and the pictorial versions. However, a closer examination is also advisable in this case. The pictorial folios were neither added to the manuscript in one coherent block, nor were they inserted into the manuscript at equal intervals. If one judges on the basis of the present condition of the manuscript, they are spread over eight of the thirteen fascicles, the number of pictorial folios per fascicle varying between one and four.[17] To quote P. Gichtel: "Even a fleeting glance must immediately reveal that the distribution of the folios in the manuscript is very uneven; one could almost speak of accumulations of illustrated folios."[18] Gichtel has demonstrated this feature of the manuscript by counting the folios of text between the pictorial folios: 2, 0, 3, 14, 6, 8, 20, 8, 5, 3, 3, 10, 2, 2. Nevertheless, he was able to show that an uneven distribution of the pictorial folios in the manuscript does not imply an uneven illustration of the text. In only three cases are the pictorial folios inserted (approximately) in the middle of the corresponding section of text. They are in fact mostly included in the relevant section but in such a way that a clear majority of lines either precedes or follows them. And finally, there are cases in which the pictorial folios lie outside the relevant sections, either before or after them.[19] Again quoting Gichtel: "These circumstances lead to a large degree of compensation, resulting in a generally balanced illustration of the text."[20]

Following the practice of the Lauber workshop, recently described in detail by Lieselotte Saurma-Jeltsch, the Brussels manuscript is also *hübsch gemolt* (nicely illuminated).[21] Containing ninety-one full-page miniatures, it originally had an additional minature on the verso side of the above-mentioned torn out leaf between folios 411 and 412. We cannot rule out the possibility that one of the three missing final folios was reserved for a miniature, which — similar to the Cologne codex — would have completed the cycle with an image of the two dead lovers. However, there is no evidence for such a final miniature, which would have been an exception to the rule deduced by Saurma-Jeltsch from a number of Lauber manuscripts and explicitly declared valid by her for the Brussels manuscript:

> Already in their function as a structuring device the miniatures have a substantial effect on the perception of the text, as they interrupt the flow of the text and divide it optically into certain sequences.—The miniatures offer a completely original, even unconventional version of the topic, combining the traditional Tristan story with other subjects closer to their time and thus transfer the Tristan story into other categories.[22]

It is the relation of the miniature-universe and the text-universe that is again under discussion. Are the results and Saurma-Jeltsch's evaluation correct?

At a first glance, the results seem indisputable. There are, however, some details that should be taken into account. To begin with, there are 184 chapters and originally 92 miniatures; both the heading and the number of a chapter are rubricated, regardless of whether a picture follows.[23] All headings are thereby given the same significance. As far as is discernible, those beginnings of chapters equipped with miniatures are marked by bookmakers. In addition, the production process of the manuscript becomes clear. We can take for granted that the scribe, probably the same individual as the rubricator, first wrote the text, leaving a specially indicated space for each miniature, which in a second and final step was supplied by the illuminator.[24]

Therefore, the question arises as to how the pictures were distributed in the manuscript, that is, in the texts. Ninety-two full-page miniatures is hardly a negligible amount. What were the criteria according to which the scribe chose the space for the miniatures? According to Saurma-Jeltsch, the miniatures have been arranged so that — regarded on their own — they build an integrated whole and divide the text "optically into certain sequences" following rules determined by features

that are contemporary with but independent from the Tristan tradition.[25] Yet this is not correct, as we shall show. Once again: Where
did the scribe get the criteria used to integrate the miniatures into the
text? We believe that these criteria were derived from the partly re-
constructible archetype of the written tradition of Gottfried's *Tristan.*

As is commonly known, a system of initials and slightly smaller
paragraph signs is used in the manuscripts of Gottfried's *Tristan,* from
the earliest to the latest (with the exception of the abridged version in
the Munich, Cologne, and Modena manuscripts). This system of initials served as the basis of both Marold's and Ranke's editions, derived,
as Ranke has shown, from the Heidelberg manuscript of the X-branch
and the Vienna manuscript of the Y-branch and their correspondences
with several old fragments.[26] The Brussels manuscript, with its chapter divisions, definitely follows the system of initials.

Admittedly, the Brussels manuscript did not transform all initials
into beginnings of chapters. Seven initials were adopted without mu-
tating into openings of chapters; many but not all of the paragraph
signs were taken over. Moreover, twelve chapters or their beginnings
appear in no other manuscript except the Brussels text. Nevertheless,
this means that the Brussels manuscript belongs to an astonishingly
constant system of initials, which can be attributed to the archetype of
an even earlier authority. Apart from the prologue, that is, the acrostic,
about 150 or even 168 of the 184 chapters of the Brussels manuscript
derive from the initials of the Heidelberg/Vienna manuscript tradition
and further manuscripts. This structure—obviously created according
to the contents, that is, according to the characteristics of the text—is
also decisive for the Brussels manuscript. To suggest that the miniatures structure the text is thus a distortion of the evidence arising from
the adoption of a specific disciplinary perspective.

In this way, "chapters" of different lengths emerge (apart from the
peculiarity of the three text transitions): the longest, chapter 108, contains 370 lines; the shortest, chapter 48, has only 24 lines. These very
different 184 chapters are related to the ninety-two miniatures, which
might suggest that a miniature is assigned to every second chapter.
While it has not been done so strictly, the miniatures are all in all
spread rather regularly through the text. More than three chapters in

a series are never presented without a picture, and this happens only twice. Conversely, there are only four instances in which three or four chapters in sequence are equipped with a miniature. Thus attention has been paid to a relatively regular distribution of the miniatures, which is undoubtedly related to the text and its characteristic integration of the three parts. In the Brussels Lauber manuscript, then, we have a sequence of miniatures based on the text; the structure of this sequence does not display a logic of its own, as is the case in the Cologne manuscript. There may be an accentuation of particular aspects, but these are founded in the general rules of composition of the whole cycle.

III

Let us now discuss the specific ways in which the Munich, Cologne, and Brussels manuscripts deal with the Tristan story by means of a comparative analysis of thematic units that are pictorially represented in all three. For this comparison, we have chosen the illumination of the so-called preliminary story, which focuses on Riwalin and Blanscheflur. In the Munich manuscript, it is treated in folios 7rv, 10rv, 11rv, and 15r (figs. 10.1–10.7). On the first three folios the scenes are divided into two registers; starting with folio 15, there are three registers on each page. Thus the preliminary story is *narrated* in a total of fifteen registers containing twenty-one to twenty-four scenes (depending on the count). The Riwalin-Blanscheflur story accounts for just over one-sixth of the surviving scenes; the impression that it was treated with special attention is supported by the particular care taken with these miniatures and by their high artistic quality.

If one starts by looking at the miniatures without particular consideration of the manuscript text, one is first struck by the repeated use of individual pictorial motifs and compositions. There are two occurrences each of a battle between heavily armed troops of horsemen (10r, top of fig. 10.3; 11v, top of fig. 10.6); the arrival of a messenger and the delivery of a message (10v, top right of fig. 10.4; 15r, top left of fig. 10.7); a farewell (10v, bottom left and right of fig. 10.4); a burial (11v, bottom of fig. 10.6; 15r, center of fig. 10.7); and the birth of a child (15r, top right and bottom right of fig. 10.7). In addition, situations

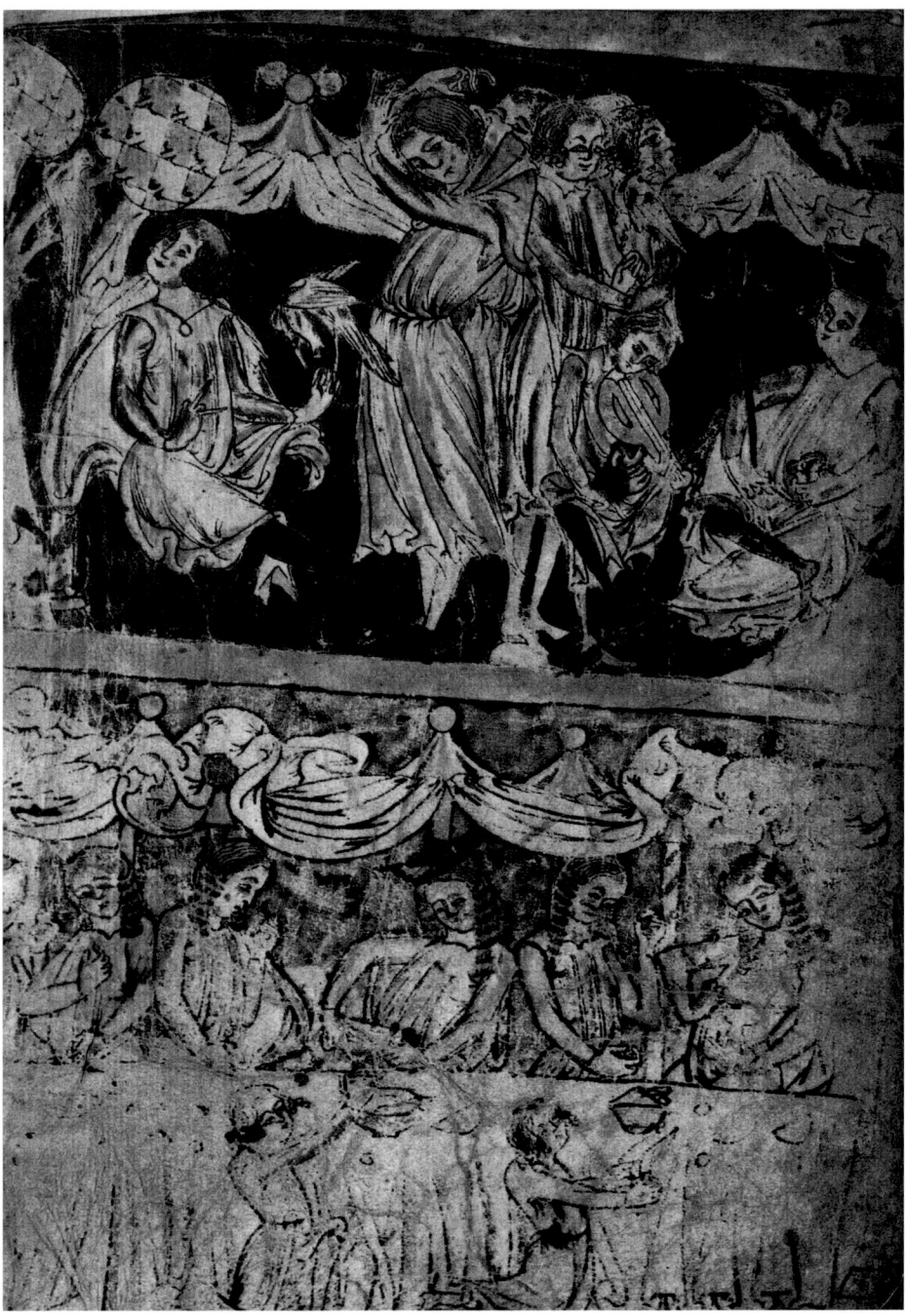

Figure 10.1. Munich, Bayerische Staatsbibliothek, Cgm 51, fol. 7r. Courtesy of
Bayerische Staatsbibliothek.

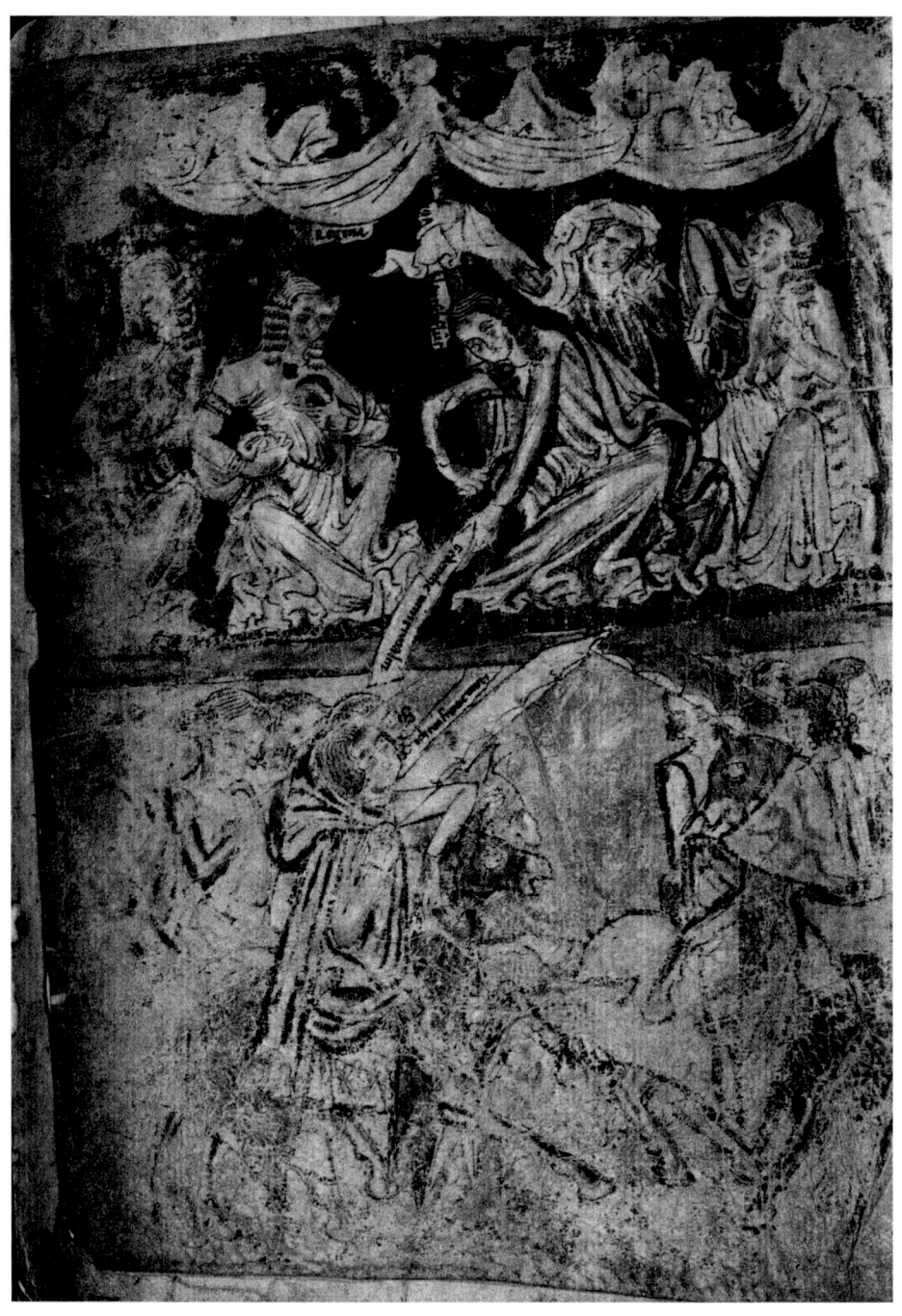

Figure 10.2. Munich, Bayerische Staatsbibliothek, Cgm 51, fol. 7v. Courtesy of Bayerische Staatsbibliothek.

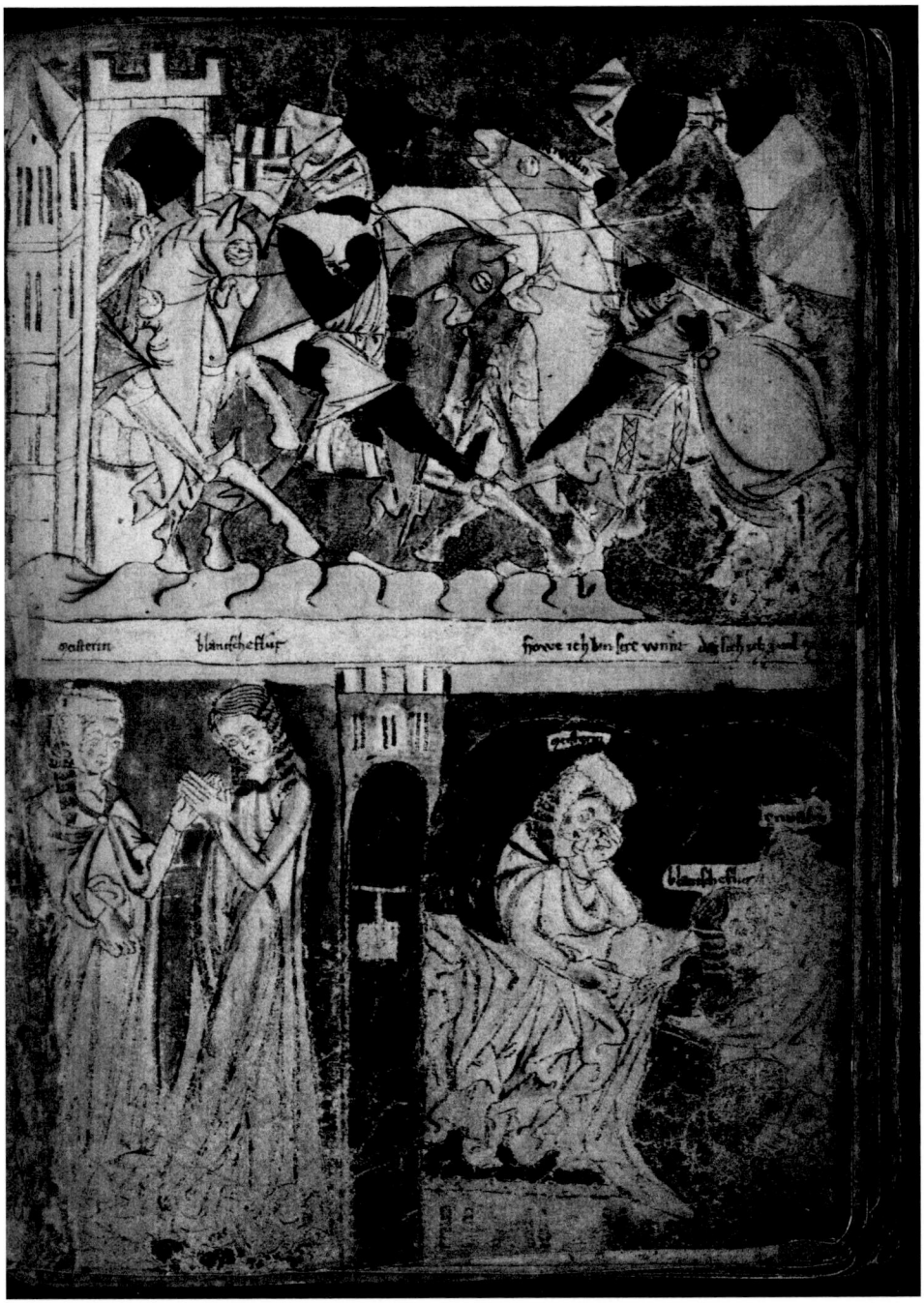

Figure 10.3. Munich, Bayerische Staatsbibliothek, Cgm 51, fol. 10r. Courtesy of Bayerische Staatsbibliothek.

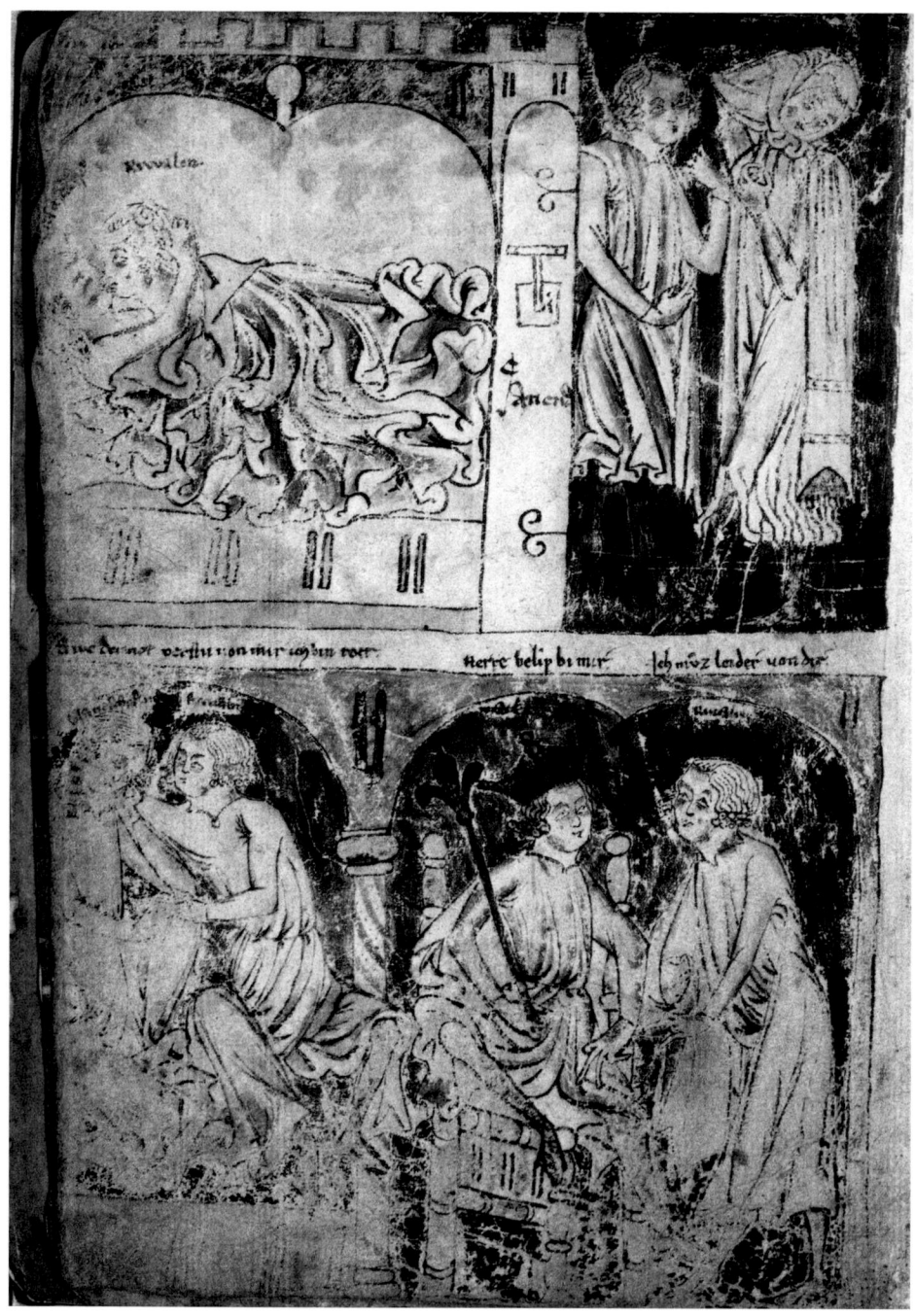

Figure 10.4. Munich, Bayerische Staatsbibliothek, Cgm 51, fol. 10v. Courtesy of Bayerische Staatsbibliothek.

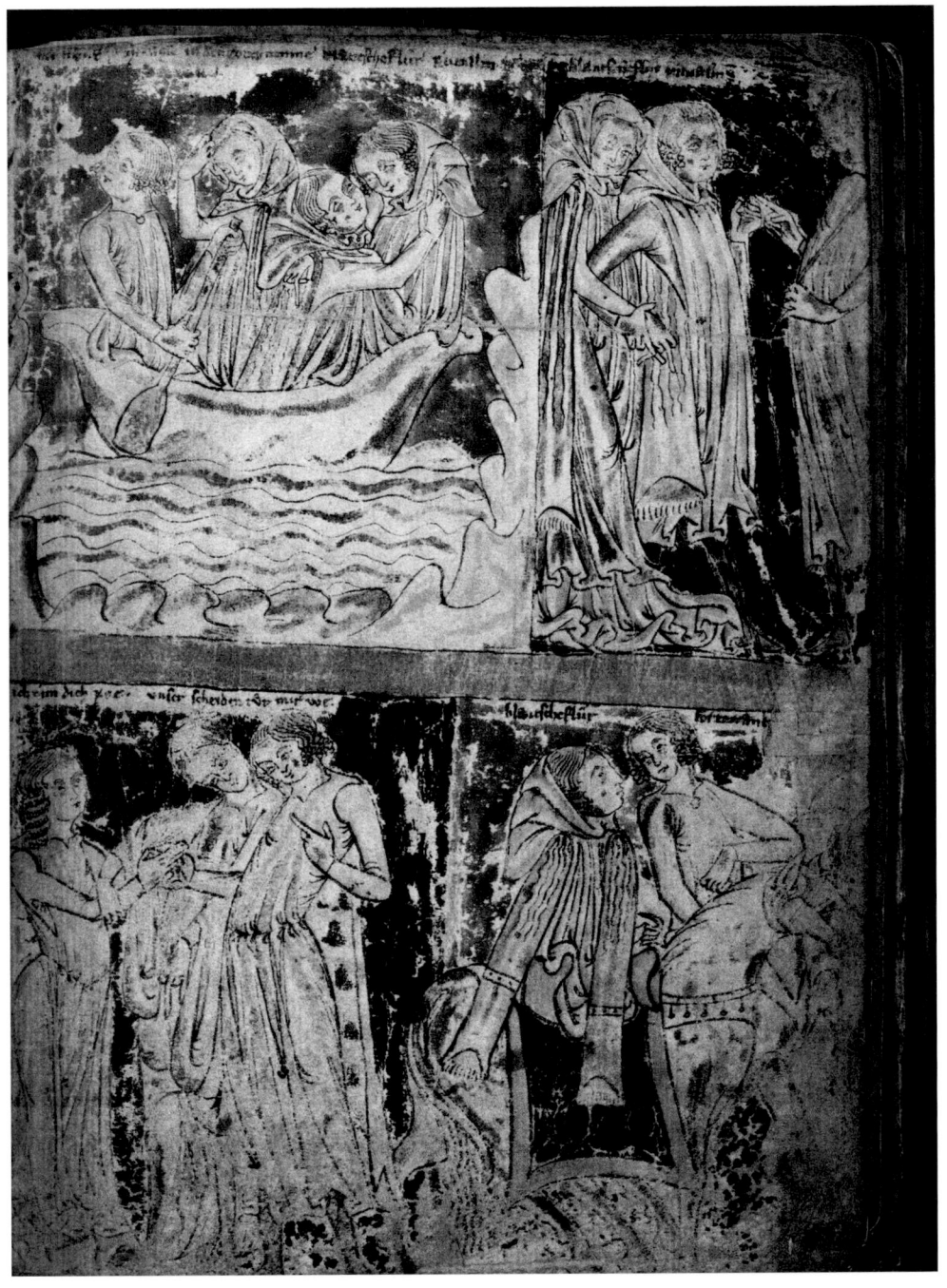

Figure 10.5. Munich, Bayerische Staatsbibliothek, Cgm 51, fol. 11r. Courtesy of Bayerische Staatsbibliothek.

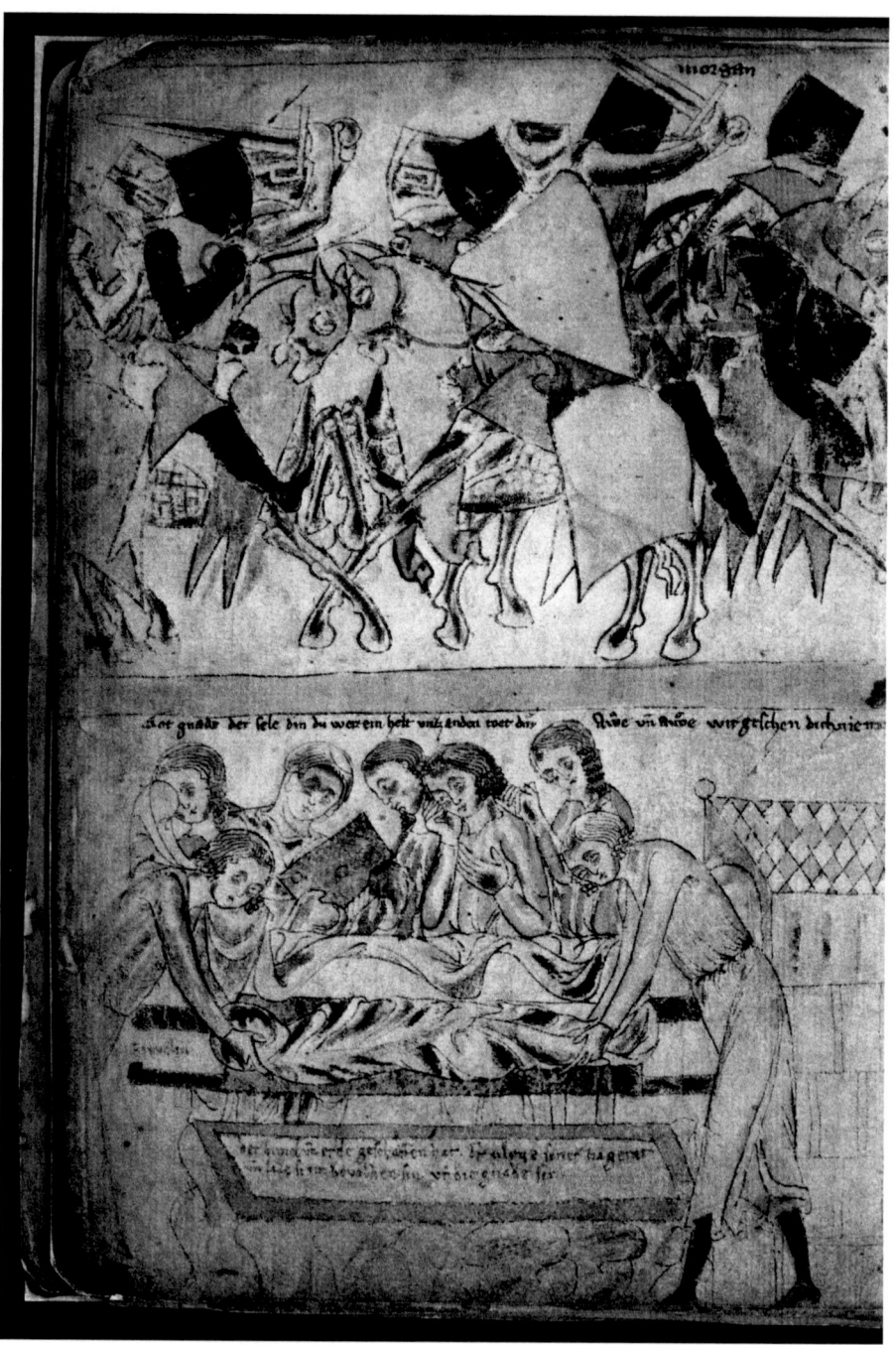

Figure 10.6. Munich, Bayerische Staatsbibliothek, Cgm 51, fol. 11v. Courtesy of Bayerische Staatsbibliothek.

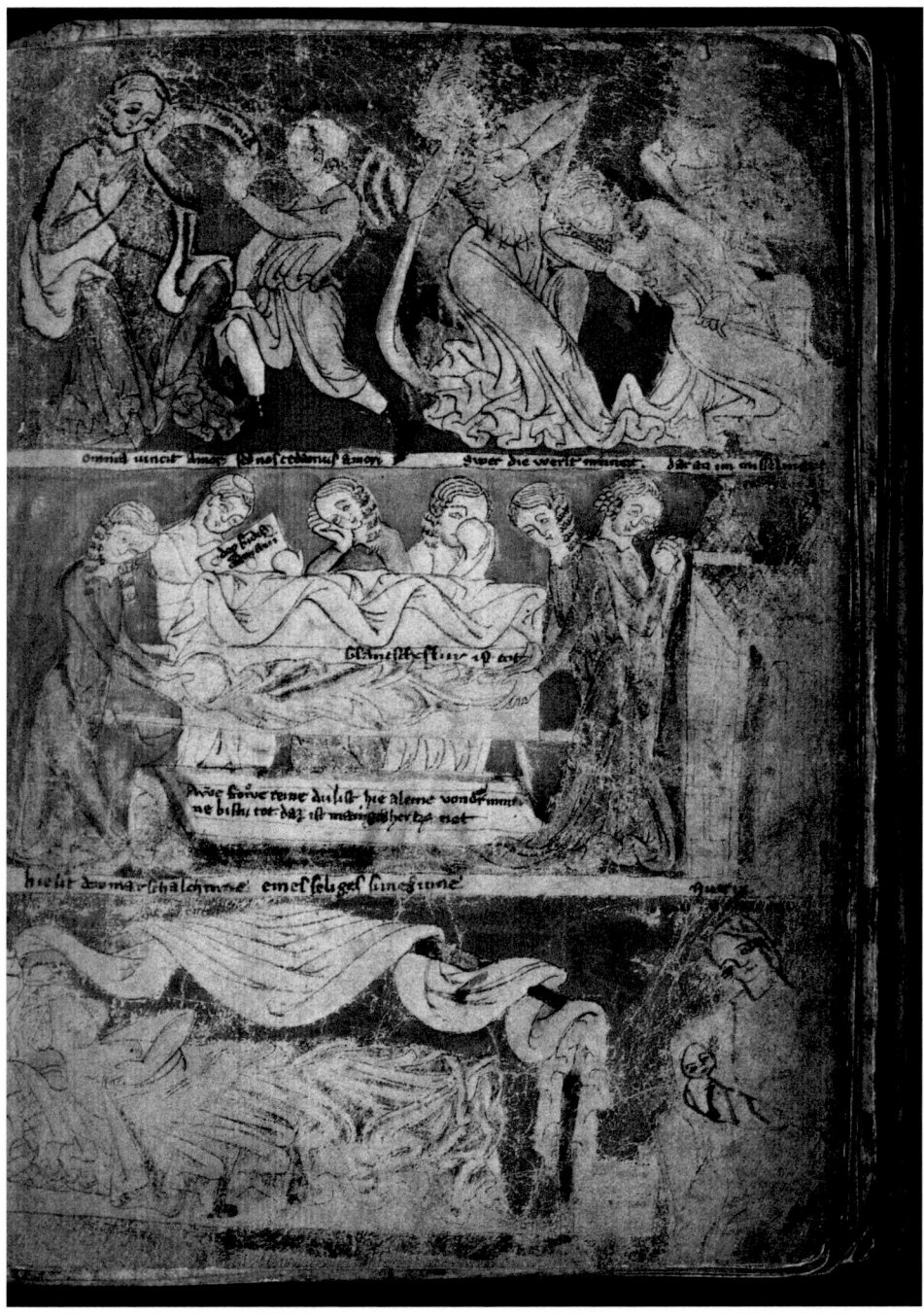

Figure 10.7. Munich, Bayerische Staatsbibliothek, Cgm 51, fol. 15r. Courtesy of Bayerische Staatsbibliothek.

concerning the transition from one place to another are depicted several times; three of the four scenes on folio 11r were designed in this way. In her study of the *Tristan* and *Willehalm von Orlens* illustrations in Munich, Cgm 51 and Munich, Cgm 63, J. C. Walworth analyzes some of these compositions in detail under the heading "Convention and Invention" and shows that their presence might, among other things, be due to the existence of iconographic traditions, conventional image types, visual topoi, and formal schemes that were familiar to the artists (and presumably also to the recipients) and which therefore could be adapted for the specific purposes of the *Tristan* illustrations.[27] A thorough study of the Munich images would have to pursue this aspect and discuss the function of repetition and variation as an artistic principle in Munich, Cgm 51.[28]

The second step is to relate the Munich images to the manuscript text, not in order to discover the extent to which the images correspond to the text, but rather in order to use the comparison between pictorial and textual *narration* to discover accentuations that might shed light on the understanding of the Riwalin-Blanscheflur story presented in this series of images. To begin with, by segmenting the preliminary story on the basis of its changes of scene one can distinguish between four passages of different lengths: (1) introduction of Riwalin (location at Parmenie [*Tristan* lines 243–332]); (2) Riwalin's attack on Duke Morgan (location at Morgan's land [lines 333–406]); (3) Riwalin's stay at King Mark's court (location at Tintajoêl/Cornwall [lines 407–1582]); (4) Riwalin's return to Parmenie, accompanied by Blanscheflur (location at Parmenie [lines 1583–91]). The narrator pays by far the most attention to the passage narrating Riwalin's life at Mark's court; the events following the return to Parmenie with Blanscheflur rank second by a substantial margin, while the introduction of Riwalin and closely connected to that the account of his attack on his liege lord, though highly significant for the logic of the following actions, are treated relatively briefly. In the miniatures, however, the introduction of Riwalin and the attack on Morgan are completely left out. The pictures concentrate on the events in Cornwall (section 3) and in Parmenie (section 4). In addition, if one takes as one's criterion the degree of detail with which the events are treated, it is clear that the pictures shift the emphasis from section 3 to section 4. The miniatures emphasize the events in Parmenie, which both conclude the story of Riwalin and Blanscheflur and begin the story of Tristan.[29]

Let us focus for a moment on the depiction of the events set in Parmenie. In principle, it follows the course of the narrative, but the selection and the design of the scenes presented in the pictorial medium show in part a striking independence from the text. Thus the first image on folio 11r (fig. 10.5) foregrounds the abduction of the pregnant Blanscheflur (which had been agreed upon by the couple). Here, the artist picks up the motif of the sea passage, highlighting an action passed over in the text. A single line — "alsus fuoren si von dan" (and so they departed from there) (Munich, Cgm 51, fol. 12vb, line 34; *Tristan* 1582) — covers the time span between the departure of the ship from Cornwall and its arrival in Parmenie. Scholars tend to explain the pictorial emphasis on transition by the need to mark the change of scene that is important for understanding the narrated events. Whether this argument is really convincing would have to be evaluated on the basis of the total pictorial inventory of the Munich manuscript.

In another case, that of Riwalin's burial (fol. 11v, bottom of fig. 10.6) and Blanscheflur's burial (fol. 15r, middle of fig. 10.7) and the mourning of the bereaved, the images emphasize precisely those moments that the narrator has refused to develop (a *brevitas* formula is used instead [see *Tristan* 1692–700, 1852–62]). Since the artist follows the pictorial convention for the burial and mourning of Christ for both depictions, Riwalin's and Blanscheflur's deaths are presented as parallel and can be perceived as similar phenomena. The narrator, by contrast, insists on difference and individuality, describing the man's death as glorious and the woman's agonizing demise as pitiful and distinguishing the intensity of the lament appropriate for each event (see Munich, Cgm 51, fol. 14ra, lines 9–17; *Tristan* 1763–71).

A comparison of word and image in the arrival scene again reveals completely different accentuations of the situation. The text is concerned with politics. Immediately upon his arrival, Riwalin is informed about the distressing condition into which he and his land have fallen due to Morgan's military action. This news causes him to send for his marshal Rûal li foitenant, whom he had deputized for the period of his absence. Rûal's account, as imparted by the narrating voice, emphasizes the threat posed by Morgan, while the words given in direct speech express confidence in the possibility of a positive turn thanks to Riwalin's timely arrival (*Tristan* 1583–1605). The conversation then turns to Riwalin's relationship with Blanscheflur, which the marshal welcomes as a great increase in his lord's *êre, werdekeit, prîs, vröude,* and *wunne* (prestige, lordship, renown, joy, and delight) and which he advises Riwalin to formalize by means of a marriage according to Christian rituals (1606–35). The corresponding picture (fol. 11r, top right of fig. 10.5) speaks in different terms. It shows Riwalin and Blanscheflur in front of Rûal, who is identified by the baton he is holding in his left hand and resting on his left shoulder. Blanscheflur and Riwalin are dressed in the traveling clothes they wore in the preceding miniature (fol. 11r, top left of fig. 10.5), so that the sequence of the scenes evokes the impression that the two have only just arrived. Blanscheflur and Riwalin stand very close to each other, with Blanscheflur half behind Riwalin's back. Riwalin's right arm is sharply bent, and he is holding her right hand, as if he were drawing her toward him in a protective manner. The artist focuses primarily on the loving couple, in full accordance with his rendering of the sea passage in the previous picture, which shows the two in a loving embrace (fol. 11r, top left of fig. 10.5). If one looks at these pictures in the context of the others used to depict the events in Parmenie, it seems as if the artist has found his own way to express the notion of the connection between love and death, between joy and sorrow, which features so prominently in Gottfried's text.

The Cologne *Tristan* manuscript, with its very few miniatures, also has a picture dealing with the preliminary story (see fig. 10.8), a fact that points to the significance that the medieval reception of the story attached to this strand of the plot. At first sight, the initial miniature lacks the precise textual reference that must otherwise be regarded as characteristic for the particular quality of the Cologne miniatures: the childbed scene with four figures does not have a direct textual equivalent.[30] On the basis of the pictorial representation alone, it would not be possible to decide whether this depicts Tristan's birth and Blanscheflur's death or Floraete's false pregnancy and delivery.

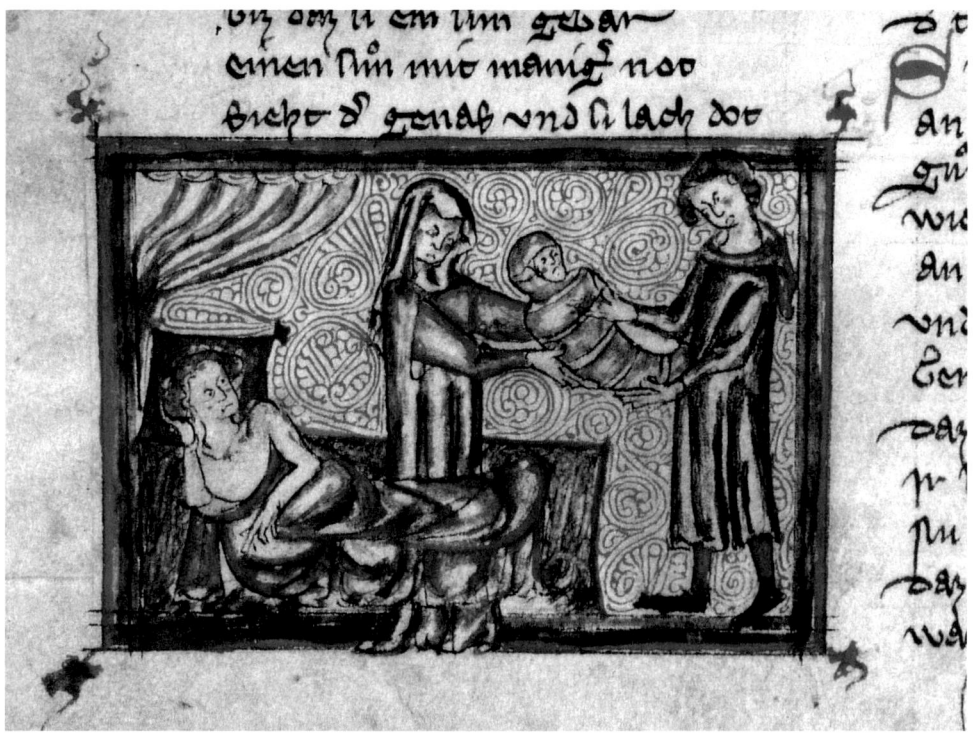

Figure 10.8. Cologne, Historisches Archiv der Stadt, W*kl.f°88, p. 22a.
Courtesy of Historisches Archiv.

The latter is treated in some depth by the text, and it also receives pictorial representation in the Munich manuscript (fol. 15r, bottom of fig. 10.7).[31] However, it is important to bear in mind that elsewhere the manuscript seems to follow the principle of choosing culmination points in the action for the miniatures, placing them in such a way that they follow the narrated action rather than anticipate it. If one assumes that this principle is also valid for the initial miniature, one must conclude that it is the pictorial realization of what has been narrated just above it on folio 22a: how Blanscheflur faints at the account of Riwalin's death and after four agonizing days gives birth to a son and, in doing so, loses her own life: "sieht der genas vnd si lach dot" (Behold, he lived and she lay dead) (Cologne, W*kl.f°88, p. 22a, line 30; *Tristan*

1748). In the context of the series of images in the Cologne manuscript, which can be understood as a heroic *vita,* the miniature highlights Tristan's birth.[32] The complex action of the preliminary story is condensed into this one moment. Accordingly, the figure of Riwalin is left out and the figure of Blanscheflur reduced to her maternal role. The extent to which the miniature might also refer to the *rebirth* with which Rûal and Floraete seek to stabilize Tristan's social position is a matter for further discussion. This miniature, which opens the image series, could then be read as a composition that both visualizes the beginning of Tristan's life and presents the precarious tension between the real descent and the manipulated biography of the hero that is inherent in the text.[33]

We turn now to the layout of the Brussels manuscript of the *Tristan* cycle, which followed two important goals. First, the miniatures were to be spread relatively regularly over the entire corpus of the manuscript. Second, the illuminations were to be related to half of the 184 chapters (i.e., to 92 chapters), themselves derived from the traditional main divisions by initials. Thus the order of the miniatures does not have a logic of its own. There is no separate logic of miniature sequences and their narration apart from the text.

An interpretation of the miniatures as a substantial transformation of the subject, as argued by Saurma-Jeltsch, can hold only if one isolates the illuminations from their closest context, that is, from the series of headings that also served as instructions for the miniaturist. For example, the story of Riwalin and Blanscheflur goes as follows in the sequence of the first headings in the table of contents (Brussels, MS 14697, fol. 1r–8v).

[1r] Das ander Cappittel Also der herre / ruwelni drú jor ritter
    was gewesen
Das dritte Cappitel Also die herē / vnd die frouwen in den ouwen /
    vnd in dem walde dantzeten mit vil / freiden
Das iiij Cappittel Also die herren von eind [gestr.] ein / ander
    schiedent vnd der dātz getō was
Das v Cappittel Von der grossen schone die fl / anscheflur an ir
    hette

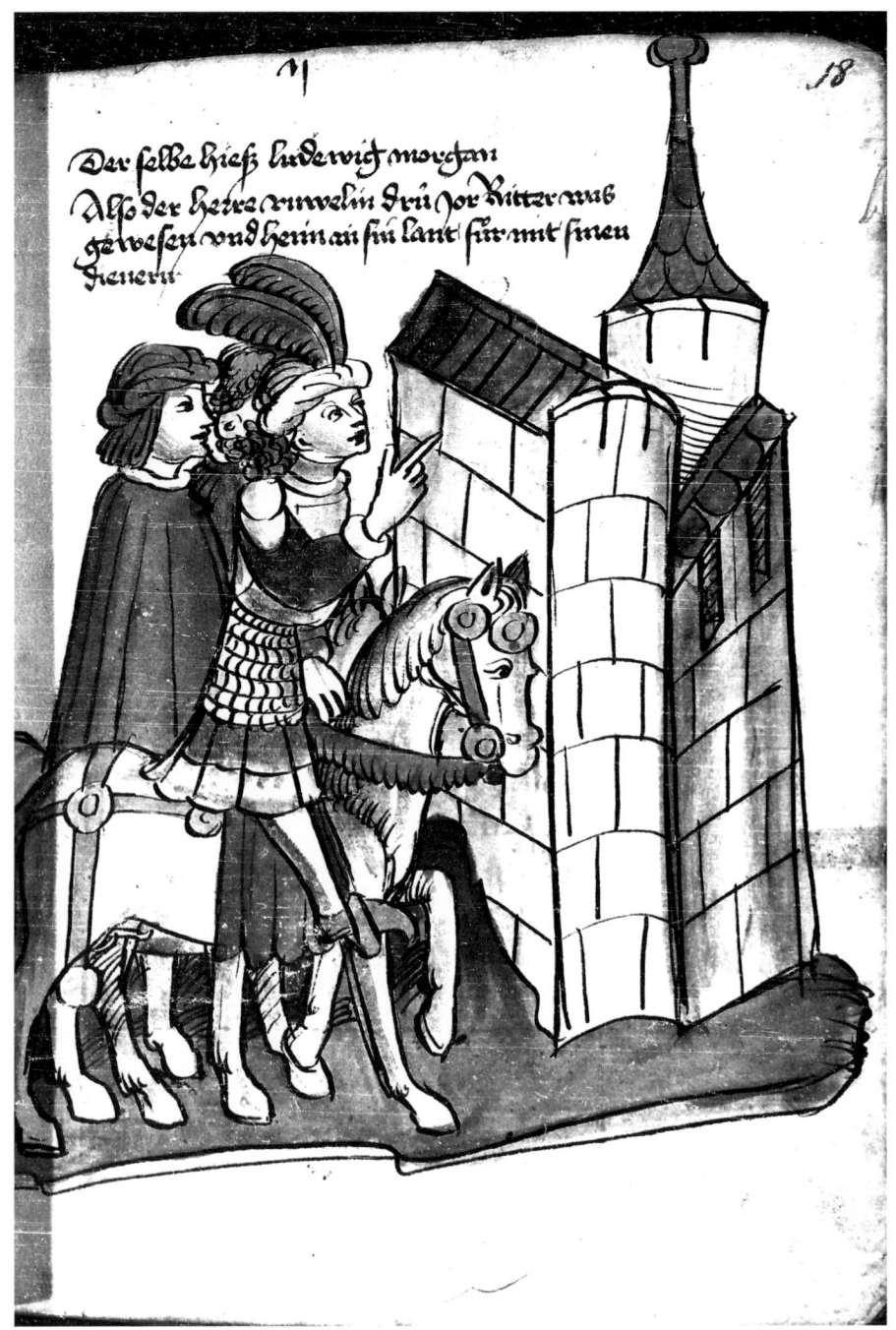

Figure 10.9. Brussels, Bibliothèque Royale de Belgique, MS 14697, fol. 18r.
Courtesy of Bibliothèque Royale de Belgique.

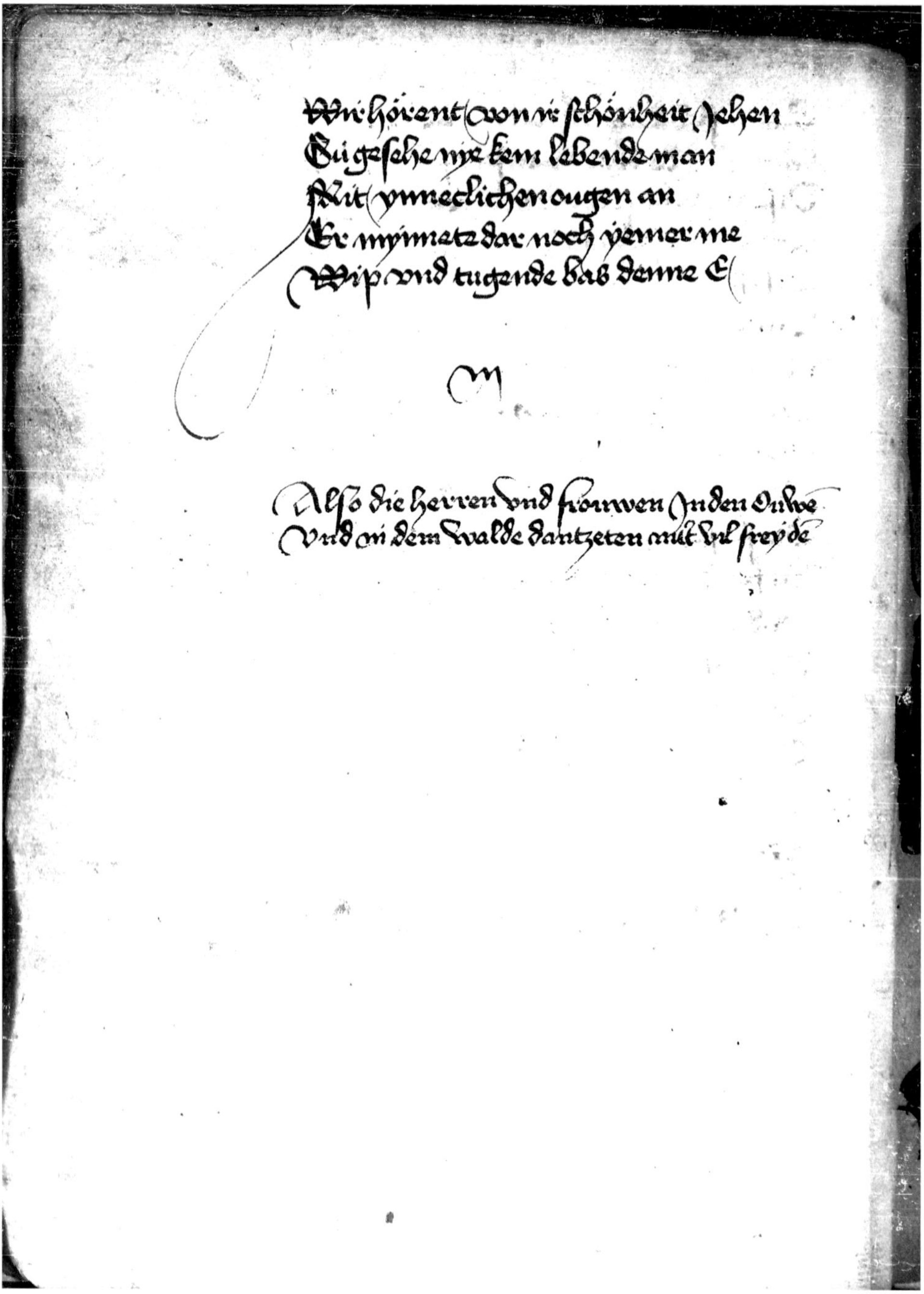

Vn horent von ir schönheit iehen
Sui gesehe nye kein lebende man
Mit ymeclichen ougen an
Er mymmetz dar noch yemer me
Wip vnd tugende bas denne E(

M

Also die herren vnd frouwen Jn den Ouwe
Vnd an dem walde dantzeten mit vil freyde

Figure 10.10. Brussels, Bibliothèque Royale de Belgique, MS 14697, fols. 25v–26r.
Courtesy of Bibliothèque Royale de Belgique.

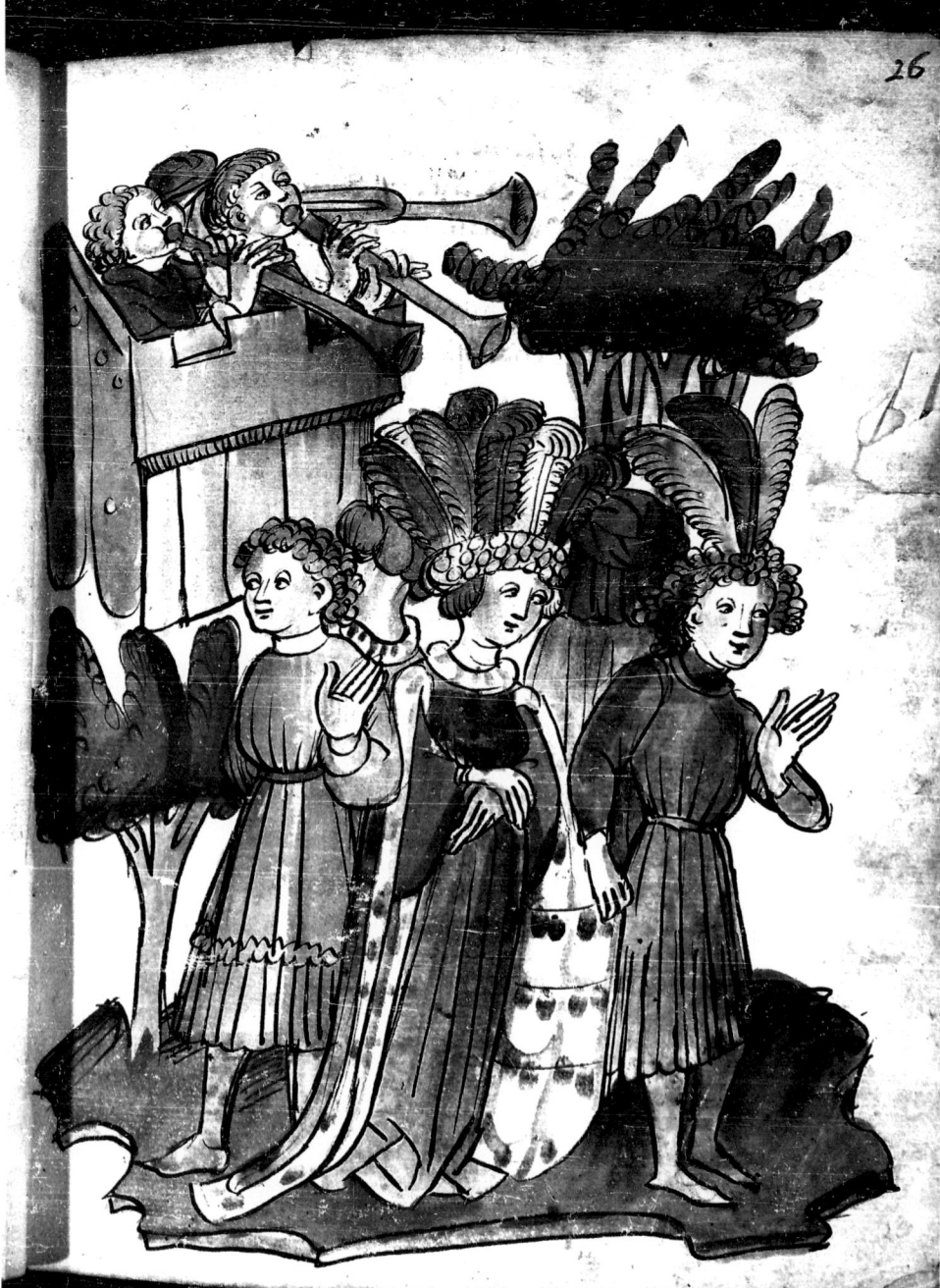

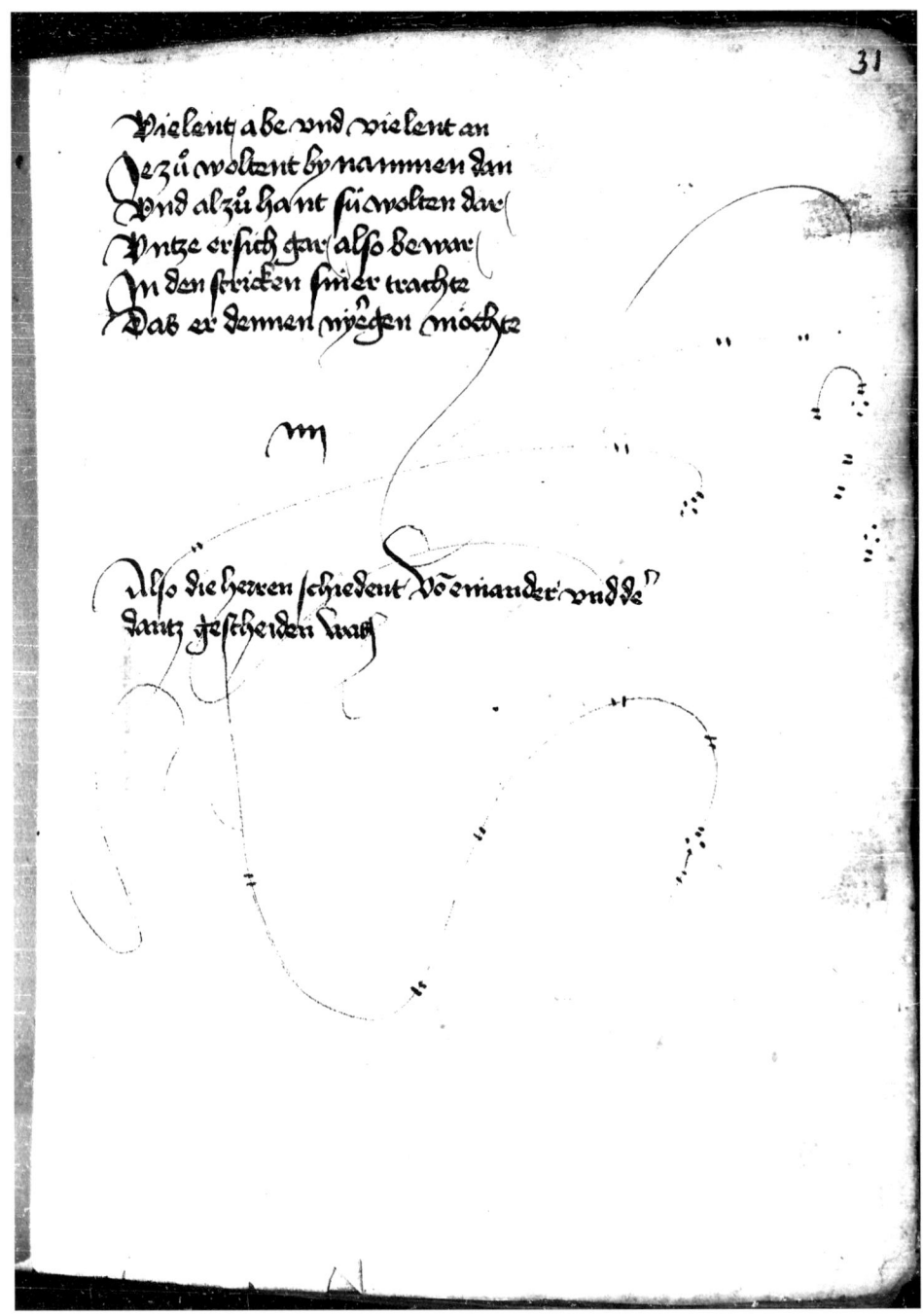

Figure 10.11. Brussels, Bibliothèque Royale de Belgique, MS 14697, fol. 31r–v.
Courtesy of Bibliothèque Royale de Belgique.

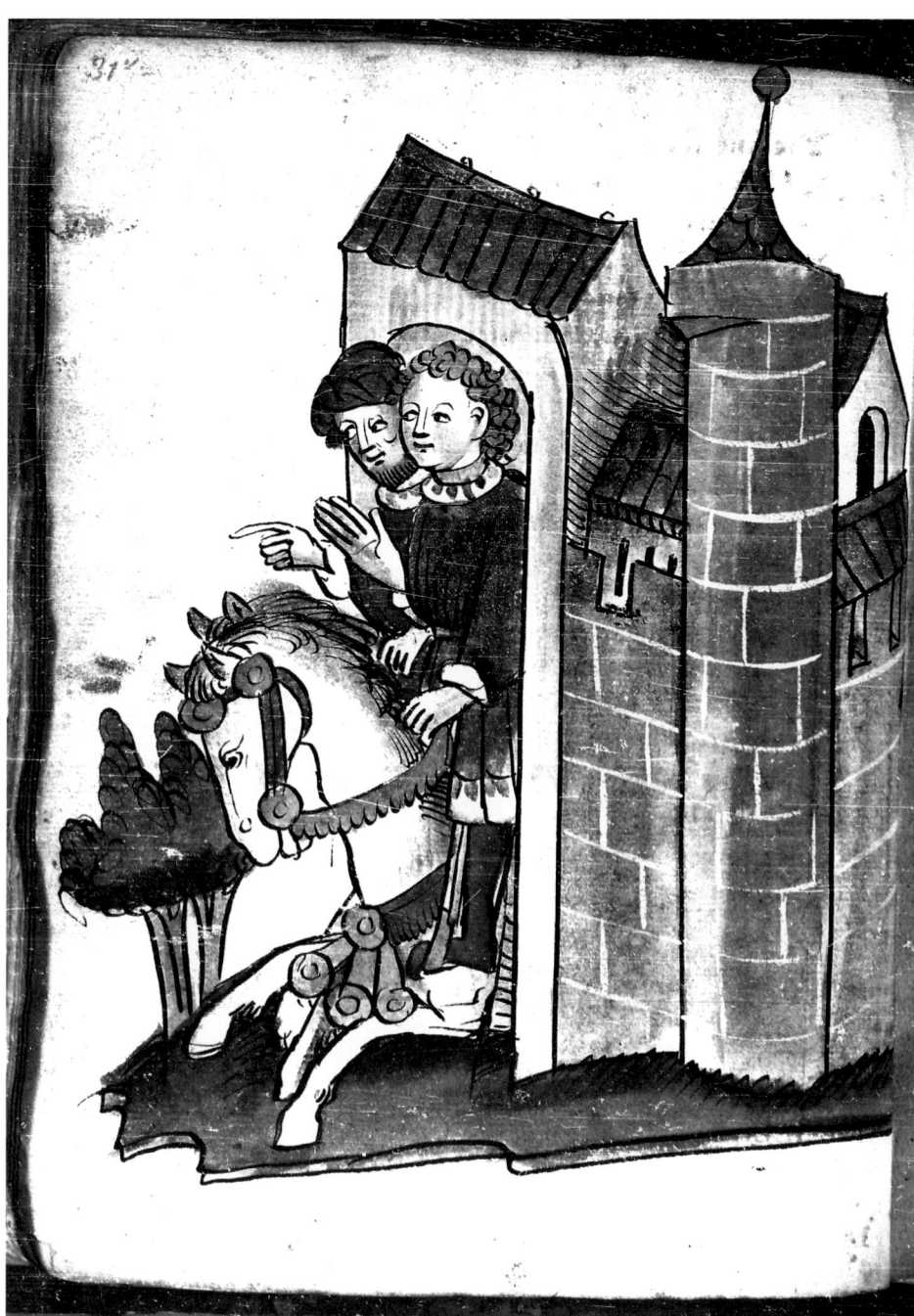

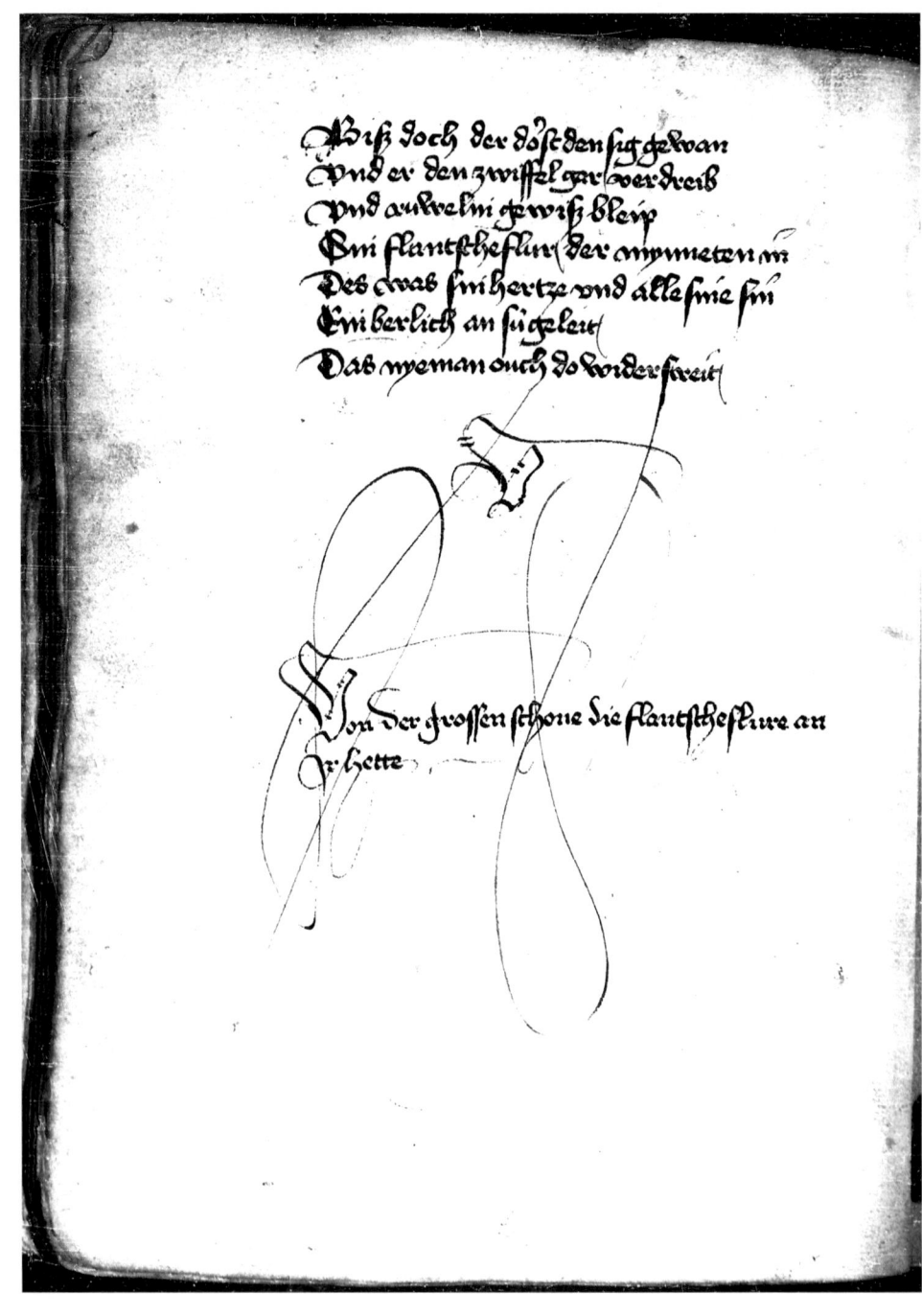

Figure 10.12. Brussels, Bibliothèque Royale de Belgique, MS 14697, fols. 33v–34r. Courtesy of Bibliothèque Royale de Belgique.

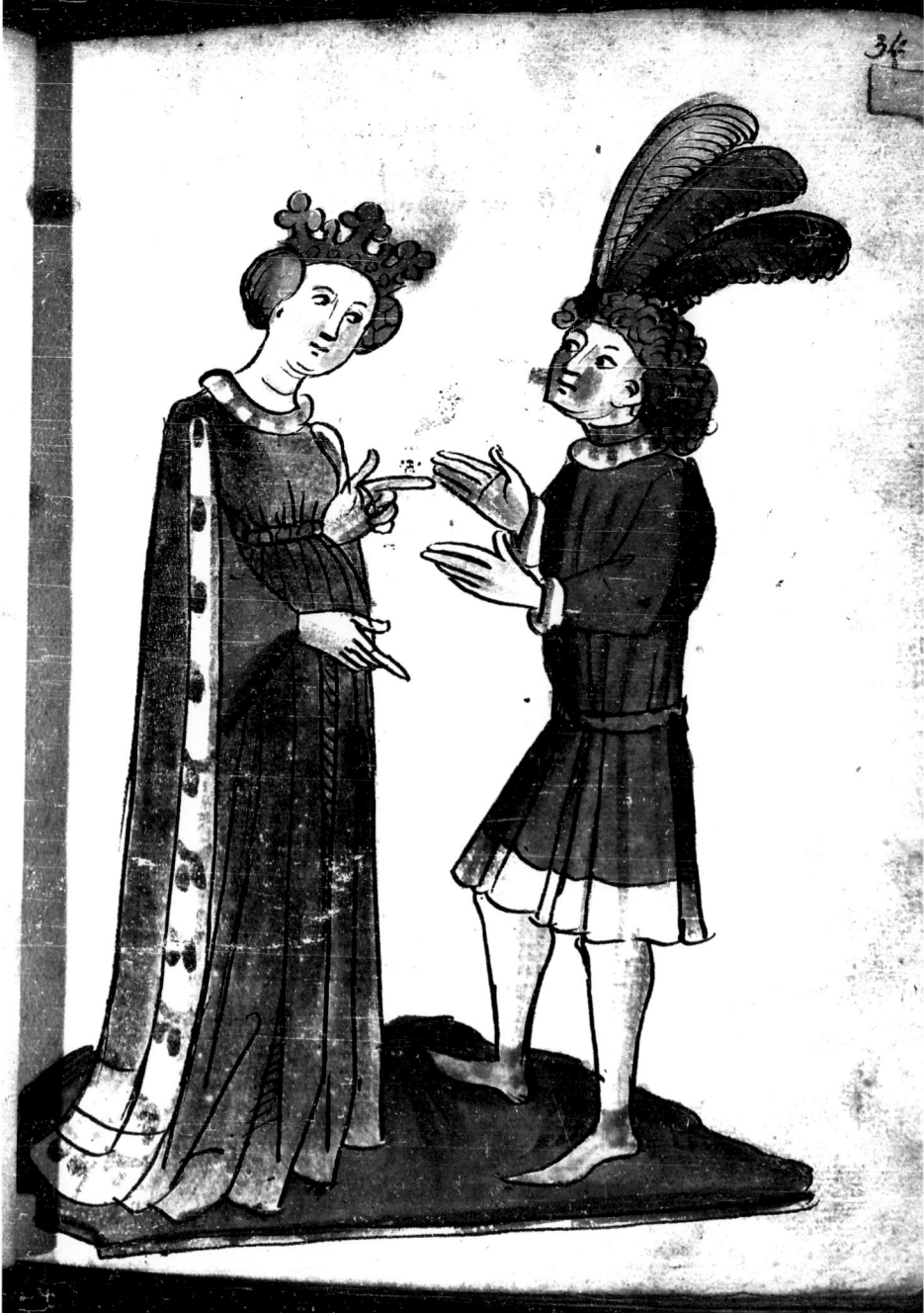

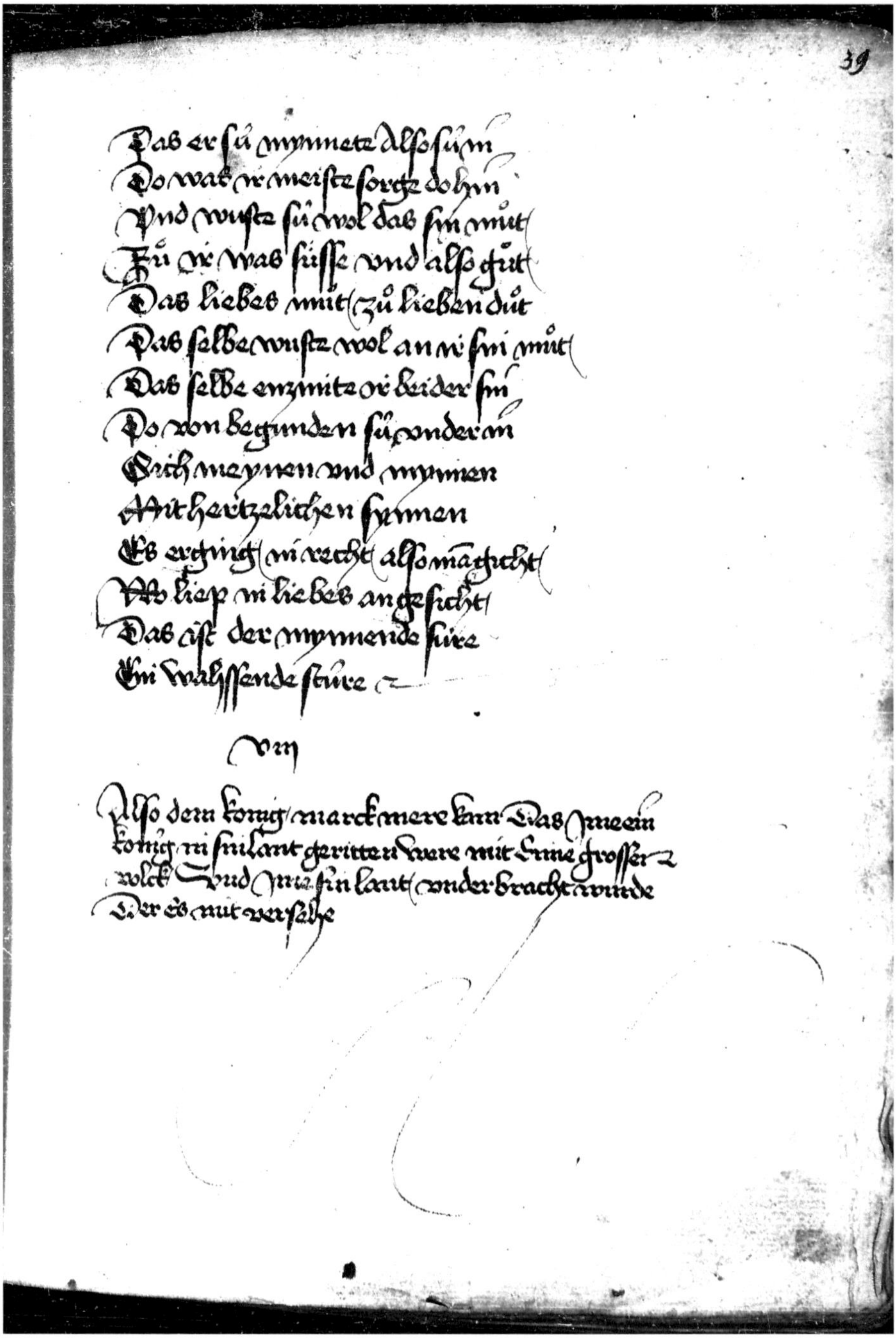

Das er sú mynnete also súzen
Do was er meister sorck do hyn
Vnd wúste sú wol das sin mút
Zú ir was sússe vnd also gút
Das liebes mút zú lieben dút
Das selbe wúste wol an ir sin mút
Das selbe enzwitz ir beider sin
Do von begunden sú sonder an
Sich meynen vnd mynnen
Mit hertzelichen synnen
Es erging ir recht also machtckt
Als liep ir liebes angesicht
Das ist der mynnende fúre
Ein wachssende stúre

Von

Also dem konig marck mere kam Das mer ein
konig in sin lant geritten were mit eime grossen
volck Snd in sin lant vonder bracht avnde
wer es mut versehe

Figure 10.13. Brussels, Bibliothèque Royale de Belgique, MS 14697, fol. 39r–v.
Courtesy of Bibliothèque Royale de Belgique.

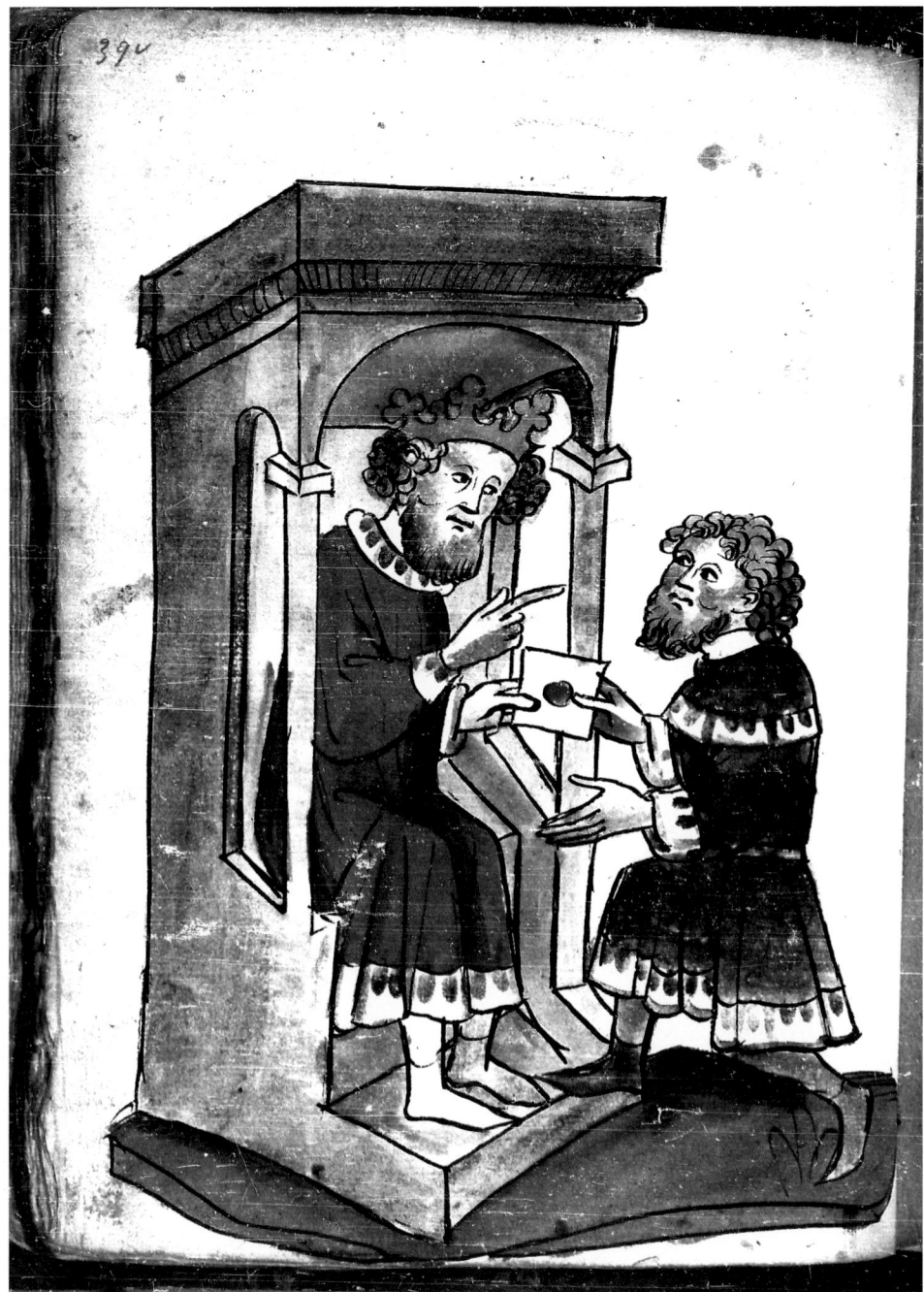

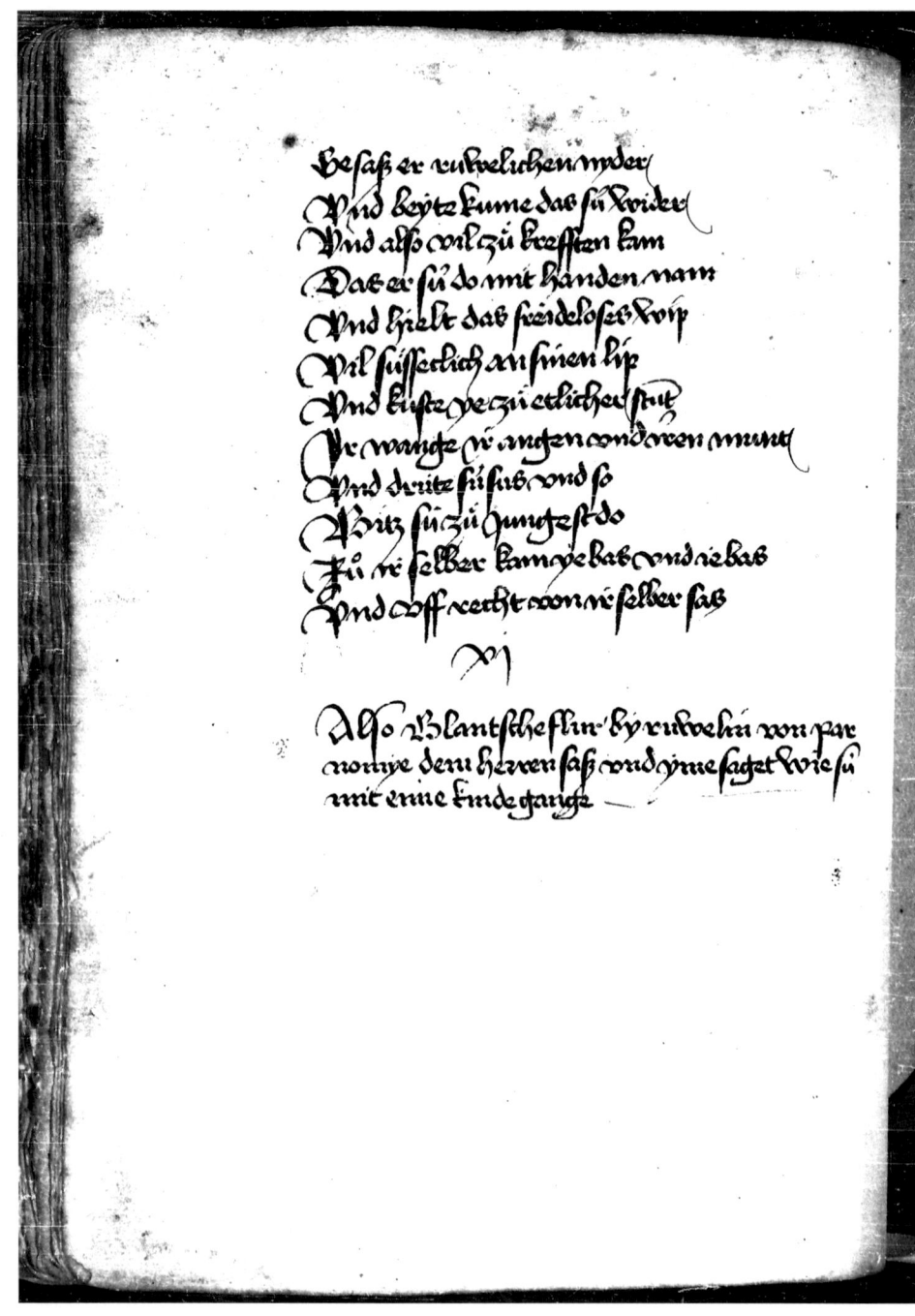

Besaß er rulvelichen nyder
Vnd beyte kume das su voider
Vnd also vrl zu kreffen kam
Das er su do mit handen nam
Vnd hielt das frendeloses wip
Vil suesserlich an sinen lip
Vnd kuste ye zu etlicher stut
Ir wange ir augen vnd iren munt
Vnd druute su sus vnd so
Untz su zu ymytzst do
Zu ir selber kam ye bas vnd ie bas
Vnd off recht von ir selber saß

Also Blantsche flur by rudvelin von par
monye dem herren saß vnd yme saget wie su
mit eine kinde gange

Figure 10.14. Brussels, Bibliothèque Royale de Belgique, MS 14697, fols. 47v–48r.
Courtesy of Bibliothèque Royale de Belgique.

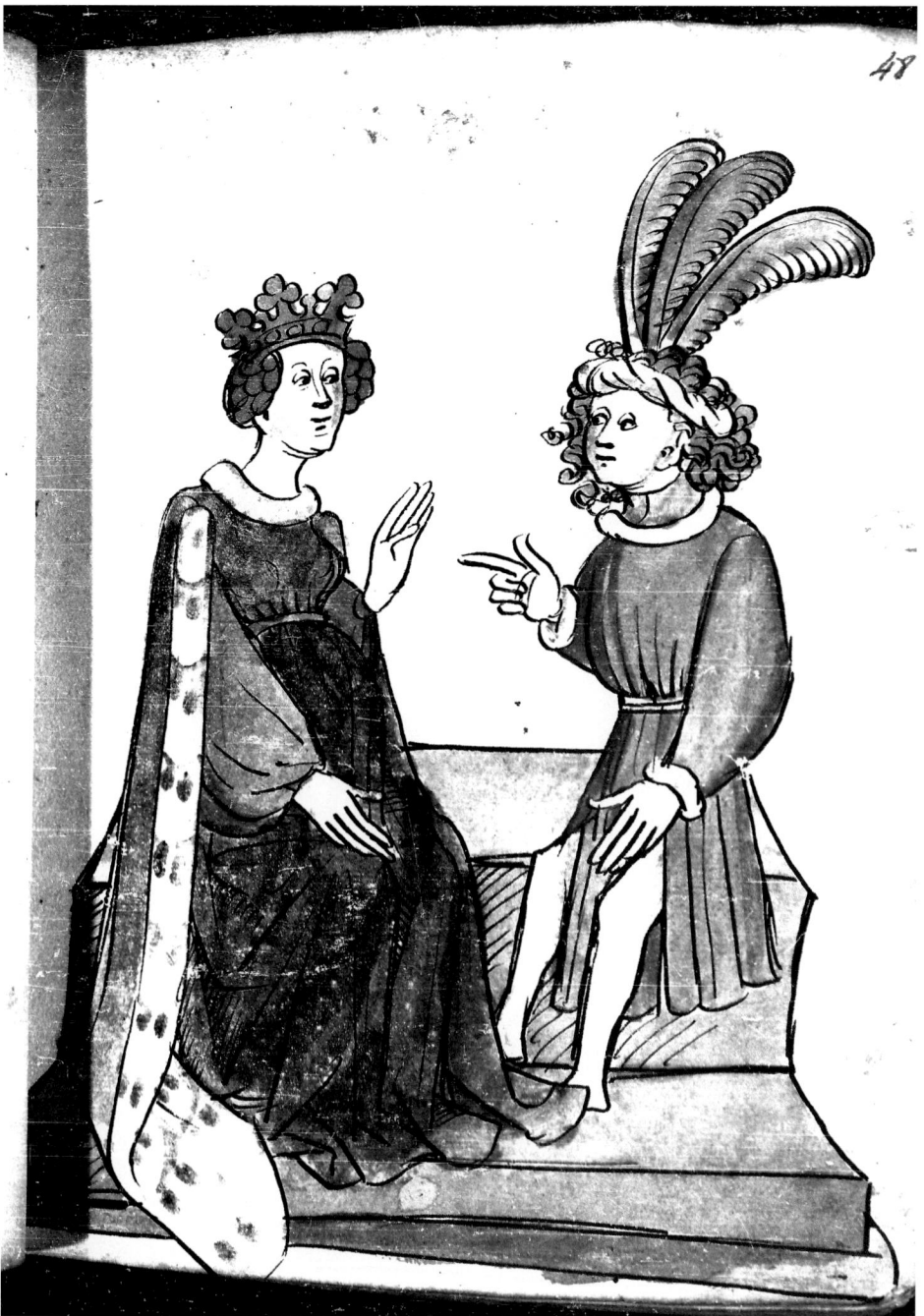

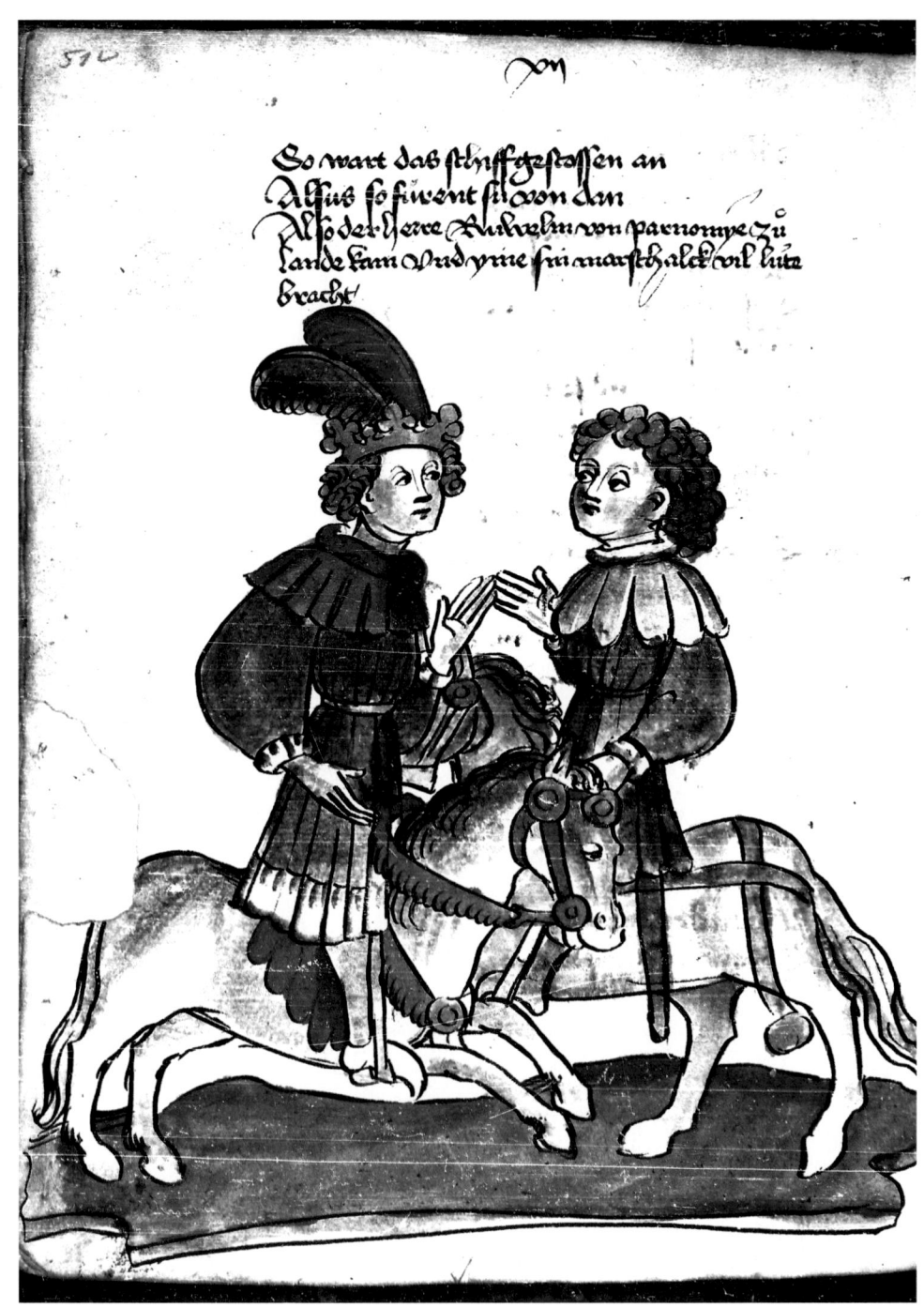

Figure 10.15. Brussels, Bibliothèque Royale de Belgique, MS 14697, fol. 51v. Courtesy of Bibliothèque Royale de Belgique.

[1v] Das vj Cappittel Also flantscheflure ir liep . . . / enschuldigete
Das es nit sin schult were das sú / in liep hette

Das vij Cappittel Also der schone ruwelin der schö= / nen
blantscheflur liep muste sin

Das viij Cappittel Also dem konnige marcke / mere kam das jme
ein konig in sin lant geritten / were mit eime grossen volck

Das ix Caꝑꝑ Also blantscheflur ir hoff meister[in] / bat das sú ir
hülff das sú mit erē zů irē liebe keme

Das x Cappil Also blantscheflur zů ruwelin / kam in sinem
grossen siechtagen Das xj Cappittel Also blantscheflur by ru= /
welin von parnomye saß

Das xij Caꝑꝑ Also der herre ruwelin von pa^s= / nomye zů lande
fur

Das xiij Cappittel Also der herre ruwelin mit / sinē dienēr dot
erslagen wart

Das xiiij Caꝑꝑ Also die schone blantscheflur / noch ruwelin irme
lieben herrē noch sime tode / gar schier starp

Das xv Cappittel Also der marschalck vnd sin / wip des jungen
herren gar sere wartetēt.

————

[The second chapter how Sir Ruwelin (Riwalin) has been a knight
for three years.

The third chapter how the gentlemen and the ladies danced in the
meadow and the woods with a lot of pleasure.

The fourth chapter how the gentlemen parted and the dance
ended.

The fifth chapter of Flantscheflur's (Blanscheflur's) great beauty.

The sixth chapter how Flantscheflur excused her lover that it was
not his fault that she loved him.

The seventh chapter how the handsome Ruwelin had to become
beautiful Blantscheflur's beloved.

The eighth chapter how King Marke was told that a king had
invaded his country with a large army.

The ninth chapter how Blantscheflur begged her lady-in-waiting
to help her reach her beloved in honor.

The tenth chapter how Blantscheflur reached Ruwelin in his
serious injury.

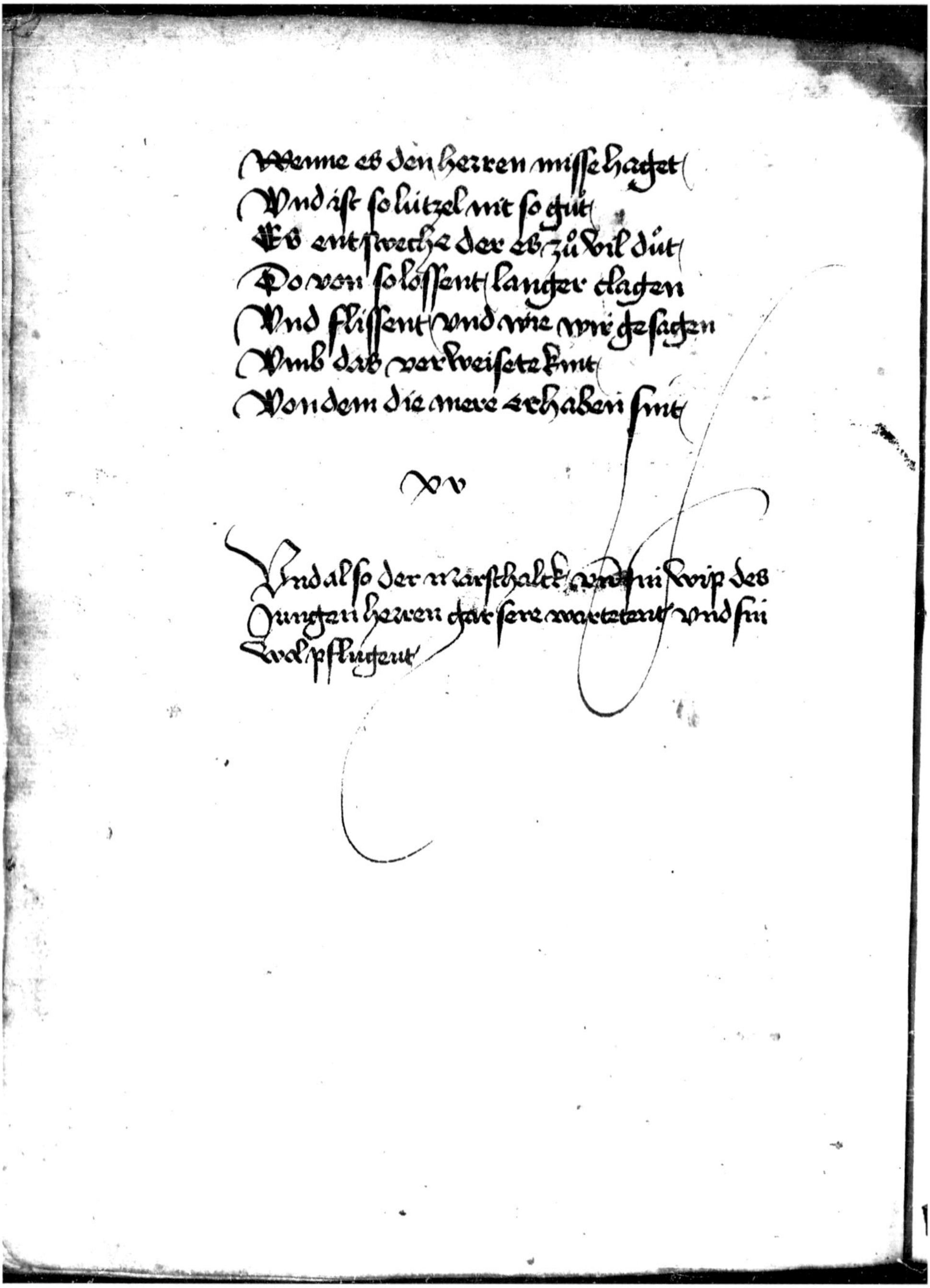

Wenne es den herren missehaget
Vnd ist so lützel mit so gůt
Es entswethe der es zů vil důt
Do von so lossent langer clagen
Vnd flissent vnd wie wir gesagen
Vmb das verweiset sint
Von dem die mere zehaben sint

xv

Vnd also der marschalk vnd ... wip des
iungen herren dar sere ... vnd sin
vol pflugent

Figure 10.16. Brussels, Bibliothèque Royale de Belgique, MS 14697, fols. 58v–59r. Courtesy of Bibliothèque Royale de Belgique.

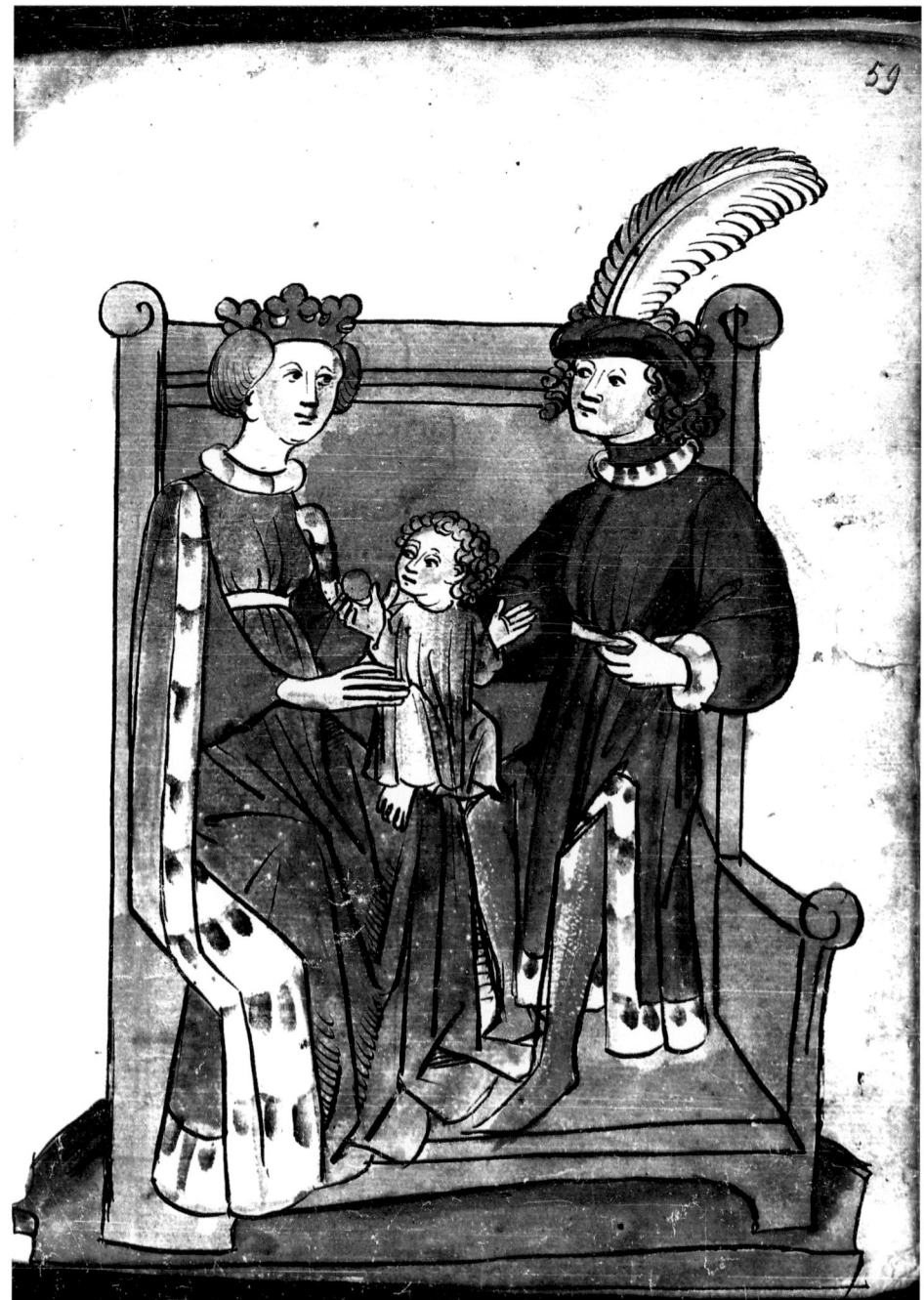

The eleventh chapter how Blantscheflur was watching over
Ruwelin of Parnomye (Parmenie).

The twelfth chapter how sir Ruwelin of Parnomye returned
home.

The thirteenth chapter how sir Ruwelin was killed with his
servant.

The fourteenth chapter how beautiful Blantscheflur died
immediately after Ruwelin's, her dear lord's death.

The fifteenth chapter how the marshal and his wife took good
care of the young lord.]

These headings are in part distinctively shortened compared to the headings in the text. But even these shortened headings present a reasonable
summary of the first part of the *Tristan* novel. This does not hold true,
however, if one takes note only of the miniatures and the headings for
those chapters provided with miniatures, namely, chapters 2, 3, 4, 5, 8,
11, 12, and 15:

ii Also der herre ruwelin drú jor Ritter was gewesen vnd heim an
sin lant fůr mit sinen dienern [fol. 18r; see fig. 10.9]

iij Also die herren vnd frouwen jn den ouwe [!] vnd in dem walde
dantzeten mit vil freyde [fols. 25v–26r; see fig. 10.10]

iiij Also die herren schiedent Vō einander vnd deˢ dantz gescheiden
was [fol. 31r–v; see fig. 10.11]

v Von der grossen schone die flantscheflure an jr hette [fols.
33v–34r; see fig. 10.12]

viij Also dem konig marck mere kam Das jme ein konig in sin
lant geritten were mit Sime grossen volck vnd wie sin lant vnder
bracht wurde Der es nut versehe [fol. 39r–v; see fig. 10.13]

xj Also Blantscheflur by ruwelin von par nomye dem herren
saß vnd yme saget wie sú mit eime kinde gange (fols. 47v–48r;
see fig. 10.14]

xij Also der herre Ruwelin von parnomye zů lande kam vnd
yme sin marschalck vil lúte bracht [fol. 51v; see fig. 10.15]

xv Vnd also der marschalck vnd sin wip des jungen herren
gar sere wartetent vnd sin wol pflugent [!] [fols. 58v–59r;
see fig. 10.16]

[2 How Sir Riwalin had been knight for three years and
   returned to his country with his servants.
3 How the gentlemen and the ladies danced in the meadow
   and the woods with great pleasure.
4 How the gentlemen parted and the dance ended.
5 Of Blanscheflur's great beauty.
8 How news came to King Mark that a king had invaded his
   country with a large army and that his country would be
   conquered if he did not defend it.
11 How Blanscheflur watched over Riwalin of Parmenie and
   told him that she was pregnant.
12 How Sir Riwalin von Parmenie returned home and his
   marshal brought him many people.
15 How the marshal and his wife took good care of the young
   lord and gave him a sheltered upbringing.]

Here, important information is missing, which cannot be supplied by
the miniatures either. The miniatures derive substantial information
from the text, most important from the distillation of the action in the
text headings and secondarily from the chapters themselves. This is
fundamentally different from the miniature cycle of the Munich *Tristan* manuscript, which is governed by divergent rules of composition
and coherence. In the Brussels manuscript, the miniatures abstain
from rendering the story with a logic of their own. Rather, they accentuate the individual chapter themes or constellations by following the
sense of the chapter headings and their instructions.

It is also true that traditional models were used for the miniatures and adapted to the conditions of the manuscript's production.
Thus themes emerge that are shared by more than one miniature.
The prominent example of this is the theme of "conversation." These
observations can be exemplified within the Riwalin-Blancheflur sequence. For example, the title of chapter 2 reads, "Also der herre ruwelin drú jor Ritter was gewesen" (How Sir Ruwelin had been a knight
for three years)—also the heading in the table of contents—and then
continues: "vnd heim an sin lant fůr mit sinen dienern" (and returned
to his country with his servants). As was the custom in late medieval

manuscripts, this heading was taken from the first lines of the corresponding paragraph, in this particular case lines 331–38 (*Tristan,* ed. Marold et al.), which read as follows in the manuscript: "Nu das der herre ruwelin / Wol vnd noch grossen eren sin / Wol drú jor ritter was gewesen / Vnd hette wol hin heim gelesen / Gentzlich kunst vnd ritterschafft / Zu vrlúge solliche krafft" (After three years of being a knight successfully and as befitted his elevated station, Sir Riwalin brought home all the arts and the chivalric retinue needed to wage war). In Marold's edition the last two lines run: "ganzlîche kunst ze ritterschaft, ze urliuge vollecliche kraft" (the whole art of chivalry, everything needed to wage war). For whatever reasons, the rubricator did not understand the line in the sense of the text, "After three years of being a knight, Riwalin brought home," that is, acquired, "the whole art of chivalry and everything he needed to wage war." Instead the rubricator understood, "After three years of being a knight, he brought his chivalry home"; that is, he represents "his chivalry" as servants. The miniature (fig. 10.9) depicts three figures on horses. The first of them, wearing a plume and armor, is put "in front of" (i.e., "above") the others, who ride behind him and seem a bit lost (one can make out nine legs of horses). Moving from left to right, they are heading for a castle, to which Ruwelin, according to the heading, points with a clear gesture. So he returns with his servants, but one cannot tell whence he has come and where he is going.

The introduction to the text of the eleventh chapter (fig. 10.14) proceeds similarly. The heading reads, "Also blantscheflur by ruwelin von parnomye saß" (How Blanscheflur watched over Riwalin of Parmenie), at which point the heading in the table of contents ends, while the introduction to the text continues, "vnd yme saget wie sú mit eime kinde gange" (and told him that she was pregnant). This is vital information for Riwalin (*Tristan* 1449–1580) but no longer for the reader, for what has been left out is the mutual decision to leave Marke's territory and to flee to Parmenie, as well as the preparations that follow and the flight itself. Following the instruction, the miniature focuses instead on the conversation scene; the text has said explicitly that Riwalin and Blanscheflur are sitting down as they speak: "gesaz er [Riwalin] riuweclichen nider" (1437) (very sad, he [Riwalin] sat down); "und [Blanscheflur] ufreht von ir selber saz" (1448) (Blanscheflur herself sat upright). Though the author of the headings may at times seem preoccupied with trivialities, these and many other examples show that he has a concise knowledge of the text. For the layout of the miniatures, the following points are significant: they focus on two figures and on the circumstances of their meeting (one may doubt whether Blancheflur is pregnant) and on their being alone, without witnesses, suggesting perhaps a moment of intimacy in their sitting together. They use simple devices of identification—the crown for Blancheflur, the plume for Riwalin—and, above all, they concentrate on the coordination of posture, line of vision, and demonstrative hand gestures. These gestures are not always explicit, and here they may indicate a question by Riwalin, a request by Blancheflur. Yet on the whole, the miniatures display a very differentiated set of hand and view gestures, partly following known, established patterns but often of a quality one might call individual.

The seventeen chapters of the Riwalin-Blancheflur sequence in the Brussels manuscript are illustrated with seven pictures corresponding to chapter headings (for comparison, the Munich manuscript provides twenty-one or twenty-four single scenes for the corresponding sequence). The miniatures are not restricted to the main characters but follow the plot and its chapter divisions. They do not indicate the main character's "bourgeois" virtues to the potential purchaser, as Saurma-Jeltsch suggests, but present, and at times even demonstrate, different characters in specific communicative situations governed by specific conditions.[34] On the whole, they are closer to the text than Saurma-Jeltsch assumes. To sum it up in a single phrase: Images of communication placing accents in the Tristan novel.

Notes

We would like to thank Selwyn Jackson, Rebecca Kroesen, Christiane Krusenbaum, and Norbert H. Ott for their assistance.

1. A survey of relevant material can be found in Michael Curschmann, "Images of Tristan," in *Gottfried von Strassburg and the Medieval Tristan Legend: Papers from an Anglo-North American Symposium,* ed. Adrian Stevens and Roy Wisbey, Publications of the Institute of Germanic Studies, University

of London 44 (Cambridge: D. S. Brewer, 1990), 1–17; reprinted in Michael Curschmann, *Wort — Bild — Text: Studien zur Medialität des Literarischen in Hochmittelalter und früher Neuzeit,* 2 vols. (Baden-Baden: Valentin Koerner, 2007), 1:227–51; Doris Fouquet, *Wort und Bild in der mittelalterlichen Tristantradition: Der älteste Tristanteppich von Kloster Wienhausen und die textile Tristanüberlieferung des Mittelalters,* Philologische Studien und Quellen 62 (Berlin: Schmidt, 1971); Doris Fouquet, "Die Baumgartenszene des Tristan in der mittelalterlichen Kunst und Literatur," *Zeitschrift für deutsche Philologie* 92 (1973): 360–70; Hella Frühmorgen-Voss, "Tristan und Isolde in mittelalterlichen Bildzeugnissen," *Deutsche Vierteljahrsschrift* 47 (1973): 645–63; and reprinted in Hella Frühmorgen-Voss, *Text und Illustration im Mittelalter: Aufsätze zu den Wechselbeziehungen zwischen Literatur und bildender Kunst,* ed. Norbert H. Ott, Münchener Texte und Untersuchungen zur deutschen Literatur des Mittelalters 50 (München: Beck, 1975), 119–39; Roger Sherman Loomis and Laura Hibbard Loomis, *Arthurian Legends in Medieval Art,* Modern Language Association of America Monograph Series (New York: Modern Language Association of America, 1938); Norbert H. Ott, "Katalog der Tristan-Bildzeugnisse," in Frühmorgen-Voss, *Text und Illustration im Mittelalter,* 140–71; Norbert H. Ott, "'Tristan' auf Runkelstein und die übrigen zyklischen Darstellungen des Tristanstoffes: Textrezeption oder medieninterne Eigengesetzlichkeit der Bildprogramme?," in *Runkelstein: Die Wandmalereien des Sommerhauses,* ed. Walter Haug et al. (Wiesbaden: Reichert, 1982), 194–239; Norbert H. Ott, "Epische Stoffe in mittelalterlichen Bildzeugnissen," in *Epische Stoffe des Mittelalters,* ed. Volker Mertens and Ulrich Müller (Stuttgart: Kröner, 1984), 449–74; Norbert H. Ott, "Literatur in Bildern: Eine Vorbemerkung und sieben Stichworte," in *Literatur und Wandmalerei I: Erscheinungsformen höfischer Kultur und ihre Träger im Mittelalter; Freiburger Colloquium 1998,* ed. Eckart Conrad Lutz, Johanna Thali, and René Wetzel (Tübingen: Niemeyer, 2002), 153–97; Maud Simon, "La mort des amants dans le *Tristan en prose*: Quand la légende révèle à travers l'image son ancrage biblique," *Le Moyen Age* 110.2 (2004): 345–66; Margaret Alison Stones, "Arthurian Art since Loomis," in *Arturus Rex II: Acta Conventus Lovaniensis 1987,* ed. Willy Van Hoecke, Gilbert Tournoy, and Werner Verbeke, Mediaevalia Lovanensia, Series 1, Studia 17 (Leuven: Leuven University Press, 1991), 21–78; Jacqueline Thibaut Schaefer, "Modulation of Moduli in the *Tristan* Illuminated Manuscripts: Secular 'Tryst' and Biblical 'Temptation' Scenes," in *Manuscripts in Transition: Recycling Manuscripts, Texts, and Images: Proceedings of the International Congress Held in Brussels (5–9 November 2002),* ed. Brigitte Dekeyzer and Jan Van der Stock (Leuven: Peeters,

2005), 139–48; Julia Caroline Walworth, "Tristan in Medieval Art," in *Tristan and Isolde: A Casebook,* ed. Joan Tasker Grimbert, Arthurian Characters and Themes 2 (New York: Garland, 1995), 255–99; Norbert Werner, "Tristan-Darstellungen in der Kunst des Mittelalters," in *Tristan und Isolt im Spätmittel-alter: Vorträge eines interdisziplinären Symposiums vom 3. bis 8. Juni 1996 an der Justus-Liebig-Universität Gießen,* ed. Xenja von Ertzdorff and Rudolf Schulz, *Chloe: Beihefte zum Daphnis 29* (Amsterdam: Rodopi, 1999), 13–59; Muriel A. Whitaker, *The Legends of King Arthur in Art,* Arthurian Studies 22 (Woodbridge: D. S. Brewer, 1990), 25–174.

2. See Ott, "Literatur in Bildern," 162 f.

3. Ibid., 172: "die in der skriptographischen Tradierung illustriert wurden mit jenen, von denen Bildzeugnisse existieren." For a survey of illuminated *Tristan* manuscripts, see Jacqueline Thibaut Schaefer, "The Discourse of the Figural Narrative in the Illuminated Manuscripts of *Tristan* (c. 1250–1475)," in *Word and Image in Arthurian Literature,* ed. Keith Busby (New York: Routledge, 1996), 174–202. See also the chapters by M. Alison Stones and Stephanie Cain Van D'Elden, this volume.

4. Ott, "Literatur in Bildern," 172: "bestimmte Deutungsabsichten, Identifikationsversuche, Ideologiemodelle."

5. Gottfried von Strassburg, *Tristan und Isolde: Mit der Fortsetzung Ulrichs von Türheim; Faksimile-Ausgabe des Cgm 51 der Bayerischen Staats-bibliothek München* (including: Textband mit Beiträgen von Ulrich Montag ["Die Handschrift Cgm 51 der Bayerischen Staatsbibliothek München, Inhalt—Beschreibung—Forschungsstand," 5–71] and Paul Gichtel ["Die Bilder der Münchener Tristan-Handschrift," 73–144]) (Stuttgart: Müller und Schindler, 1979).

6. In the Munich manuscript, Gottfried's *Tristan* appears on fols. 1ra–99rb, and Ulrich von Türheim's *Tristan* sequel appears on fols. 99rb–109ra (lines 461–2584 are missing due to a loss of pages). Citations of these works are to Gottfried von Strassburg, *Tristan,* ed. Karl Marold, Friedrich Ranke, and Werner Schröder (Berlin: de Gruyter, 1977), cited hereafter as *Tristan* by line numbers; Ulrich von Türheim, *Tristan und Isolde,* ed. Thomas Kerth (Tübingen: Niemeyer, 1979), cited hereafter as "*Tristan* sequel" by line numbers. Translations are our own. Only the most relevant recent articles on the text in the Munich manuscript can be mentioned in this context: Martin Baisch, *Textkritik als Problem der Kulturwissenschaft: Tristan-Lektüren,* Trends in Medieval Philology 9 (Berlin: de Gruyter, 2006); Alan R. Deighton, "Studies in the Reception of the Works of Gottfried von Strassburg in Germany during the Middle Ages" (Ph.D. diss., University of Oxford, 1979);

Thomas Klein, "Die Parzivalhandschrift Cgm 19 und ihr Umkreis," *Wolfram-Studien* 12 (1992): 32–66. On the phenomenon of the short versions, see Nikolaus Henkel, "Kurzfassungen höfischer Erzähltexte als editorische Herausforderung," *editio* 6 (1992): 1–11; Nikolaus Henkel, "Kurzfassungen höfischer Erzähldichtung im 13./14. Jahrhundert: Überlegungen zum Verhältnis von Textgeschichte und literarischer Interessenbildung," in *Literarische Interessenbildung im Mittelalter: DFG-Symposion 1991,* ed. Joachim Heinzle, Germanistische Symposien 14 (Stuttgart: Metzler, 1993), 39–59; Peter Strohschneider, "Höfische Romane in Kurzfassungen: Stichworte zu einem unbeachteten Aufgabenfeld," *Zeitschrift für deutsches Altertum und deutsche Literatur* 120 (1991): 419–39.

7. Karin Schneider, *Gotische Schriften in deutscher Sprache I: Vom späten 12. Jahrhundert bis um 1300; Textband* (Wiesbaden: Reichert, 1987), 152.

8. A survey of recent research is offered by Julia C. Walworth, *Parallel Narratives: Function and Form in the Munich Illustrated Manuscripts of 'Tristan' and 'Willehalm von Orlens,'* King's College London Medieval Studies 20 (London, 2007), 1–11. Also see Barbara Kunerth, "Der Bilderzyklus in der Münchner 'Tristan'-Handschrift Cgm 51" (Ph.D. diss., University of Cottbus, 1999), 21–29. Of particular interest regarding the miniatures in the Munich manuscript are Stephanie Cain Van D'Elden, "Discursive Illustrations in Three Tristan Manuscripts," in *Word and Image in Arthurian Literature,* ed. Keith Busby (New York: Garland, 1996), 284–319; Curschmann, "Images of Tristan"; Bettina Falkenberg, *Die Bilder der Münchener Tristan-Handschrift,* Europäische Hochschulschriften, ser. 28, vol. 67 (Frankfurt am Main: Peter Lang, 1986); Paul Gichtel, "Die Bilder der Münchener Tristan-Handschrift (Cod. germ. 51): Eine Bestandsaufnahme," in *Buch und Welt: Festschrift für Gustav Hofmann zum 65. Geburtstag dargebracht,* ed. H. Striebel (Wiesbaden: Harrassowitz, 1965), 391–457; Paul Gichtel, "Die Bilder der Münchener Tristan-Handschrift," in Gottfried von Strassburg, *Tristan und Isolde: Mit der Fortsetzung Ulrichs von Türheim,* 73–144; Jörg Hucklenbroich, "Einige Bemerkungen zum *Münchener Tristan,*" in *Diversarum artium studia: Beiträge zu Kunstwissenschaft, Kunsttechnologie und ihren Randgebieten: Festschrift für Heinz Roosen-Runge zum 70. Geburtstag am 5. Oktober 1982,* ed. Helmut Engelhart and Gerda Kempter (Wiesbaden: Reichert, 1982), 55–73; Kunerth, "Bilderzyklus"; Norbert H. Ott, "Bildstruktur statt Textstruktur: Zur visuellen Organisation mittelalterlicher narrativer Bilderzyklen: Die Beispiele des Wienhausener Tristanteppichs I, des Münchener Parzival Cgm 19 und des Münchener Tristan Cgm 51," in *Bild und Text im Dialog,* ed. Klaus Discherl (Passau: Wissenschaftsverlag Rothe, 1993), 53–70; Walworth, *Parallel*

Narratives; Werner, "Tristan-Darstellungen." On the binding of the images, see Ulrich Montag, "Die Handschrift Cgm 51 der Bayerischen Staatsbibliothek München: Inhalt—Beschreibung—Forschungsstand," in Gottfried von Strassburg, *Tristan und Isolde: Mit der Fortsetzung Ulrichs von Türheim,* 41–43; Gichtel, "Bilder der Münchener Tristan-Handschrift."

9. See Curschmann, "Images of Tristan," 2 f.; Michael Curschmann, "Wort—Schrift—Bild: Zum Verhältnis von volkssprachigem Schrifttum und bildender Kunst vom 12. bis zum 16. Jahrhundert," in *Mittelalter und frühe Neuzeit: Übergänge, Umbrüche, Neuansätze,* ed. Walter Haug, Fortuna Vitrea 16 (Tübingen: Niemeyer, 1999), 420 ff.; Ott, "Bildstruktur statt Textstruktur," 53 ff.

10. See Elke Brüggen and Hans-Joachim Ziegeler, "Der Tristanstoff und die Manuskriptkultur des Mittelalters: Text und Bild in der Kölner 'Tristan'-Handschrift B," in *Der "Tristan" Gottfrieds von Straßburg: Symposion Santiago de Compostela, 5. bis 8. April 2000,* ed. Christoph Huber and Victor Millet (Tübingen: Niemeyer, 2002), 24–31, as well as the survey of the textual variants of the Munich, Cologne, and Modena manuscripts on 46–49.

11. Gottfried's text in the Cologne manuscript appears on pp. 1a–234a, corresponding to Marold's edition up to line 19552; Ulrich von Türheim's text appears on pp. 234a–63b. On the design and pictorial program of the manuscript, see Brüggen and Ziegeler, "Tristanstoff und die Manuskriptkultur," as well as the secondary literature mentioned there in n. 57; Elke Brüggen and Hans-Joachim Ziegeler, "Tristan am *Niederrhein*: Die 'Tristan'-Handschrift W*kl. F° des Historischen Archivs der Stadt Köln," in *Schnittpunkte: Deutsch-Niederländische Literaturbeziehungen im späten Mittelalter,* ed. Angelika Lehmann-Benz, Ulrike Zellmann, and Urban Küsters (Münster: Waxmann, 2003), 237–67, as well as the secondary literature listed in n. 51 and the color reproductions of the miniatures on 261 ff.

12. Lieselotte E. Saurma-Jeltsch, *Spätformen mittelalterlicher Buchherstellung: Bilderhandschriften aus der Werkstatt Diebold Laubers in Hagenau* (Wiesbaden: Reichert, 2001), 1:121 n. 433, 2:13; Saurma-Jeltsch, "Der Brüsseler *Tristan*: Ein mittelalterliches Haus- und Sachbuch," in Ertzdorff and Schulz, *Tristan und Isolt im Spätmittelalter,* 249.

13. *Tristan von Meister Gotfrit von Strazzburg mit der Fortsetzung des Meisters Ulrich von Türheim in zwey Abtheilungen,* ed. Eberhard von Groote (Berlin: G. Reimer, 1821), xxx; *Tristan,* ed. Marold, Ranke, and Schröder, xlvii–li; Ulrich, *Tristan,* ed. Kerth, xi–xiii; *Tristan als Mönch: Untersuchungen und kritische Edition,* ed. Betty C. Bushey, Göppinger Arbeiten zur Germanistik 119 (Göppingen: Kümmerle, 1974), 6–12; René Wetzel, *Die handschriftliche*

Überlieferung des "Tristan" Gottfrieds von Straßburg: untersucht an ihren Fragmenten, Germanistica Friburgensia 13 (Freiburg: Universitätsverlag, 1992); Saurma-Jeltsch, *Spätformen mittelalterlicher Buchherstellung,* 1:121 n. 433, 2:13; Saurma-Jeltsch, "Der Brüsseler *Tristan,*" 249.

14. The chapter count starts with *Das ander Cappittel* in the table of contents and with the roman numeral II in front of line 333 of the text; the prologue is counted as the first chapter. Fitting the titles into the text, chapters 96 and 121 are counted twice; the scribe of the table of contents counted 97 twice (instead of 96) and simply left out the heading of the first chapter number 121.

15. Kurt Weitzmann, *Illustrations in Roll and Codex: A Study of the Origin and Method of Text Illustration,* Studies in Manuscript Illumination 2 (Princeton, NJ: Princeton University Press, 1947; rev. ed. 1970), 17 f.

16. See Brüggen and Ziegeler, "Tristanstoff und die Manuskriptkultur," 35–38.

17. The pictorial pages are distributed as follows: quire 2: 7, 10, 11, 15; quire 4: 30; quire 5: 37, 46; quire 8: 67; quire 9: 76; quire 10: 82, 86, 90; quire 12: 101, 104; quire 13: 107. See the survey of quires in Montag, "Die Handschrift Cgm 51," added between pp. 32 and 33.

18. Gichtel, "Bilder der Münchener Tristan-Handschrift," 81: "Auch einem flüchtigen Blick muß sofort auffallen, daß die Verteilung der Blätter sehr ungleichmäßig ist; fast kann man von Zusammenballungen der illustrierten Blätter reden."

19. Ibid., 81 f.

20. Ibid., 82: "Durch diese Umstände tritt ein weitgehender Ausgleich im Sinne einer im großen und ganzen ausgewogenen Bebilderung ein."

21. See Christoph Fasbender, *"húbsch gemolt—schlecht geschrieben? Kleine Apologie der Lauber-Handschriften,"* *Zeitschrift für deutsches Altertum und deutsche Literatur* 131 (2002): 66–78.

22. Saurma-Jeltsch, "Der Brüsseler *Tristan,*" 248:

> Bereits in ihrer Funktion als Gliederungselemente üben sie eine entscheidende Wirkung darauf aus, wie der Text aufgenommen wird, greifen sie doch in den Textfluß ein und gliedern diesen optisch in bestimmte Sequenzen.—Die Bilder liefern eine vollständig eigene, sogar eigenwillige Version des Stoffes, indem sie das Tradierte mit anderen zeitgenössisch näherliegenden Stoffen verknüpfen und so das *Tristan*-Thema in andere Kategorien umgießen.

23. *Tristan als Mönch,* ed. Bushey, 11; Ulrich, *Tristan,* ed. Kerth, xii.

24. Concerning scribe "B," see Saurma-Jeltsch, *Spätformen mittelalterlicher Buchherstellung,* 80, 87, passim.

25. Cf. Gichtel, "Bilder der Münchener Tristan-Handschrift," 82.

26. *Tristan,* ed. Marold, Ranke, and Schröder, lxvi:

> Spuren einer Einteilung in Bücher sind in den Hss. nicht zu entdecken gewesen; wohl aber sind Leseabschnitte durch Initialen oder Kapitelzeichen bezeichnet, größere Sinnabschnitte bisweilen durch größere und künstlerisch ausgeführte Initialen. Ich habe in der Abgrenzung der Sinnesabschnitte daher mich möglichst an die älteste Überlieferung [= HFW; see lxv] angeschlossen und im Variantenapparat durch Majuskel diese Kapiteleinteilung der einzelnen Hss. zu bezeichnen gesucht.
>
> ———
>
> [The manuscripts contain no traces of a division into books, yet the initials and capitals do indicate subdivisions into reading sections, and at times longer passages constituting units of meaning are indicated by larger, artistically elaborated initials. In order to delineate these reading passages, I have followed the oldest manuscripts (HFW; see lxv) as much as possible, and I have used capital letters in the list of variants to indicate the chapter divisions of the individual manuscripts.]

And see Ranke, "Überlieferung," 165–68. The *Tristan* manuscripts and their sigla mentioned in the text and here follow Ranke's stemma—which divides the manuscripts into X and Y branches—and refer to the following: Cologne, Historisches Archiv der Stadt, MS W*kl.f°88 (B); Modena, Biblioteca Estense, MS Est. 57 (E); Florence, Biblioteca Nazionale Centrale, MS B. R. 226 (F); Heidelberg, Universitätsbibliothek, Cod. Pal. Germ. 346 (H); Munich, Bayerische Staatsbibliothek, Cgm 51 (M); Brussels, Bibliothèque Royale, MS 14697 (R); and Vienna, Österreichische Nationalbibliothek, MS Vind. 2707,3 (W).

27. Walworth, *Parallel Narratives,* 129–57. See also Falkenberg, *Bilder der Münchener Tristan-Handschrift,* 185–90; as well as Kunerth, "Bilderzyklus," 167–242.

28. On repetition and variation as a poetic principle in Gottfried's *Tristan,* see Susanne Flecken-Büttner, *Wiederholung und Variation als poetisches Prinzip: Exemplarität, Identität und Exzeptionalität in Gottfrieds 'Tristan'* (Berlin: de Gruyter, 2011).

29. This concerns the following scenes: the journey from Cornwall to Parmenie (11r, top left of fig. 10.5); Riwalin and Blancheflur on their arrival in Parmenie, standing in front of Rûal (11r, top right of fig. 10.5); the

marriage of Riwalin and Blanscheflur (11r, bottom left of fig. 10.5); Rûal escorts Blanscheflur to Canoêl (11r, bottom right of fig. 10.5); Riwalin is mortally injured in the fight against Duke Morgan (11v, top of fig. 10.6); Riwalin is buried (11v, bottom of fig. 10.6); a messenger informs Blanscheflur of Riwalin's death (15r, top left of fig. 10.7); Blanscheflur gives birth to her child and dies (15r, top right of fig. 10.7); Blanscheflur is buried (15r, center of fig. 10.7); Floraete in childbed, feigned birth of Tristan (15r, bottom of fig. 10.7).

30. See Brüggen and Ziegeler, "Tristanstoff und die Manuskriptkultur," 35–40.

31. Rûal instructs Floraete to feign pregnacy so that he will be able to pass Riwalin and Blanscheflur's son off as his own child; Floraete lies down in childbed and has the bower prepared for the birth of the child; she simulates labor pains; Tristan is secretly laid beside her; only the nurse is let in on the plan.

32. See Brüggen and Ziegeler, "Tristanstoff und die Manuskriptkultur," 44 f.

33. See Brüggen and Ziegeler, "Tristan am Niederrhein," 258 f.; Monika Schausten, "*ich bin, alse ich hân vernomen, ze wunderlîchen maeren komen*: Zur Funktion biographischer und autobiographischer Figurenrede für die narrative Konstitution von Identität in Gottfrieds von Straßburg 'Tristan,'" *Beiträge zur Geschichte der deutschen Sprache und Literatur* 123 (2001): 24–48.

34. Saurma-Jeltsch, "Der Brüsseler *Tristan,*" 298: "aus dem höfischen Kontext ist ein bürgerlich-städtischer geworden"; see Saurma-Jeltsch, *Spätformen mittelalterlicher Buchherstellung,* 221, 236.

CHAPTER ELEVEN

Specific and Generic Scenes in Verse *Tristan* Illustrations

STEPHANIE CAIN VAN D'ELDEN

We often discuss written texts in terms of episodes, self-contained stories with links to other stories in the same work. An episode may consist of a series of scenes corresponding to acts and scenes in drama. A pictorial narrative may be constructed similarly; a visual episode may be depicted in one or more scenes. When literary historians work with codices, usually they can identify an illumination from its placement in the manuscript or from an accompanying rubric or inscription. When dealing with ivories, misericords, embroideries, wall paintings, and other artifacts, however, often they find no written identification on the object, in which case it is necessary to have a specific image that can be identified out of context, no matter what the medium. If a written text describes a man crossing a sword bridge, the text can only be *Lancelot*. Similarly, an image on an artifact showing a man crossing a sword bridge points to *Lancelot*.

I have divided the verse Tristan story into thirty episodes based on extant images that illustrate them.[1] Most of the episodes are generic and could appear in any medieval romance: the birth of the hero, the knighting of the hero, knights fighting or jousting, a knight wooing a maiden, a feast at court, and so on. Of the thirty Tristan episodes, there are six that I consider "specific"—that is, they occur only in the

Tristan story.[2] In the written codices, where space is no consideration, an episode may contain a number of scenes, and so it is not necessary that any of these scenes be "specific" since their content is identified in the text.[3] For example, in the episode of the love potion, three illustrated scenes in the Heidelberg manuscript follow the text quite closely, none of which specifically shows the actual drinking of the potion *at sea*.[4] The first picture shows an empty ship that fills the frame (fol. 44r); the second, Isolde and Tristan, after they have drunk the potion, lying in their separate beds looking very sick (fol. 49v; see fig. 11.1). Eilhart's text tells us that their attendants, Brangaene and Kurvenal, fear the lovers will die unless they are brought together to consummate their love. The third picture in this sequence shows Isolde, looking much better, ready to welcome Tristan as he comes into the chamber (fol. 50v; see fig. 11.2)—presumably not his first visit.

Conversely, where there is no text, such as on the Hermitage I ivory, the image of the lovers drinking the potion helps to identify the narrative and points the viewer to other specific and generic scenes forming a complete story, a story that may differ from the written texts.[5]

Specific Scenes

The following six episodes are unique to the *Tristan* corpus.

(1) Tristan cuts out the dragon's tongue. While there are numerous dragon-killing pictures in medieval art, there are very few examples of the tongue being removed from the dragon. The dragons in the *Tristan* corpus vary from short and squat to long and elegant, with curly tails. Since this episode is clearly explicated in the written texts, it is not necessary to illustrate it with a specific scene in the codices; of the six written texts, all of which portray the episode, only the Munich manuscript (fol. 67r–v) shows the specific image of the tongue being removed from the dragon.[6] One of the six woodcuts of the Sorg incunabulum depicting this episode shows the dragon with its tongue outstretched, clearly in position to be removed (fol. 26v).[7] None of the nine dragon scenes in the Brussels manuscript is specific because the tongue is not shown being removed.[8] For example, folio 238v depicts

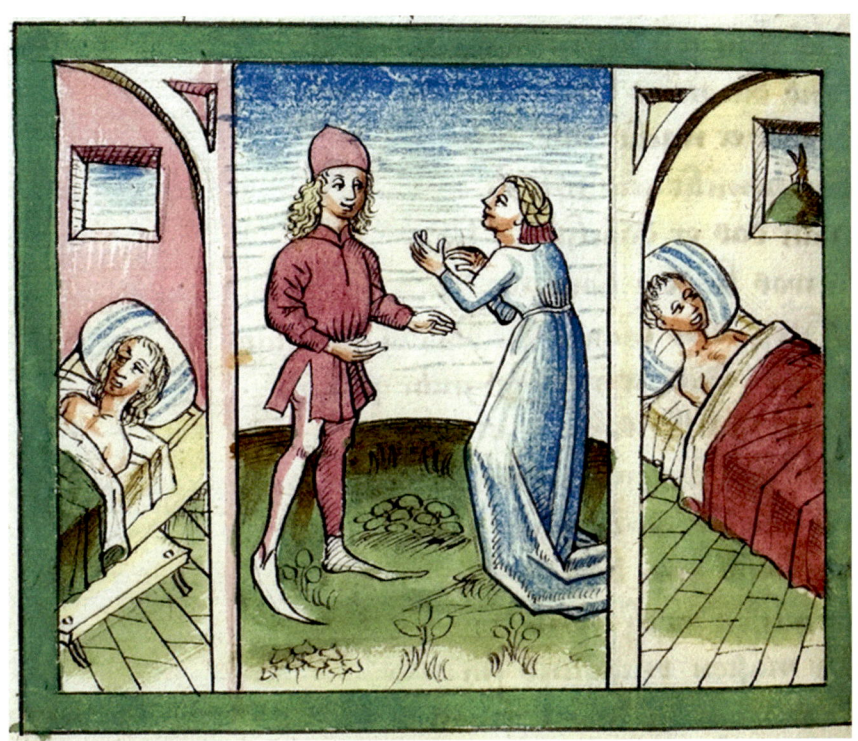

Figure 11.1. Heidelberg, Universitätsbibliothek, MS Cod. Pal. Germ. 346, fol. 49v. Courtesy of Universitätsbibliothek, Heidelberg.

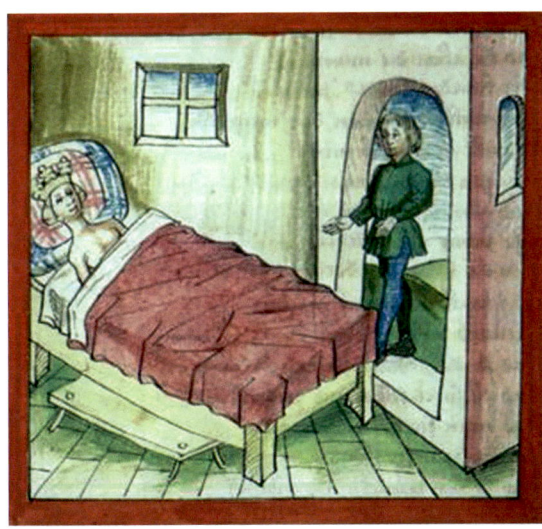

Figure 11.2. Heidelberg, Universitätsbibliothek, MS Cod. Pal. Germ. 346, fol. 50v. Courtesy of Universitätsbibliothek, Heidelberg.

Tristan piercing the dragon outside its cave; folio 244v shows the head of the dragon with its long red tongue clearly visible in a cart being paraded before the king and queen of Ireland; and folio 262r shows the seneschal presenting the green dragon's head with its long red tongue. The Runkelstein wall paintings (scene 4; see fig. 11.3), the three Wienhausen embroideries (figs. 11.4–11.7), as well as the Victoria and Albert embroidery (fig. 11.8) and the Erfurt tablecloth, contain specific scenes of this episode.[9] In each one, Tristan holds firmly to the dragon's tongue as he cuts it out with his sword (his knife in the Runkelstein painting).

(2) Isolde recognizes Tristan in the bathtub as the killer of her uncle, and she attempts to kill him. The sight of a bathtub, a barrel, could point to the baptism of John the Baptist or even a martyrdom. The nick in the sword, which is crucial to the advancement of the plot, is not depicted in all the illustrations—possibly due to miscommunication between the designer and the artist. There is some disagreement regarding the women in the illustrations—is Brangaene or Queen Isolde restraining Isolde?—that could possibly be explained by different versions of the story.[10]

(3) Tristan and Isolde drink the love potion at sea. The defining element of this episode is that the lovers are drinking at sea. The vessel from which they drink is rendered pictorially in different ways—a urine specimen bottle, a chalice, a bottle with a hole in it.[11] In some images the couple is alone in the boat; in others they have an audience. In several instances the results of the love potion are illustrated, such as in the Brussels and Heidelberg manuscripts, which lack a specific scene, and the Hermitage I ivory and Sorg incunabulum, which feature a specific scene as well as a depiction of the results. On the Erfurt tablecloth (scene 18), Queen Isolde is depicted handing the potion, which looks like a green hot water bottle, to Brangaene as the ship is about to depart Ireland.

(4) The assignation of Tristan and Isolde standing under the tree, with Mark and the dwarf Melot looking on from the branches (the so-called trysting or orchard episode).[12] There are numerous images of two lovers standing or sitting under a tree. Many eager fans of the Middle Ages have spotted such a generic scene and jumped erroneously

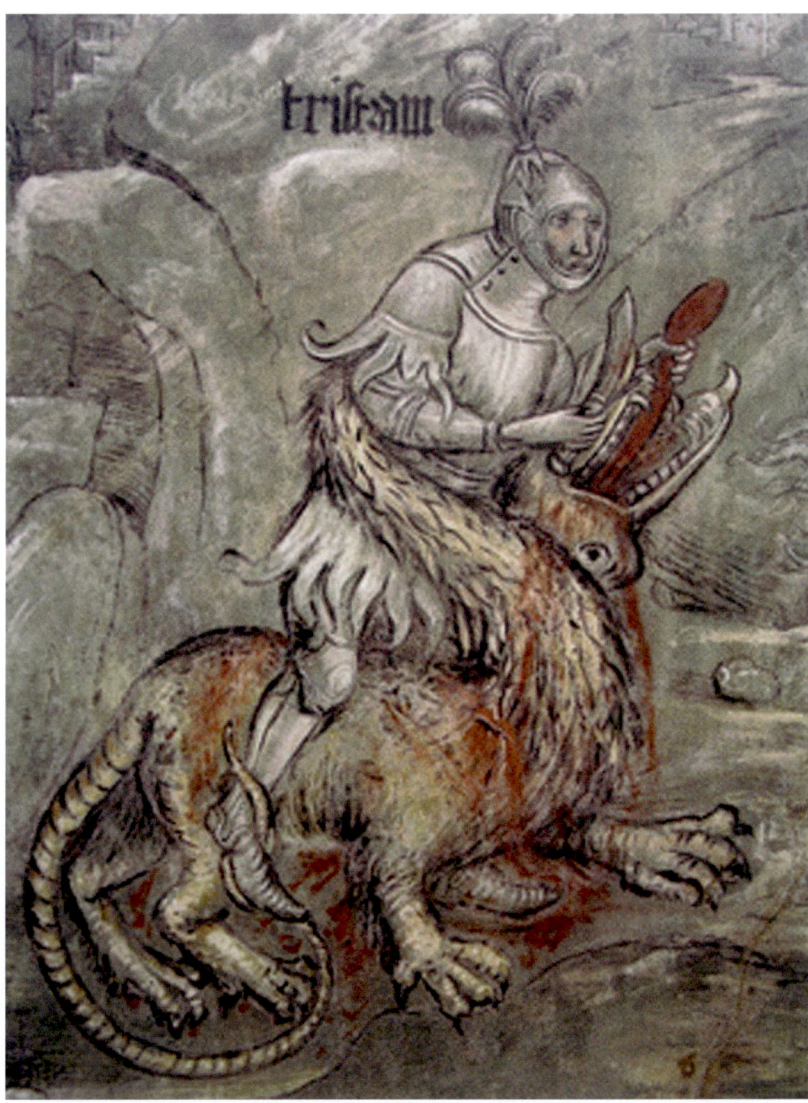

Figure 11.3. Castle Runkelstein near Bolzano, Italy, wall paintings, scene 4.
Courtesy of Fondazione Castelli di Bolzano. All rights © City of Bolzano.
Photo by Augustin Ochsenreiter.

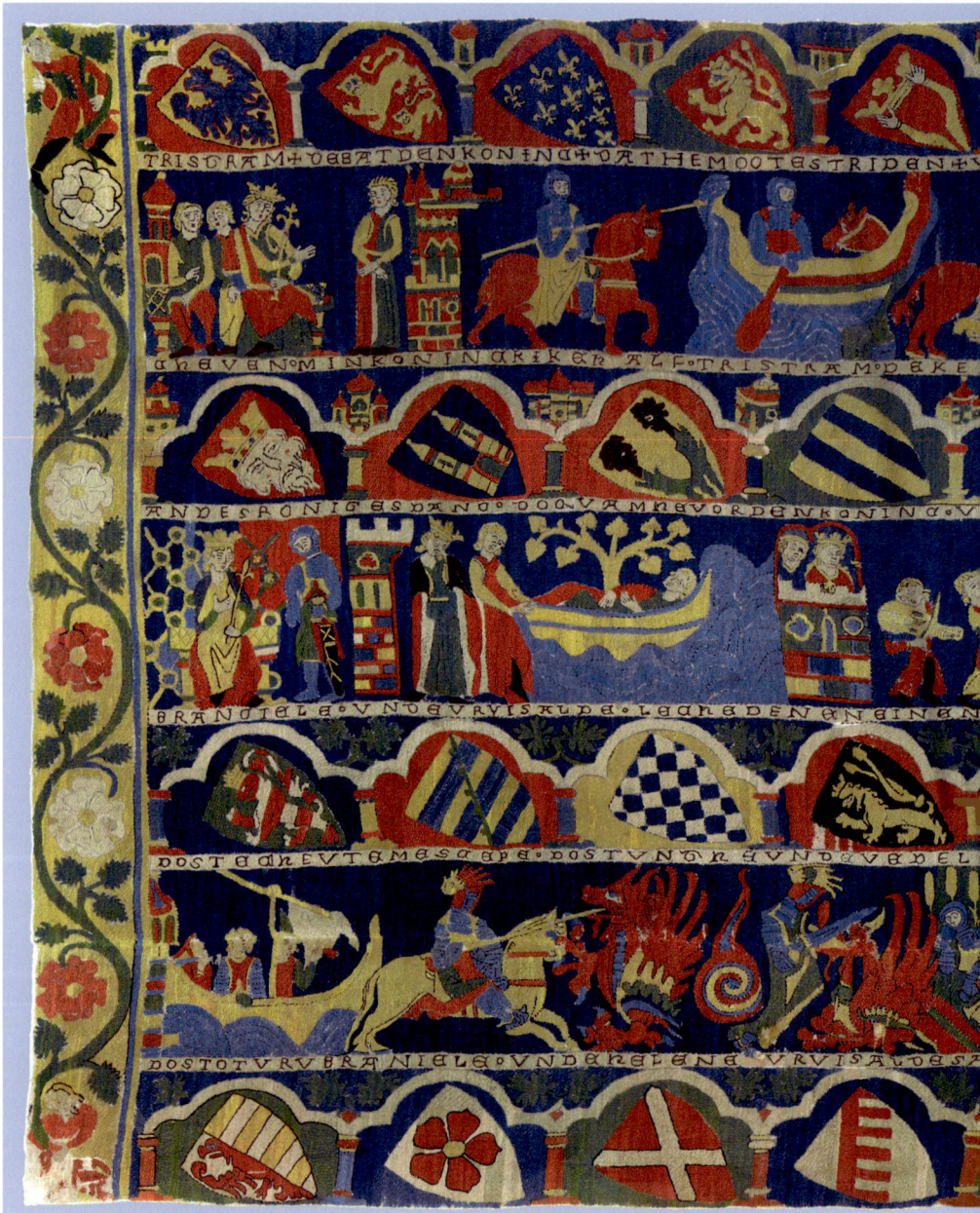

Figure 11.4. Wienhausen, Klosterverwaltung, Wienhausen I embroidery.
By permission. Image © Kloster Wienhausen. Photo: Loeper, Celle.

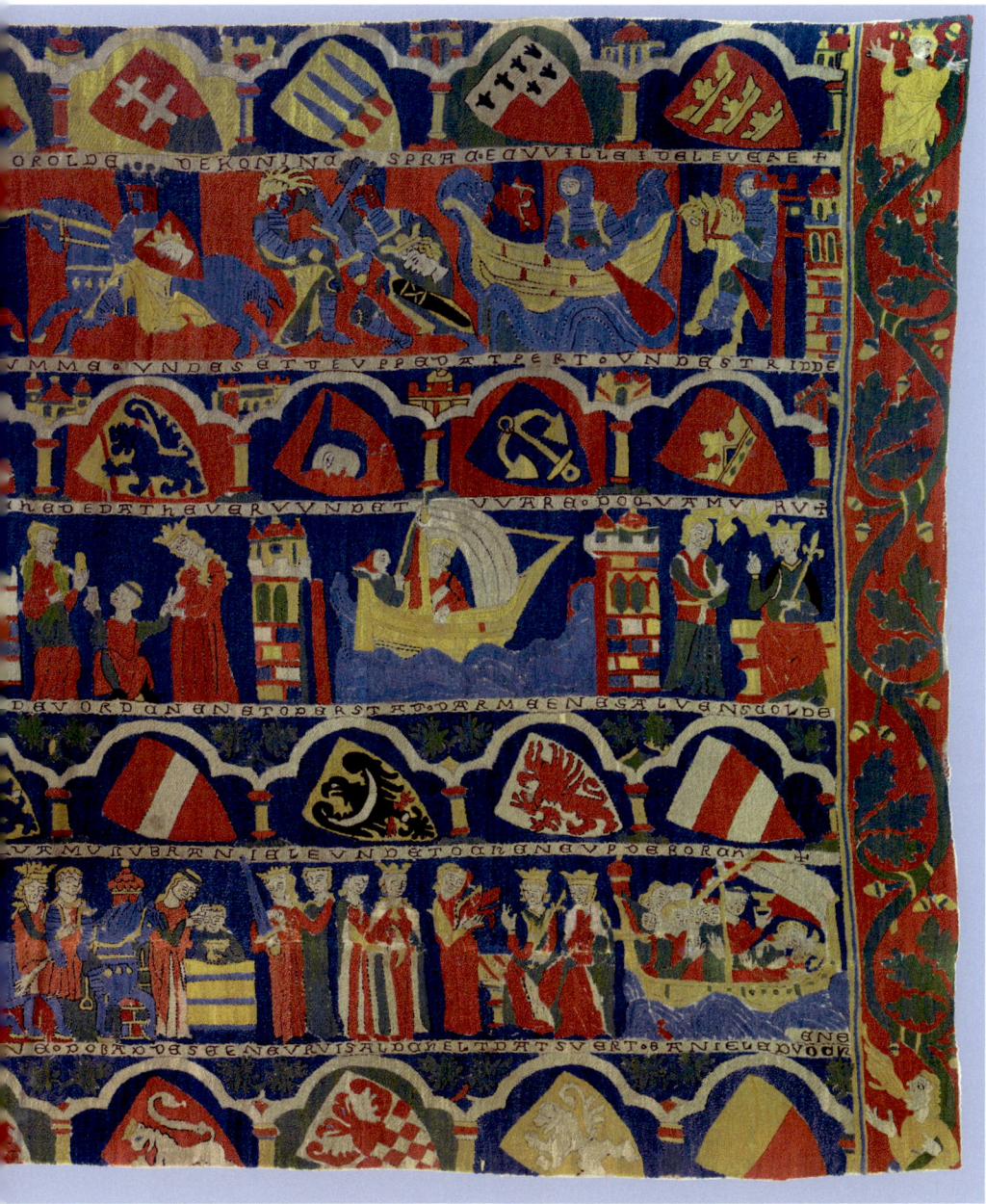

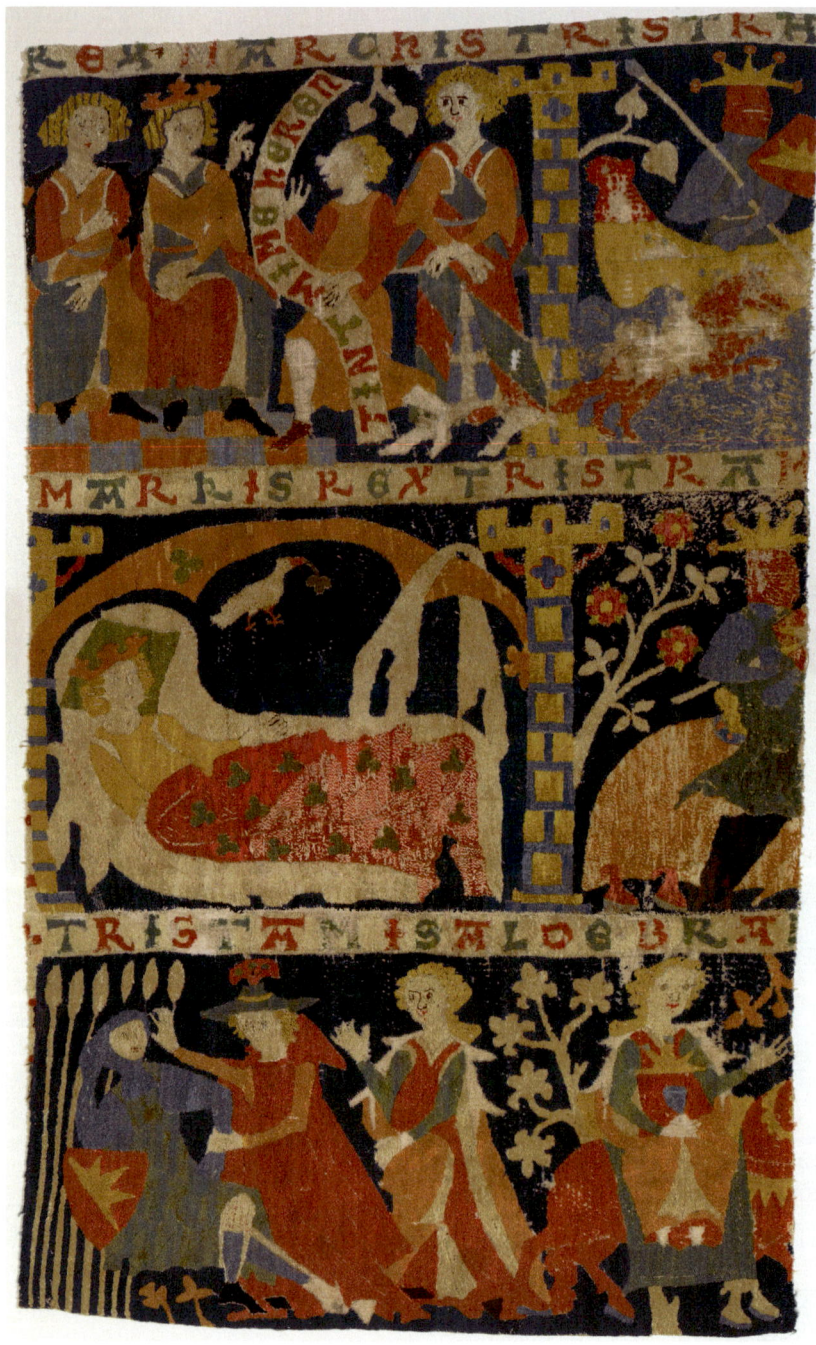

Figure 11.5. Wienhausen, Klosterverwaltung, Wienhausen II embroidery, left. Image © Kloster Wienhausen. Photo: Loeper, Celle.

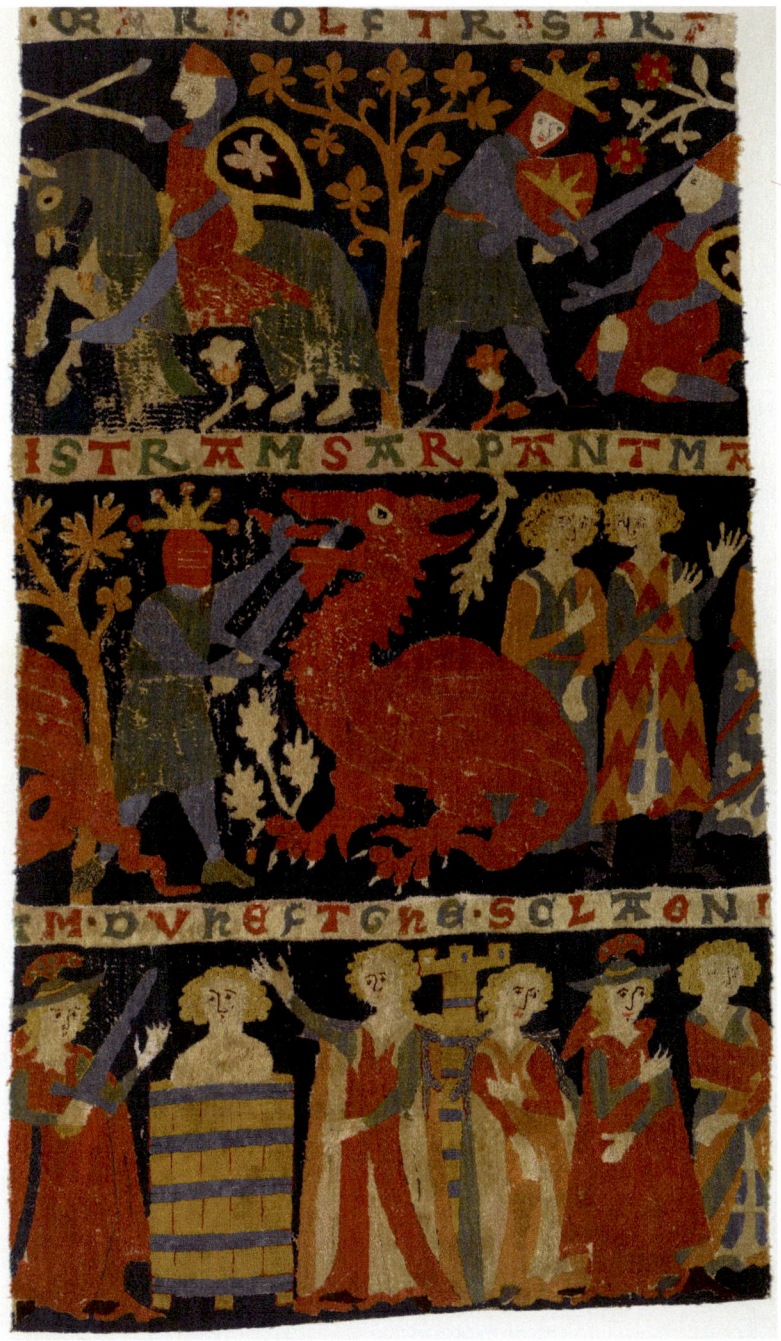

Figure 11.6. Wienhausen, Klosterverwaltung, Wienhausen II embroidery, right. Image © Kloster Wienhausen. Photo: Loeper, Celle.

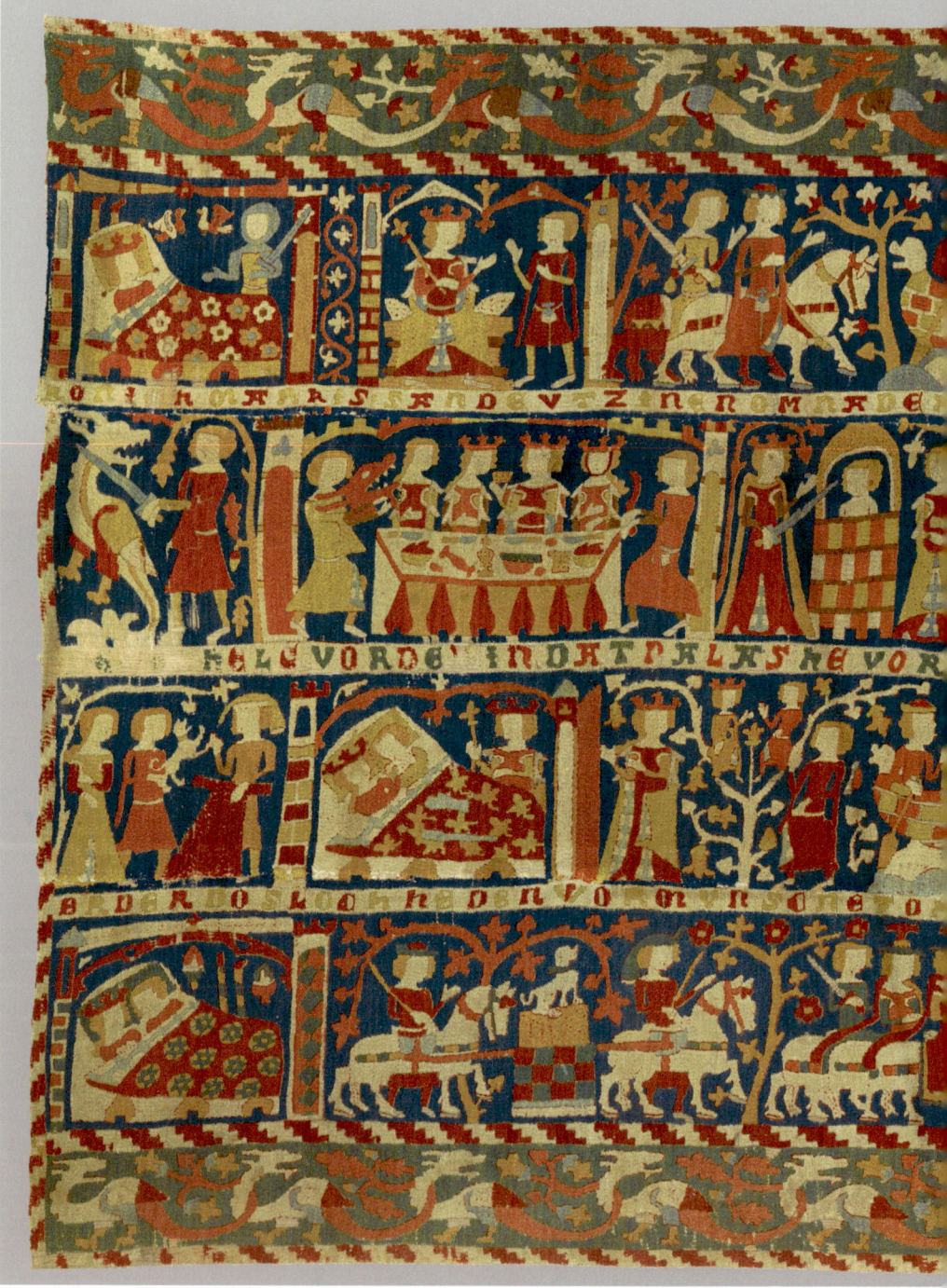

Figure 11.7. Wienhausen, Klosterverwaltung, Wienhausen III embroidery.
Image © Kloster Wienhausen. Photo: Loeper, Celle.

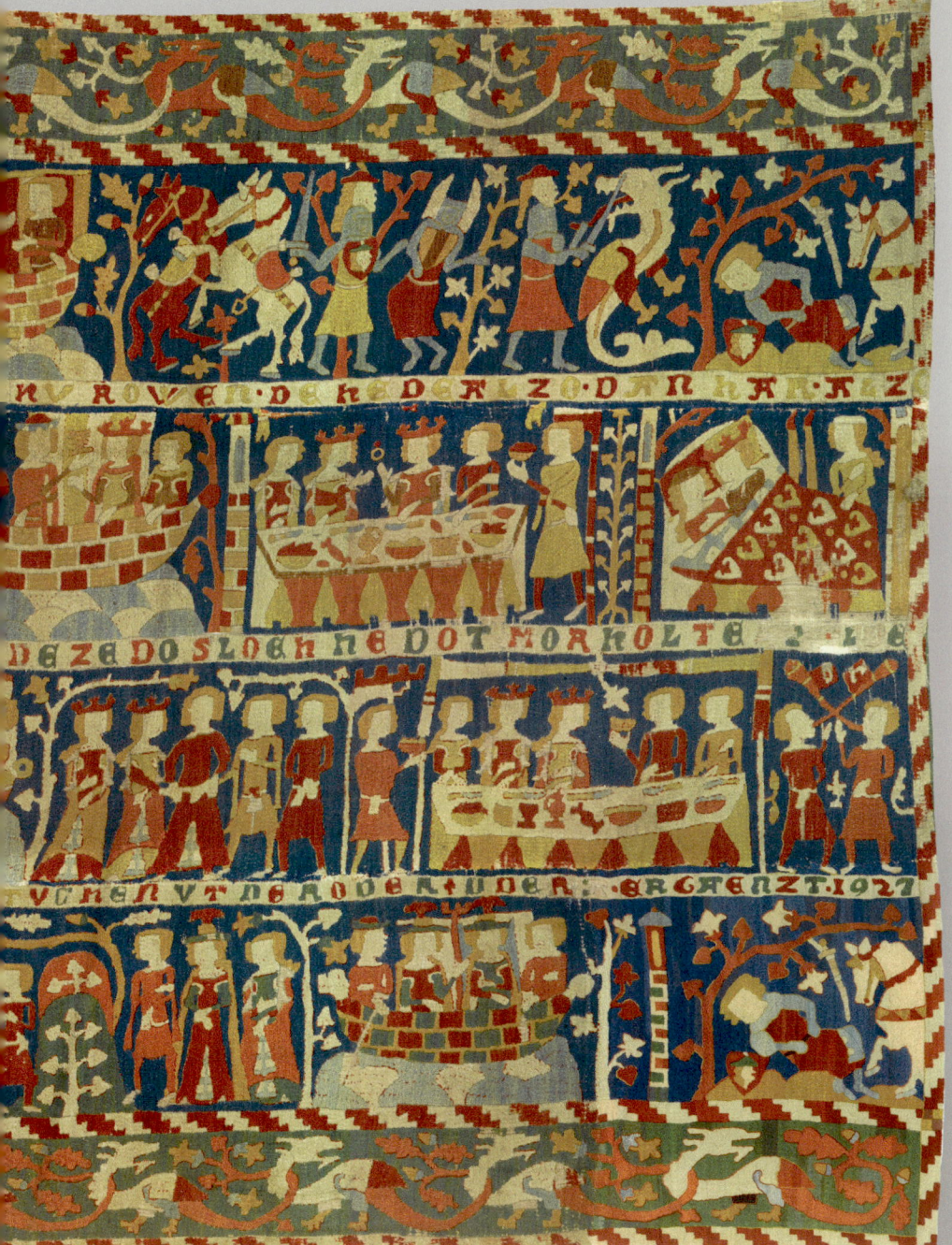

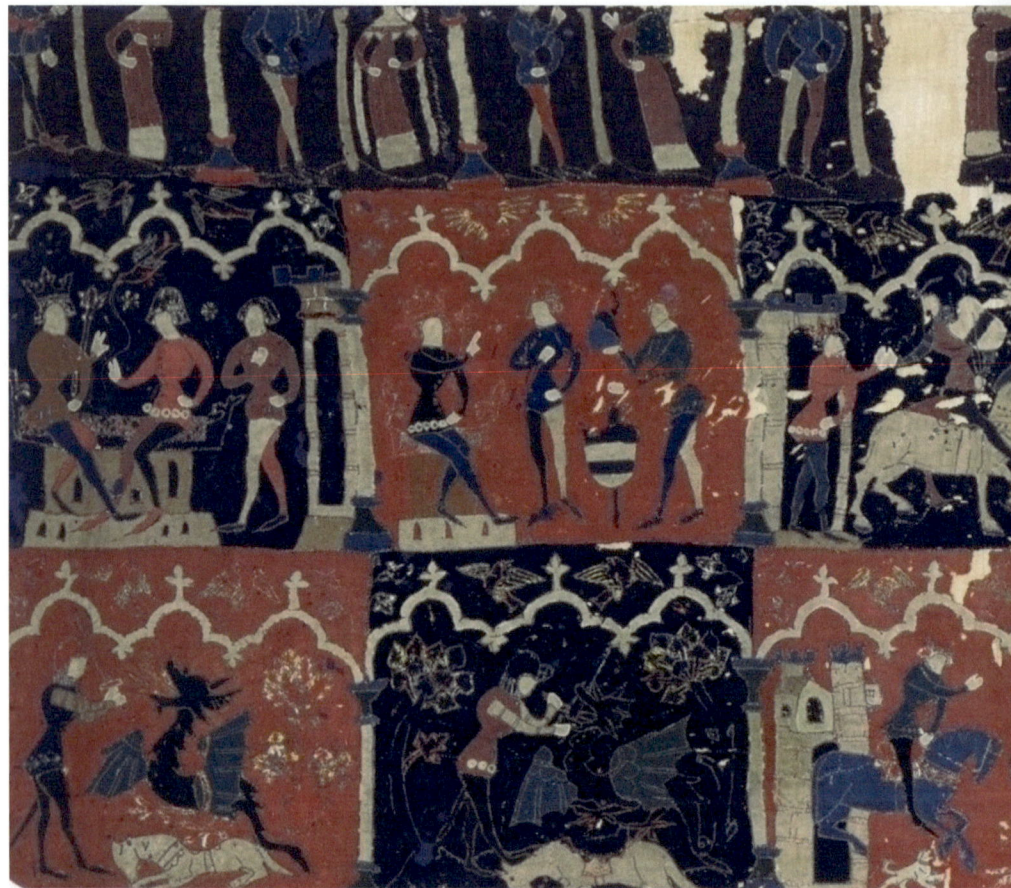

Figure 11.8. London, Victoria and Albert Museum, embroidery. Courtesy of the Victoria and Albert Museum.

to the conclusion that it must represent Tristan and Isolde. The defining elements here are one or two heads in the tree and the reflection beneath the tree of one or two heads. Interestingly, very seldom are all the text elements found in a single image — knight, lady, two heads in the tree, two reflections beneath the tree. The Erfurt tablecloth (scene 25) contains all the elements, and the episode is portrayed with an additional three scenes. Consider the Turin ivory, the Metropolitan Museum casket, the Heidelberg manuscript, the Bruges corbel, the

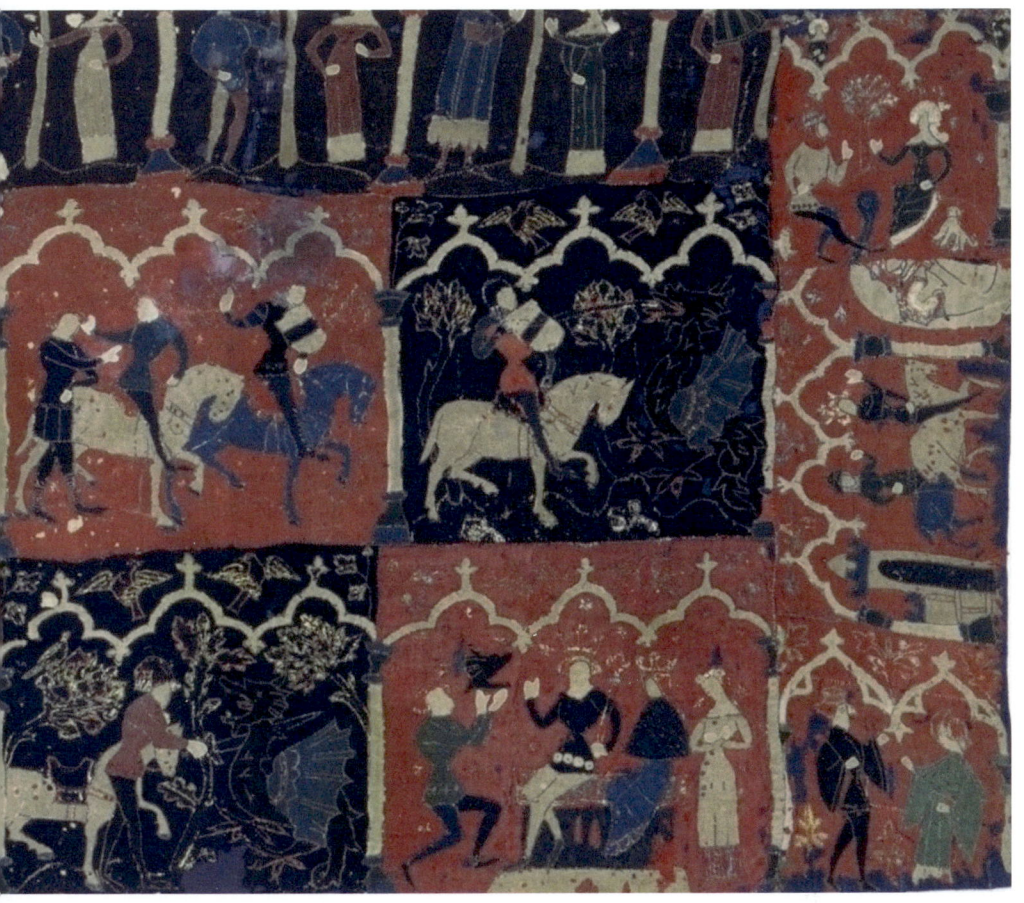

Cluny mirror case for examples of this scene, none of which has all the elements, but where the intention is clearly to represent the Tristan story.[13]

(5) Tristan and Isolde sleep in the grotto with the sword between them. Even though Gottfried von Strassburg and Eilhart von Oberg/Béroul describe the episode quite differently—an idyllic temple of love or a primitive hut—the details of Mark finding the sleeping lovers with the sword between them are very specific in all versions.[14]

In the Wienhausen III embroidery (scene 15; see fig. 11.7), the sword is not between the lovers but rather on the bedcover to the side; however, the figure of Mark and the glove he leaves behind to show his presence definitely point to this episode.

(6) The coffin(s) with the rosebush and the grapevine entwined. This poignant conclusion was undoubtedly familiar to all. According to the text of Ulrich von Türheim, "One saw the rose and the vine intertwined on top of the grave such that they could not be wound any tighter. Never has it been found since the world first came to be, that two people loved each other so much after their death."[15] This episode appears infrequently in the illustrated corpus. The Heidelberg (fol. 174r) and Munich (fol. 107v) manuscripts show plants growing and entwining from a single casket.[16] The Cologne manuscript shows the vines growing from the hearts of the dead lovers.[17] The plants themselves are generic and do not resemble a grapevine or a rosebush. Where there are multiple scenes of this episode, Isolde appears first in a boat and then showing her dismay at finding the dead Tristan.[18] The penultimate scene (scene 23) on the Wienhausen III embroidery (see fig. 11.7) shows Isolde coming to cure the dying Tristan; the final scene of the embroidery is missing and probably would have shown the specific image of the lovers in their coffins.

Generic Scenes

Generic scenes, in contrast to specific ones, cannot be identified without some sort of inscription, rubric, identifier, or chronological position in the story. They may serve as filler, they may serve to organize or outline the text, or they may simply decorate.[19] They interrupt the writing on the manuscript page and give the reader's eyes a rest. Sometimes single or multiple generic scenes illustrate a specific episode. In this case the subject of the episode must be deduced from other evidence. In the codices, especially Heidelberg, Brussels, and Sorg, generic scenes play all these roles.

Most popularly illustrated generic scenes in the verse *Tristan* corpus include the birth of Tristan, the combat of Tristan and Morolt, Tristan in his various disguises, and depictions of harps and chessboards and boats, which probably do not pertain to the Tristan story at all. The Cologne manuscript shows a generic birth, Blanscheflur reclining on a bed, a female attendant handing baby Tristan to a male figure. This is comparable to many birth scenes found in Bible illustrations, the birth of Moses, for instance. The three registers of folio 15r of the Munich manuscript depict Blanscheflur after hearing of Riwalin's death; she bears Tristan and dies; she is buried; and finally, Floraete simulates Tristan's birth.[20] Both of these manuscripts include the text by Gottfried von Strassburg. The Sorg incunabulum (fol. 3r) and the Leipzig embroidery (scene 2) illustrate Eilhart's text, which describes Tristan's cesarean section birth at sea and the resulting death of his mother. In a boat full of people there is a well-formed little boy Tristan emerging from his mother's womb. Among the people on board is Tristan's father, King Riwalin.

Most of the narrative sequences contain scenes pertaining to the episode of the duel between Tristan and Morolt. There is very little in this episode that could possibly be specific — the fact that Tristan kills Morolt with a blow to the head, leaving a piece of his sword, perhaps. The Munich manuscript follows best the details of Gottfried's text (fol. 46r). Tristan and Morolt approach the island in their separate boats; they fight each other on horseback with lances; on foot Tristan plunges his sword into the half-severed head of Morolt; Tristan and his horse sail back to Cornwall in Morolt's red boat. The effective symmetry and flow of the scenes is characteristic of much of the Munich manuscript.[21] All these five scenes are generic. The Brussels manuscript illustrates the episode with six generic scenes — from a discussion of the terms of combat to the return of Tristan after the battle — only comprehensible from the elaborate rubrics (fols. 172r, 174v, 179r, 184r, 189v, 197r). In the Cologne (p. 89) and Heidelberg (fols. 10v, 15r, 17r) manuscripts, Tristan and Morolt fight on foot with swords.[22] In the Sorg incunabulum (fols. 13v and 16r) and the Leipzig embroidery (scenes 7 and 8), they fight on horseback with lances; the next scene then shows Isolde mourning her dead uncle. The Morolt episode was especially important for the designers of the three Wienhausen embroideries: eight scenes in Wienhausen I, four in Wienhausen II and III (see figs. 11.4–11.7). It was perhaps for all the artists the easiest episode to illustrate with the common accumulation of generic pictures.

The codices abound with generic, so-called dialogue scenes: two or three figures standing or sitting as if in conversation. An example is the scene on folio 10v of the Heidelberg manuscript, in which a crowned man is seated while two men stand before him. The written text says that this represents Tristan asking Mark's permission to fight Morolt. Another example, from folio 115r, shows two men on horseback facing each other. The text states that this is Kehenis confronting Tristan about his unconsummated marriage with Isolde Whitehands. Narrative sequences on artifacts, where space is an important consideration, tend to avoid strictly decorative scenes. At most they show comings and goings or fighting on horseback and on foot. The Brussels manuscript contains ninety-one illustrations, only one of which is specific. While no picture is repeated exactly, they mainly show knights on horseback, two people standing next to each other, people meeting each other in an exterior setting or talking to each other in an interior setting, two knights fighting, many knights fighting, and so on. The very detailed rubrics at the beginning of the chapters tell the reader what each illustration is supposed to represent. The Heidelberg and Sorg codices are similar in this respect, but they often illustrate precisely the action of the story.

Quasi-Specific Scenes

A third type of scene, quasi-specific (or quasi-generic), accurately illustrates details of the story but cannot be classified as specific because it cannot be identified out of context. For example, folio 40r of the Sorg incunabulum (see fig. 11.9) shows a woman with a pail near a stream, a couple of men, and a little dog peeking out from behind a wall. The rubric explains that this represents the attempted murder of Brangaene. It is then clear that the men are the knights who were instructed to kill the first person drawing water from the stream, namely, Brangaene. The man with sword upraised is about to kill her, and the dog's liver will be removed to provide evidence that Brangaene has been killed. The Heidelberg manuscript contains three scenes illustrating this episode (fols. 55v, 56v, 57v). Brangaene holds a water pitcher at a spring while two men stand behind her, one with a sword at his waist. Then follow two totally generic scenes showing a

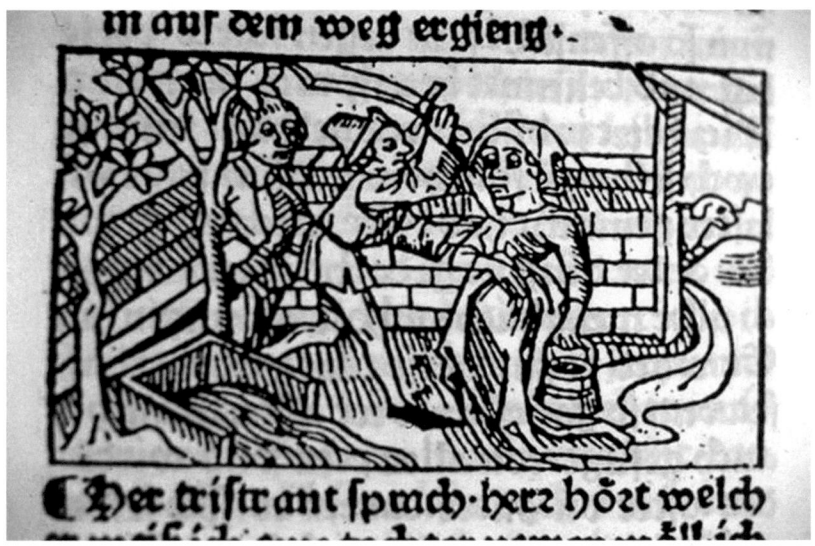

Figure 11.9. Berlin, Staatsbibliothek zu Berlin Preußischer Kulturbesitz, Inc 138, *Tristrant und Isalde* (Augsburg: Anton Sorg, 1484), fol. 40r. Courtesy of Staatsbibliothek zu Berlin Preußischer Kulturbesitz, Berlin.

man reporting to Isolde and a scene depicting the two women, Isolde kneeling before Brangaene asking her forgiveness. Scene 14 on the Wienhausen III embroidery (fig. 11.7) shows on the left Brangaene standing, in the middle a man holding a white dog, and on the right another man holding a bloodied dress.

Illustrations of two men seated opposite each other with one or two birds flying above would merely be puzzling, if one did not realize in the context of the story that the men are Tristan and King Mark, that the birds represent the swallows carrying a golden hair in their beaks, and that King Mark agrees to marry the woman whose hair matches this one.[23] Although this scene represents an important motivating element in the Tristan romance, it would not be recognizable alone, especially if the man is in bed and the pigeon-looking bird has a leaf in its beak, as in the Wienhausen III embroidery (scene 1; see fig. 11.7); perhaps the artist did not understand the story or knew a version that we do not have. In the Wienhausen II (scene 5) and III embroideries (see figs. 11.5 and 11.7), King Mark is in bed, perhaps suggesting a dream, for which there is no textual precedence.

The episode in which Tristan leaps into Isolde's bed to avoid making footprints in the flour scattered on the floor is, needless to say, difficult to execute pictorially. In two examples, Heidelberg manuscript, fol. 73v (see fig. 11.10), and Sorg incunabulum, fol. 77r, Melot is depicted hiding under the bed, as suggested in Eilhart's version. In Gottfried's version, Melot takes Mark to matins while Tristan jumps into Isolde's bed. The leap across the beds is depicted in two scenes in the Munich manuscript (fol. 76v)—Tristan about to leap and Tristan in Isolde's bed (coincidentally, following the color scheme of the page, the bedsheets are red). The Runkelstein wall paintings illustrate the episode in scenes 17 and 18.

Other examples of quasi-specific scenes are the following:

(1) Two men, one with a sword, stand in front of a chapel. One of the windows has been torn out and thus expanded; behind the chapel is a man on horseback leading a second horse; a fourth man is shown swimming in a river. This represents the episode in which the prisoner Tristan asks permission to pray in a chapel. As his guards wait outside Tristan jumps out the window into the water to be rescued by the waiting Kurvenal (Sorg incunabulum, fol. 83r; see fig. 11.11).

(2) In an exterior space with green grass two men in nightshirts and one naked man with a cloth wound around his body show off their bleeding right feet. This represents three Arthurian knights, including Keie and Walwan (Gawan), displaying solidarity with Tristan by claiming they too were caught in the wolf's trap, thus preventing Mark from discovering Tristan's deceit (Heidelberg manuscript, fol. 102r).

(3) On the left half of a woodcut a man and a crowned woman are seated in intimate conversation; on the right half, divided by a wall, a man and a woman are shown shooting arrows at a target mounted on the wall. This represents the episode in which Cainis, Tristan's brother-in-law, makes love to Gardeloye, wife of King Nampecenis, while Tristan amuses the people of the castle with his skill at archery (Sorg incunabulum, fol. 176v).

In her very persuasive essay comparing the illustrations of the Heidelberg manuscript and the Sorg incunabulum, Doris Fouquet demonstrates that many of the illustrations from the end of the fifteenth century were in common use. A generic event, part of the

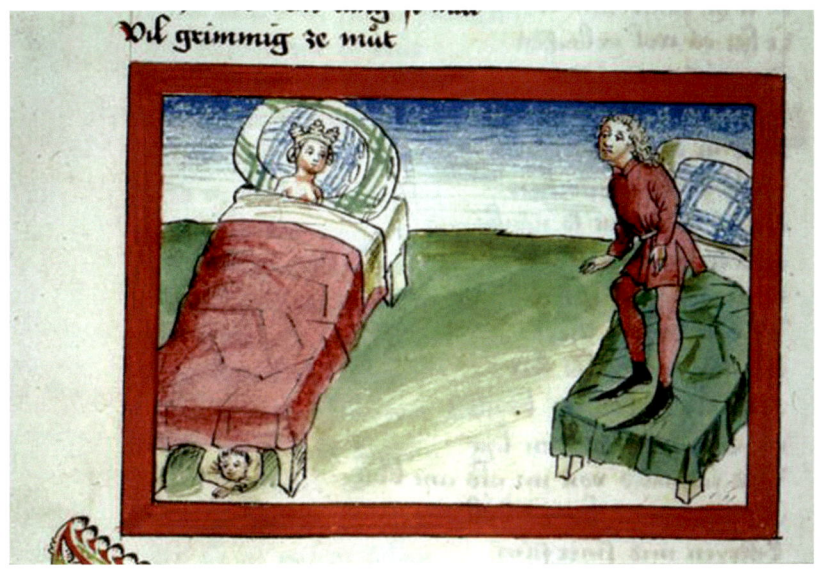

Figure 11.10. Heidelberg, Universitätsbibliothek, MS Cod. Pal. Germ. 346, fol. 73v. Courtesy of Universitätsbibliothek, Heidelberg.

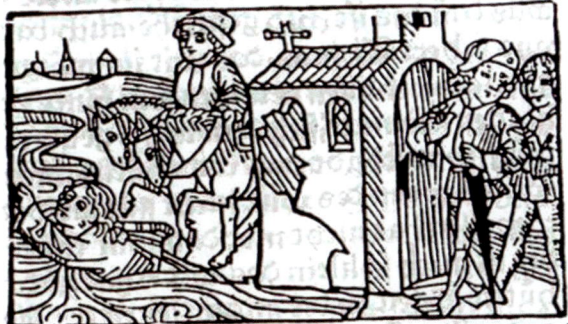

Figure 11.11. Berlin, Staatsbibliothek zu Berlin Preußischer Kulturbesitz, Inc 138, *Tristrant und Isalde* (Augsburg: Anton Sorg, 1484), fol. 83r. Courtesy of Staatsbibliothek zu Berlin Preußischer Kulturbesitz, Berlin.

episode in which Tristan goes to Ireland to be cured and on the return trip buys supplies for the starving Irish, is illustrated in the Sorg incunabulum (fol. 20r); the model for the woodcut may be a similar one by Guido de Columna illustrating a loading of heavy sacks from the *Historia Troiana* from 1482.[24] Both illustrations depict the action of the story but could not be identified outside of their context.

Discussion

If one looks at the very large Wienhausen I embroidery (see fig. 11.4) and disregards the inscription, which is not terribly useful but does identify the story, one cannot identify a single specific scene until the bottom narrative register—Tristan cutting the tongue out of the dragon. Then follow in rapid succession the bath episode and the love potion being drunk at sea. Once the story has been established by these specific scenes, it is not difficult to follow the action from Tristan setting out to fight Morolt to his winning of the bride. Tristan fiddling at the walls of Dublin, the two swallows fluttering over King Mark and Tristan, Tristan lying comatose in the rushes, and the seneschal presenting the dragon's head to the king and queen are all scenes that aptly illustrate the story. However, if they were not part of a consecutive sequence, they could not, with certainty, be identified as Tristan. Note that there are eight scenes narrating the episode of Tristan and Morolt, none of which is specific.

British Library, MS Add. 11619

There are very few narrative sequences in this corpus that have no identifying text or inscriptions. When Tony Hunt came upon four folios of illustrations in a manuscript in the British Library (Add. 11619) with no accompanying text, he was able to identify a Tristan narrative sequence by two specific scenes: The first scene depicts Tristan in the bath with a nicked sword; the second scene illustrates the tryst in the orchard with King Mark standing full figured in the tree and the reflection of the dwarf in the water.[25] Additional corroboration was supplied by the scene of Tristan killing the dragon. This is not a specific scene according to my definition since he is not shown cutting out the tongue, but it provides some additional weight to the argument. Even with the specific bath and trysting scenes as anchors, it is extremely difficult to place the other scenes—a king with crossed legs with councilors and couriers, a man in the process of being beheaded, two pictures of boats, and another court scene. Indeed Hunt has identified the beheaded man as Duke Morgan, while Alan Deighton sees him as the seneschal being punished for his fraud.[26] I tend to agree with Deighton, first because of the order; this scene follows the killing of the dragon. And second, the Erfurt tablecloth (scene 17) also depicts the seneschal being punished by having his head cut off after being exposed for his fraud.

The Hermitage I Ivory Casket

The drinking of the love potion at sea is represented in two scenes on the Hermitage I casket: the drinking at sea and the rapturous embrace following it. The story continues with the wedding of Mark and Isolde (see fig. 11.12); the uncrowned Brangaene in bed with crowned Mark, crowned Isolde pointing this out to Tristan (see fig. 11.13); a scene with Tristan and Isolde in bed, presumably leading up to the trial by hot iron; Tristan disguised as a pilgrim carrying Isolde to her trial; the trial with Isolde swearing on a Bible (see fig. 11.14); Tristan and perhaps Kaedin disguised as pilgrims carrying staves and wearing conical hats and Isolde placing a purse into his begging bowl (see fig. 11.15). The lid with the specific classic trysting scene and the grotto scene has been identified as a forgery, but even so the subject of the casket is established with the love potion.

The Victoria and Albert Embroidery

In the Victoria and Albert embroidery (see fig. 11.8), which has ten scenes, only scene 7 is specific; it depicts a knight cutting out the tongue of the dragon. From this scene one can work forward and backward to construct a little story: the episode in which Tristan wins Isolde for his uncle Mark by killing the dragon. Interestingly Isolde appears only in the last scene.

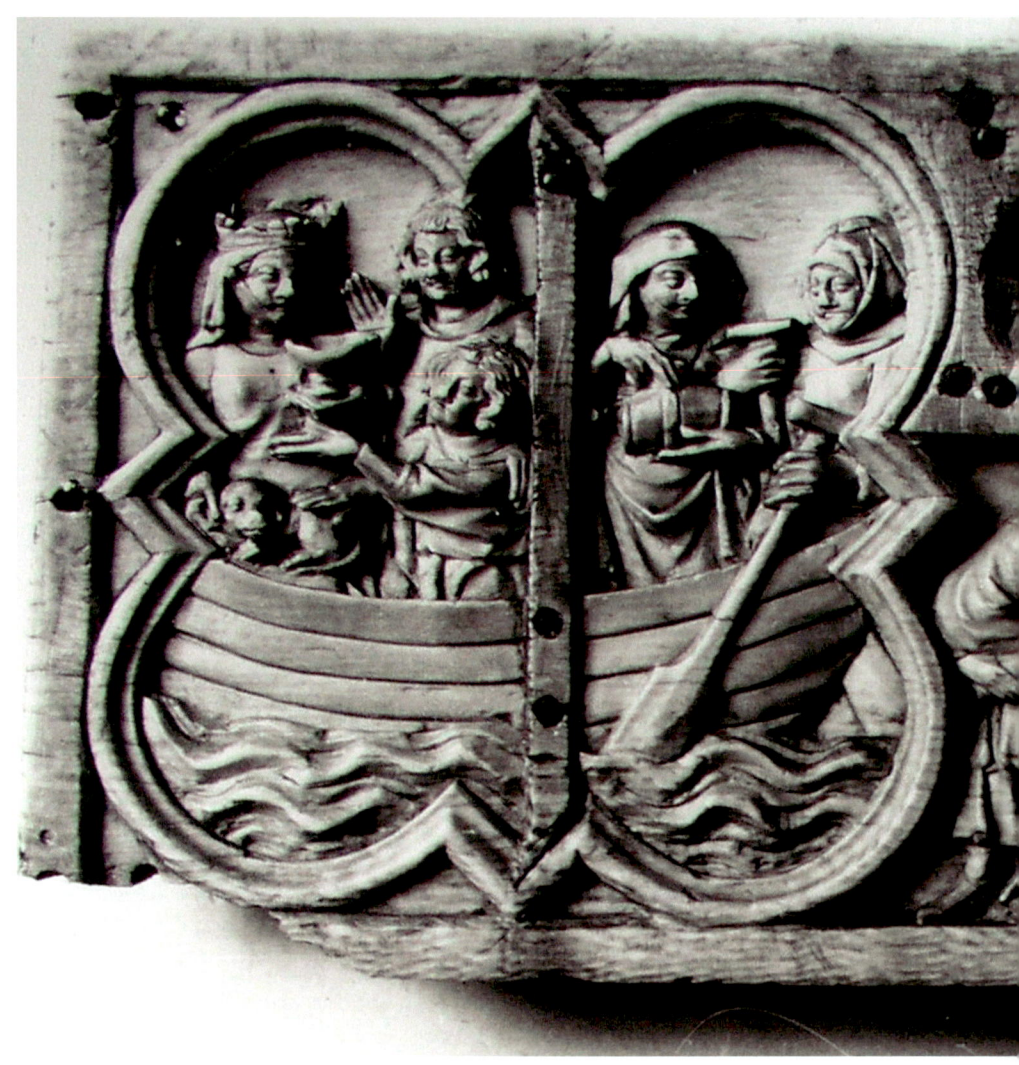

Figure 11.12. Hermitage Museum, St. Petersburg, Hermitage I ivory casket, front. Courtesy of The State Hermitage Museum, St. Petersburg (figs. 11.12–11.15).

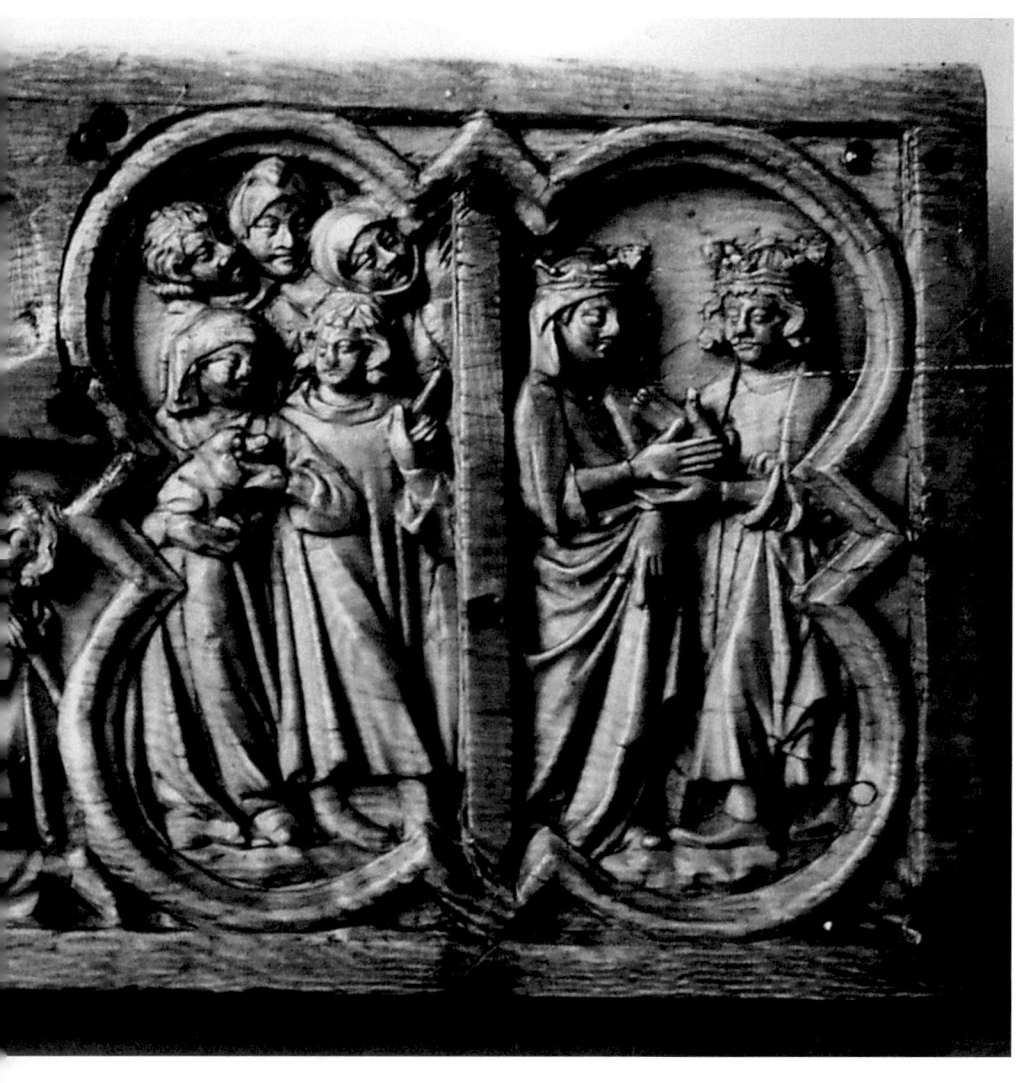

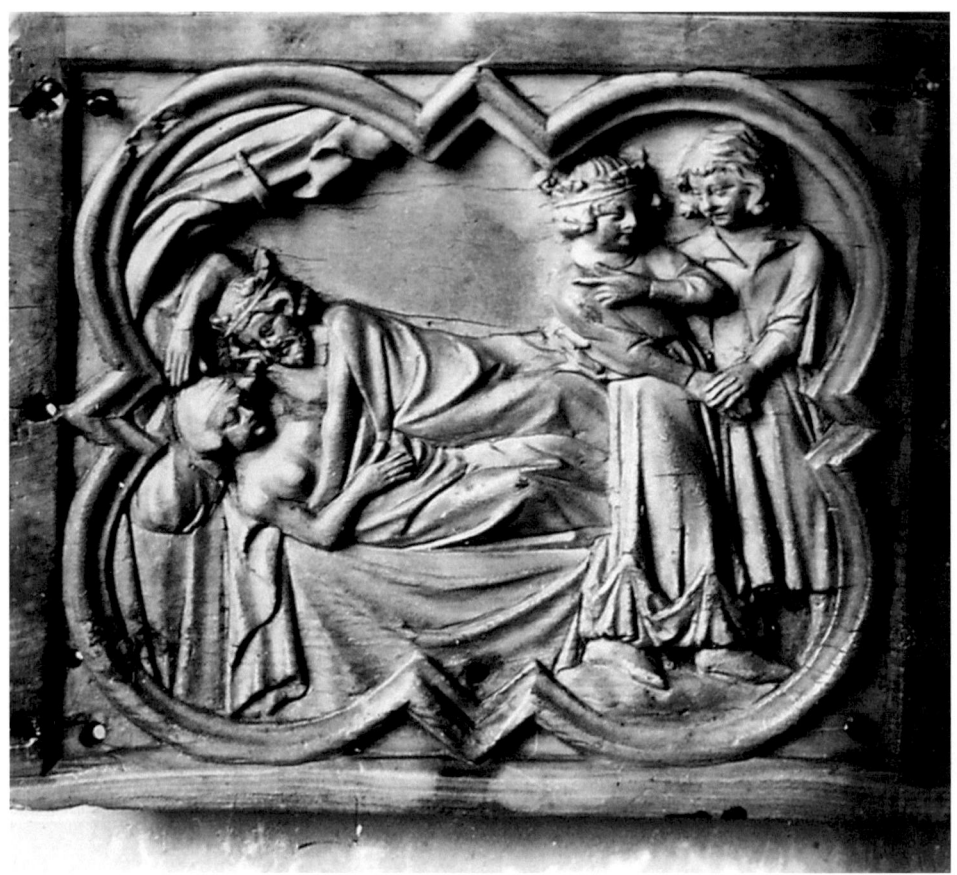

Figure 11.13. Hermitage I ivory casket, left.

WE MAY SURMISE FROM THIS EXAMINATION OF SEVERAL ILLUMINATED codices and artifacts that specific scenes immediately identify a story. Wherever these scenes are found, in isolation or in a narrative sequence, it is clear that the subject is Tristan and Isolde. Specific episodes sometimes contain only generic scenes. They can usually be identified in the context of a manuscript with inscriptions and rubrics. Or if the subject of a narrative sequence has been established, one can deduce the contents of various scenes even if they are generic. In addition, quasi-specific (or quasi-generic) scenes may precisely illustrate the

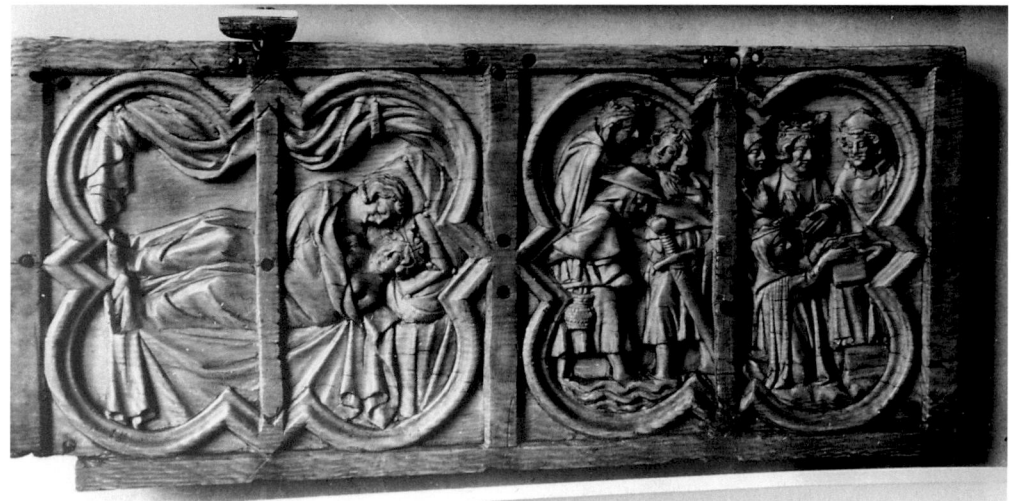

Figure 11.14. Hermitage I ivory casket, back.

action of the story. These are especially interesting, as the examples above suggest, but they are not specific since they cannot be identified out of context. The notion of an alternation between specific and generic discursive scenes provided both the literary and visual composer with a structural framework for representing his version of the story and today provides both the literary historian and the art historian with a valuable tool for interpreting a medieval narrative such as the Tristan story. On the one hand, the literary and visual narratives must portray the specific in order to be recognizable. On the other hand, generic elements provide the necessary framework for interpreting the specific. In isolation specific scenes have no meaningful context (other than representing the entire narrative); in isolation generic scenes have no identification or differentiation.[27]

The scenes discussed above can be considered illustrations of a given text of a known author only when they are embedded in a manuscript or incunabulum of that text. The illuminated folios of the Munich manuscript that are separated from the text tell, I believe, a different story from the written text—based on another written version or on the artist's notion of the story. Artifacts portraying narrative

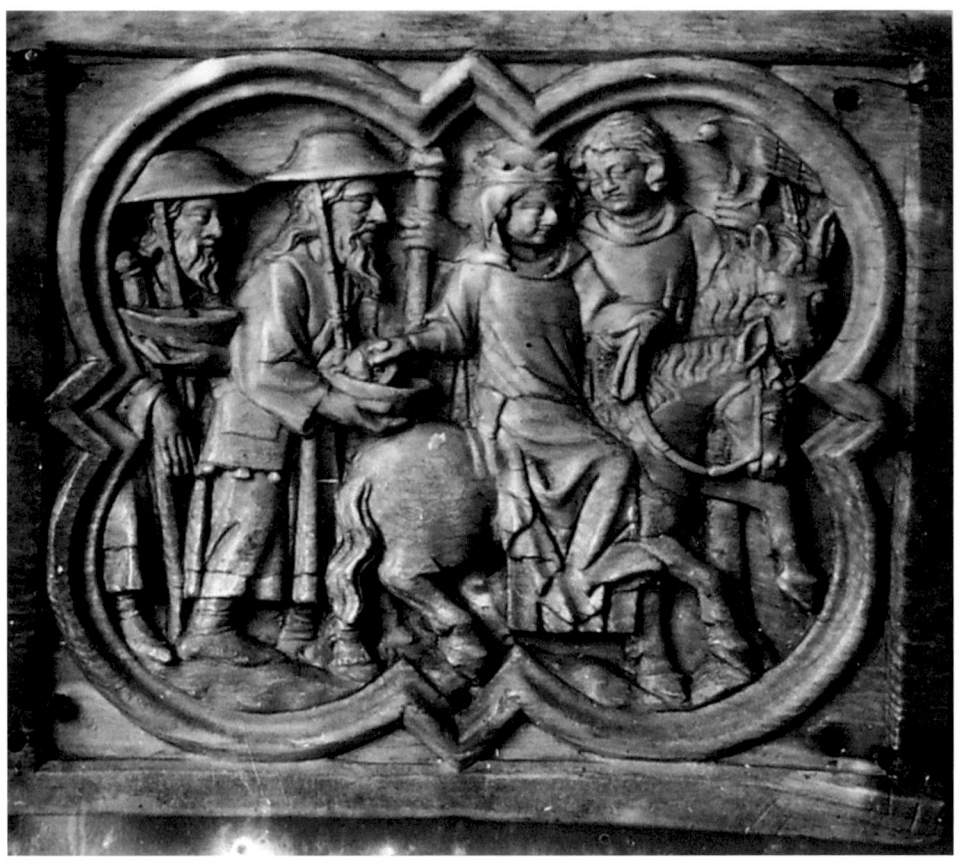

Figure 11.15. Hermitage I ivory casket, right.

sequences may be based on a written text, but it is more likely that the designer was relying on his memory from an oral rendering. Thus the Tristan stories vary from a simple courtly love story of winning a bride by killing a dragon, to a complex and often troubling story of adultery, intrigue, attempted murder, trial by ordeal, unconsummated marriage, and finally the death of Tristan and Isolde. It must be kept in mind that "images derived from narrative materials are not, even when they illustrate books, direct translations of texts into pictures. Instead, they are generated by the interaction of narrative tradition, iconographic tradition, the unique problems of the visual medium, and the individual literary and functional context of each work."[28]

Notes

1. Transmission of the text of the verse *Tristan* is complicated and somewhat problematic. Many scholars suggest that a prototype or archetype of
the Tristan story was composed by the middle of the twelfth century. It was
added to and disseminated orally until written versions appeared at the end
of the twelfth century. However, today we do not have a single complete text
earlier than the fifteenth century. That text in German by Eilhart von Oberg
is based on thirteenth-century manuscript fragments probably copied from
an archetype from about 1170–90. There are two French texts extant now in
fragmentary form: one by Thomas d'Angleterre (ca. 1175) and another by
Béroul (between 1176 and 1202). Gottfried von Strassburg composed his German version about 1210, based, he says, on Thomas. However, only 114 lines
of Thomas compare to 814 lines of Gottfried. Gottfried's version was not
completed, either because he died or because he was unwilling to commit to
the transmitted ending. It was continued and completed by Ulrich von Türheim (ca. 1235) and Heinrich von Freiberg (ca. 1290). In addition, there are
versions in Old Norse by Brother Robert (based on Thomas) and in English,
Sir Tristrem (late thirteenth century), which has often been considered a poor
adaptation of Thomas (although more recent scholarship views it as a parody),
that are important for text reconstruction, but they are not illustrated. Scholars speak of two branches, a courtly one exemplified by Thomas and Gottfried and a common or primitive one based on Eilhart and Béroul. While the
basic outline of the story is the same, the two branches or traditions treat the
details somewhat differently.

2. On the images discussed in this chapter, see, generally, Roger Sher-
man Loomis and Laura Hibbard Loomis, *Arthurian Legends in Medieval Art,*
Modern Language Association of America Monograph Series (New York:
Modern Language Association of America, 1938). In addition to manuscript
illustrations, see Norbert H. Ott, "Katalog der Tristan-Bildzeugnisse," in
Hella Frühmorgen-Voss, *Text und Illustration im Mittelalter: Aufsätze zu den
Wechselbeziehungen zwischen Literatur und bildender Kunst,* ed. Norbert H.
Ott, 140–71, Münchener Texte und Untersuchungen zur deutschen Literatur
des Mittelalters 50 (München: Beck, 1975), who has listed fifty-seven known
artifacts devoted to the Tristan story as well as twenty-eight questionable
items; and Hella Frühmorgen-Voss, "Tristan und Isolde in mittelalterlichen
Bildzeugnissen," *Deutsche Vierteljahrsschrift* 47 (1973): 645–63; reprinted in
Frühmorgen-Voss, *Text und Illustration im Mittelalter,* 119–39.

3. "Munich manuscript": Munich, Bayerische Staatsbibliothek, Cgm 51
(mid-13th cent.), 109 folios, 23.5 x 16 cm, 118 scenes (Gottfried von Strassburg

and Ulrich von Türheim). The illuminated folios of the Munich manuscript of *Tristan* are not placed next to their logical position in the text. Consequently, each specific episode contains a specific scene for identification among the generic ones.

4. "Heidelberg manuscript": Heidelberg, Universitätsbibliothek, Ms Cod. Pal. Germ. 346 (1460–75), 175 folios, 30.6 x 21.1 cm, 91 scenes (Eilhart von Oberg).

5. "Hermitage I ivory": Hermitage Museum, St. Petersburg, ivory casket (ca. 1325), 8.2 x 18.5 x 10 cm, 10 scenes, including two forgeries.

6. See Stephanie Cain Van D'Elden, "Discursive Illustrations in Three Tristan Manuscripts," in *Word and Image in Arthurian Literature,* ed. Keith Busby (New York: Garland, 1996), 284–319, fig. 9.29.

7. "Sorg incunabulum": Berlin, Staatsbibliothek, Inc 138, *Tristrant und Isalde* (Augsburg: Anton Sorg, 1484), 187 folios, 18.1 x 13.6 cm, 60 scenes (Eilhart von Oberg).

8. "Brussels manuscript": Brussels, Bibliothèque Royale, MS 14697 (ca. 1455–60), 597 folios, 27.5 x 21 cm, 91 scenes (Gottfried von Strassburg, *Tristan als Mönch,* and Ulrich von Türheim).

9. "Runkelstein wall paintings": Castle Runkelstein near Bolzano in the Italian Tyrol, wall paintings (ca. 1400), life size, 20 scenes. "Wienhausen embroideries": Kloster Wienhausen, Klosterverwaltung, Wienhausen I embroidery (1300–1330), 233 x 404 cm, 23 scenes; Wienhausen II embroidery (mid-14th cent.), left, 136 x 84 cm; right, 138 x 77 cm, 12 scenes; Wienhausen III embroidery (1350–1400), 245 x 402 cm, 23 scenes. "Victoria and Albert embroidery": London, Victoria and Albert Museum, embroidery (ca. 1375), 101 x 241 cm, 10 scenes. "Erfurt tablecloth": Erfurt, Katholisches Dompfarramt, tablecloth embroidery (late 14th cent.), 93 x 428 cm, 26 scenes.

10. See Brussels manuscript, fol. 268v; Munich manuscript, fol. 67v; Erfurt tablecloth, scene 13; Wienhausen I embroidery, scene 20; Wienhausen II embroidery, scene 11; Wienhausen III embroidery, scene 10; and Runkelstein wall painting, scenes 6 and 7.

11. See Cologne, Historisches Archiv der Stadt MS W*kl.f°88, p. 142, in Van D'Elden, "Discursive Illustrations in Three Tristan Manuscripts," fig. 9.24; Sorg incunabulum, fol. 43r; Wienhausen I embroidery, scene 23; Leipzig embroidery, scene 20. Leipzig, Museum des Kunsthandwerks (1539), left, 77 x 415 cm; right, 76 x 187 cm; 21 scenes.

12. See Michael Curschmann, "Images of Tristan," in *Gottfried von Strassburg and the Medieval Tristan Legend: Papers from an Anglo-North American Symposium,* ed. Adrian Stevens and Roy Wisbey, Publications of the In-

stitute of Germanic Studies, University of London 44 (Cambridge: D. S. Brewer, 1990), 1–17; reprinted in Michael Curschmann, *Wort–Bild–Text: Studien zur Medialität des Literarischen in Hochmittelalter und früher Neuzeit,* 2 vols. (Baden-Baden: Valentin Koerner, 2007), 1:227–51; Stephanie Cain Van D'Elden, "Is a Tree Just a Tree?" (unpublished paper, Eleventh Triennial Congress of the International Courtly Literature Society, Madison, WI, August 3, 2004).

13. For all these artifacts, see Frühmorgen-Voss, *Text und Illustration im Mittelalter.*

14. See Munich manuscript, fol. 90r; Heidelberg manuscript, fol. 87r; Sorg incunabulum, fol. 92v.

15. Ulrich von Türheim, *Tristan und Isolde,* ed. Thomas Kerth (Tübingen: Niemeyer, 1979), 3696–99; thanks to Christina White for the translation.

16. See Van D'Elden, "Discursive Illustrations in Three Tristan Manuscripts," fig. 9.30.

17. "Cologne manuscript": Cologne, Historisches Archiv der Stadt MS W*kl.f°88 (1323), 263 pages, 21 x 14.4 cm, 9 scenes (Gottfried von Strassburg and Ulrich von Türheim). See Van D'Elden, "Discursive Illustrations in Three Tristan Manuscripts," fig. 9.28.

18. See Munich manuscript, fol. 107v; Heidelberg manuscript, fols. 171v, 172v, 173r; Sorg incunabulum, fols. 182r, 184v, 186r; and even the Chertsey tiles from the Benedictine abbey at Chertsey, Surrey, now in the British Museum.

19. Lieselotte E. Saurma-Jeltsch, "Der Brüsseler *Tristan*: Ein mittelalterliches Haus- und Sachbuch," in *Tristan und Isolt im Spätmittelalter: Vorträge eines interdisziplinären Symposiums vom 3. bis 8. Juni 1996 an der Justus-Liebig Universität Gießen,* ed. Xenja von Ertzdorff and Rudolf Schulz (Amsterdam: Rodopi, 1999), 103–39, strongly suggests that the generic scenes in the Brussels manuscript have an important role in outlining the story, pulling it along from one episode to the next.

20. On these images, see Brüggen and Ziegeler, this volume.

21. The facsimile edition, *Tristan und Isolde: Mit der Fortsetzung Ulrichs von Türheim; Faksimile-Ausgabe des Cgm 51 der Bayerischen Staatsbibliothek München,* ed. Ulrich Montag and Paul Gichtel (Stuttgart: Müller und Schindler, 1979), contains an essay by Ulrich Montag describing the contents and state of research (5–72) and an essay by Paul Gichtel describing the illustrations (73–144). See also Bettina Falkenberg, *Die Bilder der Münchener Tristan-Handschrift,* Europäische Hochschulschriften, ser. 28, vol. 67 (Frankfurt am Main: Peter Lang, 1986); Julia Caroline Walworth, *Parallel Narratives:*

Function and Form in the Munich Illustrated Manuscripts of "Tristan" and "Willehalm von Orlens" (London: King's College, 2007); and Norbert Werner, "Tristan-Darstellungen in der Kunst des Mittelalters," in von Ertzdorff and Schulz, *Tristan und Isolt im Spätmittelalter,* 14: "als bewußter Akt der Dramaturgie."

22. See Van D'Elden, "Discursive Illustrations in Three Tristan Manuscripts," fig. 9.22, for the illustration in the Cologne manuscript.

23. See Erfurt tablecloth, scene 1; Victoria and Albert embroidery, scene 1, Fig. 11.8; Wienhausen I embroidery, scene 14, Fig. 11.4; and Heidelberg manuscript, fol. 27r.

24. Doris Fouquet, "Spätmittelalterliche Tristan-Illustrationen in Handschrift und Druck: Die Bilder der Heidelberger Eilharthandschrift pal. germ. 346 und der Augsburger Wiegendrucke; mit siebzehn Abbildungen," in *Gutenberg-Jahrbuch* (Mainz: Verlag der Gutenberg-Gesellschaft, 1972), 300. She contends that the incunabulum was not based on the earlier manuscript but rather that both works come from a common tradition.

25. Tony Hunt, "The Tristan Illustrations in MS London BL Add. 11619," in *Rewards and Punishments in the Arthurian Romances and Lyric Poetry of Mediaeval France: Essays Presented to Kenneth Varty on the Occasion of His Sixtieth Birthday,* ed. Peter V. Davies and Angus J. Kennedy (Cambridge: D. S. Brewer, 1987), 43–60. For images from BL Add. 11619, see Van D'Elden, "Discursive Illustrations in Three Tristan Manuscripts," figs. 9.12–9.19.

26. Hunt, "Tristan Illustrations in MS London BL Add. 11619"; Alan R. Deighton, "The Tristan Illustrations in MS London, BL Add. 11619, the *Roman de Tristan en Prose,* and the German Tristan Tapestries," *Tristania* 18 (1998): 17–35.

27. See Stephanie Cain Van D'Elden, "Specific and Generic Scenes: A Model for Analyzing Medieval Illustrated Texts Based on the Example of *Yvain/Iwein,*" *Bibliographical Bulletin of the International Arthurian Society* 44 (1992): 255–69.

28. James A. Rushing Jr., "Adventures beyond the Text: Ywain in the Visual Arts" (Ph.D. diss., Princeton University, 1988), 221.

CHAPTER TWELVE

The Artistic Context of Some Northern French Illustrated *Tristan* Manuscripts

MARGARET ALISON STONES

The beginnings of *Tristan* illustration have left few traces, but they are important indicators that the story circulated outside the British Isles and northern France in a period prior to that of the earliest surviving manuscript copies. Similarly, the topos of the Tryst beneath the Tree has an atextual history not reflected in most French versions of the story but compellingly illustrated as a stand-alone subject for depiction in a variety of contexts on objects made for personal use in France and elsewhere. When it comes to a consideration of the manuscripts of the French versions of the story of Tristan, a surprising number of copies were made and illustrated for patrons living outside the hexagon of today. I list all these in an appendix and concentrate here on an examination of the illustrated *Tristan* manuscripts made in France and their artistic context. My questions are these: What contributions do the illustrations make to the reception of the Tristan story? And how do the *Tristan* manuscripts compare with the manuscripts of the other popular prose romance, the *Lancelot-Grail,* and other books made for the patrons of *Tristan*? Some of the manuscripts have received a good deal of attention; others remain relatively unknown. Here I survey the illustrated copies, their chronology and their context, and offer some pointers toward a comparative study of *Tristan* iconography.

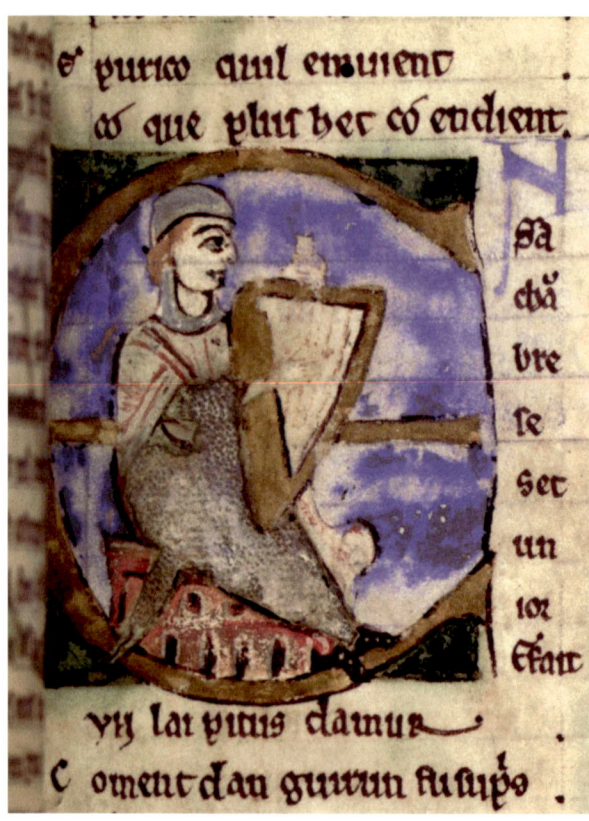

Figure 12.1. Oxford, Bodleian Library, MS Bodl. Fr. d. 16, fol. 10. Courtesy of the Bodleian Library.

Unlike the famous early-thirteenth-century illustrations in the Munich manuscript of Gottfried von Strassburg's *Tristan* (Bayerische Staatsbibliothek, Cgm 51), the earliest French versions of the story offer little illustration, and none of it is properly narrative. Only the single portrait in the *Tristan* of Thomas, depicting Tristan harping (and singing? his mouth looks closed, but the illustration is poorly preserved), attests to the desire to illustrate this compelling story. The sole historiated initial, placed in the text body, at line 834 in Gregory's edition, serves to mark the introduction of Tristan's musical accomplishments as he sings a lay (fig. 12.1).[1] For the medieval viewer, the parallel with Old Testament King David, commonly depicted since Carolingian times as a harpist at the opening of the psalms that are ascribed to his authorship, would have been obvious.[2] In the prose *Tristan*

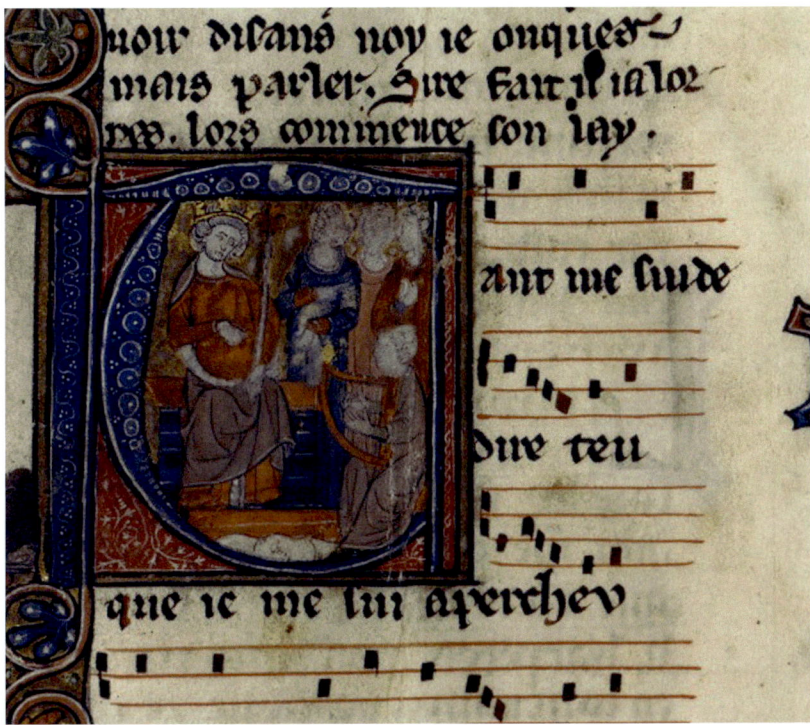

Figure 12.2. Paris, Bibliothèque Nationale, MS fr. 776, fol. 271v. Courtesy of Bibliothèque Nationale de France.

the harping motif is also common. There, the musician is more usually shown playing to an audience: Tristan or Dinan playing to King Mark, like David playing before King Saul, another common topos in biblical illustration (fig. 12.2).[3] And the episodes and their illustrations gave many variants on the harping and listening motif, whether Tristan, or Iseut, or another musician was playing, and whether Iseut, or another woman, or another man, or a group of people were listening (figs. 12.3, 12.4).

If the portrait of Tristan in Thomas's manuscript is the earliest depiction of Tristan as harpist, another of Tristan's accomplishments, namely, his strength as a warrior, is the focus of the Tristan scenes once adorning the north transept columns at the Cathedral of Santiago de Compostela. Several sculpted fragments show the aftermath of

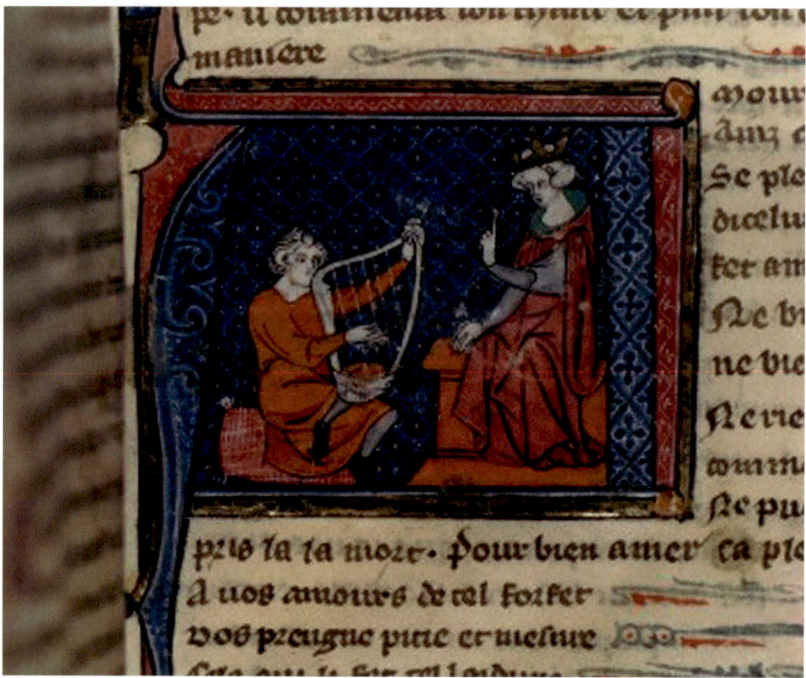

Figure 12.3. Paris, Bibliothèque Nationale, MS fr. 334, fol. 184. Courtesy of Bibliothèque Nationale de France.

Tristan's combat with the Morhaut, where the hero, accompanied by his horse, lies exhausted in his boat, holding his sword with the notch in the blade (see fig. 12.5). These have been dated circa 1100–1117, which makes them the earliest surviving depictions of Tristan, antedating any of the written versions.[4] Significantly, neither of these early depictions — the sculptures or the Thomas initial — focus on Tristan's love for Iseut but rather on Tristan's accomplishments, be they musical or heroic. In this respect they are linked to the Chertsey tiles, which Loomis has shown also reflect the *Tristan* of Thomas.[5] They again concentrate on Tristan's heroic and musical activities rather than on the love interest.

From the earliest dated illustrated prose *Tristan* manuscript, Paris, BNF fr. 750 (MS I), written by a Norman scribe, Pierre de Tiergeville,

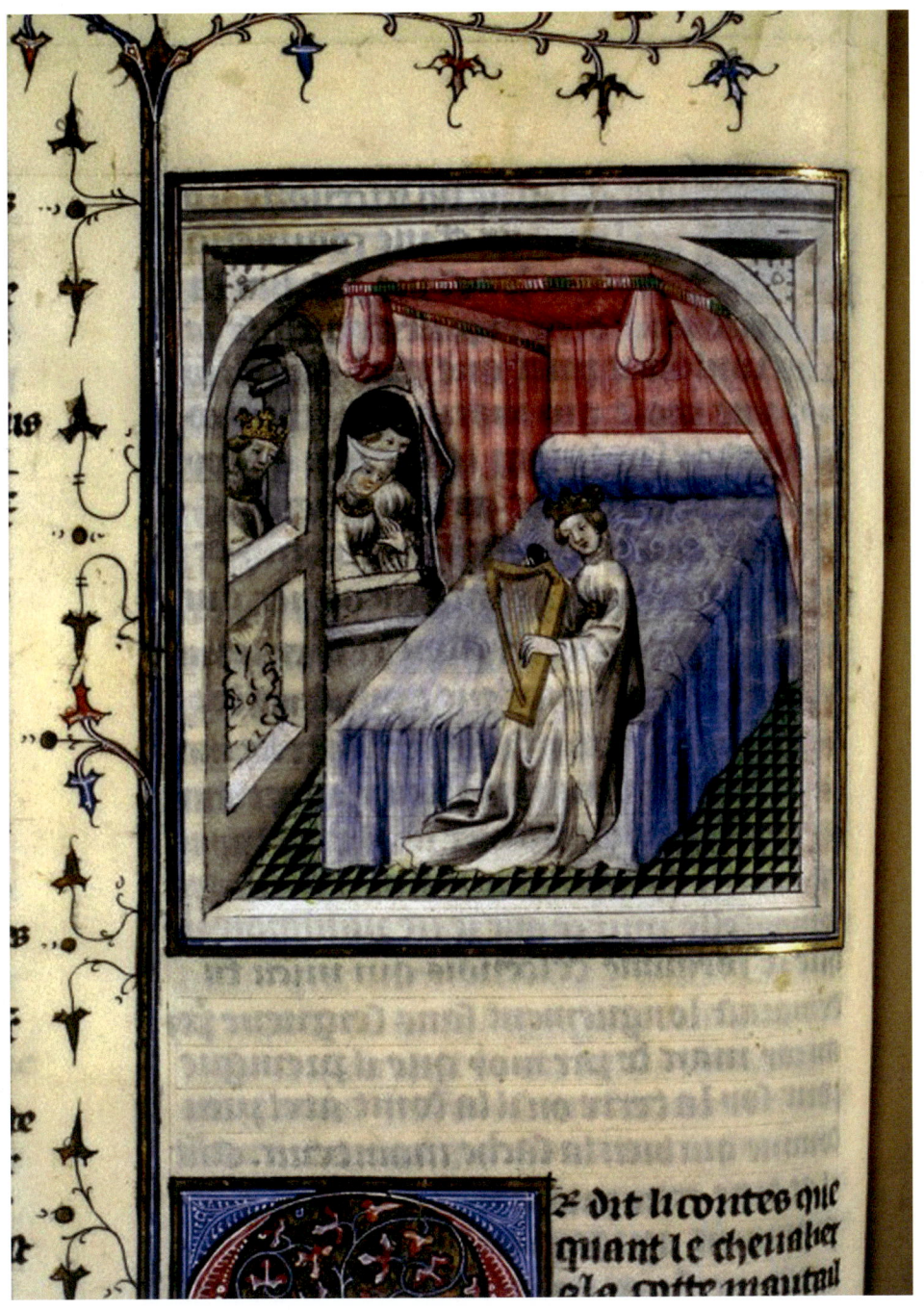

Figure 12.4. Paris, Bibliothèque Nationale, MS fr. 100, fol. 172v. Courtesy of Bibliothèque Nationale de France.

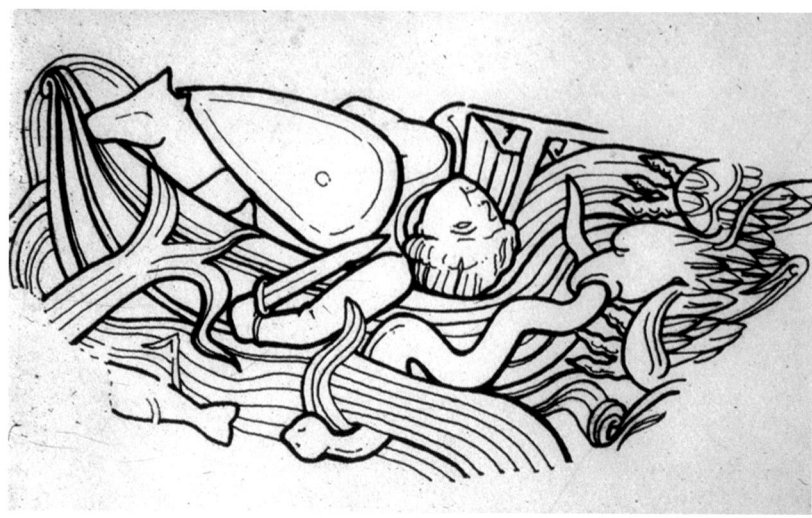

Figure 12.5. Santiago de Compostela, Cathedral, North Transept sculpture. Drawing by Serafín Moralejo, used by permission.

but illustrated either in southern Italy or the Holy Land, most manuscripts include narrative illustrations.[6] By comparison with the *Lancelot-Grail* romances, the beginnings of *Tristan* illustration are late: the *Lancelot-Grail* was already illustrated with a series of historiated initials in the earliest surviving copy, Rennes BM 255, made, I have argued, around 1220.[7] What is surprising about the *Tristan* manuscript tradition is that the earliest manuscripts, like the earliest depictions referred to above, were made outside France. Closely related textually to BNF fr. 750 is BNF fr. 12599 (MS d), written by Oddo, and made in Italy,[8] and several more Italian copies followed in the last quarter of the thirteenth century and the beginning of the fourteenth. At this time, too, numerous *Lancelot-Grail* manuscripts were also produced in the same Italian workshops, as Avril and Gousset have shown.[9] But unlike the *Lancelot-Grail* romances, of which several illustrated copies were also produced in England, only a single later English *Tristan* appears to have survived, the unillustrated London, British Library Harley 49, made in the fifteenth century.

The beginnings of *Tristan* production in France are obscure. Among the earliest manuscripts is BNF fr. 759 (version g in Curtis's edition of *Roman de Tristan en prose,* no siglum in Ménard's), but it is poorly preserved and hard to place, and it contains an abridged version of the text, so little attention has been accorded it by textual scholars. Two additional thirteenth-century manuscripts, BNF fr. 1628 and nouv. acq. fr. 5237, are also hard to place and were also considered unworthy of sigla. It is only in the last quarter of the thirteenth century that several illustrated copies can be assigned to well-known centers of production and related to the work of artists who, if not known by name, may be recognized for illustrating other texts. Thus Paris emerges as a possible center of production around 1270–80 for MS L, BL Royal 20. D. II, whose illustrations have been attributed to the Hospitaller Master, a distinctive artist working in Paris in the 1270s, then in the Holy Land up to the fall of Acre in 1291, after which he appears to have moved to Cyprus and perhaps back to Paris. Among his secular manuscripts are two copies of the *Lancelot-Grail* romance, Tours, BM 951 (with a southern Italian or Cypriot artist), and Paris, BNF fr. 12580.[10]

Certainly Parisian is MS O, Paris, BNF fr. 772, a manuscript much used and consequently poorly preserved. It was assigned to the last quarter of the thirteenth century in Paris by Blanchard; I refine that attribution here, assigning the illustrations to an artist known as the Méliacin Master for his work in the *Roman de Méliacin* by Girart d'Amiens and first recognized by Vitzthum in 1907.[11] A very substantial corpus of manuscripts of all kinds has been ascribed to this artist since then, but this is his only *Tristan,* and, surprisingly, no copy of the *Lancelot-Grail* by him has so far come to light.[12] The opening miniature in fr. 772 spreads over two columns of text and depicts the Tryst beneath the Tree, a revealing choice of subject rarely paralleled in the prose *Tristan,* as an account of this famous episode figures only in a few manuscripts of the prose text (fig. 12.6). The meeting of the lovers at a fountain where they see reflected in the water the image of King Mark, spying on them from a tree, has long been recognized as an immensely popular topos of love and an evocation of the Tristan and Isolde story. It was depicted as a single scene or as part of a cluster of literary and romantic subjects on all manner of objects for secular use. I list several in the appendix where the vast literature on the subject is referred to. In the prose versions, however, the love of Tristan

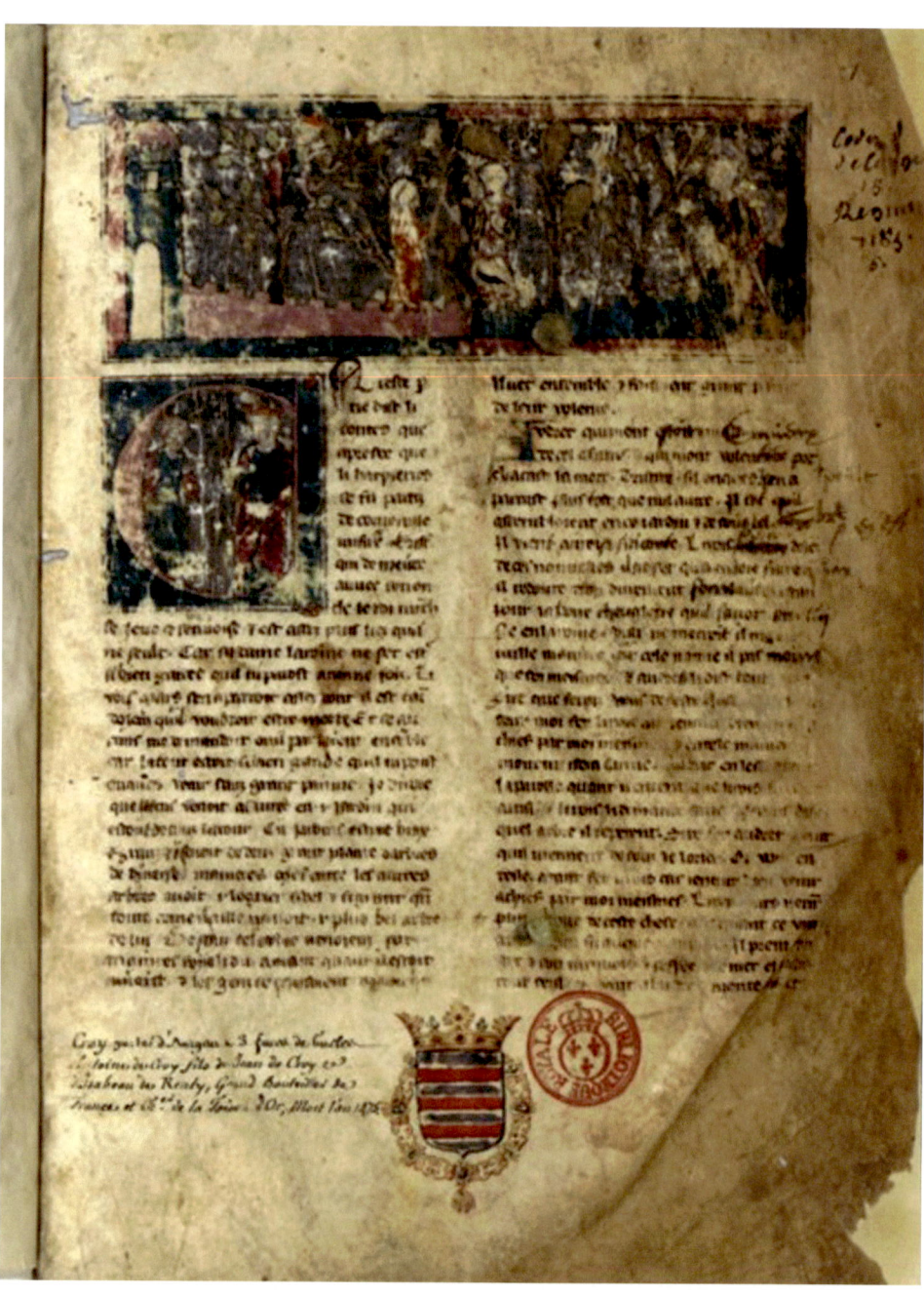

Figure 12.6. Paris, Bibliothèque Nationale, MS fr. 772, fol. 1. Courtesy of Bibliothèque Nationale de France.

and Iseut is simply a "given," and it has become almost a leitmotif rather than a central issue in the romance. In consequence it is seldom the focus of illustration. Nevertheless, a variant is included as part of the "deux captivités de Tristan" episode in seven manuscripts, where Tristan and Iseut both see King Mark hiding in a laurel as they arrive beneath it in turn for their tryst.[13] The fountain motif is absent. In BNF fr. 772 the episode comes right at the beginning of the manuscript, and the picture is closely dependent on it, depicting Mark in the tree and Tristan and Iseut below, with Audret off to the right, and the whole garden enclosed behind a crenellated wall. So far as I know the only other depiction that reflects elements of the Tryst episode in a prose *Tristan* manuscript occurs in MS K, Paris, BNF fr. 97, where King Mark is in the tree and the lovers below, again without the fountain (fig. 12.7). So the presence of this subject in the opening miniature of BNF fr. 772, and the decision to begin the manuscript at this point in the story, is of great interest and links this copy to the secular objects, many of which must have been in the making in Paris at the end of the thirteenth century, when this book was produced. The rest of the illustration in fr. 772 mostly takes the form of historiated initials (fig. 12.8), some of which are quite well preserved and enable the three-quarter profiles of the figures with their characteristic drooping chins and the maroon-blue-gray color range of the Méliacin Master to be clearly recognized.

Paris workshops of the early fourteenth century also produced illustrated copies of the prose *Tristan*: MS F, BNF fr. 334, with historiated initials as its illustrative format, has been attributed to the Papeleu Master, so named for his participation, as one of several painters, in the *Bible historiale* written in 1317 by Jean de Papeleu, Paris, Bibl. de l'Arsenal 5059. The Papeleu artist (one of at least two working on the *Bible historiale*) also painted a number of secular manuscripts, prominent among which is a copy of *Perceval* by Chrétien de Troyes, Paris, BNF fr. 1453. Another *Tristan* now in the J. Paul Getty Museum, Getty Ludwig XV. 5, adopts a different format, that of single-column miniatures, apart from a multicompartment opening page (fig. 12.9). It has been attributed to a large commercial workshop employing many artists, one of whom (fig. 12.10) shares similarities with another copy of Chrétien's *Perceval,* Paris, BNF fr. 12577.[14] Finally

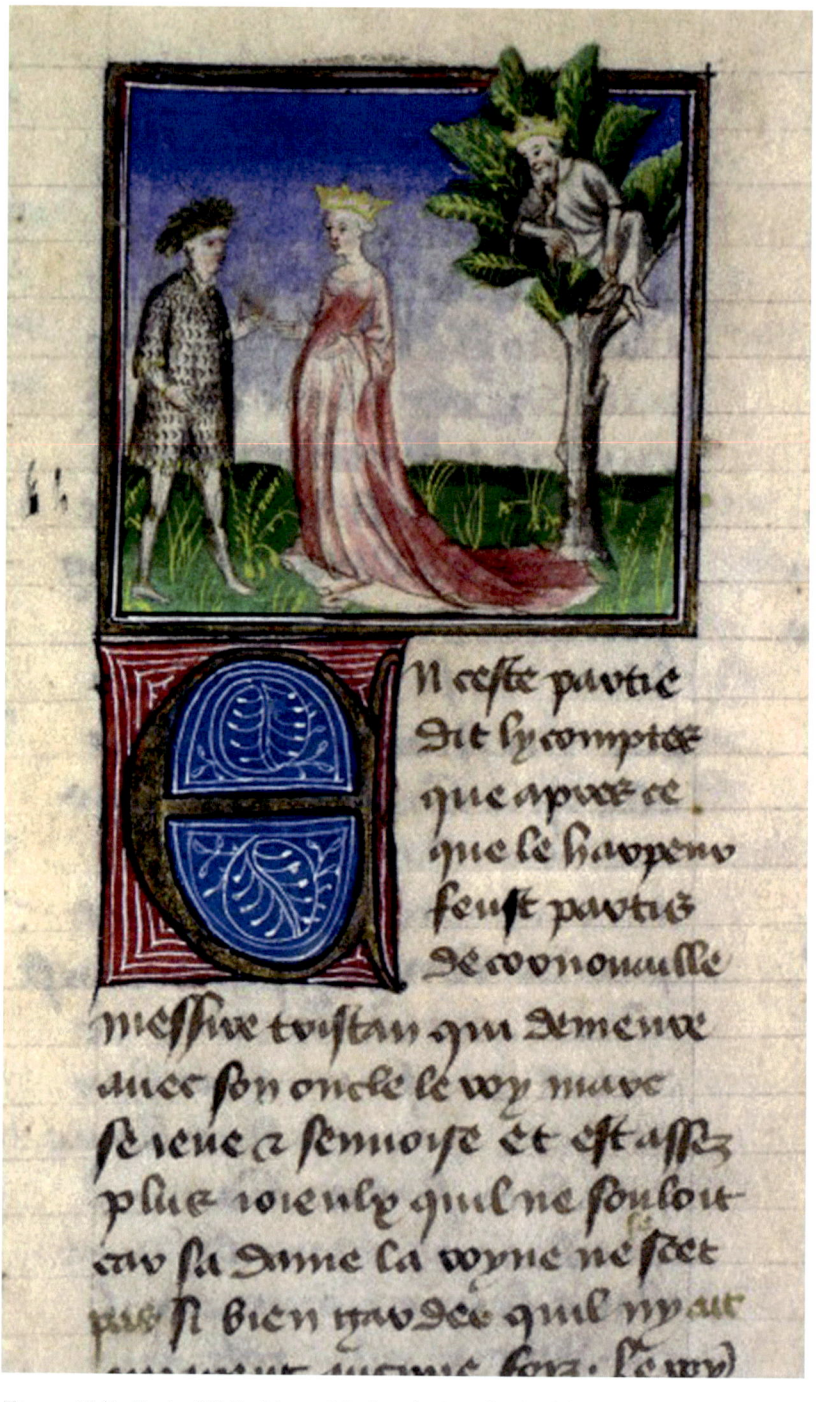

Figure 12.7. Paris, Bibliothèque Nationale, MS fr. 97, fol. 279. Courtesy of Bibliothèque Nationale de France.

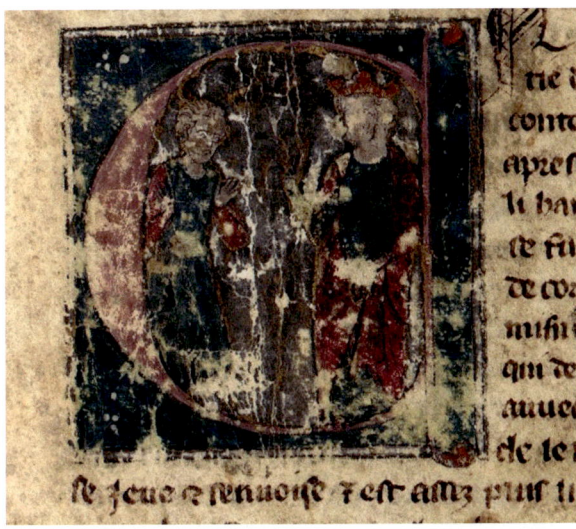

Figure 12.8.
Paris, Bibliothèque
Nationale,
MS fr. 772, fol. 1
detail. Courtesy
of Bibliothèque
Nationale de
France.

there is one of the Vatican copies of *Tristan,* Pal. lat. 1964, whose single opening miniature I have attributed to the Maubeuge Master, another distinctive painter active in early-fourteenth-century Paris who can be traced across many other secular manuscripts and in a few religious books as well. He also participated on at least one *Lancelot-Grail* manuscript, Paris, BNF fr. 9123.

Meanwhile the northeastern provinces also manifested an interest in *Tristan* manuscripts around 1300. To Arras may be attributed, by analogy with the many liturgical and devotional manuscripts made there, MS A, Vienna, ÖNB 2542, to which MS Y, BNF fr. 776 (see fig. 12.2), is closely related in format and style. Both favor historiated initials with rectilinear bar borders, apart from the opening folio of Vienna 2542, which has a four-part multicompartment miniature that has been heavily overpainted, probably while the manuscript was in the possession of Jacques d'Armagnac in the third quarter of the fifteenth century (fig. 12.11). BNF fr. 776 begins incomplete, so it is more than likely that a similar opening miniature was once part of that manuscript as well. Different in format—single-column miniatures rather than historiated initials—but similar in figure style is MS a, BNF fr. 758, which I have also attributed to Arras on the basis of its figures and minor decoration.

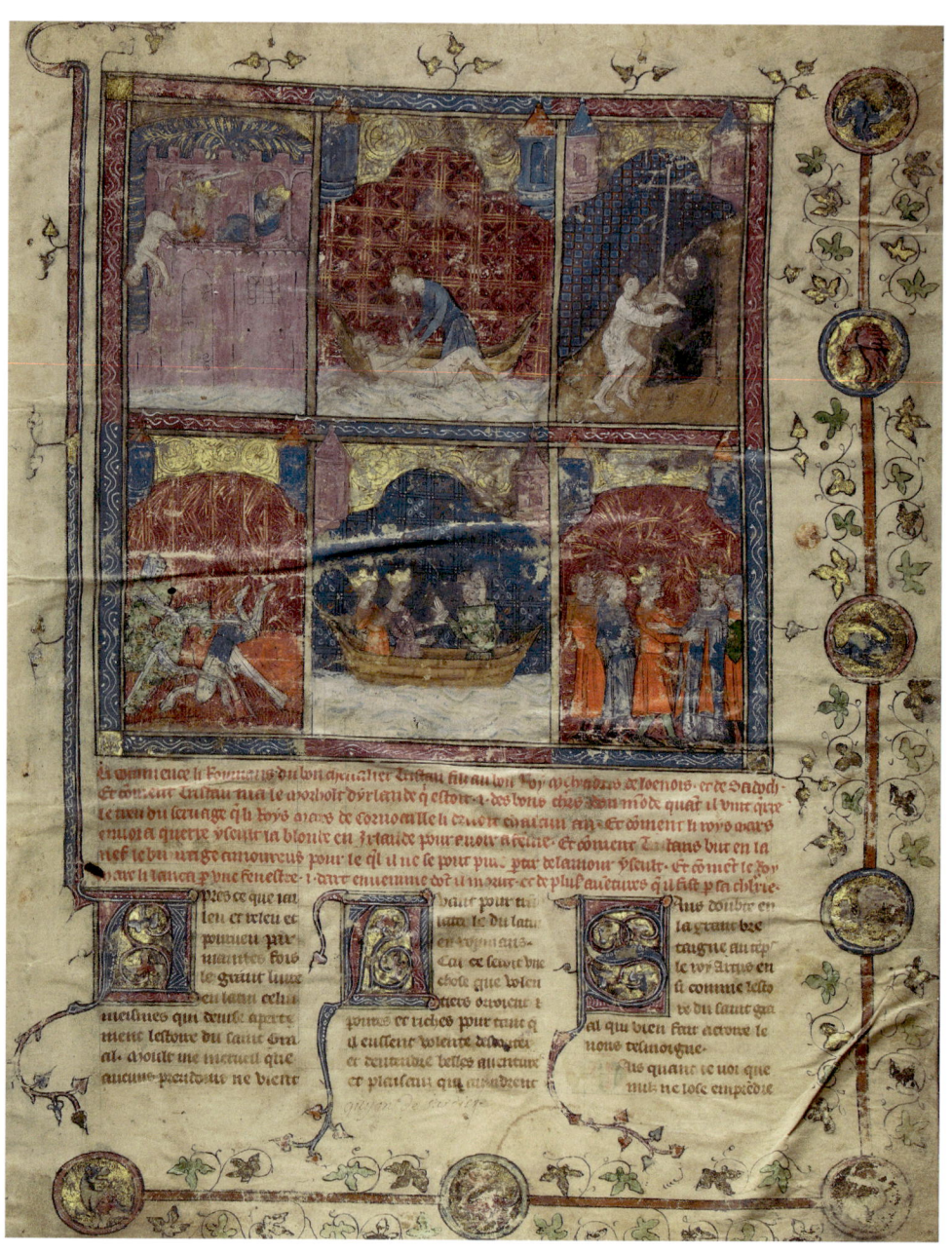

Figure 12.9. Los Angeles, J. Paul Getty Museum, Getty Ludwig XV. V, fol. 1. Courtesy of the J. Paul Getty Museum.

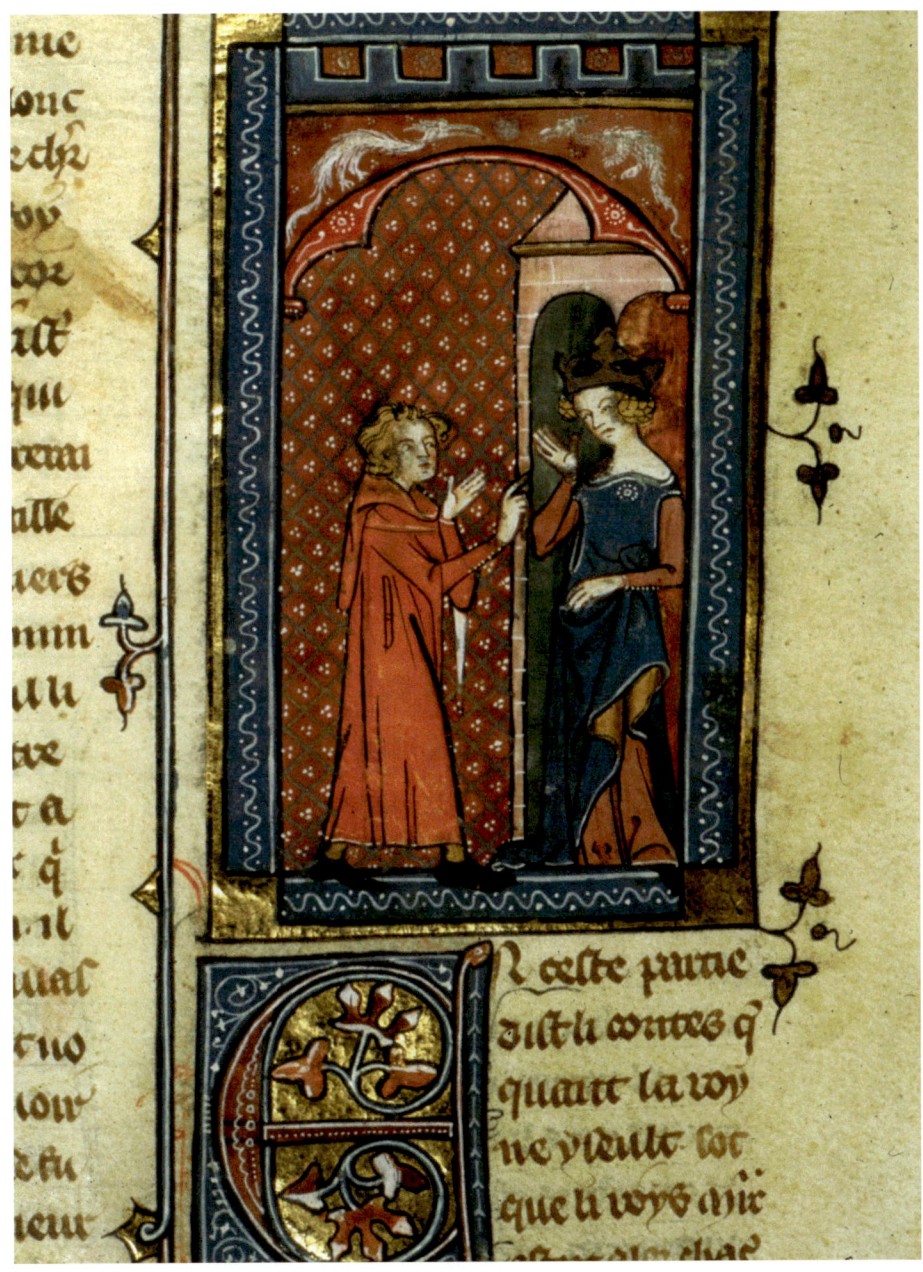

Figure 12.10. Los Angeles, J. Paul Getty Museum, Getty Ludwig XV. V, fol. 306v. Courtesy of the J. Paul Getty Museum.

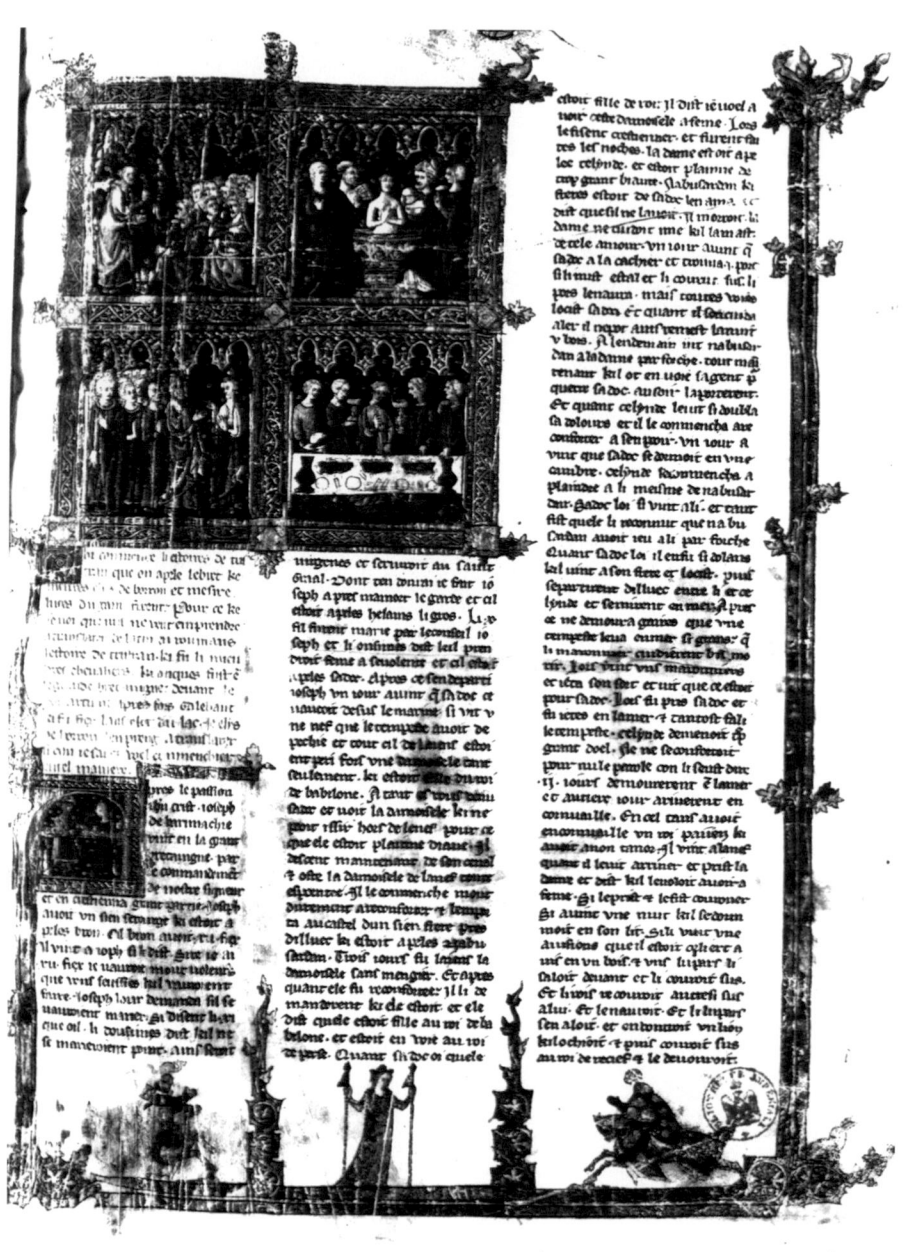

Figure 12.11. Vienna, Österreichische Nationalbibliothek, MS 2542, fol. 1. Courtesy of Österreichische Nationalbibliothek.

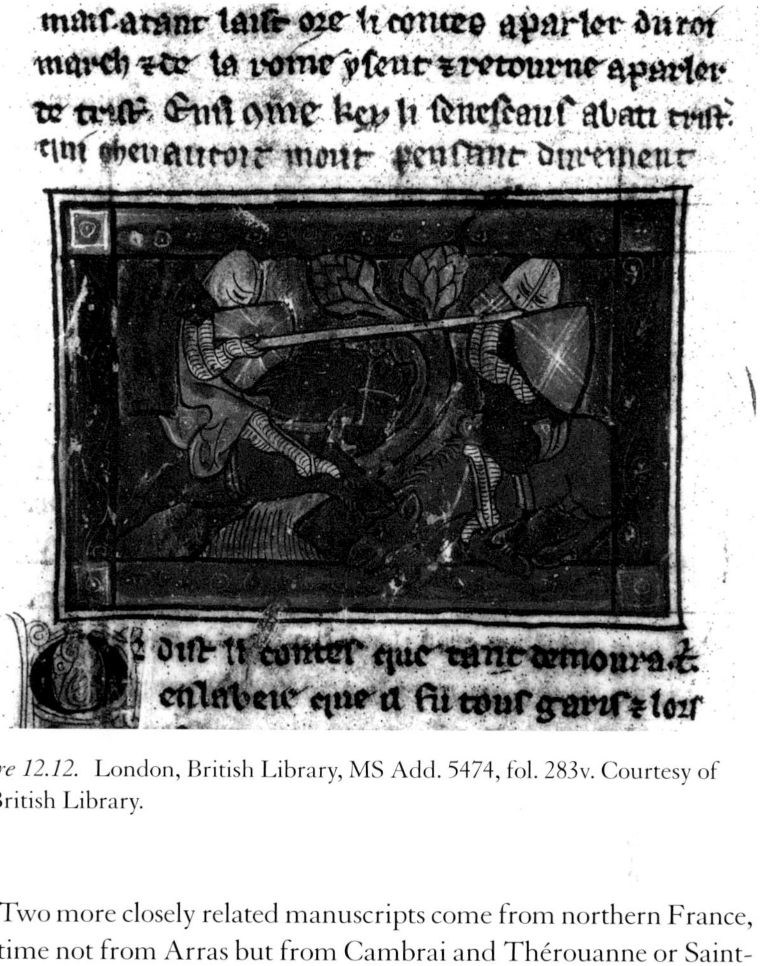

Figure 12.12. London, British Library, MS Add. 5474, fol. 283v. Courtesy of the British Library.

Two more closely related manuscripts come from northern France, this time not from Arras but from Cambrai and Thérouanne or Saint-Omer, most likely in the decade of the 1290s. They are MS M, BL Add. 5474, and BNF nouv. acq. fr. 6579 (no siglum for Ménard; Curtis's version c, MS N). BL Add. 5474 (fig. 12.12) most closely resembles the *Lancelot-Grail* manuscripts Bonn, Universitätsbibliothek 526 (written by Arnulphus de Kayo in Amiens in 1286) and BNF fr. 110. These two copies transmit the short version of the *Lancelot-Grail* and contain the entire text complete in one volume. A detailed iconographic comparison has yet to be made. Both have multiple miniatures at the openings of the branches of the *Lancelot-Grail,* accompanied by curvilinear borders, and their figure style is distinctive for its short, squat figures who are nevertheless lively in gesture and action and easily recognized. BNF fr. 110 looks somewhat later than Bonn 526 and is close to the *Guillaume d'Orange* compilation Boulogne-sur-Mer, BM 192, which was written in 1295. I have proposed that Boulogne 192 is most likely the manuscript made for Guillaume d'Avesnes, bishop of Cambrai (1286–96), and mentioned in his will of 1296, and Busby has suggested that the emphasis on Guillaume texts about converting pagans would have held particular resonance for a clerical recipient of the same name.[15] The same artist also participated in the literary miscellany BNF fr. 24403 with an Arrageois painter.[16] Many other vernacular books may also be attributed to him, some dating to the 1270s. Two missals, Cambrai, BM 153 and 154, made for Cambrai use, are also by the same artist and suggest a provenance for the group, but a number of related small devotional books, among which are Morgan Library, M. 79, and Arras, BM 47, are for use at Saint-Omer.

BNF nouv. acq. fr. 6579 belongs broadly speaking to the same stylistic current as BL Add. 5474 and also has single-column miniatures (fig. 12.13). In figure style it is especially close to the devotional books of Saint-Omer and Thérouanne use while retaining the illustrative format of MS M and its associates rather than adopting the historiated initials of the devotional books and of some of the related secular manuscripts made in Thérouanne or Saint-Omer. Among the latter is the Vincent of Beauvais, *Speculum historiale,* Boulogne-sur-Mer, BM 131, written for Eustache Gomer de Lille, abbot of Saint-Bertin, at Saint-Omer in 1297. The psalter-hours BNF lat. 1076 and Marseille, BM 111, made for Thérouanne use before 1297, is a prominent member of this group and provides further evidence for its likely provenance. Most closely related to lat. 1076 and Marseille 111 is the pair of *Lancelot-Grail* manuscripts, BNF fr. 95 and Yale Beinecke Library 229. In relation to these, however, BNF nouv. acq. fr. 6579 is less elaborate in treatment—using single-column miniatures like BL Add. 5474 rather than the exceptional format of BNF fr. 95 and Yale 229, with their double-register miniatures for the most part and their elaborate borders supporting all kinds of marginal figures. So, in the last analysis, BNF nouv. acq. fr. 6579 may be thought of as occupying an intermediary position between BL Add. 5474 and its group, dating between the 1270s and 1295, and these other Saint-Omer/Thérouanne

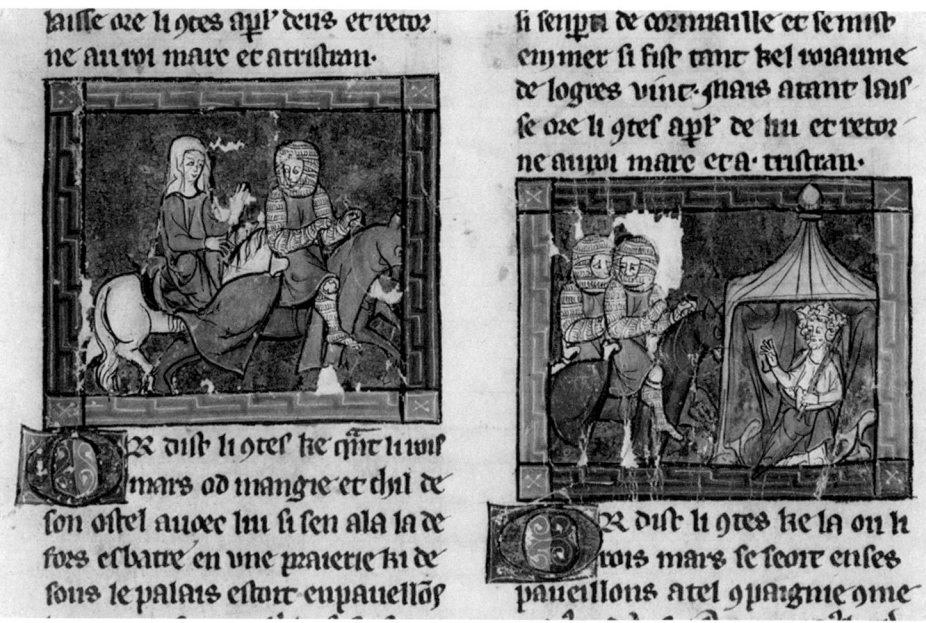

Figure 12.13. Paris, Bibliothèque Nationale, MS nouv. acq. fr. 6579, fol. 80. Courtesy of Bibliothèque Nationale de France.

books of the late 1290s. Many other manuscripts belong to these prolific groups, and further refinements are called for; I offer a more detailed analysis elsewhere.

The late fourteenth century is something of a lacuna in *Tristan* illustration until the emergence in the early years of the fifteenth century of the line-drawing and color-wash group, centered on Jean de Berry's copy, MS C, Vienna, ÖNB 2537, brought to prominence by Dagmar Thoss.[17] Four more copies have been compared to this one, ranging in date from 1400 for MS B, BNF fr. 335–36, to 1466 for MS D, Vienna, ÖNB 2539–40, and including the two copies that form Ménard's Version III: MS U, BNF fr. 100–101, and MS K, BNF fr. 97. MS K was referred to above for its Trysting scene, and it is also notable for including a miniature of the deaths of Tristan and Iseut, discovered by King Mark (fig. 12.14), for which, so far as I know, the only parallel is in one of Jacques d'Armagac's copies, BNF fr. 99 (fig. 12.15). The miniature has been partially defaced and the lovers have been

monde cfors la royne gemeure et la
fille au roy pelles mouvut pour ses
amoues . et . Ansi moruvent ambe
due . mais atant laisse ore li contes
A parler de et . et dissenl et l'estone
a paller du roy marc .

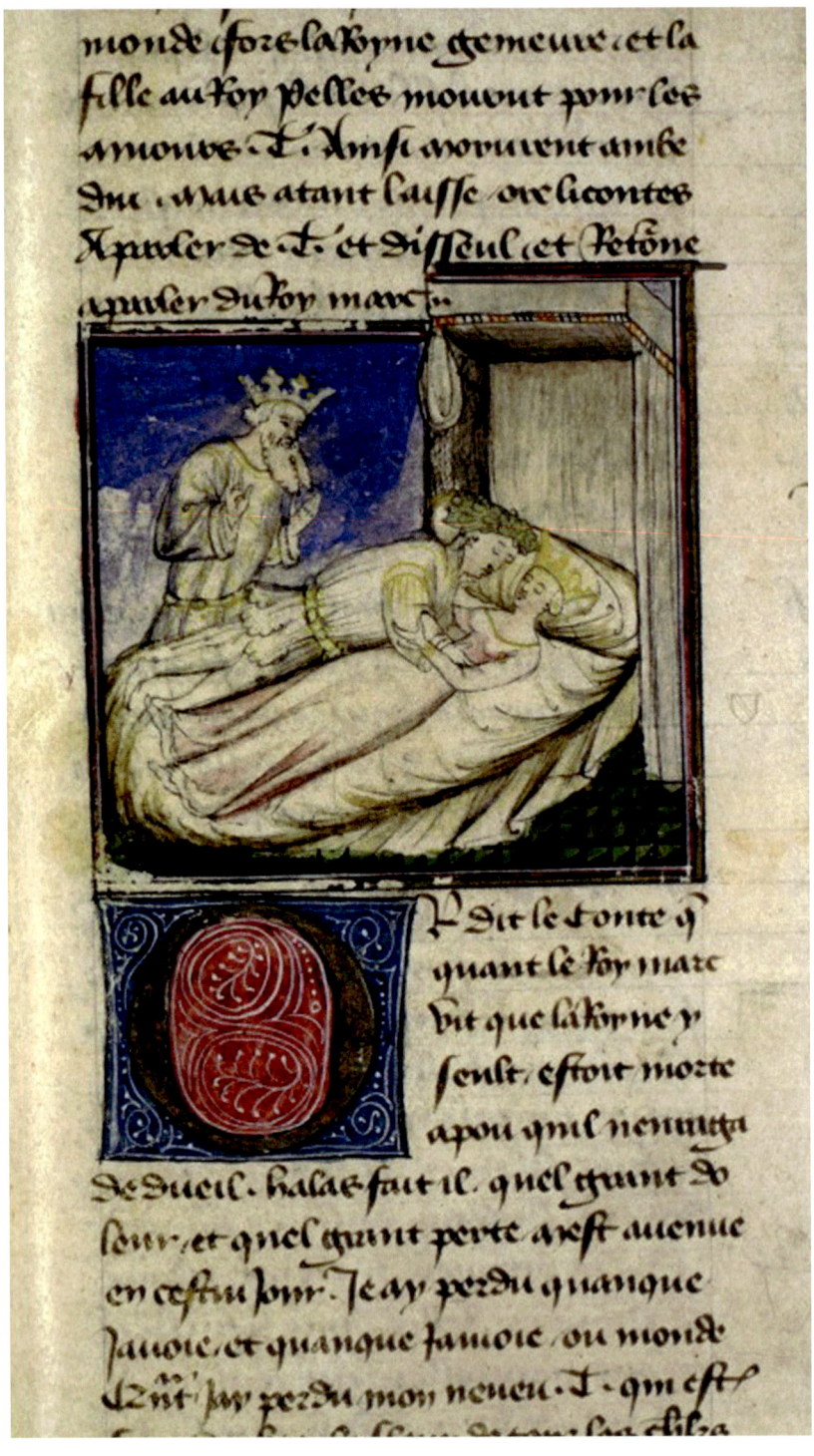

r Dit le conte q
quant le roy marc
vit que la royne y
senlt estoit morte
apou q̄l nennitta
de dueil . halas fait il . quel grant de
sour et quel grant perte a est avenue
en cestui jour . Jeay perdu quanque
Javoie et quanque Javoie ou monde
Ent say perdu mon neueu . et . q̄ est

Figure 12.14. Paris, Bibliothèque Nationale, MS fr. 97, fol. 543. Courtesy of
Bibliothèque Nationale de France.

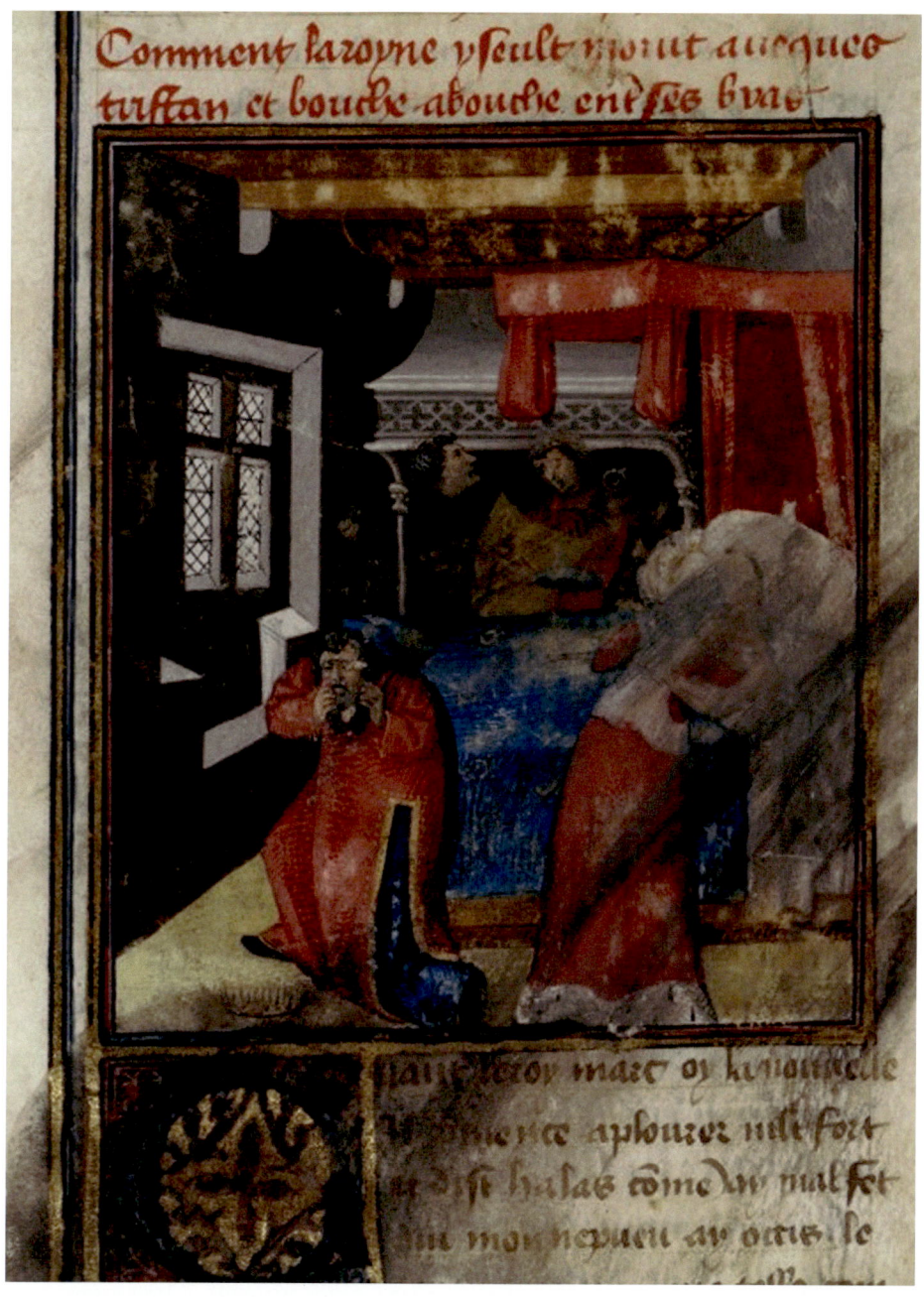

Figure 12.15. Paris, Bibliothèque Nationale, MS fr. 99, fol. 760. Courtesy of Bibliothèque Nationale de France.

damaged, as though a later owner thought their embrace was offensive. A manuscript of the compilation by Rusticien de Pise is also part of the early-fourteenth-century line-drawn group, BNF fr. 340, but no manuscript of the *Lancelot-Grail* by this artist has come to light. Jean de Berry did own a *Lancelot-Grail,* however, purchased from the Parisian bookseller Jacques Raponde around 1406, BNF fr. 117–20, whose illustrations have been attributed to the Master of Berry's Cleres Femmes.[18] It was repainted in part, circa 1470, by Berry's great-grandson, Jacques d'Armagnac.[19] A second copy of the *Lancelot-Grail* was sold by Raponde in 1405 to Jean, Duc de Bourgogne, possibly to be identified with Paris, Ars. 3479–80, and illustrated by various artists, but no *Tristan* belonging to the Duke of Burgundy has survived.[20]

The mid-fifteenth century saw the production of two *Tristan* manuscripts illustrated by the distinctive Master of Charles du Maine, younger brother of René, duke of Anjou: Dijon, BM 527, and Chantilly, Musée Condé 404. Whereas the Dijon manuscript does not figure in the manuscript lists of Curtis or Ménard, the Chantilly manuscript was included in Curtis's version e. She noted some particularly close textual links with two of the early-fourteenth-century Parisian manuscripts mentioned above, BNF fr. 334 and Vat. Pal. lat. 1964. Curtis also includes BNF fr. 104 and Geneva-Cologny Bodmer 164 in her e version. Neither is stylistically related to the rest of the e version group, and indeed they are hard to place in general. To the late 1460s belong a cluster of three *Tristan* manuscripts, all attributed to the Master of the Yale Missal (Beinecke 425): New York, the Pierpont Morgan Library M. 41, finished on April 15, 1468 (not included in Curtis or Ménard); MS V, BNF fr. 102; and Geneva, Bibl. Publique et Universitaire 189 (Curtis MS G1; no siglum in Ménard). With these groups, *Tristan* production moves away from Paris; for the Charles du Maine manuscripts, to the west; and for those of the Yale Missal Master, most likely to Bourges. Stylistically the Yale Missal Master's work approaches the artistic conventions of Fouquet while forming a subgroup somewhat apart from the works of the great master himself. The single-column miniatures are small in format, figures are diminutive, and the colors are pale, with attention devoted to landscapes and interiors. Occasionally there are touches of humor, such as Lancelot in battle disguised as a woman and shown wearing a tall pointed hennin—than which little could be more distinctive (Morgan M. 41; fig. 12.16)!

The 1470s are marked by the commissions of Jacques d'Armagnac, duke of Nemours and great-grandson of Jean de Berry. Not only did Jacques d'Armagnac have his inherited *Lancelot-Grail* manuscript repainted, but he is foremost among *Lancelot-Grail* patrons, having also commissioned BNF fr. 113–16 and the special compilation BNF fr. 112. Both were written by Michel Gonnot, who signed BNF fr. 112 in 1470, and both were illustrated by Evrard d'Espingues, who worked with collaborators on fr. 113–16.[21] BNF fr. 112 includes *Tristan* material along with its *Lancelot-Grail* borrowings and thus merits a *Tristan* siglum as MS w. It is not surprising that a *Tristan* proper was also commissioned by d'Armagnac from the same scribe, who signed in 1463, and the same artist: MS T, BNF fr. 99, referred to above for its rare depiction of the deaths of Tristan and Iseut. A second copy of *Tristan* illustrated by Evrard d'Espingues but written by another scribe, Gilles Gassien of Poitiers, was made for Jean du Mas, seigneur de l'Isle, MS h, Chantilly, Musée Condé 645–47 (315–17). Evrard d'Espingues's work makes these among the most appealing *Tristan* manuscripts for their lively action, dramatic battles, and distinctive approach to castles, tents, boats, battles, arms and armor, and for his distant landscapes and mountaintops and his seascapes, with their characteristic cusped waves (figs. 12.17, 12.18). These two *Tristan* manuscripts form Ménard's Version IV, along with the abridged copy, MS W, BNF fr. 103 (fig. 12.19). The workshop that produced MS W is not the same, however. It is of uncertain provenance, but it has attracted attention as its text version, with its final sequence, based on a verse version, was long ago noted by Bédier.[22] Equally remarkable is its full-page frontispiece miniature, which is unique in presenting on two boats the beginning of the story with Tristan and Iseut drinking the love potion, and the story's end on another boat where the bier of the lovers is borne to shore. So the image focuses not on Tristan's adventures and knightly prowess but on the love story and its dire consequences.

Manuscripts of *Tristan* continued to be copied to the end of the fifteenth century, marked, as is also the case for the *Lancelot-Grail* romance, by several paper copies without illustration. Finally, to the

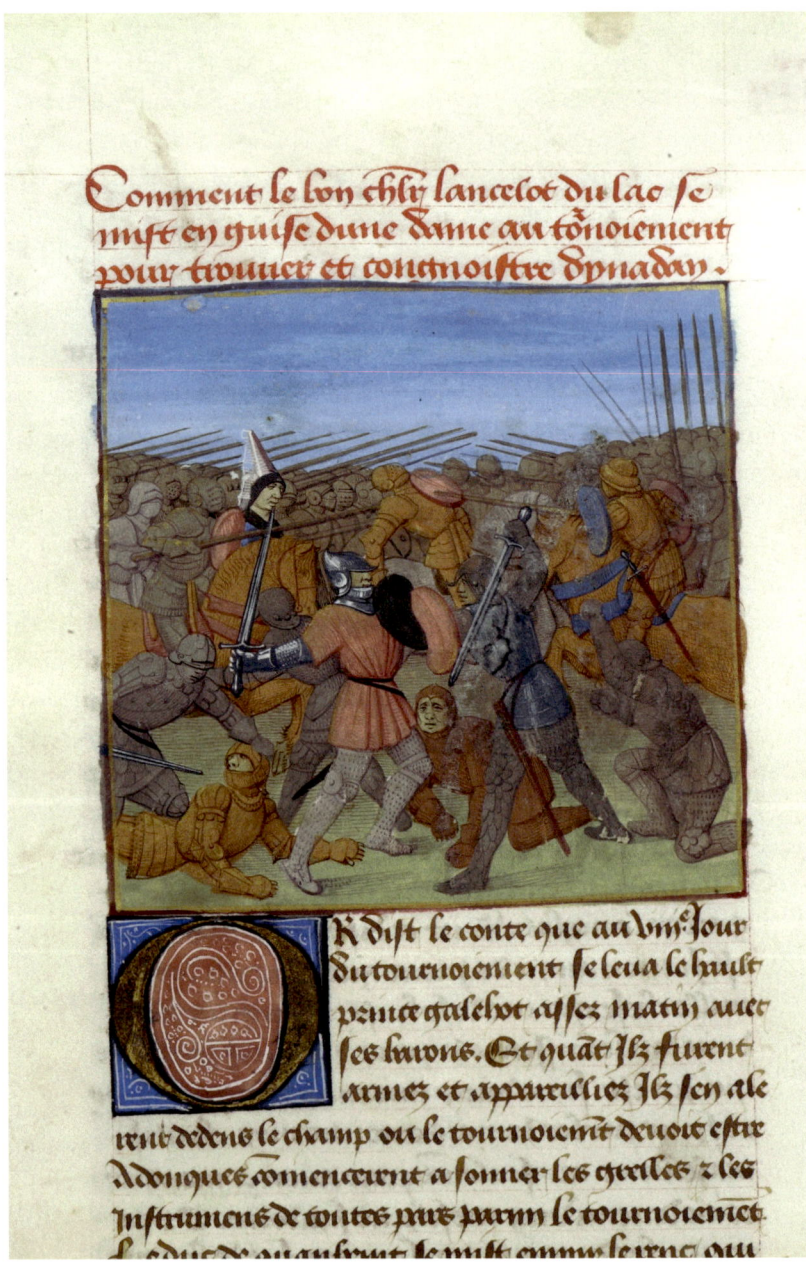

Comment le bon chlr lancelot du lac se
mist en guise dune dame au tonoiement
pour trouuer et coutnoistre dpnadan.

K dist le conte que au vm̄e iour
du tournoiement se leua le huyst
prince galelot asses matin auec
ses barons. Et quāt Ilz furent
armes et appareillies Ilz sen ale
rent dedens le champ ou le tournoiement deuoit estre
Adonques comencerent a sonner les trerlles z les
Instrumens de toutes part parmy le tournoiemēt
...dux... au aubruit se mist onmy seins...

Figure 12.16. New York, The Pierpont Morgan Library, MS M. 41, fol. 57v.
Courtesy of The Pierpont Morgan Library, New York.

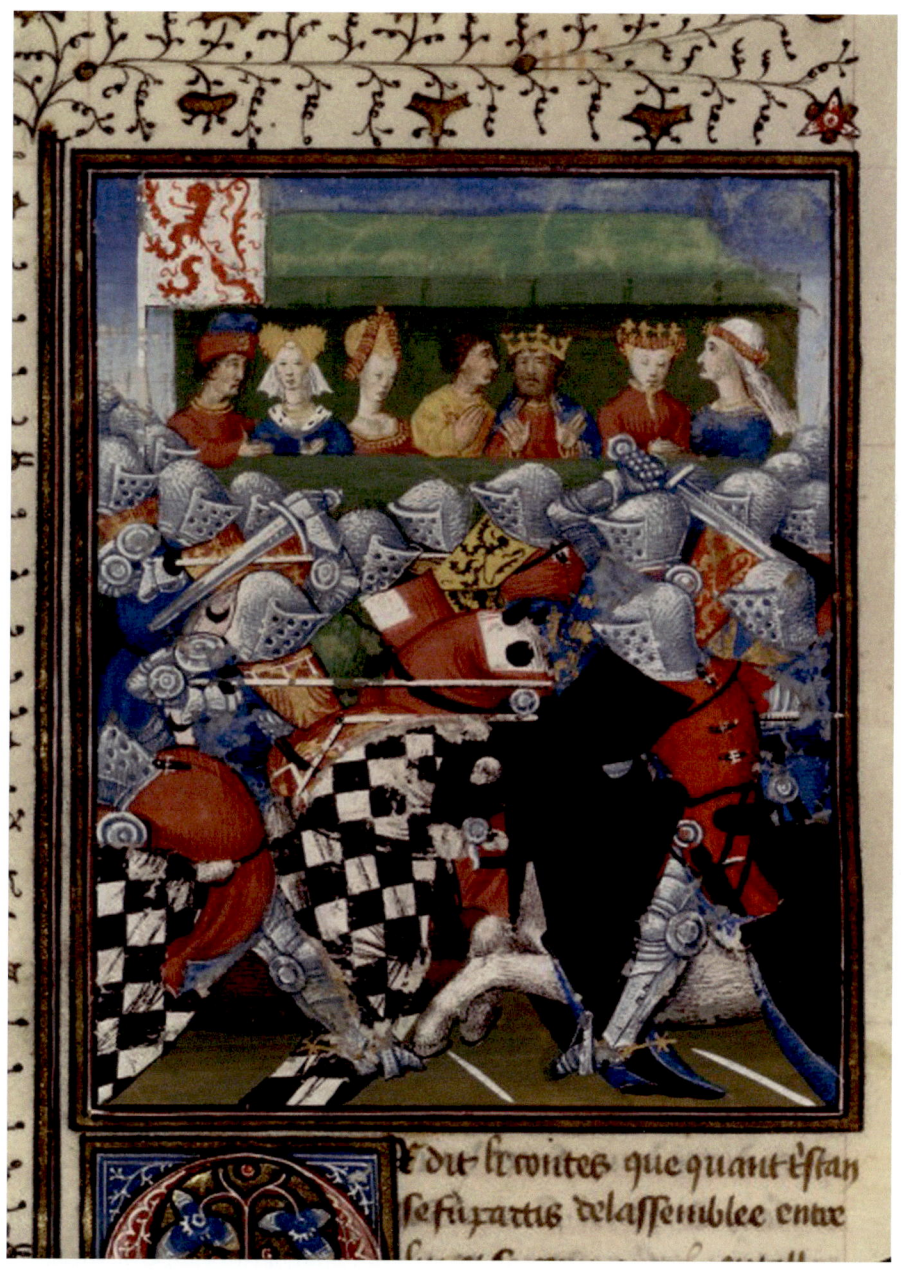

Figure 12.17. Paris, Bibliothèque Nationale, MS fr. 99, fol. 265v. Courtesy of Bibliothèque Nationale de France.

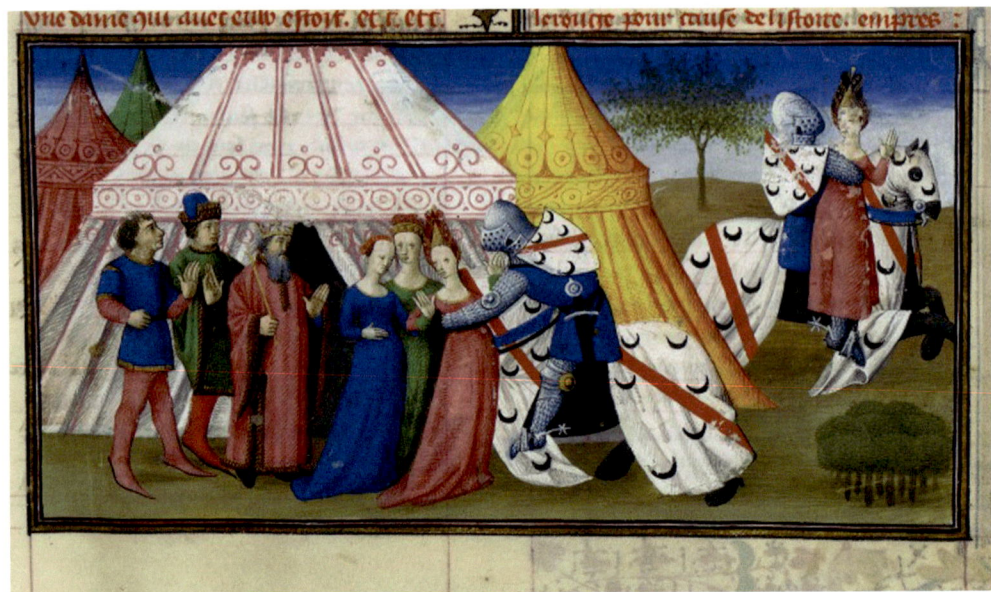

Figure 12.18. Paris, Bibliothèque Nationale, MS fr. 99, fol. 60. Courtesy of Bibliothèque Nationale de France.

1520s are ascribed two copies of the adaptation made by Pierre Sala (ca. 1455–1529), one of which he owned, Aberystwyth, NLW 443-D, and the other of which, Geneva-Cologny MS Bodmer 148, belonged to François de Tournon.[23] Both are beautifully illustrated with water color drawings and are similar to, though by a different artist than, the adaptation of the *Chevalier au lion* of Chrétien de Troyes offered around 1518 by Sala to Francis I.[24]

To a large extent, then, the patterns of production and dissemination of *Tristan* manuscripts run parallel to those of the *Lancelot-Grail* and other secular illustrated texts. In many cases they can be attributed to well-recognized artists or workshops, and sometimes particular patrons and artists can be named. Several are dated and signed by their scribes, providing anchors within workshop activity around which other books may be clustered. They span a full range of time, from the late thirteenth century through the early sixteenth. If there is a lacuna, it is in the mid-fourteenth century, a time when several

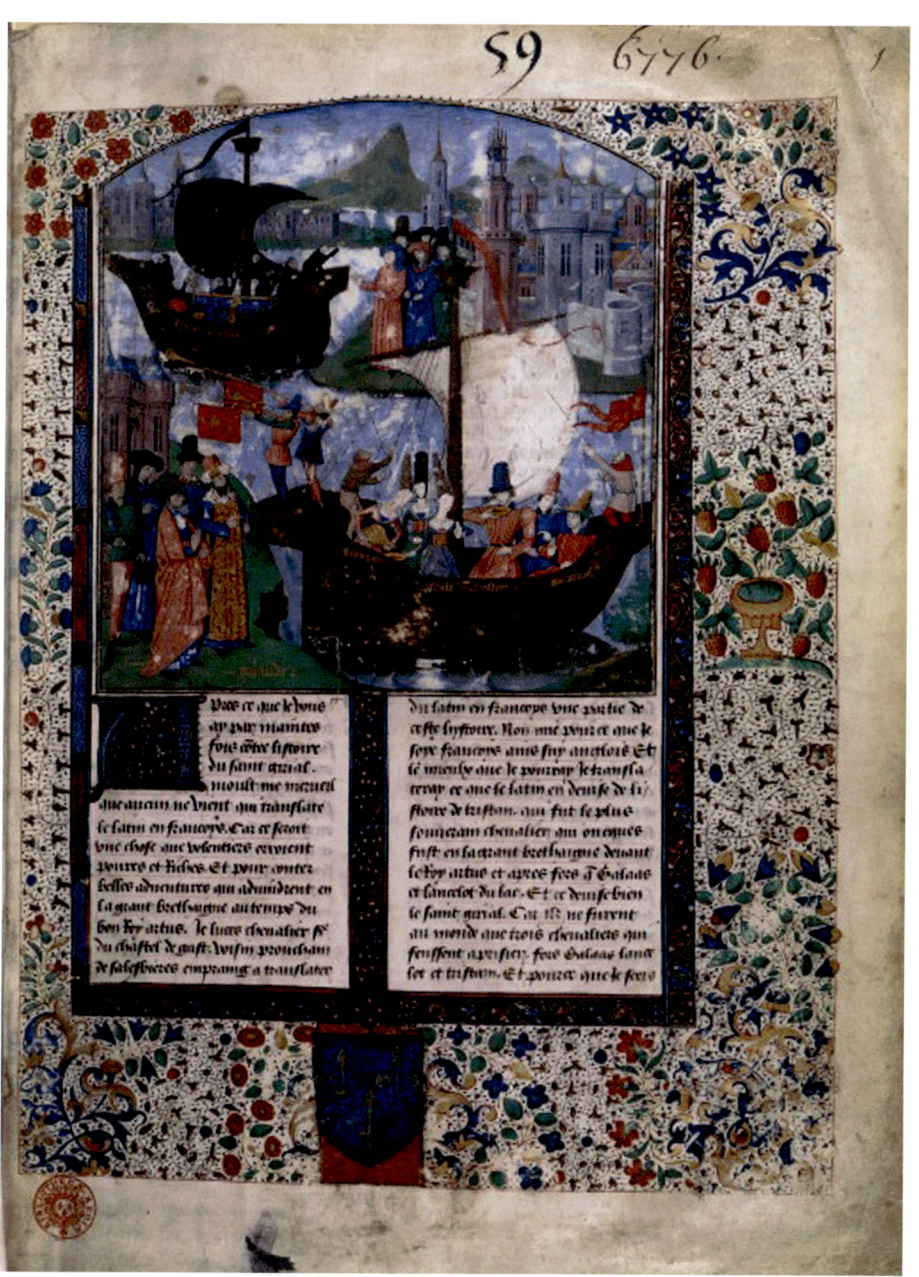

Figure 12.19. Paris, Bibliothèque Nationale, MS fr. 103, fol. 1. Courtesy of Bibliothèque Nationale de France.

important *Lancelot-Grail* manuscripts were produced, and it is surprising that few *Tristans* have emerged from this period. Like the *Lancelot-Grail,* the *Tristan* aroused considerable interest outside France, as the many Italian copies and the puzzling BNF fr. 750 attest, while the beginnings of *Tristan* illustration, unlike the early *Lancelot-Grail* manuscripts, are traceable in England. And the Trysting topos took on a life of its own, for which the *Lancelot-Grail* produced only the occasional crossing of a sword bridge with which to compare. The corpus of *Tristan* illustration in manuscripts is very substantial, and it is here that comparative work remains to be done. It has been possible to compare a few miniatures in this chapter, but no study has yet tackled the corpus as a whole, how the pictorial cycles and individual miniatures compare, whether the placing of the miniatures is the same or different, how the rubrics match or differ, and what the relationships are to the *Lancelot-Grail* manuscripts in those sections of text (esp. *Roman de Tristan en prose,* ed. Ménard, vols. 6–9) where there is so much textual borrowing from the *Lancelot, Queste,* and *Mort Artu.* Studies of *Tristan* illustration in France are only beginning to become feasible, thanks to the availability of complete editions of the text and the growing accessibility of large numbers of images online at the websites *Mandragore, Banque d'images, e-codices: Virtuelle Handschriftenbibliothek der Schweiz,* and *Enluminures.* The future for *Tristan* illustration holds great promise.

Appendix: A Chronology of Tristan in French

Texts
Béroul (ca. 1150): Paris, BNF fr. 2171, no illustrations.
ed. Muret, Ewart, Gregory.

Thomas (ca. 1173): 9 fragments, no illustrations.
ed. Michel, vol. III; Gregory.
C: Cambridge UL DD 15–12, late 13th cent., one leaf
D: Oxford, Bodl. Douce d. 6, mid-13th cent., 22 leaves
fols. 1–12c Thomas, *Tristan* (lines 1269–3086 in Gregory's ed.)
fols. 12d–19a *Folie Tristan*

fols. 19–20 debate in French verse between Pride and Humility

fols. 20v–21v prose commentary in French on the origin of the
True Cross

fols. 21v–22 short Latin text on the nature of the True Cross

Sn1, Sn2: Oxford, Bodl. Fr.d.16 14 leaves, late 12th or early 13th cent.,
one historiated initial E with a portrait of Tristan harping (at line
834 in Gregory's ed.):
'En sa chambre se set un jor
E fait un lai pitus d'amur . . . '

Str1, Str2, Str3: Strasbourg, Protestant Seminary destroyed 1870.
Binding fragment of 13th cent. according to Michel.

T1, T2: Binding fragments now lost, once in the possession of a
Turinese gentleman according to Novati, first half of 13th cent.

Carlisle, Cumbria Record Office, Holm Cultram Cartulary, fols. 1
and 286; see Benskin, Hunt, Short; ed. Short.

Marie de France, *Chevrefeuille.*
ed. and trans. O'Gorman in Lacy, pp. 184–97.
S: Paris, BNF n.a.fr. 1104, fols. 32b–172d
H: London, BL Harley 978, fols. 171d–72d

Folie Tristan
Bern, Burgerbibliothek 354 fols. 151v–56v, 13th cent., second quarter
(*Folie Tristan* is among various brief works in verse that occupy
fols. 1r–175v; they are followed by *Le roman des sept sages de
Rome* [fols. 184r–205r] and by Chrétien de Troyes, *Perceval*
[fols. 208r–83v]), eastern France?
ed. Michel, I, 215–41; Hoepffner; Morf.
Oxford Bodl. Douce d. 6, fols. 12d–19a, Anglo-Norman
ed. Michel, I, pp. 80–137; Hoepffner; Lecoy.
Cambridge Fitz. 302, fol. 100v, Anglo-Norman
ed. Dean and Kennedy.

Tristan Rossignol (part of *Le Donnei des Amants,* lines 453–660)
Geneva, Bodmer 82 (ex-Phillipps 3713), fols. 20ra–21rb
ed. and trans. Fresco.

Tristan Menestrel (part of Gerbert de Montreuil's Continuation of
Chrétien de Troyes's *Perceval,* lines 3309–4832)
Paris BNF fr. 12576 (folios not given by Fresco).
Paris, BNF n.a.fr. 6614, fols. 165vb–71vb (Fresco's MS de base)
ed. and trans. Fresco.

Luce de Gast (ca. 1230s) and Hélie de Boron (ca. 1240), *Le Roman de
Tristan* (in prose)
ed. Curtis (based on Carpentras, Bibl. Inguimbertine, MS 404,
    unillustrated).
ed. and dir. Ménard, 1987–97, based on MS A, Vienna ÖNB 2542,
    and 1997–2003, based on MS N, Paris, BNF fr. 756-757.
For the illustrated prose *Tristan* manuscripts, see below.

Early Iconography
ca. 1102–17, Spain: Santiago de Compostela, Cathedral, north portal,
    column fragments.
late 12th cent., England: Oxford, Bodl. Fr. 6. 16: f. 10, E initial, Tristan
    harping and singing.
mid-13th cent., England: London, British Museum and Halesowen
    Abbey: Chertsey tiles (Shurlock; Loomis 1916 and 1938: 44–48;
    Eames I: 141–71; Age of Chivalry, 333, nos. 60, 320 by John Cherry).
mid-13th cent., England: London, BL Add. 11619, fols. 6r–9v, full-
    page miniatures without text (Hunt, Deighton).
ca. 1280, France: Paris, BNF fr. 2186, *Roman de la Poire,* one Tristan
    miniature, fol. 5v, depicting Tristan and Isolde seated, and Mark
    discovering them in the Cave of Love (Tibaut ed. Marchello-Nizia,
    Huot 174–93, Guilhaume, Keller).

The Tryst beneath the Tree Topos
(cf. Germany and Italy, which are omitted here)
(Loomis, Newstead, Curschmann, Furrow, Walworth, and references
    below)

Manuscripts
mid-13th cent., England: London, BL Add. 11619 (see above).
ca. 1320: France, Paris: Chantilly 1078–9, *Ci nous dit,* one miniature
    (Loomis 28, fig. 120).

Ivory boxes, France (Paris?), early 14th cent.

St. Petersburg, Hermitage Museum I, Inf. N T. 60 (Koechlin I, 517; Loomis 55, figs. 87–90, without the Tryst); Hermitage Museum II, Inf. N. T. 61 (olim Basilwesky Collection: Loomis 57, fig. 91); New York, Metropolitan Museum, Inv. 17. 190, 173 (Loomis 66, fig. 122; Carns); Walters Art Museum, Inv. 71. 264 (Loomis 66; Randall 224, no. 324); London, British Museum, Inv. 368 (Loomis 66, fig. 121); Cracow, Cathedral Treasure (Loomis 66); Birmingham, Barber Institute of Fine Arts, Inv. N. 39.26 (olim Mrs. St. John Mildmay) (Loomis 66); London, Victoria and Albert Museum, Inv. 146–1866, 35549 (Loomis 66); Florence, Museo Bargello, Inv. 123c 248170 (Loomis 66).

Mirror cases, France (Paris?), early 14th cent.

Città del Vaticano, Museo del Vaticano, Inv. 1856–6–12 166 (Loomis 66, fig. 123); Paris, Musée national du Moyen Age (Musée de Cluny, Loomis 66, fig. 124); Perth (Hall and Owen).

Hair parter

Turin, Museo Civico, Inv. 105 (Loomis 67, fig. 125).

Comb

Boston, Museum of Fine Arts, Inv. 57.7, French, 15th cent., with inscriptions (Curschmann, 17 n. 7; reproduced and described on the Boston Museum website).

Shoes

Mechelen, Mechelse Vereniging voor Archeologie, Holland or Belgium, 15th cent. (*Arthurus Rex,* 1987, I, Cat. no. 2.2.6, pl. III.2.); cf. Dutch examples listed in Sarfatij.

Corbels

Bruges, Gruthuyse Museum, 15th cent. (Loomis 68, fig. 130).

Bourges, House of Jacques Coeur, 15th cent. (Loomis 69, fig. 124).

Goblet base

Milan, Poldi Pezzoli Museum, Inv. 355, France, 14th cent. (Loomis 67, fig. 126).

Leather case
Namur, Musée Inv. 29, France, 15th cent. (Loomis 67, fig. 127).

Wooden chest
London, Victoria and Albert Museum, Inv. 2173-'55 35791, France,
    15th cent. (Loomis 67, fig. 129).

Wall painting
Saint-Floret (Auvergne), 14th cent. (Loomis, figs. 96–98; Luyster,
    this volume),
Cf. Paris, BNF fr. 772, fol. 1r, and Paris, BNF fr. 97, fol. 279r
    (figs. 12.6 and 12.7 here).

Manuscripts of the Prose Versions, except Northern France
Sigla according to Ménard et al.

1278
MS I, written by Petrus de Tiergevilla: Paris, BNF fr. 750, southern
    Italy or Holy Land? Many illustrations (Avril and Gousset, II,
    no. 194; images on *Mandragore*).

13th cent., last quarter
Paris, BNF fr. 1463, Rustician de Pise, *Méliadus,* and *Tristan,* Italy,
    line drawings (Avril and Gousset II, no. 45; légendes on *Mandragore,*
    images on *Banque d'images*).
MS d, Paris, BNF fr. 12599, *Roman de Tristan,* special version,
    Italy, northeast? Written by Oddo (Baumgartner 63; Avril and
    Gousset II, no. 19; Haines; légendes on *Mandragore,* images on
    Banque d'images).
MS n, Paris, BNF fr. 1434, Cycle Post-Vulgate, no illustrations, Italy?

13th–14th cent.
Paris, BNF fr. 760, *Tristan,* version abrégée, Italy, Genoa (Avril and
    Gousset II, no. 46; images on *Mandragore*).
MS H, Paris, BNF fr. 104, *Tristan li Bret,* champie and penflourished
    initials, southern France?

ca. 1320–30

MS x, Paris, BNF fr. 755, *Roman de Tristan,* Italy: Milan, illustrations (Avril and Gousset III, no. 1; légendes on *Mandragore,* images on *Banque d'images*).

14th cent.

MS N, Paris, BNF fr. 756–757, Italy, probably for the Caffara family, Naples: "pour la deuxième partie du roman . . . le ms. 757 est le seul à donner intégralement la version I du texte" (Ménard I, 10, citing Baumgartner 18; Ménard et al. 1997–2003, MS de base).

London, BL Harley 4389, Italy, line drawing (Avril and Gousset, under II, no. 148).

MS y, Modena, Bibl. Estense. Est. 59 = alpha T.3.11 (cited by Loomis as T.S.1 and by Ménard as E 40), Italy, line drawing.

MS G, Aberystwyth, NLW 5667, Italy, line drawing.

MS Q, Paris, BNF fr. 94, Ménard Version II, Italy, decorated initial and shield with a lion (?) rampant (arms of Tristan?) on fol. 1 only (images on *Mandragore*).

ca. 1380–85

Paris, BNF fr. 343, Post Vulgate *Queste, Tristan* interpolations, Milan or Pavia (Avril and Gousset III, no. 30; Gousset) (reproduced on *Mandragore*).

15th cent.

London, BL Add. 23929, Italy: Milan, large author portrait on fol. 1r, thereafter historiated initials (Curtis I, 18–22: version a).

London, BL Harley 49, England, no illustrations (Curtis I, 18–22: version a, MS H1).

Mostly Illustrated Manuscripts of the Prose Versions: Northern France

13th cent., second quarter or middle, Uncertain Provenance

Paris, BNF fr. 759, abridged version, historiated initials, poorly preserved (Curtis II, 49: version g) (légendes on *Mandragore*).

Paris, BNF fr. 1628, no illustrations.

Paris, BNF n.a.fr. 5237, fols. 46r–48r, fragment, no illustrations.

13th cent., last quarter, Paris

MS L, ca. 1270–80, London, BL Royal 20. D. II, incomplete, Paris,
Hospitaller Master, small historiated initials (Folda, 121–24, 126,
128, 151, 197–98, Cat. no. 15).

MS O, Paris, BNF fr. 772, version III, dernière partie, ed. Blanchard,
illustrated by the Méliacin Master (new attribution) (images on
Mandragore).

1290s, Cambrai, Thérouanne, or Saint-Omer

MS M, London, BL Add. 5474 (cf. MS L, both abbreviated) (Stones,
"Illustrations," 223–41, 454–55).

Paris, BNF n.a.fr. 6579, miniatures, Thérouanne? (new attribution)
(Curtis I, 18–22: version c, MS N) (légendes on *Mandragore*).

13th cent., end, North France?

MS Z, Carpentras, BM 404, fragmentary, no illustrations (Curtis, MS
de base).

ca. 1300, Arras

MS A, Vienna, ÖNB 2542, opening miniature, historiated initials,
owned by Jacques d'Armagnac for whom was added a miniature on
fol. 500 (Hermann 44–64 [identified as English]; Stones,
"Illustrations," 40, 255, 261, 263, 266, 267, 490; Blackman 564–65,
Cat. no. 81; Stones, "Manuscript, Paris, BNF fr. 1588," 24 n. 71;
Fotitch and Steiner, Haines) (Ménard, MS de base).

MS Y, Paris, BNF fr. 776, historiated initials.

(Stones, "Illustrations," 255, 261, 263, 264, 66, 267, 491; Stones, "Artistic
Context," 253, fig. 87; Stones, "Manuscript, Paris, BNF fr. 1588,"
24 n. 71) (légendes on *Mandragore,* images on *Banque d'images*).

MS a, Paris, BNF fr. 758, miniatures.

(Stones, "Artistic context," 253. fig. 85; Stones, "Manuscript, Paris,
BNF fr. 1588," 35, fig. 55).

14th cent., first third, Paris

MS F, Paris, BNF fr. 334, historiated initials, Paris (Vitzthum, *Pariser
Miniaturmalerei,* 175; Stones, "Illustrations," 286; Stones, "Artistic
Context," 265, fig. 157; ead., Fauvel, 538, 558; cf. BNF fr. 1453 by the

Master of fr. 1453, alias the Papeleu Master) (légendes on
Mandragore, images on *Banque d'images*).
MS S, Città del Vaticano, BAV Pal. lat. 1964, one miniature, by the
Maubeuge Master (Stones, "Artistic Context," 545, 559, fig. 23.17;
Stones, "Manuscript, Paris, BNF fr. 1588," 24 n. 71).

ca. 1330–40, Paris
Los Angeles, J. Paul Getty Museum, Getty Ludwig XV.5, opening
multicompartment miniature, single-column miniatures (von Euw
and Plotzek, 220–21, attributed to Paris, circle of BNF fr. 12577,
Munich, BSB Clm 10177, BNF fr. 24391 [dated 1332], and the Busch
Collection *Roman de la rose*; Rouse and Rouse I, 391 n. 105, II, App.
9A [attributed to i: Jeanne de Montbaston: frontispiece and quires
30–34, 38, 39, except fol. 306r; ii: Master of BNF fr. 24388, quires 1,
except frontispiece, 2–5 (no illustrations in quire 6), 7–29; iii: the
first artist of BNF fr. 12577, quire 39, fol. 306v only, and quire 40;
iv: quires 35 (no illustration), 36 (my addition), 37, 45 (my addition),
46–48, 50, artist unrecognized—he does three-dimensional ocher
diaphragm arches and small doll-like figures with ocher curly hair
and large black eyes, and a fairy-tale castle on fol. 283v]).

early 14th cent., eastern France
MS E, Edinburgh, NLS Adv. 19.1.3, Lorraine dialect.

14th cent., Uncertain Provenance
MS J, St. Petersburg NLR, Fr. F. v. XII 2, close to Ménard's version IV.
MS R, Città del Vaticano, BAV Reg. lat. 727, abridged.
MS X, Geneva, Bodmer 164.

late 14th cent., Uncertain Provenance
MS P, Paris, BNF fr. 349, very fat! No illustrations.

The ca. 1400 Line Drawing Group, Paris
MS B, 1399, April 17 (1400 ns), Paris, BNF fr. 335–336, line drawings
(légendes on *Mandragore,* images on *Banque d'images*).
MS C, Vienna, ÖNB 2537, owned by Jean de Berry (not mentioned by
Meiss; see Thoss, *Ein Prosa-Tristan*).

MS U, Paris, BNF fr. 100–101, version III, line drawing (images on *Mandragore*).

MS K, Paris, BNF fr. 97, version III, line drawing (images on *Mandragore*).

Paris, BNF fr. 340, Rusticien de Pise, compilation (images on *Banque d'images* and *Mandragore*).

1466
MS D, Vienna, ÖNB 2539-40 (Pächt and Thoss I, 1, 13–20, figs. 1–13).

The Maître de Charles du Maine (younger brother of René d'Anjou), ca. 1450–60
(Avril in Avril and Reynaud, 121–22, no. 62 [Dijon 527], compared with Oxford, Bodl. 986, *Miroir historial abrégé*; Paris, BNF lat. 6749A, Albertus Magnus, *De natura avium* by the same artist).
Dijon, BM 527 (facsimile; images on *Enluminures*).
Chantilly, Musée Condé 404.

The Maître du Missel de Yale (Beinecke MS 425), Bourges or Tours? ca. 1470
(attributions by Reynaud in Avril and Reynaud 153).
New York, The Pierpont Morgan Library, M. 41, completed April 15, 1468 (images on Corsair).
MS V, Paris, BNF fr. 102 (images on *Banque d'images* and *Mandragore*).
Geneva, Bibl. Pub. et Univ. 189 (Curtis I, 16–18, MS G1).

Jacques d'Armagnac Group, ca. 1470–80
(Blackman; Reynaud in Avril and Reynaud, 164–65).
MS T, Paris, BNF fr. 99, for Jacques d'Armagnac, version IV, written by Michel Gonnot, signed, fol. 775v, 8 October 1463; illuminated by Evrard d'Espingues (Avril and Reynaud 164–65, no. 84) (Blackman 433–58) (images on *Banque d'images* and *Mandragore*).
MS w, Paris, BNF fr. 112, *Lancelot-Grail,* special version, *Tristan* interpolations, for Jacques d'Armagnac, written by Michel Gonnot of Crozant, signed, fol. 233r, 4 July, 1470, illuminated by Evrard d'Espingues (Blackman 458–502; images on *Banque d'images*).

Paris, BNF fr. 113–16, *Lancelot-Grail, Tristan* interpolations, for
  Jacques d'Armagnac, illustrated by Evrard d'Espingues, a follower
  of the Versailles Livy, and the Master of fr. 114 (Blackman 503–40;
  images on *Banque d'images* and *Mandragore*), ca. 1475.
MS h, Chantilly, Musée Condé 645–47 (315–17), version IV, written
  by Gilles Gassien of Poitiers, illustrated by Evrard d'Espingues, for
  Jean du Mas, seigneur de l'Isle, ca. 1470–80.

late 15th cent., Uncertain Provenance
MS W, 15th cent., third quarter, Paris, BNF fr. 103, version *tardive
  abrégée,* one opening miniature (Bédier, "La mort"; Loomis,
  Arthurian Legends, 113, fig. 304; Baumgartner 41–62) (image on
  Mandragore).

late manuscripts on paper, unillustrated
1475: London, BL Egerton 989, no illustrations, owned by Anne de
  Graville.
1488: Paris, Bibl. de l'Arsenal 3357, no illustrations, written by Groins
  Pittingin (Curtis I, 16–18, MS A).
16th cent.: Paris, BNF fr. 24400, no illustrations.

ca. 1520–29, Lyon: Pierre Sala, *Tristan*
(Muir; Suard; Burin 50).
Geneva-Cologny, Bodmer 148 (olim Phillipps 3637), 26 ink and
  watercolor drawings, owed by François de Tournon.
Aberystwyth, NLW 443-D, 25 ink and watercolor drawings, owned
  by Pierre Sala.

Notes

This essay is dedicated to the memory of Emmanuèle Baumgartner, who often
pressed me to consider the illustrated *Tristan* and encouraged me to embark
on this study. I thank Michael Curschmann, Martine Meuwese, Serafín Moralejo Álvarez, James Rushing, and Stephanie Cain Van D'Elden for much
helpful discussion of *Tristan* iconography.
  1. Gregory, Stewart, ed., *Thomas of Britain: Tristan,* Garland Library
of Medieval Literature 78, Series A (New York: Garland, 1991); reprint,

"Thomas' Tristan," ed. and trans. Stewart Gregory, in *Early French Tristan Poems*, ed. Norris J. Lacy, vol. 2 (Woodbridge, Suffolk: D. S. Brewer, 1998), 3–172.

2. See Colum Hourihane, *King David in the Index of Christian Art,* Index of Christian Art Resources 11 (Princeton: Index of Christian Art, Princeton University, in association with Princeton University Press, 2002), s.v. "As Musician," 34–76.

3. Ibid., s.v. "Playing before Saul," 207–10. This lay is accompanied by notation in MSS BNF fr. 776, fol. 271v (MS Y), and Vienna, ÖNB 2542, fol. 272v (MS A), and space for notation has been left in BNF fr. 12599, fol. 219 (MS d), as noted by John Haines, "The Lai Layout in the Paris Prose Tristan Manuscripts," *Scriptorium* 59 (2005): 16–17, table 5. It should be noted that Haines's sigla correspond neither to those used by Curtis nor to those of Ménard. Here I follow Ménard.

4. This fragment has been identified by Serafín Moralejo Alvarez, to whom I am grateful for permission to reproduce this image, one of several carvings depicting secular subjects, not all of which can be identified (Moralejo Alvarez, "Saint-Jacques de Compostelle: Les portails retrouvés de la cathédrale romane," *Les dossiers d'archéologie* 20 [1977]: 87–103). See also Margaret Alison Stones, "Arthurian Art since Loomis," in *Arturus Rex II: Acta Conventus Lovaniensis 1987,* ed. Willy Van Hoecke, Gilbert Tournoy, and Werner Verbeke, Mediaevalia Lovanensia, Series 1, Studia 17 (Leuven: Leuven University Press, 1991), 21–78, fig. 7. The north transept sculptures of Arthurian material at the Cathedral of Modena, of about the same date, also present iconography for which no textual source survives (Roger Sherman Loomis and Laura Hibbard Loomis, *Arthurian Legends in Medieval Art,* Modern Language Association of America Monograph Series [New York: Modern Language Association of America, 1938], 32–34).

5. Loomis, *Arthurian Legends,* 45. See also Merritt R. Blakeslee, *Love's Masks: Identity, Intertextuality, and Meaning in the Old French Tristan Poems* (Woodbridge, Suffolk: D. S. Brewer, 1989), 4.

6. References for the manuscripts mentioned here are given in the appendix, where they are listed in approximate chronological order with reference to the authors of the major studies and editions.

7. Stones, "The Earliest Illustrated Prose *Lancelot* Manuscript?," *Reading Medieval Studies* 3 (1977): 3–44.

8. Both these manuscripts are among the few to leave spaces for musical notation to accompany the lays (Haines, "Lai Layout").

9. François Avril and Marie-Thérèse Gousset, with Claudia Rabel, *Manuscrits enluminés d'origine italienne II: XIIIe siècle* (Paris: Bibliothèque Nationale, 1984).

10. I have published several lists of the chronological and geographical distribution of the *Lancelot-Grail* manuscripts. For the most recent list, see "*Lancelot-Grail* Intranet Site-Chronology and Geographical Distribution of *Lancelot-Grail* Manuscripts," *Lancelot-Graal Project,* 2007, www.lancelot -project.pitt.edu/LG-web/Arthur-LG-ChronGeog.html (Aug. 26, 2010).

11. Joël Blanchard, *Le Roman de Tristan en prose: Les deux captivités de Tristan* (Paris: Klincksieck, 1976), 27; Georg Vitzthum von Eichstätt, *Die Pariser Miniaturmalerei von der Zeit des hl. Ludwig bis zu Philipp von Valois und ihr Verhältnis zur Malerei in Nordwesteuropa* (Lepizig: Quelle and Meyer, 1907), 24–32, pl. III.

12. See François Avril, "Manuscrits," in *L'art au temps des rois maudits: Philippe le Bel et ses fils,* ed. Danielle Gaborit-Chopin (Paris: Réunion des Musées nationaux, 1998), 256–334, no. 174.

13. Blanchard, *Le Roman de Tristan en prose,* 9, identifies this episode in BNF fr. 757, 97, 100–101, 340, 349, 772, and Chantilly 648.

14. The parallel was reported by Anton Von Euw and Joachim Plotzek, *Die Handschriften der Sammlung Ludwig,* 4 vols. (Köln: Schnütgen Museum, 1979–85), 220–21; and further defined by Richard H. Rouse and Mary A. Rouse, *Manuscripts and Their Makers: Commercial Book Producers in Medieval Paris, 1200–1500,* 2 vols. (Turnhout: Harvey Miller, 2000). However, the Getty manuscript consistently uses diaphragm arches to frame its small miniatures and this format is never found in BNF fr. 12577. Whereas the figures on fol. 360v offer a degree of similarity, it is unlikely in my view that the distinctive first artist of fr. 12577 was actually a participant, rather than a distant echo, in the Getty *Tristan.* For a comparison with Chantilly, Musée Condé 645, and Paris, BNF fr. 99, see Sylvie Fabre-Baudet, "Mise en texte, mise en page et construction iconographique dans les manuscrits enluminées conservant la version IV du Roman de Tristan en prose (ms. Getty Ludwig XV-5, Paris, BnF, Fr. 99 et Chantilly, Musée Condé, 645)," in *Du scriptorium à l'atelier: Copistes et enlumineurs dans la conception du livre manuscrit au Moyen Age* Pecia 13. Le livre et l'écrit (Turnhout: Brepols, 2010), 345–66.

15. M. Alison Stones, "The Illustrations of the French Prose *Lancelot*" (Ph.D. diss., University of London, 1970–71), 9 n. 10, 30, 119, 208, 212, 215, 217–22, 454–55; Keith Busby, *Codex and Context* (Amsterdam: Rodopi, 2002), 181, 383, 386–89, 392, 534, 741–42.

16. M. Alison Stones, "The Artistic Context of *le Roman de Fauvel* and a Note on *Fauvain,*" in *Fauvel Studies,* ed. Margaret Bent and Andrew Wathey (Oxford: Clarendon Press, 1998), 253–54, figs. 78–84.

17. Dagmar Thoss, "Ein Prosa-Tristan aus dem Besitz des Duc de Berry in der Österreichischen Nationalbibliothek: cod. 2537" (offprint from *Codices manuscripti* 1977/3) (Vienna: B. Hollinek, 1977).

18. Millard Meiss, *French Painting in the Time of Jean de Berry, I: The Late Fourteenth Century and the Patronage of the Duke* (London: Phaidon, 1967), 252, 312.

19. Susan Amato Blackman, "A Pictorial Synopsis of Arthurian Episodes for Jacques d'Armagnac Duke of Nemours," in *Word and Image in Arthurian Literature,* ed. Keith Busby (New York: Garland, 1996), 3–57.

20. Meiss, *French Painting in the Time of Jean de Berry,* 356, attributes Ars. 3479 to the Master of the Cité des Dames, suggesting that it was probably the manuscript provided by Raponde (371 n. 137).

21. The illustrations are fully analyzed and tabulated in Blackman, "Pictorial Synopsis of Arthurian Episodes."

22. Joseph Bédier, "La mort de Tristan et d'Yseut d'après le manuscrit fr. 103 de la Bibliothèque nationale comparé au poème allemand d'Eilhart d'Oberg," *Romania* 15 (1886): 481–510.

23. These are listed but not discussed in Elizabeth Burin, *Manuscript Illumination in Lyons 1473–1530,* Ars Nova: Studies in Late Medieval and Renaissance Northern Painting and Illumination (Turnhout: Brepols, 2001), 50.

24. François Suard, "Notice sur le manuscrit B. N. fr. 1638: Pierre Sala et le *Chevalier au lion,*" *Romania* 91 (1970): 406–15; Burin, "Pierre Sala's Manuscript of *Le Chevalier au lion,*" in *Les Manuscrits de Chrétien de Troyes,* ed. Keith Busby et al., 2 vols. (Amsterdam: Rodopi, 1993).

Martin Baisch is Privatdozent at the Institute for German and Netherlandic Philology, Free University, Berlin. He has published extensively
on medieval epic, reception history, textual criticism, the relationship
between knowledge and emotion, and the cultural history of curiosity.
He has been project leader of "Fascination: An Inquiry into the History
and Empiricism of an Aesthetic Emotion" at the Free University's *Exzel-
lenzcluster* Languages of Emotion since 2009. He is the author of *Textkritik als Problem der Kulturwissenschaft: Tristan-Lektüren* (2006) and the
editor of *Aventiuren des Geschlechts: Modelle von Männlichkeit in der Literatur des 13. Jahrhunderts* (2003); *Der Tod der Nachtigall: Liebe als Selbstre-
flexivität von Kunst* (2009); *Neugier und Tabu: Regeln und Mythen des Wissens* (with Elke Koch, 2010); and *Der Jüngere Titurel zwischen Didaxe und
Verwilderung: Neue Beiträge zu einem schwierigen Werk* (2010).

Elke Brüggen is Professor at the Institute for German Studies, Comparative Literature, and Cultural Studies, University of Bonn. Her research
areas include twelfth- and thirteenth-century German literature, historical anthropology, didactic literature, and lyric. She is the author of *Klei-
dung und Mode in der höfischen Epik des 12. und 13. Jahrhunderts* (1989) and
has published numerous essays on didactic literature. She is currently
working on a translation of Wolfram von Eschenbach's *Parzival* (with
Hans-Joachim Ziegeler and Joachim Bumke, forthcoming from Reclam
Verlag).

Michael Curschmann is Professor Emeritus in the Department of Ger-
man, Princeton University, and a Fellow of the Medieval Academy of
America and Corresponding Member of the Bayerische Akademie der
Wissenschaften. His publications cover the period from the twelfth to

the sixteenth century and focus on German, Scandinavian, and Latin literature, medieval orality, literature and music, and literature and the visual arts. His most recent publications are *Das Buch am Anfang und am Ende des Lebens: Wernhers Maria und das Credo Jeans de Joinville* (2008); "Herrscherportraits in Bild und Schrift: Frühe Kulturen—abendländisches Mittelalter," in *Lesevorgänge,* edited by E. C. Lutz et al. (2010); and "Levels of Meaning and Degrees of Viewer Participation: Inscribed Images in Twelfth-Century Manuscripts," in *Qu'est-ce que nommer?,* edited by Ch. Heck (2010).

Jutta Eming, Professor at the Institute for German and Netherlandic Philology, Free University, Berlin, has worked on medieval and early modern German and French literature. Her areas of expertise include theories of performativity, the history of emotions, concepts of the marvelous, gender, incest, media theory, and late medieval passion plays. She is the author of *Funktionswandel des Wunderbaren: Untersuchungen zum Bel Inconnu', zum Wigalois' und zum Wigoleis vom Rade'* (1999) and *Emotion und Expression: Untersuchungen zu deutschen und französischen Liebes- und Abenteuerromanen des 12.–16. Jahrhunderts* (2006).

Elke Koch, Professor at the Institute for German and Netherlandic Philology, Free University, Berlin. Her research focuses on courtly romance and on medieval plays, both secular and religious. She has worked extensively on theories of performativity and textuality and on the intersection of historical anthropology and the study of medieval literature. Koch is the author of *Trauer und Identität: Inszenierungen von Emotionen in der deutschen Literatur des Mittelalters* (2006) and coeditor of *Neugier und Tabu: Regeln und Mythen des Wissens* (with Martin Baisch, 2010).

Klaus Krüger is Professor at the Art History Institute, Free University, Berlin. He has worked on theories of the image, sculpture, and visual media in the Middle Ages and Renaissance; Italian art from the Middle Ages through the Baroque; and the cultural semantics of premodern art, modern art, and art and film. He is the author of *Das Bild als Schleier des Unsichtbaren: Ästhetische Illusion in der Kunst der frühen Neuzeit in Italien* (2001), which has been translated into English under the title *Unveiling the Invisible: Image and Aesthetic Illusion in Early Modern Italy* (New York: Zone Books, 2011).

Ludger Lieb is Professor in the Department of German Language and Literature, Ruprecht-Karls-University, Heidelberg. He works on narrative theory of German medieval and early modern literature and has done extensive work on *Minnereden,* a genre of short narratives that deal with love. In addition to publishing numerous essays, he has coedited *Situationen des Erzählens. Aspekte narrativer Praxis im Mittelalter* (with Stephan Müller, 2002); *Triviale Minne? Konventionalität und Trivialisierung in spätmittelalterlichen Minnereden* (with Otto Neudeck, 2006); and *Genesis— Poiesis: Der biblische Schöpfungsbericht in Literatur und Kunst* (with Manfred Kern, 2009). In 2011 he edited the largest German collection of fables from the sixteenth century, *Burkard Waldis, Esopus. 400 Fabeln und Erzählungen nach der Erstausgabe von 1548.*

Amanda Luyster is Lecturer in the Department of Visual Arts, College of the Holy Cross. Her research focuses on images of narrative in late medieval France, England, Italy, and Islamic Spain, in particular, on images and stories that cross borders— either between realms of meaning (sacred and secular) or across cultural, spatial, or religious boundaries. Luyster's recent publications include the edited volume *Negotiating Secular and Sacred in Medieval Art: Christian, Islamic, and Buddhist* (with Alicia Walker, 2009), as well as essays in the journals *Medieval Encounters* and *Word & Image.* She has held numerous prestigious fellowships and awards. A fellowship from the National Endowment for the Humanities has allowed her to further her progress on a book manuscript on painted word and painted image in wall paintings in the south of France.

Jan-Dirk Müller, Professor Emeritus, Institute for German Philology, University of Munich, is a Fellow of the Bayerische Akademie der Wissenschaften and the Göttinger Akademie der Wissenschaften. His research interests include memory, gesture, performance, writing, and narrative strategy in medieval and late medieval literature. His books include *Gedechtnus: Literatur und Hofgesellschaft um Maximilian I* (1982); *Wissen für den Hof: Der spätmittelalterliche Verschriftungsprozess am Beispiel Heidelberg im 15. Jahrhundert* (1994); *Spielregeln für den Untergang: die Welt des Nibelungenliedes* (1998), translated into English as *Rules for the Endgame* (2008); *Das Nibelungenlied* (2003/2009); *Höfische Kompromisse* (2007); and *Mediävistische Kulturwissenschaft* (2010).

Ann Marie Rasmussen is Professor in the Department of Germanic Languages and Literature, Duke University. Her research focuses on gender studies and late medieval German literature. Along with numerous articles on various aspects of medieval German literature and culture, she is the author of *Mothers and Daughter in Medieval German Literature* (1997) and coeditor of *Medieval Woman's Song* (with Anne Klinck, 2002) and *Ladies, Whores, and Holy Women: A Sourcebook in Courtly, Religious, and Urban Cultures of Late Medieval Germany, with Introductory Essays* (with Sarah Westphal-Wihl, 2010).

James A. Schultz is Professor in the Department of Germanic Languages, University of California, Los Angeles. His research interests include gender studies and sexuality studies. He is the author of *The Shape of the Round Table: Structures of Middle High German Arthurian Romance* (1983), *The Knowledge of Childhood in the German Middle Ages* (1995), and *Courtly Love, the Love of Courtliness, and the History of Sexuality* (2006), as well as numerous essays.

Kathryn Starkey is Associate Professor in the Department of Germanic and Slavic Languages and Literatures, University of North Carolina at Chapel Hill. Her research interests include word and image, material culture, language, performance, ritual, gender and sexuality, and the history of the book. She has published on all these topics and is the author of *Reading the Medieval Book: Word, Image, and Performance in Wolfram von Eschenbach's "Willehalm"* (2004). In addition, she has coedited *Visual Culture and the German Middle Ages* (with Horst Wenzel, 2005) and *Imagination und Deixis: Studien zur Wahrnehmung im Mittelalter* (with Horst Wenzel, 2007).

Margaret Alison Stones is Professor of History of Art and Architecture at the University of Pittsburgh. She has held several research fellowships in Oxford, Cambridge, and Paris to pursue her research on illuminated manuscripts. Stones is a Fellow of the Society of Antiquaries of London and the Société nationale des antiquaires de France. Among her publications are *Les manuscrits de Chrétien de Troyes* (edited with Keith Busby, Terry Nixon, Lori Walters, 1993); *Le livre d'images de Madame Marie*

(Paris, BN n.a.fr. 16251) (1997); *The Pilgrim's Guide to Santiago de Compostela, a Critical Edition* (with Jeanne Krochalis, 1998); and *Gautier de Coinci: Miracles, Music, and Manuscripts* (edited with Kathy Krause, 2006). She has developed two websites: www.medart.pitt.edu/index.html and www.lancelot-project.pitt.edu/lancelot-project.html.

Stephanie Cain Van D'Elden is Professor (retired) in the Department of Foreign Languages and Literatures, University of Minnesota. Her research interests include illustrated manuscripts and marginal figures in German medieval literature. She has published *Peter Suchenwirt and Heraldic Poetry* (1976) and a translation and edition of *Moritz von Craûn* (1990). She has also coedited the volumes *The Dark Figure in Medieval German and Germanic Literature* (with Edward R. Haymes, 1986) and *The Stranger in Medieval Society* (with F. R. P. Akehurst, 1997). She is currently working on a catalog of illustrations of the story of Tristan.

Haiko Wandhoff is Privatdozent at the Institute for German Literature, Humboldt University, Berlin. His research focuses on medieval epic and lyric, word and image, ekphrasis, heraldry, printing and literary communication in the sixteenth century, and the theory and history of media and communication. He is the author of *Der epische Blick: Eine mediengeschichtliche Studie zur höfischen Literatur* (1996) and *Ekphrasis: Kunstbeschreibungen und virtuelle Räume in der Literatur des Mittelalters* (2003). Wandhoff is the editor of *Zur Bildlichkeit mittelalterlicher Texte*, a special issue of *Das Mittelalter* (2008); and coeditor of the volume *Licht, Glanz, Blendung: Beiträge zu einer Kulturgeschichte des Leuchtenden* (with Christina Lechtermann, 2008).

Hans-Joachim Ziegeler is Professor at the Institute of German Language and Literature, Cologne University. His areas of interest are narrative and genre, theoretical approaches to medieval German literature, courtly romance, short epic, and passion plays. Ziegeler is the author of *Erzählen im Spätmittelalter: Mären im Kontext von Minnereden, Bispeln und Romanen* (1985) and editor of the anthology *Ritual und Inszenierung: Geistliches und weltliches Drama des Mittelalters und der Frühen Neuzeit* (2004).

INDEX

Page numbers in italics refer to the illustrations on those pages.